TOP SECRET CANADA

Understanding the Canadian Intelligence
and National Security Community

National security in the interest of preserving the well-being of a
country is arguably the first and most important responsibility of any
democratic government. Motivated by some of the pressing questions
and concerns of citizens, *Top Secret Canada* is the first book to offer a
comprehensive study of the Canadian intelligence community, its
different parts, and how it functions as a whole. In taking up this
important task, contributors aim to identify the key players, explain
their mandates and functions, and assess their interactions.

Top Secret Canada features essays by the country's foremost experts on
law, foreign policy, intelligence, and national security, and will become
the go-to resource for those seeking to understand Canada's intelligence
community and the challenges it faces now and in the future.

(IPAC Series in Public Management and Governance)

STEPHANIE CARVIN is an assistant professor at the Norman Paterson
School of International Affairs at Carleton University.

THOMAS JUNEAU is an associate professor at the University of Ottawa's
Graduate School of Public and International Affairs.

CRAIG FORCESE is a professor in the Faculty of Law at the University of
Ottawa.

IPAC
The Institute of
Public Administration of Canada

IAPC
L'Institut d'administration
publique du Canada

The Institute of Public Administration of Canada Series
in Public Management and Governance

Editors:

Peter Aucoin, 2001–2
Donald Savoie, 2003–7
Luc Bernier, 2007–9
Patrice Dutil, 2010–18
Luc Juillet, 2018–

This series is sponsored by the Institute of Public Administration of Canada as part of its commitment to encourage research on issues in Canadian public administration, public sector management, and public policy. It also seeks to foster wider knowledge and understanding among practitioners, academics, and the general public.

For a list of books published in the series, see page 319.

Top Secret Canada

*Understanding the Canadian
Intelligence and National
Security Community*

EDITED BY STEPHANIE CARVIN,
THOMAS JUNEAU,
AND CRAIG FORCESE

IPAC
The Institute of
Public Administration of Canada

IAPC
L'Institut d'administration
publique du Canada

UNIVERSITY OF TORONTO PRESS
Toronto Buffalo London

© University of Toronto Press 2020
Toronto Buffalo London
utorontopress.com
Printed in the U.S.A.

ISBN 978-1-4875-0764-0 (cloth)   ISBN 978-1-4875-3666-4 (EPUB)
ISBN 978-1-4875-2527-9 (paper)   ISBN 978-1-4875-3665-7 (UPDF)

Library and Archives Canada Cataloguing in Publication

Title: Top secret Canada : understanding the Canadian intelligence and
    national security community / edited by Stephanie Carvin, Thomas
    Juneau, and Craig Forcese.
Names: Carvin, Stephanie, 1978– editor. | Juneau, Thomas, editor. |
    Forcese, Craig, editor.
Series: Institute of Public Administration of Canada series in public
    management and governance.
Description: Series statement: The Institute of Public Administration
    of Canada series in public management and governance | Includes
    bibliographical references and index.
Identifiers: Canadiana (print) 20200358367 | Canadiana (ebook)
    20200358375 | ISBN 9781487507640 (hardcover) | ISBN 9781487525279
    (softcover) | ISBN 9781487536664 (EPUB) | ISBN 9781487536657 (PDF)
Subjects: LCSH: Intelligence service – Canada. | LCSH: National security –
    Canada. | LCSH: Internal security – Canada.
Classification: LCC JL86.I58 T66 2021 | DDC 327.1271 – dc23

University of Toronto Press acknowledges the financial assistance to its
publishing program of the Canada Council for the Arts and the Ontario
Arts Council, an agency of the Government of Ontario.

**Canada Council   Conseil des Arts
for the Arts   du Canada**

**ONTARIO ARTS COUNCIL
CONSEIL DES ARTS DE L'ONTARIO**

an Ontario government agency
un organisme du gouvernement de l'Ontario

Funded by the   Financé par le
Government   gouvernement
of Canada   du Canada

Canadä

Contents

Foreword

National security has always been a fundamental responsibility of the modern state. However, in Canada as in many other countries, the national security and intelligence community has grown in power, resources, and reach since 2001. New organizations have been created, others have been merged and, as recently as 2019, the mandates of some of its core agencies have been expanded. The kind of technological innovation that has led to the emergence of new threats in recent years is also providing security and intelligence professionals with new and potentially more intrusive tools to practise their craft. Essential to our collective safety, security and intelligence agencies also operate with considerable secrecy as they wield powers and tools that, if used inappropriately, can be injurious to our fundamental rights. For these reasons, ensuring their democratic accountability and the legality of their actions is as vital as it is challenging. In sum, the agencies entrusted with security and intelligence functions have been fast evolving, their effectiveness remains vital to the interests of Canadians, and their operation raises significant challenges of democratic governance.

Given this importance, it is surprising that the Canadian national security and intelligence community is not better known. Even taking into account the difficulties created by its secrecy, the academic literature dedicated to understanding its practices, challenges, and impact remains remarkably limited. It is partly for this reason that *Top Secret Canada* is such a welcome addition to the IPAC Series in Public Management and Governance. By providing a comprehensive overview of the state of the national security and intelligence community as it stands in 2020, this volume will not only be of interest to specialists seeking an up-to-date scan of the latest developments, key trends, and challenges faced by the field's professionals, but it will also provide an invaluable one-stop overview of this sector to a broader readership of public servants, scholars, and concerned citizens interested in gaining a measure of "security and intelligence literacy."

To bring us this analysis of the state of intelligence and security organizations, Stephanie Carvin, Thomas Juneau, and Craig Forcese brought together a select group of academics and experienced professionals. Bringing different backgrounds, disciplinary expertise, and experiences to their task but using a common analytical framework, the authors deliver a wide-ranging and well-grounded diagnostic of these organizations. In doing so, they allow the reader to appreciate the unique circumstances of each organization while simultaneously identifying some common challenges, notably problems related to the retention, management, and motivation of personnel, as well as persistent difficulties of inter-organizational cooperation and coordination. Readers who are less familiar with the sector will also better appreciate the complexity of the legal environment in which these public organizations operate. Moreover, the book clearly shows the significance of the reforms adopted over the last few years to improve the transparency and accountability of the main security and intelligence agencies. While the effectiveness of these overdue changes remains to be seen, the book helps the reader understand the intent and significance of these developments.

In sum, *Top Secret Canada* is a valuable and timely book, providing us with an unprecedented, comprehensive, and insightful assessment of the state of play in this important and fast-changing sector of the federal bureaucracy. By including it in the IPAC Series in Public Management and Governance, we hope to contribute to a better understanding of this important area of public administration by academics, practitioners, and the broader public, but also to encourage more scholars and students to dedicate their research efforts to this understudied area of government activity.

Luc Juillet, PhD
University of Ottawa
Editor, IPAC Series in Public Management and Governance

TOP SECRET CANADA

Understanding the Canadian Intelligence
and National Security Community

Introduction

STEPHANIE CARVIN, THOMAS JUNEAU,
AND CRAIG FORCESE

This book is the result of a project funded by the Social Sciences and Humanities Research Council (SSHRC) that initially brought together some of Canada's foremost scholars on security and intelligence issues to create the first comprehensive public document on our national security and intelligence community. In putting this edited volume together, we had three goals: first, to provide a guide for public servants, academics, students, and the interested public who want to know more about how national security is managed in Canada; second, to enhance public discussion of Canadian national security and intelligence issues generally; and third, to analyse the similarities and differences between the various agencies, as well as current trends, by looking at the community as a whole. In these ways, our book seeks to address a gap during a time of fundamental transition within the intelligence and national security community in Canada.

The lack of literature on Canadian intelligence and national security is puzzling. Although Canada is often described as a "middle power," when it comes to intelligence, the story is more complicated. Canada is a member of the most elite intelligence-sharing arrangement in the world – the "Five Eyes" partnership – along with Australia, New Zealand, the United Kingdom, and the United States. We are also a member of the world's most successful alliance, the North Atlantic Treaty Organization (NATO), and we benefit from our close relationship with the United States. Our national security and intelligence agencies, such as the Canadian Security Intelligence Service (CSIS) and the Communications Security Establishment (CSE), are also well regarded around the world for their professionalism and capabilities.

At the same time, unlike most of its partners and allies, Canada does not have a foreign intelligence agency dedicated to the collection of human intelligence (HUMINT). Moreover, our ability to gather foreign intelligence is strictly limited by law. This is a product of our colonial history (during which the United Kingdom took the lead for defending Canadian security up until the Second World War) and perhaps also of the idea that spying on friends and foes is somehow beneath the model global citizen standard that Canadian leaders want to live up to (or at least portray). While the Department of National Defence (DND) and the Canadian Armed Forces (CAF) can gather foreign intelligence as relates to their mandate, CSIS may gather information only as relates to threats (terrorism, espionage and clandestine foreign influence, and subversion) to the security of Canada. The sole exception to this is that CSIS may collect "foreign intelligence" upon the request of the ministers of national defence or foreign affairs under section 16 of the *CSIS Act*, but this is limited to individuals within Canada. However, Canada excels at collecting foreign signals intelligence (SIGINT) through CSE.

As Canada finds itself within the most complex threat environment in a generation, the Canadian intelligence community is also facing unprecedented challenges. New threats such as online clandestine foreign influence operations are rising, while older challenges such as terrorism are not going away. At the same time, citizens have greater expectations that their privacy will be respected and that national security and intelligence services will enhance their public engagement activities. Finally, while all of this is going on, Canada has been undertaking the most significant transformation of its national security architecture since 1984. Legislation enacted by Parliament during the Justin Trudeau government (especially the *National Security Act, 2017*, an omnibus statute discussed further below) gives some agencies, like CSE, offensive cyber powers and creates stronger review and oversight.

In this context, we asked the authors in this volume to focus on the following five areas:

Mandate: Many national security agencies were formed well before 2001; as national security threats have evolved, so have their mandates. How well are agencies dealing with their new or evolving mandates?

Inter-agency Cooperation: Which agencies cooperate with each other the most, and how successful are they in their inter-agency interactions?

Resources: How well resourced are the agencies? What are current resource challenges?

Current Challenges: What are the main current challenges faced by each agency? What is their primary threat? How is it evolving?

How is the evolving nature of threats challenging these agencies to do their job?
Controversies: What recent controversies have affected Canada's national security agencies? Are they engaged in controversies around surveillance? Data collection and retention? The treatment of their own employees and/or subjects of investigation?

Key Themes

The chapters in this book identify a number of common challenges that affect all or most government departments in the national security community.

A first major overarching theme concerns efforts to adapt to the evolving threat environment. The intelligence community significantly shifted its attention to counterterrorism in the wake of the attacks of 11 September 2001, but there has been a growing recognition in recent years that this should not come at the expense of paying attention to other traditional and emerging threats. The latter – such as online foreign meddling in elections – also raise new challenges for the national security community: they call on its core organizations to learn to work with new, non-traditional partners who also have a role to play in addressing such threats (e.g., other federal government departments, as well as the private sector and provincial and territorial governments).

The distribution of roles and responsibilities within the Canadian national security community also raises questions. Both Public Safety Canada (PSC) and the national security and intelligence advisor (NSIA) to the prime minister, who works in the Privy Council Office (PCO), are tasked with a coordinating function within the national security realm. On paper, PSC plays this role with regard to its portfolio agencies (chiefly, CSIS, the Royal Canadian Mounted Police [RCMP], the Canada Border Services Agency [CBSA], and Correctional Services Canada), and the NSIA to the community as a whole. In practice, however, there is some overlap between the coordinating functions of PCO and PSC, since an important proportion of the agencies PCO is tasked with coordinating are found in the PSC portfolio. How well is this division of labour managed?

In parallel to the issue of coordination and complementarity among mandates and responsibilities is the issue of the community's ability to work together to mount whole-of-government responses to address threats to Canada's national security. As many chapters in this volume explain, most contemporary public safety and security concerns are multifaceted and complex, and tackling them requires that different departments and agencies work closely together. But – as in other realms of government activity – departments still too often, despite recent progress, work in silos, hampering their ability to achieve common outcomes.

Individual departments and agencies in the Canadian national security community all face resource challenges of one type or another. Some problems have been associated with growing pains: many, including CSIS and CSE, have grown significantly in size and budget since 2001. This has raised, for example, human resources problems (hiring the right people to fill new positions at the right moment). At the same time, the national security community has faced growing demands as threats have evolved and as workloads have surged. Air travel, for example, is expected to increase by 50 per cent by 2030, which will strain already stretched resources for CBSA.

Human resources challenges apply in particular to specialized vocations from cyber operators for the Canadian Armed Forces to analysts with skills in emerging technologies (artificial intelligence, big data, biometrics, etc.) for various departments, it is difficult to recruit, train, and retain qualified employees. It also applies to more generalist positions: intelligence analysts throughout the community often face constrained career prospects as they often reach the highest pay levels for analysts relatively early in their careers; they must then choose between moving on to management positions, leaving the intelligence world (thus depriving the community of their acquired skill and knowledge), or remaining as analysts but foregoing promotions and higher salaries. As a result, throughout the national security community, departments and agencies face high turnover rates, retention challenges, and in some instances, morale issues.

Several of the chapters in this volume also highlight the challenges posed by technology. On the one hand, it is very difficult for national security agencies to keep up with change. On the other, technology provides national security services with the ability to collect and analyse vast amounts of information. This has raised questions about trust and privacy at the same time as national security agencies are in a race to keep up with technological developments. Trying to balance security and privacy will likely be an ongoing battle for the national security and intelligence community into the foreseeable future.

Finally, national security has traditionally not been the top priority, or even among the top two or three priorities, for Canada's political leadership. There have, of course, been episodes (such as the immediate aftermath of the 11 September 2001 attacks) where it has sprung to the top of the political agenda, but these are more the exception than the norm. This has had many consequences. It implies that the level of literacy on security and intelligence issues among the country's top leadership is relatively low. This may allow the national security community to operate largely free from political interference on a day-to-day basis. But when major decisions have to be made, political considerations usually outweigh security ones in policymaking for the simple reason that the country, given its relatively secure position, can afford to do so.

The Evolving Legal Terrain

As noted above, Canadian national security law has entered its most dynamic period since 1984 and the creation of CSIS. In 1984, the *CSIS Act* constituted CSIS as a separate civilian security intelligence agency, while RCMP primacy in national-security-related law enforcement was preserved via the *Security Offences Act*.

Despite the intelligence and police failures in the 1985 Air India bombing, the field of national security law remained largely untouched thereafter until the events of 9/11. The *Anti-terrorism Act* (2001) ("Bill C-36") legislated many new terrorism criminal offences, and partially overhauled Canada's antiquated *Official Secrets Act* (renamed the *Security of Information Act*). It also placed the CSE on a statutory footing for the first time, through amendments to the *National Defence Act*. Canada's 2000 money laundering law was updated to include terrorism financing reporting among the mandates of the Financial Transactions and Reports Analysis Centre of Canada (FINTRAC). Other changes of the period included a revamped immigration security certificate process in the 2002 *Immigration and Refugee Protection Act*.

The most important institutional change of the period was, however, the creation of Public Safety Canada. In 2003, the governor in council created a new "Public Safety and Emergency Preparedness" portfolio by using the *Public Service Rearrangement and Transfer of Duties Act* to peel the then Office of Critical Infrastructure Protection and Emergency Preparedness away from the Department of National Defence, and place it into the Department of the Solicitor General. Likewise, it transferred supervision over CBSA from the minister of immigration, refugees and citizenship to the solicitor general, now styled the minister of public safety, and then transferred assorted other security and border organizations into CBSA. Subsequently, the Department of Public Safety and Emergency Preparedness was formally created by statute in 2005.

Canada then reverted to its tradition of inactivity in national security law. The most important exceptions to this were the fierce debates over re-enactment of "preventive detention" and "investigative hearing" provisions, originally created in the *Anti-terrorism Act* (2001) but that sunsetted after five years in the face of Opposition resistance to re-enactment during the Harper government minority period. Opposition to these measures become more muted by the new decade, and a majority Conservative government re-enacted both provisions in 2013, along with establishing new crimes focusing on the then-emerging problem of travel to participate in terrorist activities or with terrorist groups.

The other area of activity focused on immigration security certificates, which galvanized controversy and regular due process challenges, culminating in several Supreme Court of Canada decisions obliging renovation of the system. Most notably, a new class of security-cleared lawyers – special advocates – were invested with defending the interests of persons subject to security certificates in otherwise closed hearings.

During the period of relative inactivity between 2006 and 2015, other problems in Canadian national security law began to accrue. CSE's legislative framework introduced by the *Anti-terrorism Act* (2001) was minimalist and failed to keep pace with the explosion of electronic information and online activities. Likewise, CSIS's statute, largely untouched since 1984, was built for an analogue age, not one in which intelligence services increasingly operate in a sea of electronic data. The dated frameworks precipitated new, adverse court decisions and constitutional challenges. Meanwhile, a series of commissions of inquiry into the role of Canadian services in the mistreatment of Canadians suspected of terrorist affiliations, held in foreign jails, pointed to serious shortcomings in Canada's accountability framework. Review bodies for CSIS and CSE were impaired in their ability to integrate their reviews, and accountability review for other security and intelligence agencies was non-existent. Early in the new decade, a long-delayed inquiry into the 1985 Air India bombing identified serious shortcomings in the management of Canadian anti-terrorism investigations, and especially the challenges CSIS had in sharing intelligence with police – the "intelligence-to-evidence" dilemma. None of these developments precipitated serious legislative action – although during the Harper government, Parliament enacted a (relatively weak) form of review for the RCMP.

Thereafter, in the last year of the Harper government, 2015, Parliament enacted modest changes to the *CSIS Act* in response to adverse court decisions concerning the extraterritorial reach of CSIS's threat investigations. That change followed the Ottawa and Saint-Jean-sur-Richelieu terrorist killings in October 2014, but was not responsive to it. The legislative reaction to these events, and the by-then dominant political narrative around the Islamic State and foreign fighters, was the *Anti-terrorism Act, 2015* ("Bill C-51").

This law expanded CSIS's powers to include new physical "threat reduction" powers, and liberalized internal, federal government information-sharing on national security issues through a new information-sharing law. These, and other features, provoked considerable controversy, prompted by both their nature and their provocative drafting. For instance, the new CSIS threat reduction powers anticipated CSIS breaching any right and freedom in the *Canadian Charter of Rights and Freedoms*, so long as authorized by a Federal Court judge in a closed hearing, not subject to appeal.

The *Anti-terrorism Act, 2015* also failed to address the reality of security in an online world by updating antiquated legal provisions. Moreover, it was silent on the accountability shortcomings identified more than a decade before by commissions of inquiry. Nor was it responsive to the Air India commission's recommendations about addressing information-sharing challenges between the RCMP and CSIS – the new information-sharing act did not negate the "intelligence-to-evidence" dilemmas deterring CSIS information-sharing with police.

The new Liberal government pledged a renovation of the 2015 law to address its "problematic" aspects. The result was the *National Security Act, 2017* ("Bill C-59"). This omnibus statute, amending several statutes and enacting several new ones, constituted the most ambitious overhaul of national security law in a generation. Among other things, it remade CSE under a new statutory framework that greatly expanded its mandates while also anticipating constitutional flaws in the manner it had collected foreign intelligence that might include Canadian information. It also placed CSIS threat reduction on a more plausible constitutional foundation, while creating a new regime for CSIS to ingest datasets (digital data collections) and apply big data analytics. Controversial, these powers at least included checks and balances that made them more likely to survive constitutional challenge than the powers created by the *Anti-terrorism Act, 2015*. Moreover, the *National Security Act, 2017* addressed stalled accountability reform, creating the new National Security and Intelligence Review Agency, which has an all-of-government subject-matter mandate to review federal security and intelligence activities. This new entity supplemented the National Security and Intelligence Committee of Parliamentarians, created earlier during the Trudeau government as a first-ever classified setting for select parliamentarians to engage in national security review.

At this writing, other legal issues remain unresolved, including intelligence-to-evidence and concerns about encryption and the inability of agencies to access the content of even lawfully intercepted communications. It is expected that such issues will remain a pressing issue into the foreseeable future.

The Book Ahead

When organizing the workshop that led to this book, we faced a number of challenges. Perhaps the most significant was establishing who, exactly, the Canadian intelligence community is. One of the trends over the last two decades has been for some departments to establish their own intelligence capabilities (in many cases, assessment units) to inform their responsibilities. This includes Transport Canada and Fisheries and Oceans Canada. Also, as noted above, some departments are increasingly working with security and intelligence partners for the first time, such as Elections Canada and Canadian Heritage.

Ultimately, we chose to focus on federal agencies with a primary responsibility for collecting or analyzing intelligence, law enforcement, or policy coordination and advice on national security issues. Every chapter discusses a department or agency, with a focus on issues found under the *CSIS Act*: violent extremism, espionage, and clandestine foreign influence. We did not include departments and agencies with small units who produce or use intelligence only for their own broader mandates.

A second challenge was determining the order of the chapters. Canada does not have a hierarchy for its national security institutions. It does, however, have a centre, the Privy Council Office, which consume and produces intelligence analysis for the prime minister and their advisors, as well as the Prime Minister's Office (PMO), which provides political advice for key policy decisions, incorporating the information and intelligence it receives. Ultimately, we decided to categorize the chapters by departmental or agency function, loosely structured around the intelligence cycle – policy priorities, collection, analysis, operations/ enforcement, and review.

Part One examines the role of the central agencies with a coordinating function as well as a mandate to provide advice to the prime minister. How well do these agencies interact with the national security community? And how well are they supported in their tasks? Greg Fyffe looks in chapter one at PCO within the larger context of the evolution of the Canadian national security and intelligence community. In chapter two, Meredith Lilly then provides a unique perspective – that of political consumers of intelligence in PMO who face their own challenges in dealing with complex issues in a high-pressure environment.

Part Two focuses on national security agencies with a core intelligence collection function and/or advisory role. While these agencies were created with an intelligence collection mandate in mind, CSIS has now been tasked with "disruption," and CSE has seen its role in cyber offense (active cyber) and defence expand. What do we know about how these agencies are managing their evolving functions? How are they affected by concerns around information-sharing? How well do they support policymakers and enforcement agencies? Jeremy Littlewood first looks at the role of CSIS, Canada's most recognized intelligence service. In chapter four, Bill Robinson sheds light on the lesser-known CSE and notes that it has gained considerable influence in recent years. Despite a lack of publicly available information, Stephanie Carvin then looks at the evolving role of the Integrated Terrorism Assessment Centre and the difficulties of producing threat-related intelligence. John Pyrik discusses in chapter six the structural challenges faced by FINTRAC in countering threat finance in Canada.

National security operations, enforcement, and community engagement are the focus of Part Three. These agencies not only have national security responsibilities, but are also often the point of contact between the government and public on these issues. Yet the RCMP and CBSA have recently come under scrutiny for their behaviour toward employees and because of media stories about staff morale. How well are they meeting these challenges? At the same time, Public Safety Canada and its Canada Centre for Community Engagement and Prevention of Violence are newer agencies with an important role as a link between national security agencies, government, private industry, and local communities. What are the main challenges they face?

Kent Roach looks in chapter seven at the challenges faced by the RCMP, including inter-agency cooperation, the complexities of national security investigations, and the difficulties with community engagement, observing that it is not clear that the force has the resources to deal with these. Christian Leuprecht, Kelly Sundberg, Todd Hataley, and Alexandra Green raise similar issues with CBSA, which has witnessed two decades of an evolving mandate and a shortage of resources in the context of the increasing political salience of border issues. Alex Wilner then looks at challenges faced by Public Safety Canada, which is tasked with playing a coordinating role. In chapter ten, Brett Kubicek and Michael King provide an insider's view of setting up an office dedicated to countering violent extremism (CVE), the Canada Centre for Community Engagement and Prevention of Violence.

Part Four focuses on government departments with broader mandates but important national security functions. How do these agencies manage national security tasks within their larger mandates? How well do they interact with collection and enforcement agencies? Thomas Juneau looks at how the Department of National Defence and the Canadian Armed Forces – and specifically the Canadian Forces Intelligence Command, or CFINTCOM – function and the challenges they face in terms of resources and attention in a country that has traditionally felt well protected by geography and by its allies. Michael Nesbitt then analyses Global Affairs Canada's role as a national security actor that is not always perceived as one, including its consumption of intelligence and its production of political reporting. Similarly, Craig Forcese and Jennifer Poirier discuss the national security functions of the Department of Justice, including the dual hat role of the minister of justice/ attorney general amid the increasing judicialization of this space.

Finally, Part Five examines national security in an era of reform. In particular, it focuses on the role of accountability and public expectations in an era of declining trust in government. In chapter fourteen, Leah West analyses the new oversight and review bodies (the National Security and Intelligence Committee of Parliamentarians, the National Security and Intelligence Review Agency, and the Intelligence Commissioner). Given the changes in the *National Security Act, 2017*, is there adequate review of our national security agencies? Finally, Alex Boutilier discusses the role of the media in communicating security issues to Canadians and in holding national security agencies to account, as well as challenges in covering very secretive organizations.

As a final note, the editors wish to thank those who helped to make our workshop and this publication possible. This includes the Social Sciences and Humanities Research Council, the Privy Council Office's Intelligence Assessment Secretariat, CSIS's Academic Outreach program, the Canadian Association for Security and Intelligence Studies, the University of Ottawa's Centre for International Policy Studies, and Carleton University. In particular, Kyla Reid at the Carleton University Research Office was extremely helpful in assisting the editorial team to obtain the SSHRC funding. In addition, the editors would like to thank Mark Farfan de los Godos, who provided outstanding support as our research assistant, including logistical support and background research used in the preparation of these chapters. We also would like to thank those in the security and intelligence community who came to the workshop to offer honest and helpful feedback.

PART ONE

Central Agencies and Advice to Policymakers

1 The Privy Council Office (PCO)

GREG FYFFE

Canada's Privy Council Office (PCO) coordinates public service support for the prime minister (PM) and Cabinet. The clerk of the Privy Council heads PCO and is the principal public service advisor to the prime minister.

Since PCO coordination serves the prime minister, the Cabinet, and Cabinet committees, it covers all the functions requiring public service input into decision-making at the senior political level of government. These include ensuring that important government decisions are discussed by the PM and Cabinet and enforcing submission standards and deadlines. PCO secretariats press departments to resolve as many issues related to a submission as possible so that limited discussion time can focus on major questions. Secretariats and special purpose offices carry out these tasks, prepare agendas and records of decisions, verify follow-up, track the passage of the government's legislative program through Parliament, provide legal advice to the prime minister, and recommend senior government appointments.[1]

PCO's coordination role in the security and intelligence (commonly referred to as S&I) realm is required by the unique nature of the community and the importance and sensitivity of its activities. Indeed, this role, led by the national security and intelligence advisor to the prime minister (NSIA), exceeds the usual PCO mandate in other sectors. The NSIA is an important counsellor to the prime minister and is responsible for coordinating the work of the intelligence and security community. To reflect this, the NSIA is staffed at the most senior public service levels and is accountable only to the clerk of the Privy Council and the prime minister. Overall, for 2018 the various functions under the NSIA were staffed at 89 FTEs (full-time equivalents) and a budget of $10,988,011. Many of the FTEs serve routine internal security functions.[2]

The Development of the Canadian Community

Allied intelligence cooperation during the Second World War evolved into the Five Eyes partnership, consisting of the United States, the United Kingdom, Canada, Australia, and New Zealand. Membership has provided Canada with access to a volume of intelligence well beyond what could be obtained solely with Canadian resources. Canada has contributed to the Five Eyes, notably, through the ability of the Communications Security Establishment (CSE) to use Canada's far north to intercept the electronic communications of the Soviet Union. The Department of National Defence (DND) has been both a user and generator of intelligence, and the Royal Canadian Mounted Police (RCMP) and later the Canadian Security Intelligence Service, or CSIS, have focused on internal security and liaised with similar partner services.

Membership in the Five Eyes has been beneficial to Canada. This does not mean that Canada is seen inside or outside government as having an exceptional need to access intelligence to protect its vital interests. Canada is almost alone among nations in that it faces no enduring threat from its immediate neighbours. Our only land border is with the United States, and three oceans separate us from other land-based military threats. Existential perils, such as the proliferation and potential use of nuclear weapons, are common preoccupations for all nations. Our international interests have often been pursued through diplomacy, without the focus on intelligence characteristic of our allies.

Before the attacks of 11 September 2001, successive Canadian governments had not felt pushed to dramatically increase funding to the intelligence apparatus, and the machinery was slow to evolve. A low level of interest in intelligence and security produced a community that had to push intelligence products rather than react to a strong client pull. This in turn encouraged a culture of excessive secrecy and a disconnect from potential users. The Department of External Affairs (now Global Affairs Canada or GAC), whose counterpart in most countries is a primary client for intelligence, has traditionally viewed the Canadian community as excessively influenced by the gigantic American intelligence enterprise and liable to a perspective owing too much to American security priorities and the conclusions of American intelligence analysts.

This limited role for the intelligence community and its low public profile changed in response to major shifts in the international and domestic environments. The rise of al-Qaida, culminating in the 9/11 attacks in the United States, made terrorism geopolitically significant and a direct threat to North America. Canada needed to be seen as a fully committed partner in the anti-terrorism campaign; meeting this commitment became a foreign policy, trade, and defence priority. A $7.2 billion investment in intelligence and security capacity thus followed the attacks. Among the many institutional responses that followed was the creation of the Integrated Threat Assessment Centre, which later became the Integrated Terrorism Assessment Centre (ITAC, discussed in chapter five).

The need for quality intelligence, and independent intelligence assessment, was made clear by the invasion of Iraq in 2003. Canada did not participate in the invasion – a political and diplomatic decision supported by Canadian intelligence analysis, which dissented from that of its American, British, and Australian colleagues on the issue of weapons of mass destruction in Iraq.

Canada did participate in operations in Afghanistan, which advanced inter-agency intelligence coordination in the field. The Afghanistan mission underlined both the necessity and the difficulty of accurately assessing the future potential of military success against a non-traditional enemy within a country riven by ethnic feuds and corruption. Many countries of intelligence interest have a similar profile.

Since 9/11, the number of departments with an important intelligence need has also increased significantly: many departments found that they could not respond to the terrorism threat, global health crises, illegal fishing, human rights abuses, and many other core mandate issues without better access to intelligence. This has emphasized the requirement for central community coordination.

Canada's secure geographic position, in particular, has been no protection against ceaseless cyber-attacks on government operations and private sector intellectual property. The emergence of the cyber domain has transformed the nature of intelligence competition and introduced a security threat that in its dimensions and possible consequences is without precedent. Canada has thus had to make substantial investments in its cyber-defences to protect Canadian assets.

The period of American global dominance after the end of the Cold War has proved to be brief. Russia now threatens global stability by its military interventions, but also its information operations. China is a formidable intelligence power, and it has used cyber-penetration to acquire technology to advance its economic and military progress.

Canada also has to deal with numerous domestic threats, including terrorism, espionage, and organized crime. International organized crime has also increased as an RCMP preoccupation. Many criminal activities, such as weapons and people smuggling, cyber-crime, and the drug trade, also have intelligence and security dimensions.

Changing immigration patterns have generated tensions within Canadian society. These tensions have played out, for example, in the Air India bombing, anti-immigrant attacks, and the involvement of Canadians in supporting or participating in terrorist organizations outside Canada. Some ethnic communities are actively tracked by their country-of-origin security services or other organizations, and may be tempted, or forced, into activities inimical to Canadian interests.

Finally, Canada's shift from classic peacekeeping operations to peace-enforcement and stabilization operations has increased the need for tactical, operational, and strategic military intelligence, and has raised the level of the intelligence function within DND. This has increased the overall capacity of the community.

The Canadian response to the 9/11 attacks and other trends since marks a clear divide in the history of the Canadian intelligence and security community, and subsequent developments have continued to raise the community's profile and importance.

Community Coordination Needs

The historical path toward centralization has ebbed and flowed, but Canada and its Five Eyes intelligence partners have all placed the leadership of the security and intelligence function close to the prime minister or president. There are compelling structural reasons explaining this important role that PCO plays in coordinating the work of the S&I community in the federal government.

Several agencies specialize in aspects of security and intelligence, but no agency has a coordination role for the entire community. CSE and CSIS are collectors. The RCMP is a police force. ITAC is an aggregator of talent in analysing terrorism. GAC is a primary customer, and an important contributor of information through diplomatic reporting. DND integrates intelligence into all aspects of its activities. Numerous other departments also have internal intelligence units to support their mandates, such as Transport Canada and Fisheries and Oceans Canada.

Public Safety Canada serves a coordinating function for its portfolio agencies (CSIS, the RCMP, Correctional Services Canada, the Parole Board, and the Canada Border Services Agency [CBSA]), but not GAC, DND, CSE, or the many departmental intelligence units. Public Safety can give direction and resolve portfolio issues that do not require senior-level discussion with other departments. Those that do will move to one of the PCO-level structures. Public Safety may also take on major tasks, such as the consultations, policy, and legislation for the intelligence and security reforms carried out by then-Minister Ralph Goodale during Prime Minister Trudeau's first term (2015–19). PCO has the mandate and structures to facilitate the discussion and resolution of issues involving major policy decisions, the setting of government-wide S&I priorities, and the handling of sensitive files. It does not have the resources to carry out all phases of a major system reform, and may defer to Public Safety for the development of important files requiring the level of resourcing available within that department.

The overall coordination role can, therefore, be realized only by the Privy Council Office, but Public Safety is responsible for many of the S&I agencies (as discussed in chapter nine). Where it is not the final voice on coordination issues, it is a major contributor to Cabinet- and deputy-minister-level deliberations.

Different countries provide for security and intelligence leadership in different ways, but the challenges are similar. Detailed priorities must be agreed on to provide guidance for collectors and analysts, and for the allocation of resources to intelligence and security operations. Intelligence judgments must be integrated into the decision process. The agencies themselves have to develop the pathways for sharing information gathered from multiple sources. Distribution channels must be rapid and secure. Community leaders need structures to facilitate the discussion of key issues, whether immediate or long term. For Canada, allied relationships are also particularly important.

It is essential that activities within the community not conflict with other government priorities, particularly those in foreign policy, and support decision-making in critical areas, such as the acceptance or rejection of foreign investment proposals. Central leadership also promotes community professionalism, including the development of training programs, and recommends who should be named to senior positions. The NSIA must also be able to quickly convene those needed to deal with a crisis.

It is PCO's responsibility to ensure that the community makes the best use of its resources to pursue Canada's security and intelligence goals. PCO's S&I coordination objectives include all those normally fulfilled by any other PCO secretariat, but it exerts a greater degree of active leadership of the S&I community. Not only is security a primary concern of government, and intelligence input an important resource, but security and intelligence issues also have a unique potential for embarrassing governments. Action or inaction by an intelligence and security agency may appear to compromise public safety, undermine citizen rights, insult a particular ethnic or social group, or damage foreign relations. The prime minister and key ministers thus need to be briefed at the right level of detail on sensitive files and kept informed on possible developments.

Prime Ministers and the National Security and Intelligence Advisor

The increase in the importance of intelligence within the federal government has been further driven by an increase in prime ministerial interest, and a corresponding shift in the role of the NSIA.

Prime Minister Jean Chrétien (1993–2003) was a sceptic of the value of intelligence, but was responsible for the massive funding increase for the community after 9/11. Prime Minister Stephen Harper (2006–15), on the other hand, appreciated intelligence and expected PCO to play a strong role in community coordination. Prime Minister Justin Trudeau (elected in 2015) has made intelligence briefings a part of the information base for himself and his staff.

The position of intelligence and security coordinator was created within PCO in 1985 and endured in name until 2004, when the designation was changed to "national security advisor" (NSA). The role varied in rank from assistant deputy minister to senior deputy minister. In 1993, the coordinator gained responsibility for a central office for intelligence assessment. The Intelligence Assessment Secretariat (IAS) was formed within PCO when budget cuts led to the elimination of the analytical unit in the Department of External Affairs.

The position of coordinator was often doubled up with another PCO responsibility, such as associate clerk or legal counsel. This diluted its focus but gave it weight within the PCO structure. At the time of 9/11, the coordinator was Richard Fadden, who had served previously in the Security and Intelligence Secretariat. He was simultaneously legal counsel to the prime minister and deputy secretary for legislation and house planning. His triple responsibilities therefore put him at the centre of the government response to 9/11, including the financial, legislative, and policy elements.

After 9/11, there was a high turnover of individuals holding the coordinator and then NSA position, but this hides an important element of continuity within the senior ranks of the intelligence community. Some officials have held the senior PCO position more than once, and several have served in other senior positions within the community – in CSIS or DND, for example – or in other agencies with a significant intelligence or security component, such as Transport, Immigration, and the Food Inspection Agency. Their personal relationships over a prolonged period, in related roles, have been an important factor in building community linkages.

The change from "coordinator" to "national security advisor" signalled an increased attention to intelligence coordination in PCO by emphasizing the function of providing advice to the prime minister. It also made the functional link to similar offices in allied governments clearer. In 2017, the name was changed again, to "national security and intelligence advisor," symbolically emphasizing the importance of intelligence.

The prime minister's foreign affairs role has long been supported by the Foreign and Defence Policy (FDP) Secretariat in PCO. This secretariat is traditionally headed by a career diplomat, the prime minister's foreign policy advisor, with a senior officer from the Canadian Armed Forces as the deputy head.

In 2012, under Prime Minister Harper, the Foreign and Defence Policy Secretariat was added to the mandate of the NSA. As noted below in more detail, this has integrated foreign policy and intelligence briefings and made preparation for international meetings more comprehensive. The move completed the triad of secretariats under the NSA: Security and Intelligence, Intelligence Assessment, and Foreign and Defence Policy.

Prime ministers meet frequently with foreign leaders, who are usually well informed by briefings that include intelligence materials, prepared by officers similar to the NSIA. Placing Foreign and Defence Policy under the NSIA also made the incumbent the most senior PCO official responsible for advice on foreign policy, and a potential senior envoy for the prime minister in special circumstances.

Incoming Prime Minister Trudeau was briefed on the importance of intelligence by his transition advisor, Peter Harder. The prime minister and his team, and NSA Richard Fadden and his group, established a good working relationship, which continued with the next NSIA, Daniel Jean. The appointment of Daniel Jean as NSA/NSIA put a senior Global Affairs official at the head of the intelligence and security community. This appeared to follow the precedent of many of Canada's allies in naming a senior foreign affairs official to lead the intelligence community, but was more attributable to the importance of his personal credentials as an experienced official with credibility within the government and internationally. His successor as NSIA, Greta Bossenmeier (appointed in 2018, she retired in late 2019), held senior positions in the Canada Border Services Agency, PCO, and Global Affairs before being named chief of CSE in 2015. Finding the right person for national security and intelligence advisor will always be difficult. Only a small number of deputy ministers (DMs) are senior enough and have experience in all the areas the NSIA is responsible for coordinating – security and intelligence, foreign policy, and defence.

Bossenmeier was replaced in February 2020 by Vincent Rigby, who was until then an associate deputy minister at PSC and has wide-ranging experience in defence, foreign affairs, development, public safety, and intelligence analysis. It appears, however, that the Foreign and Defence Policy Secretariat will not report to him, but will instead report directly to the clerk. At the time of writing, it remains too early to assess the implications of this decision to hive FDP off from the NSIA's portfolio.

The NSIA Secretariats

Coordination structures in the S&I branch in PCO serve the related functions of facing inward to serve the prime minister and Cabinet, and outward to promote community coherence. The three secretariats – Foreign and Defence Policy, Security and Intelligence, and Intelligence Assessment – work closely together and attend each other's briefings and meetings on a regular basis. (The Security and Intelligence Secretariat is also known, like the community, as "S&I"; this chapter refers to it as PCO-S&I to avoid confusion.) There is no echo of the earlier period in which the security and intelligence function was a mystery to others in PCO. The NSIA structure provides secretariat functions to related Cabinet committees, and leads community-oriented committees designed to promote maximum communication among senior officials.

The NSIA and the three secretariats work directly with the prime minister and the prime minister's staff. There is a regularly scheduled weekly meeting of the NSIA with the PM, and other meetings take place as necessary. PCO-S&I and IAS staff brief the PM's senior advisors, particularly those responsible for issue management and policy, and are regularly contacted by PMO staff for further information and briefings. Sometimes the prime minister is briefed directly by staff.

In the durability of its mandate and core functions, the Security and Intelligence Secretariat is the most stable element of the Privy Council Office S&I structure. Its current responsibilities are comparable to those it has traditionally had, albeit with a substantial increase in the volume of its work and capacity. PCO-S&I deals with many of the urgent and contentious files, particularly domestic operational ones. It must simultaneously be able to serve the Cabinet committees that are focused on longer-term priorities. To be able to do so, it is responsible for overall community coordination, policy development, Cabinet committee support, and management of operational issues, urgent files, and special projects. Its staff are usually seconded from other S&I departments and agencies, positioning it as an office that helps create networks across the community. PCO-S&I is alert to the needs of different departments, including many only partially or temporarily involved in an S&I issue. It bears the responsibility for refining the coordination machinery and addressing gaps. PCO-S&I meets weekly with the PMO to brief on outstanding issues and is present when the Intelligence Assessment Secretariat briefs on intelligence assessments.

The capacity of the Intelligence Assessment Secretariat increased significantly with new funding after 9/11. Staff may enter by competition, or be seconded from other departments and agencies. Source departments include GAC, CSE, DND, CSIS, and ITAC. The flow of analysts also goes in the reverse direction. The IAS is one of the main entry points for subject matter experts from university programs into the S&I community. Currently there is always one person seconded from GAC's Global Security Reporting Program (GSRP), which makes it easier to integrate GSRP reports into the information flow to the prime minister. The IAS also produces intelligence assessments for the community, with a growing focus on the needs of the prime minister. It has increasingly used infographics to summarize complex issues, backed up by written papers.

The IAS issues a short daily classified intelligence summary to members of the community and provides a weekly classified summary to the prime minister. The IAS also coordinates the production of community assessments. Many of its papers are subjected to a community review process, with the IAS responsible for decisions on the final product. The IAS also takes the lead in delegations to assessment meetings with allies, and is able to extend networks by including representatives of other agencies. The IAS is, moreover, responsible for the IALP, the Intelligence Analysts Learning Program, which offers courses on intelligence analysis to all departments requiring training in writing assessments. The fundamental principle for intelligence assessments, in Canada as elsewhere, is to be "policy relevant, but policy neutral." Sound assessments are written to provide the intelligence foundation for policy discussions, not to support or oppose a policy direction.

Foreign and Defence Policy was, until early 2020, the third secretariat under the NSIA. The foreign policy advisor is, as noted above, an experienced diplomat, either a senior assistant deputy minister or a deputy minister. In addition to regularly briefing the PM and travelling with him on foreign visits, the foreign policy advisor is frequently in contact with the equivalent senior advisor to the president or prime minister in other countries.

This separate role of the foreign policy advisor continues, but adding FDP to the NSIA portfolio provided a link between intelligence production, intelligence assessments on international issues, and foreign policy advice. It provided a channel for intelligence input at the highest level of foreign policy management, and gave the NSIA a direct link to the prime minister's thinking on foreign policy and experiences and needs in travelling abroad, and more precision on briefing requirements. It raised the value of intelligence assessments, as their production became more closely tied to the PM's diplomatic role and foreign travel. The structure combining intelligence assessment and foreign policy advice created a risk that intelligence assessments could be toned down in some circumstances, but this did not appear to be an issue. The assumption remained that intelligence assessments must be independent in judgment and explicit in expressing conclusions from the intelligence, whether or not their analysis confirms foreign policy judgments.

The Committee Structure

The NSIA, in addition to their direct contacts with colleagues, works through a committee structure that has become more defined in recent years.

PCO secretariats serve Cabinet committees by following important portfolio developments and by working with the committee's Cabinet minister chair to oversee the preparation of issues for committee discussions. This includes ensuring that proper consultations have taken place, arranging the agenda, making sure documentation is properly prepared and circulated, taking notes, distributing decisions, and following up on key issues.

Cabinet committees relevant to the S&I community include those responsible for intelligence and security policy and the setting of intelligence priorities, and subject committees covering foreign affairs, trade, and defence. All may draw on intelligence material. As of August 2018, the relevant committees were the Cabinet Committee on Canada in the World and Public Security and the Cabinet Committee on Canada-US Relations, Trade Diversification and Internal Trade. The former Cabinet Committee on Intelligence and Emergency Management (CCIEM) reviewed intelligence reports, S&I priorities, preparedness for terrorist incidents, and the response to emergencies and national security issues. It had the power to establish ad hoc committees do deal with specific incidents. The policy responsibilities and priority functions were transferred to the Cabinet Committee on Canada in the World and Public Security (now Global Affairs and Public Security). A separate Incident Response Group was set up to deal with emergency situations, to parallel similar committees established by Canada's Five Eyes partners such as the UK's COBR/COBRA (described by the acronym for the Cabinet Office Briefing Rooms in which it meets). This removed the need to appoint ad hoc committees and underlined the PCO role in managing community issues.

Since the Cabinet Committee on Global Affairs and Public Security now covers foreign policy and the policy aspects of the former Cabinet Committee on Intelligence and Emergency Management, it is supported by both the Foreign and Defence Policy Secretariat and the Security and Intelligence Secretariat. CCIEM also examined special issue briefs named Security Intelligence Reviews. At CCIEM, deputy ministers sat at the table with ministers, an arrangement that reflected their special expertise and that has been traditional when community priorities have been discussed at the Cabinet committee level. This is an unusual practice for Canadian Cabinet committees, but sensible when it is the senior public servants who have detailed knowledge of S&I community preoccupations and capacities.

The mandate of Global Affairs and Public Security now includes setting intelligence priorities. Intelligence priority-setting can be frustratingly complex as it involves assessing priorities across domestic and international threats with an appreciation of the capacity needed to meet possible future threats. New priorities may arise without any certainty that previous ones can be set aside. An intelligence priority process must be able to document client department needs, match needs with community capabilities, and make sure that there is a way to obtain the needed intelligence. This involves examining departmental capabilities, intelligence received from allies, and the potential for developing new capacity if budgets can be augmented or shifted. Under the process now in place, priorities are reviewed every six months. Every year progress against the priorities is reviewed, and a new priorities process takes place every two years.

For community coordination, there are three deputy-minister-level committees under the NSIA, backed by parallel assistant deputy minister committees. PCO can also set up a special body to manage a particular issue, such as an ad hoc committee of DMs.

1.) The Deputy Ministers National Security Committee (DMNS) includes a large group of DMs and works from a standard agenda that allows for the discussion of new and hot files, and substantive longer-range issues. A round table at every meeting gives an opportunity for all departmental issues to be brought forward.

2.) The Deputy Ministers Operations Committee (DMOC) includes the core DMs in the S&I sector and examines operational issues, including the management of critical files and incidents, the forward Cabinet agenda, consular files, support for prime ministerial travel, and relations with the US. It can also support an operation or an exercise.

3.) The Deputy Ministers Intelligence Assessment committee (DMIA) meets once a month, usually discussing two important peer-reviewed

National Intelligence Assessments, drafted by IAS. The committee also plans a forward agenda for other priority assessments.[3]

When he was the NSA, Richard Fadden started off his tenure with a retreat on national security, with wide representation from DMs and other branches of PCO. This has now been institutionalized, and the intention is to schedule at least two such retreats per year.

As in other areas, PCO is also a natural place for special advisor functions. Toward the end of a long career in security and intelligence, Ward Elcock was federal coordinator of Olympic and G8/G20 security (2007–10) and then special advisor on human smuggling and illegal migration (2010–16). Putting special coordination functions in PCO underlines their importance to the government, and gives the official responsible the structure and authority to carry out special mandates.

These changes to PCO machinery, and the cooperative spirit that has driven them, have increased the effective interaction of senior officials in the S&I sector, made it easier for departments and agencies to bring forward important issues, and provided the means to overcome the barriers to communication and information-sharing that are inevitable in a community that is both extensive and organizationally diverse.

Challenges

PCO has steadily improved its coordination machinery as it has augmented its ability to serve the prime minister and his office. It may be that future prime ministers will not wish for intelligence briefings with the same enthusiasm as Prime Ministers Harper and Trudeau, but most of the factors that have led to the increased need for PCO leadership will persist.

Coordination can be improved, but there is no finish line. In meeting current responsibilities, the resources allocated to PCO are seen internally as appropriate. If Canada's need for intelligence increases, or the security threat level goes up, the Security and Intelligence Secretariat might need to grow to enable the NSIA to lead an even more complex community. The Intelligence Assessment Secretariat could find that its relatively small size handicaps it as other departments, such as DND and GAC, increase their analytical capacity.

The security and intelligence community struggles to recruit the right people and to retain them. PCO is at the centre of this dilemma, as it recommends senior appointments to the prime minister. Sometimes there is a limited number of experienced candidates for senior positions. Rotating officials into senior positions in intelligence and security from other departments can be difficult, as an operational understanding of the sector cannot be easily acquired. Bringing in new recruits from outside government is frustrated by the lengthy period needed to complete security clearances. Some vital skills, such as intelligence analysis, provide limited opportunity for advancement, driving many analysts to move on to other positions. Government needs highly skilled cyber experts and must compete with the private sector, which needs them as badly but can often pay more. Private sector companies are expanding their capacity to respond to a growing number of security threats. Operational veterans from the government security and intelligence agencies are targets for recruitment.

An important unknown is the extent to which new review and oversight structures – the National Security and Intelligence Committee of Parliamentarians (NSICOP) and the National Security and Intelligence Review Agency (NSIRA), discussed in this volume in Leah West's chapter – will challenge the coordination responsibilities of PCO. Many more departments and agencies with an intelligence function are now subject to hearings by the committee and review by NSIRA. However, pressure from parliamentarians and other review bodies may be a positive stimulus to the community and push even greater coordination.

Conclusions

The PCO structure has evolved to serve the needs of the prime minister and of the wider community. Changes in structure will, therefore, continue. The ultimate question is whether coordination will continue at the level now in place, or move to a higher level. An example of greater coordination is the UK model, with a common intelligence budget and the centralization of the community through the Joint Intelligence Committee. Form does follow function, which in turn follows need. The need for coordination is surging, not receding.

For the time being, the need is being met: the machinery serves the purposes of PCO and the community. Changes in committee structures and processes have steadily increased the interaction level between PCO and the other departments and agencies in the security and intelligence community. Resource investments, legislative changes, and machinery adjustments have improved Canada's credibility with its allies.

NOTES

This chapter draws on the experience of the author as executive director of the Intelligence Assessment Secretariat in PCO from 2000–8, on continued contact with people in the intelligence and security community after 2008, and on interviews with current and former government officials familiar with recent developments and structures.

1 There are a few public sources on the structure of PCO and its operations, but very few for the intelligence function. PCO's role within the Canadian government has changed over time, and its structure changes as priorities change. The PCO website describes its functions in detail. See in particular https://www.canada.ca/en/privy-council/corporate/mandate.html and https://www.canada.ca/en/privy-council/corporate/organizational -structure.html. While Cabinet committees are listed at https://pm.gc.ca /en/cabinet-committee-mandate-and-membership, the operation of the structure is not described in public sources. Books that help understand the role of PCO and the Prime Minister's Office include Eddie Goldenberg, *The Way It Works: Inside Ottawa* (Toronto: McClelland & Stewart, 2006), and more recently, Ian Brodie, *At the Centre of Government: The Prime Minister and the Limits of Political Power* (Montreal and Kingston: McGill-Queen's University Press, 2018). Brodie's book is in part situated as a counterpoint to the writings of Donald Savoie, and the theme in his many books, such as *Governing from the Centre* (Toronto: University of Toronto Press, 1999), on the centralization of the Canadian government under the prime minister. This chapter maintains that the centralization of leadership of the security and intelligence community in PCO is explained by reasons special to that community.

2 Governments are intentionally imprecise about the amounts spent on security and intelligence so that capabilities cannot be inferred. Information on PCO can be found on the "Open Government" website at https:// open.canada.ca/data/en/dataset/e03ef931-c096-4710-bc4a-1fcd0cc0ea00. FTEs are projected as the same for 2019–20, with expenditure reduced to $10,771,907.

3 The committee structure described here was in effect at the time of writing in 2019, but will inevitably change.

2 The Prime Minister's Office (PMO)

MEREDITH B. LILLY

Introduction

When originally asked to contribute this chapter on the use of intelligence in the Prime Minister's Office of Canada (PMO), I declined. Security and intelligence policy is not a focus of my research, nor do I have a strong personal drive to address issues surrounding the operation of Canadian intelligence agencies. Despite this, I have had the rare experience of being one of a small group of individuals to directly advise a Canadian prime minister on foreign policy matters that use and apply intelligence gathered by Canada's various agencies. Through this experience, I developed some unique insights into how intelligence is used at the nexus of political advice and public policymaking.

This chapter diverges from the format of other chapters in this volume for several reasons. First, while many individuals may be interested in reading about who received official intelligence in Stephen Harper's PMO, how it was used, and what classified files I worked on – there is little upside to Canadian national security interests or to me personally for disclosing such information. Thus, this chapter does not offer a "who's who" of Stephen Harper's PMO from an intelligence perspective.

Second, every PMO is temporary and operates differently. I can speak only about my experience serving as a policy advisor to Stephen Harper from 2012–15 as a political staffer. In the Canadian context, political staff comprise a small group of employees who combine advice from the non-partisan public service with additional analysis of the political factors that may influence government decisions and public communication. Political staff are usually hired from outside of government specifically to advise political leadership and ensure delivery of the government's mandate. They tend to be less constrained than public service counterparts to draw information rapidly from a variety of sources – the public, experts, stakeholders, and business – to offer additional advice to politicians directly. As Mr. Harper's foreign affairs and international trade advisor, I oversaw the international trade, foreign affairs, and international development portfolios within PMO. I accompanied the prime minister on most foreign trips, including to war zones and international summits, and also participated in all incoming visits by foreign leaders. I had regular interaction with the security and intelligence staff of the Privy Council Office (PCO) during that period. My personal reflection on the use of intelligence represents a very small window into the broader PMO in which I worked, and may offer no additional insights into continuing PMO operations today.

The PMO is involved in the full range of national security and intelligence functions, which affect a range of files: domestic security and border control; foreign and domestic terrorism and counterterrorism; emergency preparedness and response; health pandemics; national defence; critical infrastructure; foreign investment and trade; and espionage and foreign political interference. Most of the time, relevant files are managed independently by line departments and agencies. Nevertheless, Canada's prime minister often advances bilateral and multilateral interests on the world stage and is Canada's ultimate spokesperson on international affairs. Therefore, policy staff in the PMO must work closely with the foreign affairs department and its minister, remain apprised of relevant security and intelligence developments, and sometimes lead on specific files when the prime minister's direct engagement is needed. Similarly, on the domestic side, the prime minister is expected to lead and manage any response to a major security event or tragedy in Canada. At such times, files are swiftly moved from line departments and agencies to the PMO and PCO for overall coordination. In their entirety, security and intelligence policy functions in the PMO tend to be allocated across several staff and their superiors in the PMO structure.

With the above caveats, I offer several reflections on the interplay between PMO and PCO in the use of intelligence, as well as on political staff in related departments and the departmental officials who support their work. I offer four lessons that may be of interest to those working in the field. While my comments are specific to the use of foreign intelligence in the management of international files, there may be application for domestic security and intelligence processes as well.

1. Tell Me What I Need to Know, Not What You Want to Tell Me

Political staff are busy. Really busy. Part of their duty is to be accessible at all times to political colleagues within PMO and elsewhere on the Hill, and most importantly in my case, to the prime minister. This has implications for the format in which officials convey intelligence to political staff as well as the amount of time political staff can devote to receiving sensitive intelligence.

Aside from the Cabinet processes and specific policy files that are brought to PMO's attention, there are several ways in which intelligence staff brief political staff on ongoing foreign intelligence developments. One is in the form of regular written foreign intelligence briefs, which offer basic information about geopolitical conflicts and issues as well as some economic information. These briefs can be highly useful for political staff because they can be read when it suits the staffer's limited availability. A quick skim is often all that is necessary, and staffers do not always have the flexibility to read every report every time. For this reason, these briefs should be regarded as "information only" by respective agencies and should not supplant other types of briefs on important intelligence developments, especially if it is anticipated that departmental action will be required on a given file.

To clarify, "information only" documents are provided to ministers and political staff literally for their information. It may be helpful to think of "information only" documents as private, client-focused news feeds: they contain news that the client is likely to be interested in, but that may never be read. Similarly, though the intelligence analysts preparing the briefs see obvious links between the "news feed" item and the target reader's role and responsibilities, the "client" staffer may not see any direct relevance. This may be because both the motivations and focus of the intelligence agencies providing the information and the political staffer receiving it are different and often poorly understood by both sides. It then follows that if public servants believe it is *important* for a minister or their advisors to possess specific intelligence – even if no action is required – then the public service should provide that intelligence via a different mechanism than the "information only" brief.

All the same, the "information only" brief can be highly useful over time, as political staff become familiar with which world hot spots are getting "hotter" or "colder," which in turn provides context for broader media narratives and geopolitical events. This offers political staff a level of literacy that then allows them to read public news sources more intelligently, ideally avoiding being surprised by emerging events in foreign countries such as military coups, et cetera.[1]

The other standard practice used by officials of offering in-person briefings in windowless rooms without access to mobile phones can be more problematic for political staff. Certainly, the rationale for observing such security protocols is obvious and clear. However, the capacity of political staff to cut themselves off from their political colleagues and their minister or prime minister for 30 minutes or more in the middle of a business day is extremely limited. In order to justify that use of a senior political staffer's time, the intelligence being shared in such briefings must be carefully prioritized by officials. It should be *important*, not simply *interesting*, and intelligence officials should err on the side of sharing only information that staff *"need to know"* rather than what may be *"nice to know."* Since receiving and working with intelligence forms only a very small component of any political staffer's role, senior staff in the PMO simply do not have the flexibility to receive "nice to know" briefings.

So what does a senior political staffer charged with intelligence functions in the PMO "need to know"? Obviously, within the realm of intelligence that is gathered according to approved procedures, political staff advising the prime minister need to know about events that are certain or very likely to impact Canada in the very near term (days or weeks, not months, away). For example, is there any country on the verge of political collapse that is likely to require Canadian intervention (because Cabinet or the prime minister will need to make a decision on aid or military assistance)? Are national elections being held where the result is likely to be contentious or vulnerable to fraud (because it would be embarrassing for Canada's prime minister to publicly congratulate the victor only to find out the outcome was fraudulent)? Are there private sector deals on the horizon that will affect Canada's critical infrastructure or national security interests (because these may come to Cabinet for decision under the *Investment Canada Act*)? Have any Canadians been unlawfully detained by authorities overseas in countries of concern (because the PMO will be asked for comment and the prime minister may need to intervene)? Political staff also need to be informed about any significant security and intelligence breaches suspected of being carried out by foreign governments or their operatives in Canada.

How do the above examples differ from what is simply "interesting"? Events or trends that should be categorized as "interesting" are not likely to have a direct impact on Canada, are not likely to affect Canada for a delayed period of time, or are unlikely to require the prime minister's personal attention. These may pertain to civil unrest in a small country with few historic ties to Canada, routine overseas election results, or scientific technologies being developed with long-term national security implications. All of these items may potentially be relevant to Canada, but none are time sensitive and often can be handled at the ministerial level or by departmental staff directly. Therefore, the best place to brief on "interesting" matters that are not time sensitive is in written form, such as the "information only" daily briefs described above, rather than in person.

Timeliness of information and appropriate classification of intelligence so that it can be used in a timely fashion are also critical.[2] It should go without saying that intelligence that is delivered to PMO too late to be useful to the prime minister's work is neither "important" nor "interesting" to political staff and, if deadlines have been missed, it would be better to leave "information only" briefs undelivered altogether. I recall several instances when, regrettably, intelligence briefs containing information that was directly relevant to a meeting with a foreign leader were delivered to my office after the meeting had already taken place. Or information was so highly classified that it was difficult to deliver to the prime minister's team when travelling overseas and therefore could not be accessed when most useful. In the first case, I suspect the delay was not the fault of diligent intelligence analysts who had prepared the briefs weeks in advance, but instead the result of slow approval chains within the bureaucracy. Nevertheless, as I frequently tell my students as the reason I offer no flexibility on deadlines for assignments, the single most important rule when accompanying the prime minister overseas is "Never miss the motorcade." Put simply, intelligence is useful to political staff only if it can be used to advise the minister effectively: missing the proverbial motorcade by delivering a brief "too late" is helpful to no one and represents an enormous waste of resources.

The urgency of daily life at PMO does not imply that medium and long-term security and intelligence challenges are left unaddressed. On the contrary, the Cabinet process is an important mechanism for the development of long-term plans to address societal challenges on any range of matters, including security and intelligence. The Cabinet process offers space and discipline to gather relevant information and strategies from across government, and for a variety of views to be consulted in the development of national plans. Most senior public servants and political staff would agree that Cabinet usually offers a more thoughtful and disciplined forum to address long-term issues than do

narrow discussions between PMO, PCO, and line departments. Use of
the Cabinet process is also helpful in tamping down concerns that actors
at the "'centre" (PMO, PCO, Department of Finance, or Treasury Board)
may be seeking to advance their own narrow interests or undermine the
objectives of those on the "periphery" (line departments, agencies, and
ministers) unfairly.[3]

Still, the Cabinet process is also a political process and vulnerable to
resource limitations: a minister or the prime minister must be success-
fully engaged on a file in order to advance it for presentation in that
forum. Security and intelligence challenges that intelligence agencies
may believe are priorities but that do not secure the necessary political
buy-in will face difficulties being added to the Cabinet agenda. Since
the "end run" to Cabinet is always possible if the prime minister personally chooses to prioritize a file, it is inevitable that policy staff in the
PMO get lobbied on any range of short- and long-term issues by both
the public service and external stakeholders.

Thus, returning to the title of this lesson, "Tell me what I need to
know, not what you want to tell me," it is important for both the public
service and political staff to listen carefully for the right cues in all such
lobbying efforts:

- Sometimes officials *would* tell me what I needed to know, but
  I was frankly distracted by other (equally or more) pressing
  matters. In these instances, my advice to public servants would
  be that if something's important, don't give up. Tell the staffer
  again.
- Sometimes officials would instead tell me what they wanted to
  tell me, but I mistook it for something I needed to know and acted
  accordingly. This strategy can backfire on everyone involved,
  since the full resources of the PMO are then deployed to address a
  relatively unimportant issue (the "bazooka to swat a fly" problem).
  If such mismatched interactions occur regularly, trust erodes
  between officials and staffers, which can have more negative
  consequences down the line.

To summarize, as in foreign diplomacy, I would advise public servants
against sacrificing the benefits of a strong and mutually respectful
working relationship with a political staffer for short-term, transac-
tional gains on bureaucratic priorities. Similarly, political staffers of
every party affiliation would be well served to remain open to challenging advice from officials, even if they ultimately pursue a different
direction on any given file.

2. Political Staff Are Intelligence Assets

There is an understandable hesitation in the public service around sharing highly sensitive intelligence with political staff. Intelligence officials frequently do not have a strong understanding about the level of training that political staff receive in the handling of sensitive security and intelligence information. There is also a series of protocols pertaining to accountability in the chain of sharing sensitive intelligence that likely come into play. If, for example, a Canadian intelligence official shared classified information with an untrained political staffer, and that staffer then publicly divulged the information, the official could be partially blamed and face penalties. Given the potential consequences of such breaches, it is both reasonable and valid for intelligence staff to tread carefully. However, it is also precisely for these reasons that any political staff cleared to receive highly sensitive intelligence must first complete a series of security clearance procedures and be oriented to the responsibilities and requirements associated with having such clearance.

Yet it is also important to impress upon intelligence officials my view that very senior political staff often possess the best qualities associated with protecting and securing highly sensitive information. In my experience, one of the reasons that political staff rise to the senior ranks is precisely their discretion and judgment: in protecting personal information about the politicians they serve, in handling sensitive information about Cabinet proceedings, and in demonstrating judgment in the conduct of their personal lives to avoid becoming an embarrassment to the government. Senior political staff are also not simply passive recipients of intelligence that has been gathered exclusively by Canadian intelligence officials making bureaucratically driven determinations about what is "safe" to share with them. Other parties – domestic and foreign – share delicate information with political staff directly, and they also gather sensitive information themselves from various external groups to inform their policy advice.

Despite this, senior political staff are at times excluded from important policy discussions by intelligence officials who may believe that political staff cannot be trusted.[4] Despite some of the media stories that support a contrary narrative, it was not my experience during my time in politics that political staff were untrustworthy. Certainly, some junior political staff have had very little training or experience in dealing with sensitive information. But the political staff who are selected to receive sensitive intelligence are rarely neophytes at their first job.[5] In my case, I had nearly two decades of professional experience managing confidential files and sensitive research data, in addition to doctoral training in the appropriate handling and use of private personal information.

To this end, following their departure from politics, political staff who have demonstrated success in managing intelligence files may be obvious recruits for Canada's intelligence agencies. Such individuals have already demonstrated their trustworthiness in protecting and maintaining strict confidentiality, and many have a talent for gathering intelligence themselves. Most political staff never consider careers in intelligence, but instead fall into these roles due to their other responsibilities. Still, it seems to be a lost opportunity for the Canadian intelligence agencies involved not to seek to retain staff who have demonstrated a natural aptitude for the work.

In the same fashion, as intelligence agencies are increasingly asked to engage with the public about what they do, former political staff with experience in communications can offer an important skill set. Political communications staff are individuals with years of experience engaging the media directly on controversial, confidential issues. The best ones remain employed in those positions by engaging the media effectively but without divulging either too much or the wrong kinds of information. Through experience, they have been schooled – sometimes very publicly – on what the differences are between "on the record," "off the record," and "background" media briefings and how to build mutual trust with reputable journalists over time.

A recent high-profile example in Canada of a senior public servant who briefed journalists on sensitive intelligence matters serves as a case in point. On the condition of anonymity, that individual briefed a number of journalists on a politically sensitive matter tied directly to the prime minister. Not surprisingly, the public servant was publicly identified within a matter of days, causing embarrassment to Canada's security and intelligence reputation and concerns about the possible politicization of our security and intelligence agencies.[6] The entire situation could have been avoided if the public service had employed a seasoned former political communications staffer to advise on the plan. Such an employee could easily have anticipated the high likelihood that the official would be named, and would have prepared an alternate plan that met the government's communication objectives without reputational risk to Canada's intelligence agencies.

Perhaps counter-intuitive to those with reflexively negative views about political staff,[7] consulting a former staffer (who is no longer active in partisan activity) also may have helped avoid allegations that Canada's security establishment was acting in a partisan manner in the above case. Unlike in the United States, where security and intelligence portfolios are highly politicized and concerns about the politicization of policymaking have existed for decades,[8] Canadian intelligence agencies have largely been regarded as operating in a non-partisan manner. This is positive for Canada and helps maintain public confidence in those agencies and their employees. However, this impartiality must not be taken for granted as either a natural or permanent state: it must be continually protected by the public service and the institutions created to protect its neutrality.[9] Former political staff have been trained to identify and recognize a variety of risks to public office holders:[10] once discharged from political roles, their expertise could be applied elsewhere in government to help ensure that real or perceived conflicts of interest and allegations of partisan behaviour are avoided.

3. Crisis Situations Are Well Managed and Highly Scrutinized Already

As mentioned at the outset, national security crises always involve the Prime Minister's Office. The public looks to its prime minister for guidance, comfort, and leadership in times of crisis, and therefore, the public handling of major events involving the loss of life in Canada will always involve the PMO. This was the case following the terror attacks on Patrice Vincent and on Parliament Hill in 2014, as well as the Toronto van attack and Danforth shootings in 2018. However, unlike ongoing intelligence work, which is frequently restricted to a small number of staff in PMO, many political staff are involved in the management of large-scale emergencies. For example, PMO communications and issues management staff, who engage with media and who normally do not work with intelligence files, need to be briefed up quickly about events as they unfold.

In addition, as has been outlined elsewhere,[11] Canada's PMO/PCO together comprise the "centre" of government and serve as a hub for whole-of-government communication, coordination, and direction. There is always intense interest in the handling of such major crises by the various agencies involved, and it is not uncommon for the events to become the subject of public inquiries and parliamentary committee investigations. Take, for example, the inquiry into public agency operations following the attack on Parliament Hill in October 2014.[12] Such public reports are also often paralleled by internal government audits into the management of the crisis. If legal prosecution is involved, many of the details are also made public through legal discovery processes.

For this reason, and due to the limits on what I can share with respect to my own knowledge of such events, I have not devoted any space to reflecting on specific events here. Public policy lessons to be learned are frequently captured in the public reports released, as mentioned above. There are also separate public communication lessons on offer that can be particularly relevant for the political arm of government.

I would, however, note that it has been my experience that cooperation and teamwork between the political level and public service arms of government have often been highest during these periods of crisis and heightened tension. The strong public and media calls for action and pressure for quick answers perhaps heighten the awareness between public servants and political staff that each serves an important function, and both are counting on one another for information, advice, and error-free delivery. In these high-stakes contexts, many of the layers of bureaucratic oversight that can increase opportunities for misunderstanding and often serve to frustrate both sides of the PMO/PCO divide are overcome in favour of direct exchanges with short chains of command. Finding ways to replicate this sort of rapid and collegial teamwork during everyday operations may improve workflow and quality for staff in both offices, and ultimately, the Canadians they serve.

4. Political Staff Can Be Traumatized by What They Know

Contrary to many intelligence officials, I did not seek – nor did I want – Top Secret security clearance. The Secret clearance I already possessed made me privy to enough sensitive information to last a lifetime. Nevertheless, Top Secret clearance was required for my role so that I could work on highly sensitive files effectively and quickly.

Some of the sensitive intelligence I received was graphic in detail, documenting the worst atrocities humans can commit. While many Canadians can bear witness to similar awful information by reading media accounts of genocide or the war in Syria, I found that receiving such information through classified channels was incredibly isolating precisely for its "secretiveness." I felt a deep burden and responsibility for simply possessing some of the information I knew, especially when it pertained to Canadians detained abroad. Political staff are in the unique position of offering direct advice to ultimate decision-makers charged with making difficult calls about the most tenuous and life-threatening situations. It is important for staff to find ways to cope with the constant stress induced by possessing such large quantities of negative information.

I'm sure that our intelligence agencies have considered the psychological consequences that collecting or possessing very traumatic intelligence can have on their staff. For example, in its 2017–18 report, Canada's Security Intelligence Review Committee referenced the mental health consequences to Canadian Security Intelligence Service (CSIS) operatives exposed to sensitive material during operations. The committee recommended that additional resources be dedicated to providing timely, specialized assistance.[13]

However, during my time in PMO, the only time psychological help was ever offered followed the terror attack on Parliament Hill on 22 October 2014. I, like most of my colleagues, was working in the Langevin Building when events unfolded across the street. Locked down in one of the country's most secure buildings, I never felt that my personal safety was threatened and was instead focused on doing my part to respond to the situation.

Any personal psychological stress I experienced on that day and during its aftermath was minor in comparison to the private grief and pain I experienced in dealing with a handful of sensitive foreign intelligence files. I managed those files largely alone within PMO, I couldn't speak to colleagues or family about what I knew, and I sometimes felt powerless to do anything to change the situations at hand. Certainly, the burden I experienced was nothing compared to the weight felt by politicians who are ultimately charged with making difficult decisions and taking action, the experiences of Canadians detained abroad in horrendous conditions, or the dangers that face Canadian Armed Forces members deployed overseas. Nevertheless, the experience for political staff charged with possessing the most sensitive state secrets can be very isolating, and I found it at times to be traumatizing.

Significant advances have been made in Canada in recent years to provide specialized mental health services for Canada's first responders and military beyond "employee assistance programs," which are largely inappropriate for those circumstances. It is hoped that these services are extended to intelligence officials exposed to traumatic content in their work, as recommended by the House of Commons Standing Committee on Public Safety and National Security in 2016.[14] I would further recommend these services be offered to political staff and parliamentarians who manage sensitive security and intelligence files. Recalling the limited capacity of staffers to disconnect from their duties during the workday, services must be available outside of business hours and should recognize the stigma associated with seeking help, which may discourage staff.

Conclusion

In this chapter, I have provided a glimpse into the duties and responsibilities of political staff who work with, and use intelligence in, the PMO, and lessons we might draw from those experiences.

First, to narrow down the vast amounts of intelligence provided to political staff to what is useful, intelligence analysts should focus on what a prime minister needs to know to discharge their responsibilities to Canadians rather than what the analysts want to tell the prime minister to demonstrate the value of their intelligence efforts. If agencies focus on the former, the latter will be obvious.

Second, experienced political staff should be regarded as assets to intelligence agencies both during and after their political careers. While in their roles, political staff are not passive recipients of intelligence provided to them by officials but are instead active participants in gathering, collecting, and synthesizing intelligence for policymaking purposes. Following their political careers, seasoned political staffers from across party lines could bring a unique and valuable skill set as employees of intelligence agencies, particularly to improve the public-facing functions of these organizations.

Third, by virtue of the public investigations that often follow large-scale crises and emergencies in Canada where intelligence has played an important role, much is already known about the management of these events by political actors. Much less is known about the day-to-day use of intelligence at the nexus of political and policy functions. In the future, more attention to the use and application of intelligence in daily operations would be extremely valuable.

Finally, just like their public service counterparts, political staff engaged in intelligence activities can be exposed to violent information and images, with traumatic effects. However, unlike in Canada's security and intelligence agencies, political staff who receive sensitive intelligence are often isolated from colleagues who have shared their experience. As the public service seeks to address occupational stress injuries among intelligence officials,[15] it is obligated to extend these services to political staff engaged in similar work.

While some of the lessons I have offered will be well known to security and intelligence officials who work closely with political staff, others may seem surprising. In my experience, staffers who have been entrusted with security and intelligence duties are just as committed to the safety and security of Canadians as the public servants they work alongside. Though it is fundamental to maintain clear divisions between the political and non-partisan operational arms of government, that separation should never be confused with the obligations of both sides to work collectively in the interests of national security. As I reflect on the various scandals that engulf the national security and intelligence community in the United States under President Donald Trump, I am deeply proud of our own national security apparatus and the careful steps that are taken every day by professionals on both sides of the political/public service divide to protect the integrity of our own system.

NOTES

1 Amanda J. Gookins, "The Role of Intelligence in Policy Making," *SAIS Review of International Affairs* 28, no. 1 (2008): 65–73.
2 See Gookins, "The Role of Intelligence in Policy Making."
3 Ian Brodie, *At the Centre of Government: The Prime Minister and the Limits on Political Power* (Montreal and Kingston: McGill-Queen's University Press, 2018).
4 Anna Lennox Esselment, Jennifer Lees-Marshment, and Alex Marland, "The Nature of Political Advising to Prime Ministers in Australia, Canada, New Zealand and the UK," *Commonwealth & Comparative Politics* 52, no. 3 (2014): 358–75, https://doi.org/10.1080/14662043.2014.919731.
5 R. Paul Wilson, "Research Note: A Profile of Ministerial Policy Staff in the Government of Canada," *Canadian Journal of Political Science* 48, no. 2 (2015): 455, https://doi.org/10.1017/S0008423915000293.———. "Trust but Verify: Ministerial Policy Advisors and Public Servants in the Government of Canada," *Canadian Public Administration* 59, no. 3 (2016): 337–56, https://doi.org/10.1111/capa.12175.
6 Privy Council Office, "Appearance before the Standing Committee on Public Safety and National Security (SECU)," Opening Statement by Daniel Jean, National Security and Intelligence Advisor to the Prime Minister, 16 April 2018. Available online: https://www.canada.ca/en/privy-council/news/2018/04/appearance-before-the-standing-committee-on-public-safety-and-national-security-secu.html.
7 Ian Brodie, "In Defence of Political Staff," *Canadian Parliamentary Review* 33 (Autumn 2012): 33–39, http://www.revparl.ca/35/3/35n3_12e_Brodie.pdf.
8 See Gookins, "The Role of Intelligence in Policy Making"; Bethany Eisenfeld, "The Intelligence Dilemma: Proximity and Politicization – Analysis of External Influences," *Journal of Strategic Security* 10, no. 2 (2017): 77–96, http://doi.org/10.5038/1944-0472.10.2.1583.
9 See Brodie, *At the Centre of Government*.
10 See Esselment, Lees-Marshment, and Marland, "The Nature of Political Advising."

11 See Brodie, *At the Centre of Government.*
12 Royal Canadian Mounted Police, *RCMP Security Posture, Parliament Hill, October 22, 2014: OPP Review and Recommendations* (2015). Available online: http://www.rcmp-grc.gc.ca/en/rcmp-security-posture-parliament-hill-october-22-2014. See also Standing Senate Committee on National Security and Defence, *Countering the Terrorist Threat in Canada: An Interim Report* (2015). Available online: http://publications.gc.ca/collections/collection_2015/sen/yc33-0/YC33-0-412-18-eng.pdf.
13 Security Intelligence Review Committee, *SIRC Annual Report 2017–2018* (2018). Available online: http://www.sirc-csars.gc.ca/anrran/2017-2018/index-eng.html#section_2_3.
14 Standing Committee on Public Safety and National Security, *Healthy Minds, Safe Communities: Supporting Our Public Safety Officers through a National Strategy for Operational Stress Injuries* (2016). Available online: https://www.ourcommons.ca/Content/Committee/421/SECU/Reports/RP8457704/securp05/securp05-e.pdf.
15 See Standing Committee on Public Safety and National Security, *Healthy Minds, Safe Communities.*

PART TWO

Core Collection and Advisory Agencies

3 The Canadian Security Intelligence Service (CSIS)

JEZ LITTLEWOOD

The Canadian Security Intelligence Service (CSIS) was established by an Act of Parliament (the *CSIS Act* [1984]) and began its formal existence on 16 July 1984.[1] At its founding it had 1,968 staff,[2] of whom approximately 95 per cent were from the RCMP Security Service,[3] which had been disbanded and replaced by CSIS following a Royal Commission into illegal activities by the Royal Canadian Mounted Police (RCMP, discussed in chapter seven). Upon its establishment, CSIS had an estimated budget of $115 million.[4] Today, it employs over 3,200 individuals and has a budget allocation slightly over $589 million.[5] The consolidated public accounts for 2018–19 indicate that CSIS's total allotment in that fiscal year was over $607 million.[6]

CSIS is arguably the best-known core intelligence agency of Canada's national security community. Together with the Communications Security Establishment (CSE) and the RCMP, it represents the front line of intelligence. The Service, as CSIS is often called, is a security intelligence agency, meaning its mandate relates to threats to the security of Canada. Those threats are defined, broadly, in the *CSIS Act* and cover espionage, foreign influence and interference, terrorism and political violence, sabotage, and unlawful covert acts to undermine Canadian democracy.[7] Beyond these, public reports have also identified the proliferation of chemical, biological, radiological, and nuclear (CBRN) weapons, cybersecurity, and critical infrastructure protection as national security issues.[8] Like all intelligence organizations, CSIS draws upon all sources to collect, analyse, and develop intelligence, but it is the recruitment and use of human sources that is its principal niche. It is not a law enforcement agency and has no powers of arrest or detention. The Service has a physical presence in at least 16 locations within Canada. It also operates globally through foreign stations and security liaison officers (SLOs).

This chapter examines in turn the mandate of CSIS, its resources and footprint, its liaison and cooperation (intelligence-sharing) issues, the challenges facing CSIS, and specific controversies it is currently embroiled in. Inevitably, there is overlap between these issues; for example, threat reduction measures (disruption) are both a mandate issue and a controversy. The threads of the narrative explanation in the principal sections are brought together in the conclusion of the chapter.

Mandate

The mandate of CSIS is defined in law under the *CSIS Act*. Amendments and additions to the act since 1984, most notably in 2015 and 2019, have resulted in CSIS having four principal roles. First, as an intelligence collection and analysis agency, under section 12 of its act, it investigates and subsequently reports to and advises the government on threats to the security of Canada. This is its core intelligence function, and the threats are defined in section 2 of the act.

Second, as per additional powers under the *Anti-terrorism Act, 2015*, CSIS may undertake threat reduction measures (TRMs) against threats to national security under what is now section 12.1 of the *CSIS Act*. This activity and the mandate were initially controversial and subject to further evolution under Bill C-59 (*National Securty Act, 2017*).[9]

Third, CSIS conducts foreign intelligence activity, but to the confusion of many, "foreign" intelligence is conducted by CSIS only within Canada. It is not legally permissible under the *CSIS Act* to conduct foreign intelligence in another country. This does not mean that CSIS works and operates only in Canada. As noted, CSIS is a security intelligence agency with a primary focus on threats to the security of Canada. Its officers and staff do work outside of Canada, that is, in foreign countries, but do so only related to the security intelligence aspect of the mandate. "Foreign," in this context, means the collection of information or intelligence about the capabilities, intentions, or activities of foreign states and persons (who are not Canadian citizens, permanent residents, or a corporation) and in relation to the defence or the conduct of international affairs of Canada. This foreign intelligence activity is authorized only at the written request of either the minister of foreign affairs or the minister of national defence and with the approval of the minister of public safety as per section 16.

Fourth, CSIS is responsible for security screening activity related to most employees of the Government of Canada who have access to classified material and to individuals who require access to sensitive sites (e.g., airports, nuclear power plants), as well as security assessments related to visitors, citizenship and immigration applicants, and refugees to Canada. Each of these powers is explored below, with the exception of threat reduction measures, which are explored in the section on controversies.

Intelligence Collection, Analysis, and Advice

The core intelligence function of CSIS is, as noted above, determined by section 12 of the *CSIS Act*, whereby the Service is mandated to "collect, by investigation or otherwise, to the extent that it is strictly necessary, and analyse and retain information and intelligence respecting activities that may on reasonable grounds be suspected of constituting threats to the security of Canada and, in relation thereto, shall report to and advise the Government of Canada."[10]

CSIS's primary role in collection is via human sources, but it is not limited to collection using only human sources. It collects intelligence via investigations and other means, which include open sources and through liaison and cooperation agreements with other agencies and organizations in Canada and abroad (intelligence-sharing). Several investigation techniques, such as physical surveillance, human sources, and information received through liaison and cooperation agreements, are not subject to judicial authority and control (warrants), but are managed by internal control and compliance mechanisms and can be examined by review and accountability entities. More intrusive techniques, such as interception of communications, and access to and obtaining records, documents, or items, require a warrant to be issued by a judge of the Federal Court as per section 21 of the *CSIS Act*. Furthermore, retention of a dataset – a collection of information stored as an electronic record and characterized by a common subject matter – that is filled with primarily Canadian information is subject to judicial oversight and authorization. (Retention of foreign datasets involves the approval of the intelligence commissioner.)

Outside of the special dataset regime, collection and retention of information and intelligence are limited to "the extent that ... is strictly necessary," although what "strictly necessary" means is not clearly defined in the *CSIS Act*. That is not to say it is unimportant: in fact, the "strictly necessary" test is of fundamental importance.[11] However, it requires a contextualized interpretation and operationalization rather than a bounded legal definition, as is evident in Part II of the *CSIS Act*, relating to judicial control, and in the stipulations within the act for applications for a warrant. The concepts of "strictly necessary" and "may assist" were under examination by CSIS internally following a 2016 court ruling.[12]

CSIS also conducts analysis of the information and intelligence collected. Information is corroborated, verified, and validated as much as possible, and assessments and judgments are formed by analysis. This occurs within the Intelligence Assessments Branch (IAB) of the Service. The collection and analysis activities of the Service are limited to threats that may on "reasonable grounds be suspected" of constituting threats to the security of Canada. The Service then reports to and advises the Government of Canada about these investigations. The reporting and advice take many different forms, including written intelligence reports, oral briefings, and involvement in cross-government committees. It is, however, for the government to decide on how to respond to such advice. Information and intelligence on threats are distinct from decisions on how to respond to such threats. The latter is the prerogative of decision-makers.

CSIS identifies the key threats to the security of Canada as terrorism, the proliferation of weapons of mass destruction, espionage, foreign interference, and cyber-tampering affecting critical infrastructure.[13] Economic security is included within the understanding of national security in this context. These more specific descriptors are not immediately evident under the formal definitions of the CSIS Act, which define threats to the security of Canada in more generic terms. However, the act has the advantage of being well understood in legal, policy, and operational environments and establishes the agreed boundaries of threats. Lawful advocacy, protest, and dissent are not considered threats to the security of Canada, and CSIS is prevented from investigating such activity unless it is carried out in conjunction with the defined threat activities. However, historically and contemporaneously there is an inherent fuzziness in determining whether any threatening sharks are swimming with or alongside the inoffensive fish involved in lawful advocacy, protest, and dissent,[14] which has raised legal issues for CSIS and other organizations involved in national security.[15]

Foreign Intelligence

In its 2011–13 public report, CSIS described foreign intelligence as "information about the capabilities, intentions and activities of foreign states or entities."[16] Canada has no equivalent to the Secret Intelligence Service (SIS) of the UK or the Central Intelligence Agency (CIA) in the United States. In a narrow sense, Canada does not have an intelligence organization with a primary mandate of recruitment of covert human sources for foreign intelligence in the economic, military, and political realms. This should not be construed as Canada lacking any foreign intelligence capability: as is clear from the other chapters in this book, Canada does gather foreign intelligence from all sources, and collectively the Canadian intelligence community is able to provide the Government of Canada with foreign intelligence through open source reporting and diplomatic channels, through the technical and signals intelligence capabilities of CSE, through technical and other capabilities related to defence via Canadian Forces Intelligence Command (CFINTCOM), and through allies and other intelligence cooperation arrangements.

CSIS also plays a role in foreign intelligence under section 16 of the *CSIS Act*, which permits it to conduct foreign intelligence within quite tight boundaries. As noted, this can be confusing because CSIS's foreign intelligence activity is not conducted in any foreign country, but in Canada, and when a CSIS officer (employee) is working in another (foreign) country abroad, they do so as part of the security intelligence mandate of the Service. Under its mandate, "the Service may, in relation to the defence of Canada or the conduct of the international affairs of Canada, assist the Minister of National Defence or the Minister of Foreign Affairs, within Canada, in the collection of information or intelligence relating to the capabilities, intentions or activities of (a) any foreign state or group of foreign states; or (b) any person other than (i) a Canadian citizen, (ii) a permanent resident ..., or (iii) a corporation incorporated by or under any Act," collect intelligence and information on the "capabilities, intentions or activities of" any foreign state or group of foreign states or any person (except a Canadian citizen, a permanent resident, or a corporation) if it is "in relation to the defence of Canada or the conduct of the international affairs of Canada, [to] assist the Minister of National Defence or the Minister of Foreign Affairs."[17]

Thus, CSIS's foreign intelligence collection activities may occur only in Canada, against someone who is not Canadian or a permanent resident, and by request, in writing, of the respective ministers of national defence or foreign affairs. They also may occur only with the consent of the minister of public safety.

In 2009, CSIS's former review body, the Security Intelligence Review Committee (SIRC, now replaced by the National Security and Intelligence Review Agency, NSIRA, discussed in chapter fourteen) examined the evolution of CSIS's role in foreign intelligence and reported that the "collection of foreign intelligence is no longer as limited as it once was."[18] SIRC stated it had reported to the minister of public safety that there were now "questions about whether there should be a dedicated foreign intelligence service in Canada."[19] These questions arose from the emergence of what CSIS referred to as "blended collection," or the linking of its security intelligence and foreign intelligence activities because of increased demand for intelligence across government. This "melding," as SIRC referred to it, could give rise to CSIS becoming "what Parliament never intended it to be: namely, a Service with equal security and foreign intelligence mandates."[20]

The requirement for a dedicated foreign intelligence service like the CIA is a long-standing debate in Canada, which periodically reanimates after its apparent death. In the wake of 9/11, the possibility of establishing a foreign intelligence service was part of the platform of the Conservative Party in the 2006 federal election, and it is a staple of the academic literature about intelligence in Canada.[21] The lack of action by successive governments suggests that ministers have determined that the existing structures and mandates suffice. However, court rulings may result in the issue reappearing in the future.[22]

Security Screening

The Service is also responsible for security assessments of individuals. These take two forms: government security screening (GSS) and immigration and citizenship screening (ICS). Data is reported in CSIS's public reports and the reports of SIRC. In GSS, the role of CSIS is to assess employees of the Government of Canada who require lawful access to classified information or other individuals who work in sensitive sites, such as major ports, airports, nuclear facilities, or the Parliamentary Precinct.[23] In total over 60,000 requests per year relate to the federal government, and a further 140,000 per year to other entities. CSIS also supports both Immigration, Refugees and Citizenship Canada (IRCC) and the Canada Border Services Agency (CBSA) by providing assessments on citizenship, permanent resident, and temporary resident visa applicants (whether visitors, students, or temporary workers) and persons applying for refugee status in Canada. The last available public report from CSIS indicated 250,000 requests in 2015–16, 223,000 in 2016–17, and over 300,000 in 2017–18.[24] This implies that, taken together, the Service screens nearly 10,000 people per week, a significant increase beyond what was reported in 2004, when there was an average of 7,500 screenings per week.[25]

Resources

Resource allocations have a significant influence on the conduct of intelligence. As noted, the original budget for CSIS (1984–85) was estimated at $115 million ($255 million in 2019 dollars). In 2018, CSIS was allocated

Figure 3.1. CSIS expenditure 2001–7. Figures in millions of C$. Data from CSIS public reports and GC InfoBase.

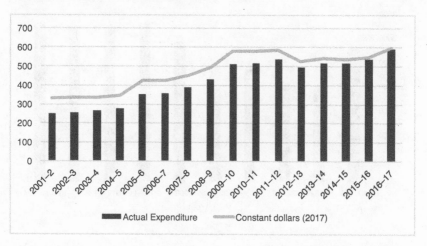

$570.3 million in the main estimates, but additional commitments brought the allocation to $599.5 million for fiscal year 2018–19. This accounted for 0.2 per cent of the $284 billion budget of the federal government.

Allocations have been rising, and the five-year trend (between fiscal years 2014–15 and 2018–19) indicates an increase of 13.8 per cent.[26] Over the last five years, CSIS has not used all its allocation and has underspent by approximately 4 per cent per annum ($25 million on average).[27] Federal accounting breaks down CSIS program spending into two areas. In 2016–17, of the $589,416,000 allocated, the Intelligence Program accounted for $546,128,000 and the Security Screening Program for $42,288,000, indicating that security screening consumed over 7 per cent of expenditures.

Staffing

Approximately 62 to 65 per cent of CSIS's expenditures appear to be in salaries: thus, any increase in resources must be considered in line with the increase in staff. At its establishment, the Service had 1,968 staff. In 1992–93, it employed 2,760 people, its high point until 2008–9, when it reported 2,910 employees.[28] The 2014–15 public report indicated 3,217 employees, but opacity has crept in and now staffing levels are reported as "over 3,200." Figure 3.2 provides data on select years to illustrate the steady increase in the number of employees over time.

Figure 3.2. CSIS employee numbers. Data from CSIS public reports.

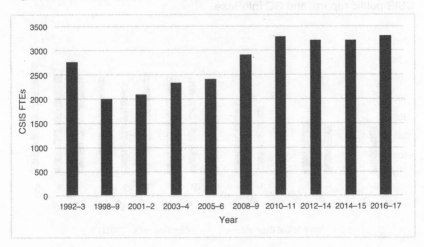

Of the employees in 2015–16, approximately 48 per cent were female, 2 per cent Aboriginal/First Nations peoples, 4 per cent persons with disabilities, and around 480 members of visible minorities (15 per cent).[29] More recent data indicates a slight increase in employees who are members of a visible minority.[30] Over two-thirds of staff are bilingual (69 per cent), and 18 per cent have an additional foreign language to French or English. Data indicates over 100 languages are spoken by CSIS employees.[31]

The number of employees in the Service does not easily map on to any given period of crisis. Recruitment is a process that can take between twelve to eighteen months, and for intelligence officers (IOs) the basic training is understood to last one year. Thus, budgetary resources were increased after 9/11, but CSIS employee numbers did not significantly increase until 2003–4.

CSIS staff are located across Canada and the world. The headquarters is in Ottawa, and there are six regional offices, in Halifax, Montreal, Ottawa, Toronto, Edmonton, and Burnaby, covering respectively the Atlantic Provinces (Nova Scotia, New Brunswick, Newfoundland and Labrador, and Prince Edward Island), Quebec, Ottawa, Toronto, the Prairie region (covering Ontario north and west of Thunder Bay, Manitoba, Saskatchewan, Alberta, and the territories of Yukon, Northwest Territories, and Nunavut), and British Columbia. Regions also have district offices located in Newfoundland and Labrador (St. John's), New Brunswick (Fredericton), Quebec (Quebec City), Ontario (Niagara Falls; Windsor),

Manitoba (Winnipeg), Saskatchewan (Regina), and Alberta (Calgary). In addition, there are "several Airport District Offices, including those at Toronto's Pearson International Airport and at Vancouver's International Airport."[32] Assuming that "several" means more than two but fewer than ten, Canada's principal international airports likely have a CSIS presence.

As noted in chapter twelve, CSIS also operates abroad in foreign stations and with staff acting as SLOs. The Service has identified only the United States (Washington), the United Kingdom (London), and France (Paris) as foreign stations, but it has in the past acknowledged temporary stations and deployments in Afghanistan and Lebanon. The foreign footprint is quite small: in its 2008–9 report the Service noted that of its "2,910 employees, more than 50 CSIS Foreign Officers were located abroad ... in approximately 30 countries."[33] Notwithstanding the decade since then, the foreign footprint is probably still below 5 per cent of employees. Overall, a staffing level of 3,200 combined with the number of locations where CSIS has a physical presence implies that employees are spread thinly in certain places. Deployments abroad require cross-government liaison, most notably with Global Affairs Canada (GAC) and, presumably, SLOs are based out of diplomatic stations given the requirements for a secure physical location, IT and communications equipment that can handle classified information, administrative support, and a whole-of-government response to a variety of issues. SLOs are most likely in locations where there is a nexus between intelligence priorities and threats to the security of Canada that emanate abroad.

Cooperation

Cooperation is essential to intelligence collection, analysis, and reporting. There are at least three broad areas of cooperation to consider: first, intra-CSIS cooperation, that is, cooperation within the Service itself across regional and district offices and foreign stations, and within operations; second, cooperation with other departments, agencies, and organizations of the federal government and cooperation with provinces, territories, municipalities, and other public sector organizations, as well as with the private sector; and third, cooperation with agencies of other governments.

Intra-CSIS Cooperation

Intra-organizational cooperation is as important as inter-organizational cooperation. Inquiries into intelligence failures and strategic surprise in democratic states often reveal error within, as well as dysfunction and rivalry between, organizations involved in national security.[34] However, "knowledge of the inner workings of ... [CSIS] ... is minimal, not only in the population at large, but also in academia and even within the federal government itself."[35] Indeed, outside of the public reports of SIRC and commissions of inquiry, little is known about cooperation within CSIS, even though such cooperation is evident from its organizational structure, successful national security court proceedings, and SIRC reports.

In 2012, a change in the HQ–regional offices relationship gave regions flexibility in turning principles and guidance from HQ into reality on the ground in order to emphasize "collaboration and integrated approaches" in operations: upon reflection, "this has been a positive development."[36] Intra-Service cooperation also faces challenges beyond organizational structure and resources: a consistent issue within CSIS is professional culture and the separation between IOs and non-IOs. SIRC reported in 1999 that IOs are treated differently in terms of salary, training, and career advancement,[37] and a 2017 workplace climate assessment in the Toronto region office and districts did nothing to dispel the understanding that, within CSIS subcultures, IOs, non-IOs, and managers clash and that an "old boys network" mentality and "a culture still permeated with its militaristic past"[38] remain in existence. CSIS leadership has publicly acknowledged some of these problems and has stated that it has begun a process to try to address them.[39]

A further challenge to internal cooperation is resourcing, with some units in the Toronto office being understaffed and smaller regional and district offices struggling to implement business modernization.[40] This resource issue can be seen in other SIRC reports over the years. A final example, relevant to warrant controversies, is the inevitable silos that emerge in any large organization that relies on both generalists and specialists (legal, IT, etc.): with regard to warrants, SIRC has suggested that legal experts may not always fully understand the modalities of intrusive communications surveillance and data management, whereas technical experts may lack details of the legal environment CSIS operates within.[41] This is not to say that specialist communities are ignorant of or careless about the issues. Rather, it underlines that intra-Service cooperation is essential to avoid failures and running afoul of the law. In this regard, although intra-CSIS cooperation is clearly evident, even the sparse information in SIRC reports and other material points to challenges in coordinating complex issues, resources, and workplace culture.

In one sense, this should be expected given the complexity of the national security environment, the legal and political context of intelligence collection, and the size and organizational structure of CSIS. However, in a political culture where the mere whiff of wrongdoing is fodder for the media and others to hark back to the barn burning and burglary days of the

RCMP Security Service, intra-CSIS cooperation is likely to be more heavily scrutinized in the coming years. This, together with court rulings and a wider transparency agenda around national security,[42] may account for the emergence of an operational compliance framework within the Service.[43]

CSIS Cooperation with Other Canadian Actors

The Service cooperates with a host of other federal departments and agencies. At the very least, this involves the 17 entities identified in the *Security of Canada Information Disclosure Act* (2015),[44] now the *Security of Canada Information Disclosure Act*, although up to 100 organizations are potential partners in Canada for CSIS.[45] CSIS's relationships with the RCMP and CSE have more significant operational implications.

Historically the focus of concern in this area has been the CSIS–RCMP relationship. The *CSIS Act* requires CSIS and the RCMP to work collaboratively because the former has no powers of arrest or detention, while the latter maintains the law enforcement role. While guidance to both was provided by the solicitor general in 1984[46] and SIRC reports note an ongoing evolution of the relationship, one assessment suggests that when and how to cooperate "was largely left to the leadership [of CSIS and the RCMP] and the rank and file of the two agencies, with only occasional prodding from the outside."[47] Other views, notably from SIRC's quite regular assessments of the relationship, are more positive.[48] Post-9/11, the imperative to share intelligence to counter terrorism resulted in a new CSIS–RCMP memorandum of understanding (MOU) in 2006. Subsequently, experience, the tempo of operations, and various inquiries gave rise to the "One Vision" framework in 2012 and the development of "One Vision 2.0" in 2015.[49]

Accompanying the evolving CSIS–RCMP relationship post-9/11 were larger developments, including the creation of the Integrated Terrorism Assessment Centre (ITAC) and the emergence of the Integrated National Security Enforcement Teams (INSETS): indeed, from the fall of 2001 much of the reform in Canadian national security has been driven by a need for greater integration in order to deliver effective and efficient responses to threats.[50] Successful terrorism prosecutions since 9/11 indicate that the intelligence to law enforcement relationship works but is not without major challenges. The CSIS–RCMP relationship is not one of seamless intelligence-sharing, for legal, structural, and cultural reasons, and at the heart of these lies the perennial intelligence-to-evidence challenge.[51] Nevertheless, the relationship exists within an overarching political, legal, and societal framework beholden to the wrongdoings of the 1960s and 1970s as its principal frame of reference. Intelligence-to-evidence is a significant challenge, but CSIS and the RCMP are not *the* problem, even though they are an important piece within that challenge, which requires legal and political overhauls rather than simple inter-institutional fixes.

The Service's other key relationship lies with CSE, which possesses extraordinary expertise in the protection, exploitation, and interception of what it calls the "global information infrastructure." Under its existing mandate, CSE may assist CSIS upon request and subject to legal authorizations of the activities (i.e., warrants). Prior to 9/11, it was likely that the CSE–CSIS relationship was more limited: even in redacted form, the MOU from 1990 is relatively sparse. Post-9/11, the shift to enhanced cooperation and coordination between national security agencies and the rise of information technology increased CSE's relationships with other parts of the intelligence community, but a new MOU did not emerge until 2012. Since 2014, CSIS and CSE have been located in adjacent buildings, leading one journalist to characterize their relationship as "extremely cozy."[52] The revelations of Edward Snowden and the Federal Court's apparent displeasure with the lack of candour by CSIS with regard to its use of CSE and other Five Eyes partners to collect signals intelligence on CSIS targets abroad, together with the changes to the *Security of Canada Information Sharing Act* (2015) (which became the *Security of Canada Information Disclosure Act* in 2019), have brought greater attention to the extent of CSIS–CSE relations.

Coziness between the Service and CSE should be expected; indeed, in an era of complex and multiple threats, technological ubiquity, and expectations of coordinated government responses, if the Service and CSE were at cross purposes there would be significant reason for concern. The importance of exploiting the global information infrastructure to contemporary intelligence is difficult to understate. In addition, cybersecurity has risen to the top of many national security threat assessments. The protection of the federal government's most important IT infrastructure is the responsibility of CSE, which devotes around one-third of its budget to IT security. With the formation of the Canadian Centre for Cyber Security in 2018, CSE has taken on a more public role, and one consequence is that CSIS's role in investigating and advising on cyber threats to the government and other actors (e.g., provincial and municipal governments, critical infrastructure providers) is likely to evolve substantially in the coming years. The role of CSIS is likely to be niche, but the CSIS–CSE relationship will be even more important as threats to the security of Canada and foreign intelligence will have a cyber dimension.

CSIS Cooperation with Other States

In a briefing provided to the minister of public safety in 2015, CSIS reported that it had over 300 information-sharing agreements with

156 countries and territories.[53] Liaison and cooperation allows the Service to both push (send) and pull (request) intelligence from other states. The thwarted Khawaja and VIA Rail terrorism plots and the Delisle espionage case all point to intelligence-sharing being of central importance in Canadian national security, with these cases involving UK and US cooperation.

One area of concern post-9/11 has been the relationships between CSIS and states with poor human rights records, as revealed in public inquiries and other documents.[54] As a result, ministerial direction was updated in 2017[55] and again in 2019, underlining clear expectations.[56] In a recent report, SIRC "found no evidence that CSIS used information obtained by torture and other cruel, inhuman, or degrading treatment, nor directly contributed to human rights abuses," but identified procedural and policy shortfalls. CSIS is currently adapting its approach to ensure adherence to the ministerial direction of 2017.[57]

The Omar Khadr case illustrates many issues related to information-sharing.[58] The case illustrates how political pressure, human rights, fear of terrorism, the need for information and intelligence, the expectation of a whole-of-government approach, and the roles of individuals all play out together under certain circumstances. No agency or department was reflected in a positive light by the Khadr case. CSIS took the brunt of opprobrium but had also been pulled by its imperative to collect information and intelligence. SIRC's review outlines that the case "brought to the forefront [that] information-sharing with foreign partners, especially in cases where there are human rights concerns, dealing with youth, and interacting with detainees in foreign jurisdictions, do not have easy answers or solutions."[59] One outcome of the case, which also considered the impact of legal decisions not directly related to CSIS activity, was that "CSIS can no longer undertake its activities solely through the insular lens of intelligence-gathering, rather it must consider the wider environment and implications within which its work is carried out."[60] Looking forward, a key challenge for CSIS and other national security partners is thus balancing this requirement to fulfil their role and mandates while acting in a complex, multijurisdictional environment.

Current Challenges

CSIS faces political, legal, and organizational challenges. An additional perspective on the challenges posed to CSIS in a complex security environment can be gleaned from target and warrant data. Table 3.1 indicates the breakdown of authorized targets,[61] whereas rounded numbers for the last decade are provided in Table 3.2.

58   Jez Littlewood

Table 3.1. Authorized targets (2005–6)

Branch	Individuals	Organizations	Issues/Events	Totals
Counterintelligence	152	36	4	192
Counterproliferation	55	6	6	67
Counterterrorism	274	31	30	335
Totals	481	73	40	594

Table 3.2. CSIS targets (rounded to nearest ten) as reported in the SIRC annual reports

Year	2007–8	2008–9	2009–10	2010–11	2011–12	2012–13	2013–14	2014–15	2015–16	2016–17	2017–18
Targets	610	530	480	470	410	500	400	590	550	560	500

Target and warrant information must be treated with caution, and the limits of the available data understood: this is especially true in light of changes in reporting about warrant numbers, which account for the apparent decrease since 2016–17 in Figure 3.3.[62]

From the data, we can see that CSIS has on average 510 targets in a given year, with the lowest number being 410 and the highest 610. In a similar vein, warrants granted to CSIS rarely fall below 200 per year, but do not exceed 300 per year over the last two decades. A further element of continuity is indicated by the fact that most warrants are replacements or renewals of existing authorities. While the overall numerical range of targets and warrants is relatively stable, it is not clear from the data whether this is due to decline and emergence of specific targets over time or whether the numbers reflect budgetary and resource constraints that bound operational activity. Both are possible inferences, but assuming 500 targets a year, and assuming at best 50 per cent of CSIS's 3,200 staff are directly involved in operational activity, the data still points to an agency stretched thinly at times.

Controversies

Any reading of media reports, academic studies, or the annual reviews produced by SIRC (and since 2019, NSIRA) reveals a number of quite serious as well as routine concerns about the operations and activities of CSIS.[63] To be fair, these reports often note the general compliance of CSIS and, in many cases, efforts made in good faith by the Service to

Figure 3.3. CSIS warrants, 1998–2018

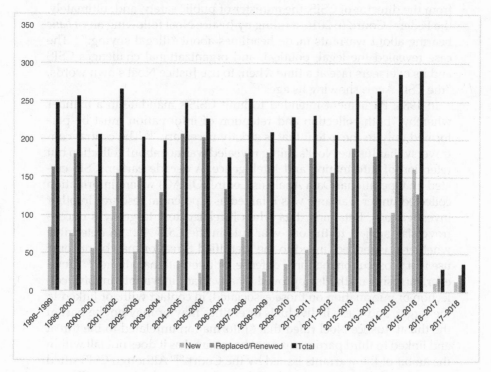

act within its mandate, in accordance with ministerial direction, and within the law. Independent but still critical assessments of CSIS's known activities also suggest compliance overall – "CSIS is generally law-abiding" – but this "means it has acted improperly at times."[64] In this context, it would be an exaggeration to claim that CSIS ignores the law or runs amok over rights and liberties of Canadians. Developing a complete list of concerns or controversies is a work in itself, but three recent issues illuminate where CSIS runs afoul of its overseers and political masters.

Warrant Compliance

Warrant application procedures are resource-intensive and complex undertakings that work their way through approval processes within CSIS. Targeting and, if required, warrant applications are subject to oversight that involves CSIS and others,[65] and warrants require approval from the director of CSIS, the minister of public safety, and, ultimately, the Federal Court. In 2016, a ruling by Justice Noël following an *en banc* hearing about warrants made headlines about "illegal spying."[66] The case revealed the legal, political, and organizational challenges CSIS and its overseers face at a time when, to use Justice Noël's own words, "the CSIS Act is showing its age."[67]

In 1984, Parliament intended to limit CSIS's mandate in a manner whereby "both collection and retention of information must be performed only to the extent that is strictly necessary."[68] The central controversy that Justice Noël's ruling revealed was not about collection but retention of information and intelligence. A decade earlier, CSIS created an Operational Data Analysis Centre (ODAC) where information collected under warrants was retained as a potential resource in other investigations. Retaining data when it related to a target was uncontroversial, subject to the one-year rule in the *CSIS Act* "to determine whether it is indeed linked to the identified threat or may be of some use to a prosecution, national defense, or international affairs."[69] However, intrusive methods approved by a warrant inevitably involve collection of information on those associated, in contact with, or linked to the target, and these individuals or entities may or may not be part of the threat. Justice Noël ruled that "information unrelated to the threat and linked to third parties must not be retained as it does not fall within the ambit of the warrants issued by the Court."[70] Although CSIS sifted through and deleted the details of data where these had no significance within the investigation, it retained the metadata, which Justice Noël ruled was not within its "strictly necessary" mandate.[71]

The ensuing headlines claimed illegal spying: as Colin Freeze reported, "it appears the spy agency was secretively holding onto phone logs and e-mail trails that it had mapped out around targets of past investigations ... Retaining such communications metadata ... would appear to mean the government is keeping records relating to the family, friends and acquaintances of former terrorism suspects."[72] While these headlines were accurate in pointing out illegality, they implied that the issue was collection and ongoing surveillance when it was in fact retention of metadata and how that may be used, legally, as a resource in future investigations.

This example points to three challenges for CSIS and its overseers. First, operationalization of intelligence collection needs close attention over time and continuous assessment and review by authorities. Although it took a decade from ODAC being established to the court ruling on its legality, the architecture of accountability eventually worked.

The follow-on impacts are, moreover, evident in the dataset regime of the *National Security Act, 2017*. Second, as SIRC remarked in its 2016–17 report, "a gap has slowly developed between CSIS's use of technology and the management of critical compliance functions," and "these retention errors continued unnoticed for so long [because] employees with expert knowledge of intercept technologies and CSIS databases had incomplete knowledge of warrants, while those employees who knew about the importance of warrant precepts had incomplete knowledge about the technologies used for collection and retention."[73]

The third issue illustrates the tensions between a complex threat environment, the evolution of practices (and policy) to respond to dynamic threats, and the stasis of law. As the redacted court documents reveal, "evidence was produced establishing that the processing and analysis of associated data has yielded some useful intelligence results."[74] Indeed, there is an inherent logic in mapping and retaining information about targets and their acquaintances, as terrorism cases in the UK and Canada denote.[75] One of the striking aspects of the 2016 FC 1105 warrants application was the reliance on and interpretation of the intentions of decision-makers and meaning of words over 30 years old vis-à-vis "strictly necessary." This is not criticism of Justice Noël: he noted that an appropriate balance between national security and liberties must entail intelligence agencies having "the proper tools for their operations"[76] and that that may require a change in law; how "strictly necessary" was meant to be understood in 1984 is not automatically how it should be interpreted now. In some respects, the *National Security Act, 2017* is an attempt to resolve the problem of ensuring data retention, but post-*en banc* efforts within CSIS related to the management, assessment, and use of datasets are a time-consuming and resource-intensive process.[77] Data management is supposed to make national security more effective and efficient; the reality is evidently that it makes it less so.

Sources

Human sources are key to the work of CSIS.[78] Human source recruitment does not require a warrant, but internal oversight and accountability procedures are in place. Such sources were central to the prosecutions in the "Toronto 18" case and the VIA Rail plot, and were at the heart of the decision to stay the case against Nuttall and Karody with respect to the 2013 Canada Day plot in British Columbia. In the latter two cases, the sources were undercover law enforcement personnel, whereas in the Toronto 18 case both human sources were individuals persuaded to assist CSIS and later the RCMP. Controversy surrounding human sources is a permanent feature of Canada's intelligence history: Marc-André Boivin and the alleged targeting of labour unions in 1987, Grant Bristow and the neo-Nazi Heritage Front (1994), and a Kurdish refugee who refused to become a source for CSIS (Suleyman Govan, 1994–2006) have all generated headlines.[79] More recently, an alleged CSIS source was uncovered in Turkey assisting three British women in their efforts to join the Islamic State in Syria. After a flurry of reporting, the issue went cold, and whether or not the claims were correct is currently unknown.[80]

Controversies around human sources are less prevalent than those related to intrusive interception techniques, but this may be a feature of the warrant process entailing judicial oversight and approval, court rulings, and other reporting that puts technical issues into the public domain. A review by SIRC of the Service's foreign-based human sources was generally complimentary,[81] and other than the Govan case and the alleged CSIS source linked to smuggling in Turkey, the post-9/11 controversies that have embroiled CSIS have, perhaps surprisingly, not involved human sources. Nevertheless, as Whitaker et al. note with regard to the Govan case, implying or threatening to withhold a clearance to enter or remain in Canada is an example of a "CSIS primary recruitment tool"[82] that will, inevitably, ensure that human sources remain a potential controversy into the future.

Threat Reduction Measures

The controversy over TRMs requires some historical context, because in many ways it is the third iteration of the issue. The first stemmed from the origins of CSIS and revelations about RCMP operations in the 1970s and the infamous barn burning action.[83] The second, from the post-9/11 period up to 2010, saw CSIS respond to the concerns of SIRC and determine that "disruption activities" did not fall within its mandate; employees were therefore "directed not to engage in such activities."[84] It should be noted that the methods and means of disruption activities up to 2010 are not detailed in public reports.

The current issues with TRMs originate in legislation passed by the Harper government, the *Anti-terrorism Act, 2015*, otherwise known as Bill C-51. This bill created section 12.1 of the *CSIS Act*, which empowered the Service to take reasonable and proportional measures to reduce threats to the security of Canada. Extraordinarily, these powers were subject to the warrant authority if the measure was in contravention of a *Charter* right or other law.

Empowering CSIS to undertake activities that in the minds of Canadians were the very reasons the RCMP was stripped of its intelligence responsibilities was compounded by the lack of explanation for why the measures were necessary, what disruption powers CSIS could use, and where the limits of disruption were bounded. Only three limitations were identified: death or bodily harm to an individual; attempts to obstruct, pervert, or defeat the course of justice; and violations of the sexual integrity of an individual. The debate over C-51 was largely vacuous, given the dearth of information provided by the government at the time to explain in detail the rationale for the far-reaching changes being made. Consequently, the information deficit led to speculation that focused on worst-case scenarios. Forcese and Roach concluded that an "uncertain but staggering range of things"[85] could be included in the new disruption powers. Evidently, however, CSIS has not made use of TRMs in the way opponents of C-51 feared: available data to March 2018 points to no warrants being issued for disruption and approximately 30 TRMs having been used.[86]

The expansive potential scope of TRMs under the 2015 act is curtailed under the *National Security Act, 2017*. As explained in the summary of that act, there are limits on these powers via "a list of measures that may be authorized by the Federal Court."[87] Nevertheless, concerns remain about how TRMs will evolve and be used in the future and the "proposed kinetic powers [that] move CSIS from the intelligence role it was designed to play."[88]

CSIS, National Security, and Civil Liberties: Conclusions

Beyond the controversies of CSIS's 30-plus years of operation is a deeper record of an intelligence agency in compliance with its mandate most of the time. While the biggest failure of CSIS occurred within eleven months of its establishment – the Air India bombing – a steady trickle of missteps is evident throughout its history. There are, equally, invisible failures, or at least invisible challenges that are hinted at, if not revealed in detail, in the reports of SIRC and, pre-2012, the inspector general of CSIS (the history and role of these two former CSIS review bodies is discussed in chapter fourteen). Running parallel to failures and controversies are the successes of intelligence that may not be appreciated because ministers, parliamentarians, the public, and the fifth estate expect CSIS to "get results, and not mess up":[89] no terrorist attacks; no targeting people who are not real threats; no espionage scandals; no sharing information that may lead to torture or inhumane treatment;

no overstepping the perceived clear mandate of the Service; no invasions of privacy; and no wrongdoing.

Problems with warrant compliance, TRMs, and the use of human sources shed light upon the perennial challenge of providing security while safeguarding rights and liberties. It is correct to note that when the state has extended its "eyes, ears, and fists" into its own civil society, the risk of abuse has not always been avoided.[90] Such controversies were at the heart of why CSIS was formed in 1984. Heightened concerns about the balance of liberties and security emerged post-9/11 and were evident in debates over the *Anti-terrorism Act* (2001) and subsequent legislation, most notably Bill C-51 in 2015. Such concerns are legitimate given historical and contemporary experience. Each controversy points to real problems, but drawing broad conclusions based only on controversies is incomplete.

Intelligence agencies are bureaucracies like other parts of government in a democratic state.[91] CSIS is both extraordinary in its powers and ordinary in its resemblance to any government entity. Slightly more than 3,000 people in an agency that accounts for 0.2 per cent of the federal budget are charged to ensure that threats to the security of Canada are detected and the government advised about them. Those threats exist at home and abroad and in the real and virtual worlds: the twenty-first century has manifested into Woolsey's "jungle filled with a bewildering variety of poisonous snakes."[92]

These 3,200 individuals work in a political culture that has traditionally been disdainful of intelligence, ignorant about its realities, and strongly influenced by the controversies of the past and the latest error revealed in the press. A more sympathetic assessment suggests CSIS has a thankless task, but empathy should not ignore the lessons of history or be sanguine about the "eyes, ears, and fists" of the state.

On balance, CSIS has achieved the objective of parliamentarians in 1984 of being a civilian intelligence agency under the rule of law. Unlike some of its counterparts in other democracies, CSIS appears to have avoided becoming one of the "toilet cleaners of globalization"[93] post-9/11, but its mistakes have had very significant consequences for individuals. Under the *National Security Act, 2017* – which others in this volume have categorized as the largest overhaul of Canadian national security in a generation – the four roles of CSIS (investigation of threats, disruption of threats, foreign intelligence, and security screening) are embedded within an enhanced reporting and accountability regime. Although many experts believe enhanced accountability is essential for the future, attention to its effect on CSIS in terms of resource reallocations, policy, and operational activities will also be required in future years.

NOTES

1 Canadian Security Intelligence Service (CSIS), "The CSIS Mandate,"
   Backgrounder Series 1, January 2005.
2 CSIS, "Human Resources," *Backgrounder Series* 4, February 2004.
3 Security Intelligence Review Committee (SIRC), *Annual Report 1984–85*
   (1985), 19. Available online: http://www.sirc.gc.ca/pdfs/ar_1984-1985
   -eng.pdf.
4 Reg Whitaker, Gregory S. Kealey, and Andrew Parnaby, *Secret Service:
   Political Policing in Canada from the Fenians to Fortress America* (Toronto:
   University of Toronto Press, 2012), 399.
5 Employment numbers are drawn from the last available public report of
   CSIS (*Public Report 2014–2016*, posted 28 February 2017). Available online:
   https://www.canada.ca/en/security-intelligence-service/corporate
   /publications/public-report-2014-2016.html. Budget allocation is reported
   at GC InfoBase at https://www.tbs-sct.gc.ca/ems-sgd/edb-bdd/index
   -eng.html#orgs/dept/94/infograph/financial.
6 Government of Canada, "Budgetary Details by Allotment," last modified
   30 December 2019, https://www.tpsgc-pwgsc.gc.ca/recgen/cpc-pac
   /2019/vol2/sp-ps/dba-bda-eng.html.
7 *Canadian Security Intelligence Service Act*, R.S.C. 1985, c. C-23 (generally
   referred to the *CSIS Act* and available at https://laws-lois.justice.gc.ca
   /eng/acts/c-23/). The act, current to 10 April 2018, was used for this
   chapter, with a version current to 1 July 2019 used to update any text.
8 CSIS, *Public Report 2013–2014* (2015). Available online: https://www
   .canada.ca/en/security-intelligence-service/corporate/publications
   /2013-2014-public-report.html.
9 Bill C-59, *An Act respecting national security matters*, received Royal Assent
   on June 21, 2019, creating the *National Security Act, 2017*, S.C. 2019, c. 13.
10 *CSIS Act*, ss. 12(1), 12(2).
11 See: *In the Matter of an Application by Xxxxx Xxxx for Warrants Pursuant to
   Sections 12 and 21 of the* Canadian Security Intelligence Act, *R.S.C. 1985,
   C. C-23 and in the Presence of the Attorney General and Amici and in the Matter
   of Xxxx Xxxxxxx Xxxxx Xxxxx Xxx Threat-Related Activities Xxxxx Xx*,
   Judgment and Reasons, 2016 FC 1105. Justice Noël provides an extensive
   summary of the importance of "strictly necessary" and its meaning in
   terms of collection, analysis, and retention in chapter 2 of the ruling, 32–99.
12 SIRC, *Building for Tomorrow: The Future of Security Intelligence Accountability
   in Canada: Annual Report 2017–2018* (2018), 31. Available online: http://
   www.sirc.gc.ca/pdfs/ar_2017-2018-eng.pdf.
13 CSIS, *Public Report 2014–2016*.
14 Whitaker, Kealey, and Parnaby, *Secret Service*, 467.

15 Mark Hume, "RCMP, Intelligence Agency Accused of Spying on
    Pipeline Opponents," *Globe and Mail*, 6 February 2014, https://www
    .theglobeandmail.com/news/british-columbia/csis-rcmp-accused
    -of-spying-on-pipeline-opponents/article16726444/; Jim Bronskill,
    "CSIS Collected Info on Peaceful Protests of Indigenous Groups,
    Environmentalists: Documents," *Global News*, 8 July 2019, https://
    globalnews.ca/news/5470406/csis-energy-industry-information/.

16 CSIS, *Public Report 2011–2013* (2013), 45. Available online: https://
    www.canada.ca/content/dam/csis-scrs/documents/publications
    /PublicReport_ENG_2011_2013.pdf.

17 *CSIS Act*, s. 16.

18 SIRC, *Annual Report 09/10: Time for Reflection: Taking the Measure of Security
    Intelligence* (2010), 7. Available online: http://www.sirc.gc.ca/pdfs/ar
    _2009-2010-eng.pdf.

19 SIRC, *Annual Report*, 7.

20 SIRC, *Annual Report*, 15.

21 See, e.g., Barry Cooper, *CFIS: A Foreign Intelligence Service for Canada*,
    (Calgary: Canadian Defence & Foreign Affairs Institute, 2007). Available
    online: https://d3n8a8pro7vhmx.cloudfront.net/cdfai/pages/41
    /attachments/original/1413661510/CFIS.pdf?1413661510; Paul Robinson,
    "The Viability of a Canadian Foreign Intelligence Service," *International
    Journal* 64, no. 3 (2009): 703–16; Stuart Farson and Nancy Steeple,
    "Increasing Canada's Foreign Intelligence Capability: Is It a Dead Issue?,"
    Intelligence and National Security 30, no. 1 (2015): 47–76.

22 Craig Forcese, "Oh, What Tangled Webs the CSIS Act Weaves: The Federal
    Court's Latest Decision on CSIS's Foreign Intelligence Mandate," *Craig
    Forcese* (blog), 19 July 2018, https://www.craigforcese.com/blog
    /2018/7/19/oh-what-tangled-webs-the-csis-act-weaves-the-federal
    -courts.html.

23 Government of Canada, "Government Security Screening," last modified
    18 July 2018, https://www.canada.ca/en/security-intelligence-service
    /services/government-security-screening.html.

24 CSIS, *2018 CSIS Public Report* (2019), 31. Available online: https://www
    .canada.ca/content/dam/csis-scrs/documents/publications/2018
    -PUBLIC_REPORT_ENGLISH_Digital.pdf.

25 SIRC, *SIRC Report 2003–2004: An Operational Review of the Canadian Security
    Intelligence Service* (2004), 7. Available online: http://www.sirc.gc.ca/pdfs
    /ar_2003-2004-eng.pdf

26 Financial information is derived from GC InfoBase and the CSIS infographic.
    Available online: https://www.tbs-sct.gc.ca/ems-sgd/edb-bdd/index
    -eng.html#orgs/dept/94/infograph/financial.

27 See Treasury Board Secretariat, "Infographic for Canadian Security Intelligence Service," accessed 3 August 2020, http://www.tbs-sct.gc.ca /ems-sgd/edb-bdd/index-eng.html#orgs/dept/94/infograph/financial.
28 CSIS, *Public Report 2008–2009* (2009), 30. Available online: https://www .publicsafety.gc.ca/lbrr/archives/cn24357-2008-2009-eng.pdf.
29 See Government of Canada, "Employment Equity Representation for the Canadian Security Intelligence Service," last modified 30 October 2019, https://open.canada.ca/data/en/dataset/d77a24fe-eb38-4d02-8e00 -32148a708b11%20for%20the%20data%20covering%201988–89%20to%20 2015/16%20years.
30 CSIS, *2018 CSIS Public Report* (2019), 39. Available online: https://www .canada.ca/content/dam/csis-scrs/documents/publications/2018 -PUBLIC_REPORT_ENGLISH_Digital.pdf.
31 CSIS, *Public Report 2008–2009*, 31.
32 CSIS, *Public Report 2008–2009*, 23.
33 CSIS, *Public Report 2008–2009*, 27.
34 For a Canadian example, see literature on the Air India inquiry: Commission of Inquiry into the Investigation of the Bombing of Air India Flight 182, *Air India Flight 182: A Canadian Tragedy*, vol. 1, *The Overview* (Ottawa: Public Works and Government Services Canada, 2010); Craig Forcese and Kent Roach, *False Security: The Radicalization of Canadian Anti-terrorism* (Toronto: Irwin Law, 2015), 46–52; Whitaker, Kealey, and Parnaby, *Secret Service*, 375–89.
35 Stéphane Lefebvre, "Canadian Security Intelligence Challenged," *International Journal of Intelligence and CounterIntelligence* 22, no. 3 (2009): 548–55.
36 SIRC, *Accelerating Accountability: Annual Report 2016–2017: Business Modernization SIRC 2016–17* (2017), 18–19. Available online: http://www .sirc.gc.ca/pdfs/ar_2016-2017-eng.pdf.
37 SIRC, *SIRC Annual Report 1998–1999: An Operational Audit of the Canadian Security Intelligence Service* (1999), 14. Available online: http://www.sirc .gc.ca/pdfs/ar_1998-1999-eng.pdf.
38 CSIS, "Director Statement on Assessment Report Regarding Workplace," 25 October 2017. Available online: https://www.canada .ca/en/security-intelligence-service/news/2017/10/director _statementonassessmentreportregardingworkplace.html. The director of CSIS (David Vigneault) discussed some of these issues in 2018 in eEpisode 36 of *Intrepid Podcast*: https://www.intrepidpodcast.com /podcast/2018/5/11/t7a66ktq1pwmscgk9hinevyhu3slcn.
39 Michelle Shephard, "Head of Spy Agency CSIS Admits 'Retribution, Favouritism, Bullying' in Workplace," *Toronto Star*, 25 October 2017,

https://www.thestar.com/news/canada/2017/10/25/csis-director
-calls-behaviour-unacceptable-after-report-uncovers-bullying-reprisals
-at-canadas-spy-agency.html.

40 SIRC, *Accelerating Accountability: Annual Report 2016–2017: Business Modernization SIRC 2016–17*, 2017, 20.

41 SIRC, *Annual Report 2016–2017*, 13.

42 Government of Canada, "National Security Transparency Commitment," last modified 18 June 2020, https://www.canada.ca/en/services/defence/nationalsecurity/national-security-transparency-commitment.html

43 CSIS, "Consultation on Operational Compliance Framework," Ref # EXE19-34602, 25 November 2019. Only the existence of a briefing note on this topic is known. See proactive disclosures of the Government of Canada related to briefing note titles and numbers, including this briefing note, at https://search.open.canada.ca/en/bn/?sort=date_received_tdt%20desc&page=1&search_text=&bn-search-orgs=Canadian%20Security%20Intelligence%20Service.

44 The 17 (as of 2015) are the Canada Border Services Agency; Canada Revenue Agency; Canadian Armed Forces; Canadian Food Inspection Agency; Canadian Nuclear Safety Commission; CSIS; CSE; Department of Citizenship and Immigration; Department of Finance; Department of Foreign Affairs, Trade and Development; Department of Health; Department of National Defence; Department of Public Safety and Emergency Preparedness; Department of Transport; Financial Transactions and Reports Analysis Centre of Canada; Public Health Agency of Canada; and the RCMP.

45 Forcese and Roach, *False Security*, 157.

46 Whitaker, Kealey, and Parnaby, *Secret Service*, 366.

47 Wesley Wark, "The Intelligence-Law Enforcement Nexus: A Study of Cooperation between the Canadian Security Intelligence Service and the Royal Canadian Mounted Police, 1984–2006, in the Context of the Air India Terrorist Attack," in *Air India Flight 182: A Canadian Tragedy*, Commission of Inquiry into the Investigation of the Bombing of Air India Flight 182 (Ottawa: Public Works and Government Services Canada, 2010), 1:178.

48 SIRC, *An Operational Audit of CSIS Activities* (1998), 27–34. Available online: http://www.sirc.gc.ca/pdfs/ar_1997-1998-eng.pdf.

49 "One Vision 2.0 (CSIS-RCMP Framework for Cooperation)," *Secret Law Gazette*, accessed 9 November 2018, https://secretlaw.omeka.net/items/show/21.

50 Reg Whitaker, "Made in Canada? The New Public Safety Paradigm," in *How Ottawa Spends, 2005–2006: Managing the Minority*, ed. Bruce Doern (Montreal and Kingston: McGill-Queen's University Press, 2005), 80–84.

51 Craig Forcese, "Threading the Needle: Structural Reform & Canada's Intelligence-to-Evidence Dilemma" (Ottawa Faculty of Law Working Paper No. 2018–19, 4 August 2018).
52 Justin Ling, "Secret Documents Reveal Canada's Spy Agencies Got Extremely Cozy with Each Other," *Vice*, 20 May 2015, https://news .vice.com/article/secret-documents-reveal-canadas-spy-agencies-got -extremely-cozy-with-each-other.
53 Colin Freeze, "Documents Reveal CSIS Wary of Bill C-51 Reforms," *Globe and Mail*, 3 March 2016, https://www.theglobeandmail.com /news/national/documents-reveal-csis-wary-of-bill-c-51-reforms /article29023837/; CSIS, "Letter to Incoming Public Safety Minister," 2015. A copy may be found at https://qspace.library.queensu.ca /bitstream/handle/1974/24354/A-2015-509.pdf?sequence=1 &isAllowed=y.
54 Commission of Inquiry into the Actions of Canadian Officials in Relation to Maher Arar, *Report of the Events Relating to Maher Arar: Factual Background*, vol. 1 (Ottawa: Public Works and Government Services Canada, 2006).
55 Public Safety Canada (PSC), "Ministerial Direction to the Canadian Security Intelligence Service: Avoiding Complicity in Mistreatment by Foreign Entities," 25 September 2017, https://www.publicsafety.gc.ca /cnt/trnsprnc/ns-trnsprnc/mnstrl-drctn-csis-scrs-en.aspx.
56 PSC, "Ministerial Direction to the Canadian Security Intelligence Service: Accountability," 10 September 2019, https://www.publicsafety.gc.ca/cnt /trnsprnc/ns-trnsprnc/mnstrl-drctn-csisacc-en.aspx.
57 SIRC, *Annual Report 2017–2018*, 16–17.
58 SIRC, *CSIS's Role in the Matter of Omar Khadr: SIRC Study 2008–05* (2008). Available online: http://www.sirc-csars.gc.ca/opbapb/2008-05/index -eng.html?wbdisable=true.
59 SIRC, *CSIS's Role*.
60 SIRC, *CSIS's Role*.
61 A "target" may equally be an individual, an organization, or an issue similar to a warrant approved by the Federal Court, which may also be an individual or an organization or a group. SIRC also rounds targeting numbers to the nearest ten.
62 SIRC changed its reporting on warrants in its 2016–17 annual report: "Historically, SIRC has provided statistics on the total number of warrants granted by the Federal Court during a fiscal year. In such instances, a single warrant may be directed toward numerous individuals. Similarly, many warrants provide for a multitude of powers, whereas others are singular in nature. Moreover, not all individuals are subject to the same number of warrants." The warrant statistics presented here represent

the total number of warrant applications submitted to the Federal Court,
independent of the actual number of warrants granted in each application
or the number of individuals who were the subject of warrants.

63 Whitaker, Kealey, and Parnaby, *Secret Service*, 365–520 provides a
comprehensive overview of issues and controversies between 1984
and 2012.
64 Craig Forcese, "CSIS and the Metadata Muddle PT3: Politics, Small and
Big 'P,'" *Craig Forcese* (blog), 8 November 2016, https://www.craigforcese.
com/blog/2016/11/8/csis-and-the-metadata-muddle-pt-3-politics-small
-and-big-p.html.
65 Stéphane Lefebvre, "Canada's Legal Framework for Intelligence,"
International Journal of Intelligence and CounterIntelligence 23, no. 2 (2010):
253.
66 Alex Boutilier, "CSIS Program Illegally Spied for a Decade, Judge Rules,"
Toronto Star, 3 November 2016.
67 2016 F.C. 1105, 124.
68 2016 F.C. 1105, 6.
69 2016 F.C. 1105, 6.
70 2016 F.C. 1105, 7.
71 2016 F.C. 1105, 118.
72 Colin Freeze, "In Scathing Ruling, Federal Court Says CSIS Bulk Data
Collection Illegal," *Globe and Mail*, 3 November 2016, https://www
.theglobeandmail.com/news/national/in-scathing-ruling-federal
-court-says-csis-bulk-data-collection-illegal/article32669448/.
73 SIRC, *Annual Report 2016–17*, 13.
74 2016 F.C. 1105, 124.
75 Ian Cobain, Richard Norton-Taylor, and Jeevan Vasagar, "MI5 Decided
to Stop Watching Two Suicide Bombers," *Guardian*, 1 May 2007, https://
www.theguardian.com/uk/2007/may/01/terrorism.politics2; Jana G.
Pruden, Colin Freeze, and Kelly Cryderman, "RCMP Face Scrutiny in
Wake of Edmonton Attack," *Globe and Mail*, 2 October 2017, https://www
.theglobeandmail.com/news/national/edmonton-attack-mounties
-face-scrutiny-in-wake-of-edmonton-attack/article36461018/; David
Anderson, *Attacks in London and Manchester March–June 2017: Independent
Assessment of MI5 And Police Internal Reviews: Unclassified* (2017). Available
online: https://assets.publishing.service.gov.uk/government/uploads
/system/uploads/attachment_data/file/664682/Attacks_in_London
_and_Manchester_Open_Report.pdf.
76 2016 F.C. 1105, 124.
77 SIRC, *Annual Report 2017–2018*, 25–31.
78 Steve Hewitt, "Forgotten Surveillance: Covert Human Intelligence
Sources in Canada in a Post-9/11 World." In Geist, Michel (ed.). *Law,*

Privacy and Surveillance in Canada in the Post-Snowden Era, ed. Michel Geist (Ottawa: University of Ottawa Press, 2015), 45–67.

79 Whitaker, Kealey, and Parnaby, *Secret Service*, 403–13, 447–8.

80 Steven Chase and Colin Freeze, "Canada Silent on Alleged CSIS Links to Man Helping Girls Go to Syria," *Globe and Mail*, 13 March 2015, https://www.theglobeandmail.com/news/world/video-shows -man-with-alleged-links-to-canada-spy-agency-help-girls-go-to -syria/article23447143/.

81 SIRC, *Annual Report 2014–15* (2015). Available online: http://www.sirc .gc.ca/pdfs/ar_2014-2015-eng.pdf.

82 Whitaker, Kealey, and Parnaby, *Secret Service*, 448.

83 Philip Rosen, *The Canadian Security Intelligence Service*, Current Issue Review 84-27E (Ottawa: Library of Parliament, 2000), 4.

84 SIRC, *Maintaining Momentum: Annual Report 2015–2016* (2016), 16. Available online: http://www.sirc.gc.ca/pdfs/ar_2015-2016-eng.pdf.

85 Forcese and Roach, *False Security*, 259.

86 SIRC, *Annual Report 2017–2018*, 23.

87 Namely: (a) interfering with communications or means of communication, (b) interfering with documents, goods, components, and equipment, (c) fabricating or disseminating information, (d) financial transactions, (e) interrupting financial transactions, (f) interfering with the movement of an individual, but excluding detention, and, (g) impersonating a person to take such measures. Bill C-59, 3 May 2018 version.

88 Canadian Bar Association, *Bill C-59 – National Security Act, 2017* (2018), 3. Available online: https://www.cba.org/CMSPages/GetFile .aspx?guid=af8ac20b-0d2a-4249-a743-0ba351012c54.

89 Whitaker, Kealey, and Parnaby, *Secret Service*, 509.

90 Whitaker, Kealey, and Parnaby, *Secret Service*, 523.

91 Martin J. Smith, "Intelligence and the Core Executive," *Public Policy and Administration* 25, no. 1 (2010): 11–28.

92 Testimony of R. James Woolsey, hearing before the Select Committee on Intelligence of the United States Senate One Hundred Third Congress First Session on Nomination of R. James Woolsey to Be Director of Central Intelligence, 2–3 February 1993.

93 Richard Aldrich, "Beyond the Vigilant State: Globalisation and Intelligence," *Review of International Studies* 35 (2009): 892.

4 The Communications Security Establishment (CSE)

BILL ROBINSON

The Communications Security Establishment (CSE) is Canada's national cryptologic agency. When it began operating in September 1946, the agency – then called the Communications Branch of the National Research Council (NRC) – was charged with two responsibilities: (1) collecting foreign intelligence by monitoring foreign radio communications and, when necessary and feasible, breaking the encryption systems protecting their contents; and (2) providing the encryption systems used by the Canadian government to protect its own communications from the activities of similar agencies in other countries. These two programs are now called signals intelligence (SIGINT) and information technology security (IT security or ITSEC).[1] The ITSEC program has grown to include protection of "electronic information and information infrastructures ... of importance to the Government of Canada" as well as the government's own systems, while the advent of the internet and ubiquitous computing has widened the agency's SIGINT focus from radio communications to all types of sensitive data stored on or transmitted among information technology systems. In 2019 CSE's mandate was extended to include a covert action role through computer network attack operations, but SIGINT and ITSEC remain CSE's fundamental missions.

Origins and Evolution

Canada first entered the SIGINT field in a serious way during the Second World War. When the United States and Britain agreed to extend their SIGINT cooperation into the post-war era – with the Soviet Union the new primary target – Canada, Australia, and New Zealand also agreed to collaborate, creating the five-nation group now known as the Five Eyes. In return for an annual contribution of around 10,000 Canadian SIGINT end product reports (EPRs, discussed below), focused for much of the Cold War on the northern Soviet Union, CSE was able to make available to Canadian intelligence consumers as many as 200,000 partner EPRs covering a much broader range of countries and topics.[2] The five SIGINT partner agencies are today known as the US National Security Agency (NSA), the UK Government Communications Headquarters (GCHQ), the Communications Security Establishment (CSE), the Australian Signals Directorate (ASD), and New Zealand's Government Communications Security Bureau (GCSB). No longer focused purely on SIGINT, the Five Eyes relationship has grown over the years to encompass cooperation across a broad range of intelligence, security, and law enforcement activities involving multiple agencies.

CSE has also evolved. The agency was given its current name in April 1975, when the Communications Branch was transferred from the NRC to the Department of National Defence (DND). It became a stand-alone agency in November 2011, still housed in the portfolio of the minister of national defence but no longer part of the department. Meanwhile, the arrival of the internet in the 1990s transformed the nature of SIGINT operations. Tight budgets and outdated legal authorities had initially left CSE hobbled in its efforts to reorient itself to the emerging global information infrastructure, but all that changed in September 2001. In the wake of the 9/11 attacks, terrorism and other security issues became the new top priority, and CSE received its first statutory mandate, new powers to intercept communications, and a huge increase in resources.[3]

Mandate

The omnibus *Anti-terrorism Act* passed in December 2001 amended the *National Defence Act* to establish CSE's three-part mandate, previously laid out in classified directives, in statutory form, authorizing it to (a) collect foreign intelligence from the global information infrastructure; (b) protect electronic information and information infrastructures of importance to the Government of Canada; and (c) provide technical and operational assistance to federal law enforcement and security agencies.[4] These three elements are commonly referred to as Parts A, B, and C of the CSE mandate (or sometimes simply Mandates A, B, and C).

Additional amendments empowered the minister of national defence to issue ministerial authorizations permitting CSE to collect "private communications" in the course of targeting foreign entities located outside Canada. (A "private communication" is an electronic communication not intended for broadcast that has at least one end in Canada.) Prior to the amendment, if an al-Qaida recruiter in Sudan that CSE was monitoring telephoned, or was telephoned by, a number in Toronto, it was illegal for the agency to intercept that communication. The ministerial authorization regime removed that limitation, but direct CSE targeting of entities located in Canada (or Canadians located anywhere) remained illegal, except under Part C.

In 2019, a new, free-standing statute for CSE was enacted.[5] Among other changes, the *Communications Security Establishment Act* added a fourth element to the agency's mandate: cyber operations, divided into "active" and "defensive," with the former corresponding to cyber operations in support of the SIGINT program or other national objectives and the latter to operations in support of IT security. These additional authorities are referred to as Part D of the CSE mandate. The *CSE Act* also modified the ministerial authorization regime, requiring foreign intelligence and cybersecurity authorizations for all Part A and B information collection by the agency (excluding "publicly available" information).

Part A

Part A is CSE's foreign intelligence mandate. The Canadian government defines foreign intelligence as "information or intelligence about the capabilities, intentions or activities of a foreign individual, state, organization or terrorist group, as they relate to international affairs, defence or security."[6]

Canadian intelligence priorities are developed in the Privy Council Office (PCO) in consultation with major intelligence producers and consumers and approved by Cabinet on a biennial basis. Guidance on the priorities relevant to CSE is then transmitted to the agency in the form of a directive from the minister of national defence.[7] Typically seven or eight priorities per year have been identified for CSE in recent years, encompassing subjects like indications and warning (I&W) intelligence, North American perimeter security, cybersecurity, terrorism and extremism, proliferation of weapons of mass destruction, support to military operations (SMO), foreign espionage and interference, and diplomatic and prosperity issues.[8]

Additional guidance comes from a PCO-led interdepartmental process that translates the priorities set by Cabinet into a detailed list of standing intelligence requirements (SIRs) that is updated at least every six months. There are currently over 400 SIRs.[9]

Finally, working in consultation with its key SIGINT clients, CSE compiles a tiered list of standing and ad hoc SIGINT requirements – essentially a summary of the applicable SIRs – called the National SIGINT Priorities List (NSPL).[10] Since 2011–12 the NSPL has also included Canadian Forces requirements for operational and tactical SIGINT, "thus eliminating duplication and increasing efficiencies."[11] CSE also responds to specific requests for intelligence-related information made during the year by CSIS and other clients when resources are available and the request is consistent with the NSPL.[12]

CSE uses the NSPL to guide its collection of foreign intelligence-related communications and metadata at radio and satellite monitoring sites, at physical interception points in the global telecommunications network, and via remote computer hacking (more formally known as computer network exploitation, or CNE) operations. The results are disseminated mainly in the form of EPRs. EPRs are typically short products reporting individual items of information. They usually do not contain assessments of the information's wider significance, although explanatory comments may be added.[13]

CSE provides SIGINT services to more than 2,100 clients in over 25 departments and agencies across the government,[14] ranging from major intelligence consumers like the Privy Council Office/Prime Minister's Office (PMO), the Canadian Security Intelligence Service (CSIS), Global Affairs Canada (GAC), and DND to lesser users such as the Canadian Nuclear Safety Commission.[15] CSE client relations officers (CROs) are embedded at key departments and agencies to provide personalized SIGINT delivery, mostly to senior consumers such as ministers and senior public servants. In 2015, there were CROs serving PCO/PMO, GAC, DND, CSIS, the Canada Border Services Agency (CBSA), and the departments of Public Safety, Innovation, Science and Economic Development, Aboriginal Affairs and Northern Development, Natural Resources, Fisheries and Oceans, Agriculture and Agri-Food (and the Canadian Food Inspection Agency), Transport, Environment, and Finance.[16] Other clients obtain SIGINT through SLINGSHOT, CSE's electronic EPR delivery service, database, and feedback system.

The number of Canadian EPRs released in an average year is probably around 10,000. CSE collects feedback from its clients in order to assess the value of this reporting and guide future production efforts. According to the agency, in 2014–15, 94 per cent of EPRs were read by at least one client, 76 per cent were rated as having satisfied a need, 36 per cent were rated as exceptional, and 7 per cent were rated as "actionable intelligence."[17]

A large proportion of EPRs are also made available to Canada's Five Eyes partners, who are important *de facto* clients. Since 2001, CSE has been legally required to conduct all Part A activities "in accordance with Government of Canada intelligence priorities." However, many of those priorities concern topics that are also of interest to Canada's partners, and this requirement does not prevent CSE from taking responsibility within the Five Eyes community for specific regions or topics, as long as the subject falls within one of the broad priorities identified by the government. In 2004 CSE's senior liaison officer in the United States affirmed that CSE is "always seeking opportunities to make valuable, tangible contributions to NSA."[18] Such contributions have included "open[ing] covert sites at the request of NSA."[19]

Part B

Part B comprises the cybersecurity and information assurance aspects of CSE's mandate. Originally this meant oversight of the encryption systems used by the Canadian government for its classified communications and production of the key material for those systems. Over time, however, CSE's communications security (COMSEC) role evolved to cover security of the full range of government electronic data processing and transmission systems, along with the data contained in them, and the role was renamed ITSEC.

By 2001, when CSE's mandate was first set in statutory form, the agency's ITSEC role had grown to include "advice, guidance and services to help ensure the protection of electronic information and of information infrastructures of importance to the Government of Canada." This provided a clear legal footing for ITSEC information-sharing with other levels of government and operators of critical infrastructure, such as electricity distributors and communications providers, considered to be "of importance" to the government. However, the agency's ability to provide assistance involving the interception of private communications remained limited, as the required ministerial authorizations could be issued only for protecting "the computer systems or networks of the Government of Canada."[20]

The *CSE Act* removed this limitation, authorizing the minister of national defence to issue cybersecurity authorizations that cover information infrastructures outside the federal government.[21] However, an authorization can be issued only if the owner or operator of the infrastructure submits a written request.[22]

The government has also moved in other ways to increase CSE's role. In 2018, as part of the new National Cyber Security Strategy, the ITSEC side of the agency, parts of the Security Operations Centre of Shared Services Canada, and the Canadian Cyber Incident Response Centre and Get Cyber Safe public awareness campaign of the Department of Public Safety were combined to create the Canadian Centre for Cyber Security (CCCS). The centre serves as "a single, unified source of expert advice, guidance, services and support on cyber security for government, critical infrastructure owners and operations, the private sector and the Canadian public." Although still part of CSE, the 800-employee CCCS operates under its own identity with its own "external-facing, publicly-accessible" facility.[23]

Part C

Part C of the CSE mandate authorizes the agency to provide technical and operational assistance to federal law enforcement and security agencies (LESAs) and the Canadian Forces/DND. Examples of such assistance include "collecting and processing communications, providing linguistic support, decrypting a hard drive, or designing technical solutions."[24] Whether CSE is able to respond positively to a request for assistance depends on a number of factors, including its ability to perform the requested task and the relative priority of other demands on the agency's resources. Provision of Part C support is also subject to the existence of appropriate legal authority on the part of the agency requesting the support. If the collection of Canadian communications is sought, the requesting agency must first obtain a judicial warrant and provide a copy to CSE.

All federal government departments and agencies with law and regulatory enforcement functions are eligible for part C assistance, including CSIS, the RCMP, the CBSA, the Canada Revenue Agency, Immigration, Refugees and Citizenship Canada, Health Canada, Environment Canada, Innovation, Science and Economic Development Canada, Transport Canada, the Canadian Food Inspection Agency, and Fisheries and Oceans Canada.[25] However, the primary recipients of such assistance are CSIS and the RCMP.

Statistics on part C assistance provided by CSE show that 294 new requests were made during the four-year period from 2009 to 2012: 205 (70 per cent) by CSIS; 85 (29 per cent) by the RCMP, 3 (1 per cent) by the CBSA, and 1 (0.3 per cent) by DND. All of the requests to monitor communications came from CSIS, accounting for one-quarter of the requests originating from that agency.[26] However, these statistics do not include renewed requests or ongoing assistance activities. Also, an individual request may relate to multiple active files. Thus, the scale of support provided by CSE under part C is likely to be significantly greater than these numbers suggest.

Part D

Part D is the most recent element of CSE's mandate, added in 2019. Sections 19 and 20 of the *CSE Act* expand the agency's mandate to include "defensive cyber operations" and "active cyber operations," respectively. These correspond to what are more commonly called computer network attack (CNA) activities, with defensive operations being those conducted under the IT security program and active operations those conducted under the SIGINT program in support of national objectives.

Examples of possible active cyber operations include

> action online to disrupt foreign threats, including activities to protect our
> democratic institutions, to counter violent extremism and terrorist planning,
> or to counter cyber aggression by foreign states. For example, CSE could use
> active cyber operations to prevent a terrorist's mobile phone from detonating
> a car bomb. We could impede terrorists' ability to communicate by obstruct-
> ing their communications infrastructure. Or we could covertly disrupt a for-
> eign threat actor from interfering in Canada's democratic process.[27]

Defensive cyber operations could include operations "to proactively stop
or impede foreign cyber threats before they damage Canadian systems or
information holdings ... For example, under defensive cyber operations
CSE could disable a foreign server that was attempting to steal information about Canadians from a Government of Canada network."[28]

The *CSE Act* prohibits any CSE cyber activity that would "(a) cause,
intentionally or by criminal negligence, death or bodily harm to an
individual; or (b) wilfully attempt in any manner to obstruct, pervert
or defeat the course of justice or democracy."[29] However, these prohi-
bitions do not apply to assistance provided to Canadian Forces cyber
operations via Part C of CSE's mandate. Like other military operations,
military cyber operations could seek to kill people as well as to break
things, and CSE assistance to such operations is subject only to the limitations applicable to the Canadian Forces themselves. Cyber operations
in support of CSIS "disruption" activities can also be undertaken under
Part C, subject to the limitations applicable to CSIS.

In addition to establishing a legal basis for CSE CNA capabilities and
activities, the *CSE Act* lays out a formal process for approving such
operations. Part D cyber operations require specific authorization by the
minister of national defence following consultation with the minister of
foreign affairs, and active cyber operations may be undertaken only if
the foreign affairs minister has requested or consented to the activity.[30]

Resources

CSE's staff and budget have grown dramatically since 2001. As of March
2019, the agency had a staff of 2,549, up roughly 1,600 from its pre-9/11
total and still growing (see Figure 4.1); in 2020 CSE reported that the
total had risen to 2,900.[31] The growth in the agency's budget resources
has been even more significant. In inflation-adjusted terms, CSE's budget increased from $187 million in 2000–1 to $733 million (or more) in
2019–20 (see Figure 4.2), with more growth on the way.[32]

Figure 4.1. CSE staff 1995–6 to 2018–19.

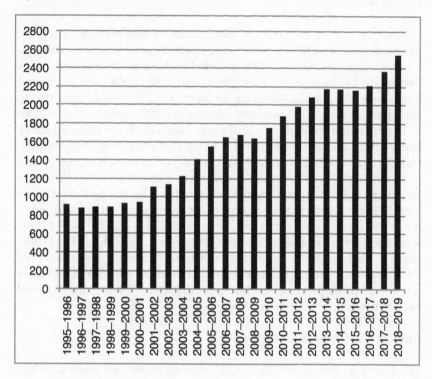

Figure 4.2. CSE Budgets 1995–6 to 2019–20. Figures in millions of C$. Grey line shows constant dollars (2019).[33]

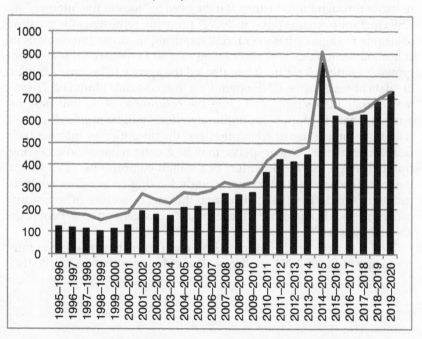

Whether a staff of 2,900, or even more, is adequate to meet the demands placed on the agency may be open to question. There is always more intelligence that might be collected and more cybersecurity work that might be done. But it is doubtful that CSE could have expanded much faster than it has. Allowing for attrition, CSE probably has had to absorb more than 3,000 new employees since 2001, amounting to close to 10 per cent of the agency's staff every year. Given the demand for IT skills within the private sector, it is likely that recruiting and retaining sufficient numbers in that field has been especially challenging.

Interestingly, despite greatly increased concern about cyber threats in recent years and the growing role assigned to CSE in combating those threats, there is little sign of change in the relative priorities assigned to the ITSEC and SIGINT programs. Between 2012–13 and 2017–18, ITSEC accounted for an average of 29.5 per cent of the CSE budget. The ITSEC share is likely to have jumped significantly following the creation of the Canadian Centre for Cyber Security, but in the absence of increases other than those promised in Budgets 2018 and 2019, it is likely to fall back to not much more than 30 per cent by 2024–25.

Current Challenges/Controversies

The primary challenge facing CSE, cutting across all aspects of the agency's activities, is the need to keep up with the constant evolution of information age technologies.

CSE's SIGINT program has had to respond to changing target technologies throughout its history. But the need to "master the Internet," as CSE chief John Adams put it in 2007,[34] probably represents the greatest challenge the agency has ever faced, requiring fundamental changes in collection technology and an ongoing race to keep pace with an ever-growing volume of traffic. It has also led the agency to become a hunter of "data at rest," using CNE operations to access data stored on IT systems rather than simply collecting the communications that pass its sensors ("data in motion"). Continuing efforts will be required to cope with the growing use of encryption and the migration of internet traffic to smartphones. One response may be greater reliance on accessing traffic through service providers or through compromise of endpoint devices. The agency is also increasingly looking to big data analysis techniques to derive intelligence from the vast quantities of communications metadata and other "data exhaust" now generated as people go about their lives.[35]

The IT security challenge posed by the information age is the mirror image of the SIGINT challenge. The techniques that CSE's SIGINT program uses against its targets are used by others against Canadian public and private sector IT systems and information holdings. This will remain an enduring problem. Internet-enabled influence operations designed to undermine Canada's political and social stability or advance other objectives could also become an important threat in coming years.[36] To the extent that the intelligence community has a role to play in protection against such operations, it is predominantly a job for CSIS. But CSE could provide valuable assistance in their detection and attribution. The challenge for the Canadian government will be finding ways to respond to such campaigns without undermining legitimate political and social discourse.

CSE's formal move into CNA roles faces technological challenges similar to those confronting the SIGINT program. The agency will also have to ensure that the effects of the cyber operations it undertakes remain limited to their specific targets, keeping them within the applicable legal limits and minimizing effects on innocent parties. The restrictions imposed on Part D operations have been criticized for their vagueness, which could lead to excessive permissiveness, but it is also possible that their relatively undefined nature will lead to a conservative interpretation of what is legally permissible to ensure that operations stay well outside the grey areas. Policy development and planning for such operations is likely to require ongoing dialogue among CSE, its minister, the minister of foreign affairs, the national security and intelligence advisor and other PCO elements, the Department of Justice, the National Security and Intelligence Review Agency (NSIRA), the National Security and Intelligence Committee of Parliamentarians (NSICOP), and eventually, perhaps, the courts. The rules and procedures governing such operations will also have to be worked out in consultation with other Canadian CNA actors,[37] and coordinated, or at least deconflicted, with the operations of the Five Eyes and perhaps select other countries. Some commentators question the wisdom of pursuing a CNA capability at all.[38]

Reconciling and balancing the sometimes complementary, sometimes competing imperatives of its SIGINT, ITSEC, and cyber operations roles will pose a continuing challenge to CSE. CSE's original SIGINT and COMSEC mandates were almost entirely complementary: the agency's knowledge of cryptanalysis and other SIGINT techniques informed its efforts to protect Canadian government communications against hostile SIGINT activities, and its knowledge of COMSEC techniques helped inform the SIGINT program. The situation is more complex now, with many of the hardware and software systems used by Canadians being the same as those used by Canadian SIGINT targets. Which side of the house will prevail when SIGINT wants to exploit a vulnerability but ITSEC would rather warn the public so Canadians can protect themselves? Similar dilemmas will arise as CSE integrates CNA activities into its operations. Is impeding the ability of terrorists to communicate justified if it means burning accesses that provide insight into current operations and future plans? For better or worse, the much greater institutional power of the SIGINT part of the agency may well exert a significant restraining effect on CSE's enthusiasm for CNA activities. Whether it will also exert a restraining effect on Canadian Forces and CSIS cyber operations remains to be determined.

CSE and Canadians

By long-standing policy and, since 2001, by law, CSE's foreign intelligence (Part A) and IT security (Part B) activities cannot be "directed at" Canadians or persons in Canada. The same prohibition also applies to the new cyber operations (Part D) mandate. But the agency does acquire a large quantity of Canadian communications, metadata, and other information about Canadians in the course of its operations.

A watchdog agency, the Office of the CSE Commissioner (OCSEC), was established in 1996 to provide public assurance that CSE obeys the law and takes adequate measures to protect the privacy of Canadians (discussed in chapter fourteen). In 2019, OCSEC's responsibilities were absorbed into the newly created NSIRA, which continues to perform this function.[39] Only once in OCSEC's two decades of existence did a CSE commissioner conclude that CSE had failed to comply with the law, and even in that case the non-compliance was ascribed to a failure of due diligence rather than determined to be an intentional violation of the law.[40] However, OCSEC did not always agree with CSE's activities or the Department of Justice's interpretation of CSE's obligations under the law. As of June 2019, commissioners had made 175 recommendations for changes in CSE's policies or practices, including in some cases calls for amendments to CSE's statute. By OCSEC's count, the government accepted and implemented or was working to address 95 per cent of those recommendations.[41] Other observers have been less sanguine. In a case still before the Federal Court at the time of writing, the British Columbia Civil Liberties Association claimed in 2014 that CSE's collection of Canadian communications metadata and its incidental collection of Canadian private communications in the absence of a system of judicial authorizations infringe the *Charter of Rights and Freedoms*.[42] Some of the provisions of the *CSE Act* were probably designed to make the agency's activities more *Charter*-compliant in these respects. The

CSE Act itself has been criticized on a wide range of grounds, however.[43] On a number of these questions the courts may yet end up deciding.

Concerns have also been expressed about the extent to which Canadian communications, metadata, and other information about Canadians may be acquired, analysed, and shared by CSE even when the agency is operating entirely within the law.

When information relating to Canadians is used in Part A and Part B reporting, the name and other identifying information of that Canadian – known as Canadian identity information (CII) – is usually "suppressed," that is, replaced by a generic reference such as "a named Canadian" as a privacy protection measure. The information is not deleted, however. It is retained by CSE and is available to clients who can demonstrate both the authority and an operational justification for obtaining it. From July 2017 to June 2018 inclusive, CSE received 1,156 requests for disclosure of CII to its Canadian clients, along with 102 requests for disclosure to Five Eyes agencies and 24 to non-Five Eyes agencies.[44] The number of items of CII actually disclosed in response to these requests was not reported.

Potentially more concerning is CSE's collection of metadata related to communications and other internet activity. It is likely that the metadata that CSE and its Five Eyes partners collect captures a very large proportion of Canadians' internet lives. When processed with, or even without, other public and government-accessible data, such information can be extraordinarily revealing.[45] Although CSE is not permitted to direct its Part A and B activities at Canadians, the analyses it conducts under these parts of its mandate may end up incorporating Canadian data, and under Part C of its mandate the agency is permitted to search or otherwise analyse its metadata holdings directly for Canadian-related information on behalf of clients like CSIS and the RCMP. No information has been released as to how often this occurs or what judicial or other processes are required to initiate such analyses.

Since passage of the *CSE Act*, the agency has also been permitted to analyse Canadian-related communications and metadata in support of investigations under the *Investment Canada Act*.[46]

The creation of the NSICOP in 2017 and the NSIRA in 2019 may help provide reassurance not only that CSE complies with the law, but that the imperatives of both security and human rights are respected. A new oversight position called the intelligence commissioner (IC) was also created in 2019.[47] The foreign intelligence and cybersecurity authorizations issued by the minister of national defence to enable CSE to collect information can take effect only if approved by the IC, based on the commissioner's assessment of the reasonableness of the minister's decision.[48] Whether the courts will consider this quasi-judicial process a satisfactory mechanism for protecting Canadians' *Charter* rights remains to be seen.

Conclusion

CSE is the primary Canadian provider of foreign intelligence information and the main Canadian contributor to the Five Eyes intelligence community, through which Canada gets access to much of the vast intelligence output of the United States and the other Five Eyes partners. The agency also provides technical and operational assistance to federal law enforcement and security agencies and the Canadian Forces/DND, including in some cases the collection of Canadian communications or other data. In 2019, its mandate was extended to include conduct of offensive and defensive cyber operations. Finally, through the Canadian Centre for Cyber Security, CSE offers cybersecurity guidance and services to the government, the private sector, and the public.

Changes in intelligence priorities and the evolution of global communications mean that CSE, which once focused almost entirely on the communications of the Soviet Union, increasingly encounters Canadians in the course of its operations, raising important human rights and privacy concerns. The agency's reluctance to provide information about the degree to which Canadians end up in its crosshairs contributes to public distrust. The changes in review and oversight of the agency enacted in 2019 may help to allay some of these concerns by providing reassurance that CSE is capable of performing its mission, is focused on the right tasks, and adequately protects the rights and freedoms of Canadians. Greater transparency on the part of CSE would also be helpful. In some respects, CSE provides less information now than it did before it became a stand-alone agency in November 2011. Yet it has also expressed a determination to become more open. CSE will always need to shroud a substantial part of its operations in secrecy, but a lot of scope remains for greater openness.

NOTES

1 Communications Security Establishment (CSE), "CSE Information Kit," last modified 18 July 2018, https://www.cse-cst.gc.ca/en/media/information.

2 Privy Council Office, *The Canadian Intelligence Community*, 16 March 1990, appendix C, p. 4, Library and Archives Canada, RG 25, BAN 2016-0149,

box 2, file 3-5-5, pt. 1. I am grateful to the Canadian Foreign Intelligence History Project for making this document available to me.

3 For more on these developments, see Bill Robinson, "From 1967 to 2017: CSE's Transition from the Industrial Age to the Information Age," in *Big Data Surveillance and Security Intelligence: The Canadian Case*, ed. David Lyon and David Murakami Wood (University of British Columbia Press, forthcoming).

4 Bill C-36, the *Anti-terrorism Act*, S.C. 2001, c. 41, received Royal Assent on 18 December 2001.

5 The *Communications Security Establishment Act* was Part 3 of Bill C-59, *An Act respecting national security matters*, which received Royal Assent on 21 June 2019, creating the *National Security Act, 2017*, S.C. 2019, c. 13.

6 *CSE Act*, s 2.

7 "Intelligence Priorities," in *CSE Briefing Binder* prepared for Defence Minister Harjit Sajjan, November 2015, released in redacted form under access to information request A-2015-00067.

8 CSE's *Annual Report to the Minister of National Defence 2014–2015* (4–10) listed eight key intelligence priorities, while the 2013–14 version (2–8) listed seven. Both documents were released in redacted form under access to information request A-2015-00086. No information about the nature of the priorities was released. However, in broad terms they were probably similar to the seven listed in the supplementary material on CSE that was published on the DND website in conjunction with the department's *2011–2012 Report on Plans and Priorities* (https://web.archive.org/web /20130522195915/http://www.vcds-vcemd.forces.gc.ca/sites/page-eng .asp?page=10414): "terrorism and extremism; mission in Afghanistan; proliferation of weapons of mass destruction; cyber security; foreign espionage and interference; Canada's Northern Strategy; and international security and prosperity interests."

9 National Security and Intelligence Committee of Parliamentarians, *Annual Report 2018* (2019),39–43. Available online: https://www.nsicop-cpsnr.ca /reports/rp-2019-04-09/2019-04-09_annual_report_2018_public_en.pdf.

10 CSE, *CSEC Foundational Learning Curriculum* (2013), 436, released in redacted form under access to information request.

11 CSE, *Annual Report to the Minister of National Defence 2011–2012* (2012), released in redacted form under access to information request A-2015-00086.

12 Office of the Communications Security Establishment Commissioner (OCSEC), *Annual Report 2007–2008* (2008), 18. Available online: https:// www.ocsec-bccst.gc.ca/a76/ann-rpt-2007-2008_e.pdf.

13 In 2015, the agency reported that "CSE is an intelligence collector and compiler; CSE does not currently conduct intelligence assessments."

See "CSE's Domestic Partnerships," in *CSE Briefing Binder* prepared for Defence Minister Harjit Sajjan. The IT security part of CSE, the Canadian Centre for Cyber Security, does produce assessments, however.

14 CSE, *Communications Security Establishment Annual Report 2019–20* (2020). Available online: https://www.cse-cst.gc.ca/en/transparency-transparence/reports-rapports/annual-report-rapport-annuel-2019-20.

15 "Communications Security Establishment" presentation, 5, in *CSE Briefing Binder* prepared for Defence Minister Harjit Sajjan.

16 "CSE's Domestic Partnerships," in *CSE Briefing Binder* prepared for Defence Minister Harjit Sajjan.

17 CSE, *Annual Report to the Minister of National Defence 2014–2015*, 4. According to the report, "SIGINT reports graded actionable intelligence (AI) have: a) identified a threat to Canadian and/or allied interests, b) resulted in significant action being taken by the GC, or c) significantly influenced decisions by the GC, the Canadian Armed Forces or an allied government. Reports graded as Exceptional or Satisfied Need have provided important context to promote situational awareness on topics of importance to the clients, and may have contributed to subsequent decision-making by clients."

18 "CANSLOW Can't Slow Down!," *SIDtoday*, 20 December 2004, https://theintercept.com/snowden-sidtoday/3676164-canslow-can-t-slow-down/.

19 This probably refers to intercept sites in Canadian diplomatic facilities. National Security Agency, "NSA Intelligence Relationship with Canada's Communications Security Establishment Canada (CSEC)," 3 April 2013, https://snowdenarchive.cjfe.org/greenstone/collect/snowden1/index/assoc/HASHadcc.dir/doc.pdf.

20 *National Defence Act*, R.S.C. 1985, c. N-5, s 273.65(3). It could, however, provide assistance to a system owner monitoring its own traffic for cybersecurity purposes.

21 *CSE Act*, s. 28(2).

22 *CSE Act*, s. 34(3).

23 CSE, "Canadian Centre for Cyber Security," last modified 16 October 2018, https://cse-cst.gc.ca/en/backgrounder-fiche-information. The number of employees was revealed by CCCS head Scott Jones in testimony before the Standing Committee on Government Operations and Estimates on 25 May 2020 (https://www.ourcommons.ca/DocumentViewer/en/43-1/OGGO/meeting-14/evidence). More information about the Public Safety cybersecurity elements that were absorbed into the Cyber Centre can be found in Alex Wilner's chapter on Public Safety Canada in this volume.

24 "*CSE Act* Mandates – Examples," in CSE, *C-59 Briefing Binder* (2017), released in redacted form under access to information request A-2017-00077.

25   CSE, *OPS-1-11: Retention Schedules for SIGINT Data* (2007), 17, released in redacted form under access to information request A-2014-00013.

26   Colin Freeze, "Spy Agency's Work with CSIS, RCMP Fuels Fears of Privacy Breaches," *Globe and Mail*, 31 January 2014, https://www .theglobeandmail.com/news/politics/spy-agencys-work-with-csis -rcmp-fuels-fears-of-privacy-breaches/article16623147/.

27   Opening statement of CSE Associate Chief Shelly Bruce to the Standing Committee on Public Safety and National Security, 13 February 2018.

28   "Foreign Cyber Operations," in CSE, *C-59 Briefing Binder*.

29   *CSE Act*, s. 33(1).

30   *CSE Act*, ss. 30 and 31.

31   CSE, *Communications Security Establishment Annual Report 2019–20*. employment information for recent years can be found on the GC InfoBase website at https://www.tbs-sct.gc.ca/ems-sgd/edb-bdd/index-eng .html#orgs/dept/110/infograph/. Not included in these figures are the approximately 900 members of the Canadian Forces Information Operations Group (CFIOG) who work with CSE on national intelligence collection activities and provide SIGINT and ITSEC services to the Canadian Forces/DND. With the Canadian Forces moving to stand up an offensive cyberwarfare capability, the size of the CFIOG may be growing.

32   Treasury Board of Canada, *2019–20 Estimates: Parts I and II* (2019), II-52. This figure does not include spending on the CFIOG, which is buried in the DND budget and probably amounts to about $150–200 million per year.

33   Budget figures compiled by the author from the DND *Departmental Performance Report* (1996) for fiscal year 1995–6 and subsequent editions up to fiscal year 2006–7; the CSE *Annual Report to the Minister of National Defence 2010–11* (2011), providing data for fiscal years 2007–8 to 2009–10; the CSE *Annual Report to the Minister of National Defence 2014–15* (2015), providing data for fiscal years 2010–11 to 2011–12; the *Public Accounts of Canada* (2013) for fiscal year 2012–13 and subsequent editions up to fiscal year 2018–19; and the *2019–20 Estimates: Parts I and II*. Constant dollars calculated by the author using the Canadian Gross Domestic Product Implicit Price Index reported by the International Monetary Fund World Economic Outlook Database (2019) (https://www.imf.org/external /pubs/ft/weo/2019/02/weodata/index.aspx). The bump in 2014–15 was the result of a one-time $300-million payment made when CSE's new HQ building was completed.

34   John Adams, testimony to the Standing Senate Committee on National Security and Defence, 30 April 2007.

35   Scott Thompson and David Lyon, "Pixies, Pop-Out Intelligence and Sandbox Play: New Analytic Methods and National Security Surveillance

in Canada," in *Big Data Surveillance and Security Intelligence: The Canadian Case*, ed. David Lyon and David Murakami Wood (University of British Columbia Press, forthcoming).

36 CSE released a public report on this issue in June 2017: *Cyber Threats to Canada's Democratic Process*, https://www.cse-cst.gc.ca/sites/default /files/cse-cyber-threat-assessment-e.pdf. An updated report was released in April 2019 ahead of the federal election in October of that year: https:// cyber.gc.ca/en/cyber-threats-and-democracy.

37 The Canadian Forces, and possibly CSIS, will have the ability to carry out CNA operations using their own authorities and resources, and both will also be able to seek CSE assistance through Part C of CSE's mandate.

38 See, e.g., Ronald Deibert, "A Close Look at the Proposed 'CSE Act,'" *Ronald Deibert* (blog), 18 December 2017, https://deibert.citizenlab.ca/2017/12 /close-look-proposed-cse-act/.

39 For more information on OCSEC and NSIRA, see Leah West's chapter on national security review and oversight in this volume.

40 OCSEC, "Commissioner Plouffe's Report Is Tabled in Parliament – 2016," 28 January 2016, https://www.ocsec-bccst.gc.ca/s41/s60/d352/eng /commissioner-plouffe-report-tabled.

41 OCSEC, *Annual Report 2018–2019* (2019), 8. Available online: https://www .ocsec-bccst.gc.ca/a308/ar-ra-2018-2019-en.pdf.

42 Notice of claim filed by British Columbia Civil Liberties Association, 27 October 2014, Federal Court File No. T-2210-14, https://bccla.org/wp -content/uploads/2014/12/20141027-CSEC-Statement-of-Claim.pdf.

43 See, e.g., Lex Gill, Tamir Israel, and Christopher Parsons, "Government's Defence of Proposed CSE Act Falls Short," *Citizen Lab* blog, 30 January 2018, https://citizenlab.ca/2018/01/governments-defence-of-proposed -cse-act-falls-short/, and Craig Forcese, "Does CSE Risk a Re X Moment with the Current Drafting in C-59?," *National Security Law* blog, 2 February 2018, https://craigsforcese.squarespace.com/blog/2018/2/2/does-cse -risk-a-re-x-moment-with-the-current-drafting-in-c-5.html. The full list of testimony and briefs submitted to the Standing Committee on Public Safety and National Security with respect to Bill C-59 can be found at https://www.ourcommons.ca/Committees/en/SECU/StudyActivity? studyActivityId=9807256.

44 OCSEC, *Annual Report 2018–2019*, 20–21. Note, however, that these figures are not the same as the number of identities requested, as the same identity may be requested by multiple clients, while a single request may encompass more than one identity.

45 Office of the Privacy Commissioner of Canada, *Metadata and Privacy: A Technical and Legal Overview* (2014). Available online: https://www.priv .gc.ca/media/1786/md_201410_e.pdf.

46 *CSE Act*, s. 23(2). I am grateful to Wesley Wark for his comments on this provision and other aspects of CSE's activities.
47 For more information on the intelligence commissioner, see Leah West's chapter in this volume.
48 However, the IC does not review authorizations for active or defensive cyber operations.

5 The Integrated Terrorism Assessment Centre (ITAC)

STEPHANIE CARVIN

Housed within the Canadian Security Intelligence Service (CSIS) building in Ottawa is the Integrated Terrorism Assessment Centre (ITAC),
one of the newest and perhaps one of the least well known of all of
Canada's national security agencies. Indeed, there is little in the way of
open-source information on ITAC; it has only one page on the government's website and, at the time of writing, the Centre is one of the few
organizations in this book that has no social media presence.[1] Further,
there is no recent publicly available information as to the number of
employees the Centre has or its budget.[2]

There is a significant degree of irony to this. ITAC was specifically designed to be an agency that would provide information to
a variety of actors on terrorist threats to the security of Canada.
There should almost certainly be more known about an agency
that describes itself as Canada's "independent, expert federal body
responsible for assessing terrorism threats to Canada and Canadian
interests globally"[3] that is also responsible for determining Canada's
National Terrorism Threat Level. And yet information about ITAC is
not only hard to come by, but often the available information is contradictory. Its relationship to CSIS, its core mandate, and what ITAC
actually does vary in descriptions of the Centre – sometimes within
the same document.

Unfortunately for ITAC, the failure to provide more information
about its core functions means that the void is filled by reports and academic scholarship, most of which is critical. Indeed, media coverage of
the Centre has largely focused on ITAC's supposed role in coordinating
information about the Occupy protests, Idle No More, and surveillance
groups.[4] As such, ITAC is sometimes presented as an all-knowing organization working on behalf of critical infrastructure in the hands of the
private sector.

This chapter argues that this sinister portrayal of ITAC is inaccurate and hides an organization that seems to have struggled with fulfilling a challenging mandate. As such, it will outline what is publicly known about ITAC, including its core functions. It will highlight some of the challenges in meeting its mandate, including difficulties communicating threat information in a democracy. It will also use the Centre as an example of how an overly secretive approach can damage an organization's own self-interest.

Mandate

ITAC has a confusing management structure. Housed physically within CSIS Headquarters in Ottawa, ITAC is a separate intelligence analysis body that is managed by its own director. The ITAC director is appointed by the national security and intelligence advisor (NSIA) in consultation with the director of CSIS. The director of ITAC is responsible to the CSIS director, as well as its management board, chaired by the NSIA and attended by the deputy ministers from participating organizations to review ITAC's performance. ITAC is also required to submit an annual report directly to the Cabinet.[5]

A large portion of ITAC analysts, with exact numbers unknown, are secondees from multiple national security and intelligence agencies in Ottawa. According to an April 2007 CSIS backgrounder (no longer available online), the departments and agencies then represented at ITAC included the Canada Border Services Agency (CBSA), Correctional Services Canada, the Communications Security Establishment (CSE), CSIS, the Department of National Defence (DND), the Financial Transactions and Reports Analysis Centre of Canada (FINTRAC), Foreign Affairs and International Trade Canada (now known as Global Affairs Canada or GAC), the Privy Council Office (PCO), Public Safety Canada (PSC), the Royal Canadian Mounted Police (RCMP), and Transport Canada, as well as two provincial police forces: the Ontario Provincial Police (OPP) and Sûreté du Québec.[6] A more recent survey of participating organization includes CSIS, CSE, RCMP, DND, Transport Canada, CBSA, GAC, the Canada Revenue Agency, PSC, and the OPP.[7] Typically, secondees serve at ITAC for two years before returning to their home agency. However, ITAC has increasingly hired its own permanent analytical and managerial staff. As will be discussed below, it is not entirely clear why this is the case.

Of all of the national security agencies in Canada, ITAC's mandate is probably the least clear, and there is the least amount of publicly available information on it out of the departments and agencies discussed in this book. Unfortunately, as noted above, information provided by the few sources available is vague and somewhat contradictory. An overview of the establishment of ITAC and its apparent evolution in the years since may offer an explanation as to why this is the case.

ITAC's origins are in the aftermath of 9/11, when a push toward integrated decision-making to handle complex security threats, especially international terrorism, was common across Five Eyes countries. Each nation established a multi-source comprehensive threat assessment agency that drew upon individuals from different departments to improve information-sharing and relationships across government. In this sense, ITAC is similar to its partners in Australia (the National Threat Assessment Centre, NTAC – established on 17 October 2003),[8] New Zealand (the Combined Threat Assessment Group, CTAG – established in 2004),[9] the UK (the Joint Terrorism Analysis Centre, JTAC – established in June 2003),[10] and the US (the National Counterterrorism Centre, NCTC – established in May 2003).[11]

To meet the need for a more integrated approach identified by the government, CSIS created the Integrated National Security Assessment Centre (INSAC) in early 2003. It was envisioned that INSAC would use intelligence from a variety of sources to produce relevant and timely analysis and assessments of threats to the security of Canada and would distribute these reports to agencies and departments with national security or public safety responsibilities.[12] In doing so, it invited several government agencies and departments to participate: the Customs and Revenue Agency (CRA), CSE, DND, the Office of Critical Infrastructure Protection and Emergency Preparedness (now folded into Public Safety Canada), the RCMP, Transport Canada, the Department of Foreign Affairs and International Trade (DFAIT – now GAC), Citizenship and Immigration Canada (CIC – now Immigration, Refugees and Citizenship Canada), the Department of the Solicitor General of Canada (now PSC), and the PCO.

According to a 2004 report from the Office of the Auditor General, it did not take long for bureaucratic politics[13] to intervene in the establishment of this new body. Neither DFAIT, nor the Solicitor General, nor PCO were keen to participate, and they did not offer a representative for the new body. CIC indicated it wished to do so but that financial resources were not available. DFAIT appears to have taken the strongest stance against participation and argued that the scarce resources of a foreign affairs ministry should not be spent on domestic agencies. At least the Solicitor General and PCO indicated that they were processing information from INSAC.[14]

However, part of the difficulty seems to have been that even from the beginning the parties involved in the creation of INSAC were unable to agree to a mandate for the organization. No one in the government appears to have objected to more information-sharing with actors who needed to protect Canada's infrastructure or safeguard the population from terrorism. Nevertheless, how this should be done, for whom, and for what purpose seem to have been elusive and possibly handicapped INSAC from the beginning.

To be fair, INSAC was not alone in its start-up difficulties. The Auditor General noted that during this period the RCMP's Integrated National Security Enforcement Teams (INSETs) and Integrated Border Enforcement Teams (IBETs) were experiencing similar problems with regard to sharing and participation. This led the Auditor General's report to conclude that while the idea of integrated agencies had promise, the execution of this principle was off to a bad start:

> While integrated units represent an improvement, in each case they were initiated by a single agency; we are concerned that participation by other departments and agencies is discretionary. We are also concerned that without an accepted framework to guide their development, such groups could proliferate and lead to duplication.[15]

Yet if there were doubts about an integrated approach, these were not seen in the Paul Martin government's 2004 national security policy, *Securing an Open Society*. The document, which was Canada's first-ever (and so far only) national security policy statement, emphasized an integrated approach to the challenges of protecting Canada after 9/11. A key feature of this policy was the creation of the Integrated Threat Assessment Centre, as it was initially known, "to ensure that all threat-related information is brought together, assessed and reaches all who need it in a timely and effective manner."[16] Noting that there "has been no comprehensive and timely central government assessment that brings together intelligence about potential threats from a wide range of sources to allow better and more integrated decision-making," the policy stated that "the integrated approach that the Government is taking will help to reduce the risk that information held by one part of the Government will fail to be provided in a timely fashion to those who can utilize it."[17] As an example, the document suggested that threat information would be provided to border services agents so they could act "to prevent people who represent a known threat from entering Canada."[18]

The presentation of ITAC as the creation of a new government body was, however, somewhat misleading; it seems that when ITAC became fully operational on 15 October 2004, it replaced the already existing INSAC. Still, *Securing an Open Society* makes it clear that the government had at least two particular purposes in mind, mirrored in other Western democracies in the post-9/11 period: eliminating information silos and improved, timely all-source assessment. In an unclassified slide presentation, ITAC described itself as "created specifically to address terrorism" and as "a community resource."[19]

However, in terms of a public description of its mandate, there was still a lot of information missing. While the 2004 national security policy stressed the importance of getting information to those who need it, just who these individuals and/or agencies were was left largely unspecified. Were ITAC's activities limited to the public sector? What about critical infrastructure? Local and provincial authorities?

Indeed, there does not seem to be a consistent description of ITAC's mandate. The April 2007 CSIS backgrounder noted above offers a description of "ITAC's Role":

> ITAC's primary objective is to produce comprehensive threat assessments, which are distributed within the intelligence community and to first-line responders, such as law enforcement, on a timely basis. Its assessments, based on intelligence and trend analysis, evaluate both the probability and potential consequences of threats. Such assessments allow the Government of Canada to coordinate activities in response to specific threats in order to prevent or mitigate risks to public safety.[20]

Two years later the Auditor General described the ITAC mandate as: "to produce comprehensive threat assessments and analysis that are distributed within the intelligence community, the private sector and to emergency services."[21] The Auditor General's report is one of the first to mention the private sector as the recipient of information. Whether this was due to ITAC wanting to keep its information-sharing decisions quiet or the inclusion of the private sector being a recent development in ITAC's mandate is not clear. As noted above, the recipients of ITAC's assessments were never specifically identified. In 2011, ITAC changed its name from the "Integrated Threat Assessment Centre" to the "Integrated Terrorism Assessment Centre" to better reflect its mandate, but publicly it was never made clear why this step was taken.

At time of writing, the most recent iteration, in December 2017, of ITAC's mandate on its website suggests a major shift has taken place. The Centre describes itself as "a federal organization responsible for

assessing terrorism threats to Canada and Canadian interests worldwide. Its products support the decision-making needs of senior federal
leaders."[22] There is no mention of first responders, the private sector,
or even lower-level public servants. This change appears to represent
something very different from ITAC's 2004 mandate.

Intelligence Products

As part of its earlier mandate, ITAC was reported to produce somewhere between 300–400 reports every year.[23] While its output under its
revised mandate is unknown, ITAC currently produces three kinds of
intelligence products:

Threat and risk assessments: Like other analytical bodies in the Canadian
government, ITAC produces assessments on threats and risk to Canada
and Canadian interests. For source material, ITAC analysts have access
to CSIS's highly classified databases. However, this is somewhat short
of the original goals of the Centre, which envisioned ITAC as having
access to multiple national security databases, including those of the
RCMP, DND, CBSA, Transport Canada, and others, and to become a
central conduit for the flow of information.[24]

One policymaker interviewed on their use of ITAC's threat and risk
assessments in 2018 indicated that while the Centre's products had previously been received on a daily basis, they were by then received on a
weekly basis in a compendium format, because "there wasn't so much
daily that it merited the daily structure."[25] Unfortunately, this means
the material may sometimes be a little stale by the time it is consumed.
However, it is not clear if this compendium format is the way material
is shared across all government departments.

National threat level: Since October 2014, ITAC has been responsible
for setting the National Terrorism Threat Level. According to the threat
level website, this represents "the likelihood of a violent act of terrorism
occurring in Canada, based on information and intelligence."[26] The levels correspond to the following five categories: very low, low, medium,
high, and critical. At time of writing, the level has never changed from
"medium" since October 2014.[27]

While the threat level is announced to inform the public, the level
requires no action from citizens. Instead, it is meant to inform "the
Canadian security and intelligence community, provincial and municipal emergency authorities, first responders and relevant stakeholders
so they can identify risks and vulnerabilities from threats and determine what measures to put in place to prevent or mitigate a violent act
of terrorism."[28] According the National Terrorism Threat Level website,

the level is calculated using current intelligence as well as information, including past trends and known intentions, capabilities, and opportunities for terrorist entities to conduct attacks. ITAC states it also uses both quantitative and qualitative methods, although none are specified.[29] The level is assessed at a minimum every four months, or more frequently if needed. Once ITAC has formulated its assessment, it sends a recommendation to the CSIS director, who then provides it to the national security and intelligence advisor to the prime minister.

Special events: ITAC participates in wider government efforts around special events, including the G7/8 and G20 summits in Canada. Typically, this involves being present at and writing analytical products for operational centres that may be set up on an ad hoc basis to support the security of these events. In addition, ITAC sets the threat level for special events in Canada (such as the 2015 Pan American Games in Toronto) or where Canada may be participating abroad (such as the 2016 Olympics in Brazil).[30] It also advises on high-level visits, either of foreign officials in Canada or of Canadian officials going abroad.[31]

Cooperation

ITAC was deliberately designed with inter-agency cooperation as part of its core mandate of providing integrated assessment. This is reflected in the original organizaton of the Centre, which was initially intended to be staffed almost exclusively with secondees. The idea behind this structure is that it will help facilitate the exchange of knowledge, experience, and contacts within the Canadian national security sector. Ideally, the secondee will bring their specific departmental expertise to ITAC and leave with a better understanding of national security priorities, as well as having developed contacts elsewhere in government.

However, there are potential downsides to staffing with secondees. First, there are serious structural barriers to implementing the original staffing model for ITAC. In particular, the process to bring someone into the CSIS building to work at ITAC is extremely cumbersome: it can take between 18 months and two years to complete the appropriate security checks, even if that person already has a government secret clearance. In this way, it makes sense to hire permanent employees rather than deal with the frustration of constant churn and the uncertainty of security clearance processes for secondees that may take longer than the duration of the actual position.

A second downside comes from the reality of self-interest within bureaucracies; it is unlikely that managers will send their best staff to another organization like ITAC for two years. Instead, they might see it as an opportunity to rid themselves of an employee who is underperforming or challenging. As ITAC is an organization traditionally staffed to a large degree by secondees, the issue of the quality of secondees has been problematic. The 2009 report by the Auditor General noted that there were questions about whether ITAC had sufficient subject matter expertise in order to fulfill its mandate.[32] Indeed, taking analysts who used to work on combating drugs, transportation issues, or crime and expecting them to develop strong analytical skills and a knowledge of the nuances of domestic and international violent extremists is ambitious. At best, they face a very steep learning curve.

There is an irony here – one of the points that critics of ITAC focus on is its "fusion" nature, which, they argue, makes the sharing and storing of information faster and easier, posing a risk to democratic protest.[33] The idea that the integrated approach suffers from problems frequently associated with bureaucratic scheming is absent. Indeed, it appears that there is friction in inter-agency cooperation that ITAC faces on a daily basis. For example, in 2005 ITAC noted that disclosure of information to ITAC from other agencies was not automatic but "governed by the home agency." In other words, partner agencies choose what information ITAC employees may see. In addition, any disclosure of information that ITAC holds "is subject to permission of [the] source agency." Although it is not clear if this is still the case, it would mean that sharing information could be more difficult than what is often believed.[34] Additionally, ITAC's revised mandate to focus on "senior policy makers" suggests that the Centre is sharing even less information and with fewer partners than before.

Resources

As noted above, information about ITAC's budget is not publicly available. It is possible that ITAC's budget is combined with the CSIS budget, but government officials have not confirmed this. According to briefing materials accompanying the 2005 slide presentation mentioned above, ITAC was provided with $30 million for the first five years of its existence.[35] In 2009, the Auditor General stated that it was not clear that ITAC had sufficient resources in order to succeed.[36] Nor is it known whether ITAC received extra funding after the terror attacks of October 2014, as did CBSA, CSIS, and the RCMP.[37]

As also noted above, there also is no current publicly available information on the number of employees ITAC has in terms of either permanent staff or secondees, or the ratio of staff to secondees. The only source of publicly available information is the same 2005 slide presentation, which states that the organization had 45 employees in total, with 20 designated ITAC employees, mostly on the administrative side. However, it is important to note that just because a position exists does not mean the position has necessarily been filled. If an organization refuses or is unable to staff a position, it may remain empty.

Controversies

It is not unusual for the Centre to find itself in the news in relation to its role in providing intelligence assessments during domestic events. Much of this coverage tends to be critical and to portray ITAC as an organization with well-established, networked connections to police, provinces, and private critical infrastructure programs that monitor domestic protests.

For example, in 2011, ITAC reportedly monitored "the potential for politically motivated violence" during the Occupy protests in Canada.[38] Media reporting indicates the Centre wrote three reports during this time that focused on potential economic disruption and whether the hacker group Anonymous would support the protests. The reports were said to "contain widely known information" and focus on the threats of politically motivated violence as a part of the protests. However, activists objected to the very existence of the reports themselves, suggesting that writing them was anti-democratic. A spokesperson for the BC Civil Liberties Association noted that these assessments increased the "hype around security threat of active dissent by citizens," which could "increase the potential justifications for very invasive policing."[39]

ITAC's information-sharing practices in relation to Indigenous protests have also been subject to criticism. ITAC wrote multiple assessments on the Indigenous National Day of Action and other protests between 2007 and 2008 and spoke about Indigenous protests under the categories of "terrorism and extremism" in its bi-annual updates.[40] Similarly, ITAC reportedly monitored Idle No More protests in 2012–13, although the Centre claimed it was not doing it because it believed the protests were a threat, but to protect activists from the violence of others, such as white supremacists who had encouraged attacks on the demonstrations.[41]

It is not unreasonable for activists to be concerned over government surveillance. During the Cold War, the RCMP engaged in large-scale surveillance of civil society groups of individuals who might have had a very tenuous link to left-wing movements and political parties, LGBTQ2 persons, et cetera.[42] Further, historical injustices and poor relations between Indigenous communities and government authorities mean that there is already very little trust between the groups. When it is revealed that a "terrorism assessment centre" is analysing protests, even benignly, this is not likely to improve the situation.

At the same time, there often seems to be, on the part of these critiques, a failure to understand how intelligence assessments work in Canada. In the first instance, assessments are often written at the requests of politicians and senior policymakers who want to know if there is a threat related to what they are seeing or reading in the news. Second, the intelligence analyst has a responsibility to try to anticipate these questions. In both instances it is the job of the intelligence analyst to explain the context of the situation and explain why there may *or may not be* a threat. The work of intelligence analysis is often to dispel concerns by explaining why there is no risk or threat.

That is not to say that intelligence assessment bodies always get it right. Assessments prepared for the 2010 G8 and G20 summits, based in part on ITAC's information, listed "embarrassment to the Canadian government" as one possible threat or risk.[43] Clearly, this is a political problem, not a national security threat. Further, including protesting groups under headings such as "extremism," even when dispelling the idea that there is a threat, can create conflation between the two issues.

However, much of the misunderstanding seems to stem from the fact that there is so little publicly available knowledge about ITAC, its mandate, and the limits of the organization. It is, as a result, not difficult for some critics to portray it as a secretive, far-reaching force within government, with considerable access to many databases. The evidence presented in this chapter suggests that this is a deeply flawed view. However, ITAC's refusal to be more forthcoming about itself and its mandate plays a large role in undermining trust in its activities.

Conclusion

It is reasonable to conclude that ITAC's future success will depend on its ability to address three key issues. First, ITAC needs to carve out a role for itself in the national security and intelligence community that moves away from its ambiguous and possibly unachievable mandate. Its historical development suggests that it is an integrated centre with an identity crisis. Where does it fit and who is it serving? Second, ITAC should address its lack of transparency to counter misleading information about its national security functions.

The third issue is one of efficacy. It appears the initial impetus behind the Centre, the creation of an inter-agency community resource that provides useful intelligence to different agencies at all levels of government, has not come into being. As explained in this chapter, this is likely due to the inherent problems of inter-agency cooperation, the difficulties of sharing information across agencies, and bureaucratic politics. In being a new kid on the block, ITAC has struggled. Individuals either currently serving or having served in several Canadian intelligence and national security agencies have noted that ITAC's reputation for analysis is poor, although there has been some improvement in recent years, particularly under the guidance of recent directors.[44]

However, it is also the case that integrated agencies designed to provide threat warning intelligence in the post-9/11 era have struggled in other countries as well.[45] While the idea of an integrated approach seems promising, in reality, there are many structural barriers in the way. First, information passed on to partners or the public can be seen as political rather than neutral. In the US, surveys show that within two years of introducing a colour-based threat warning system, 40 per cent of Americans believed that increases in the terror alert level "were either fully or partially motivated" by political gain.[46] ITAC's threat warning system is different in nature from the (now replaced) US system, but its information has certainly been portrayed as reinforcing the status quo, benefiting private sector owners of critical infrastructure protection and monitoring dissent.

Second, it often makes little sense to provide threat warning information for an entire country. This is especially the case in a country the size of Canada: conditions in Toronto are very different from those in Saskatchewan and Newfoundland. Threat warning information that is not local or specific enough does not provide enough information for local authorities to act and may therefore be ignored.[47] Relatedly, it is very difficult to get the balance of information right. Available intelligence should be disseminated to those best able to use it. In the case of ITAC, these were originally meant to be first responders. However, calibrating the amount and appropriateness of information is difficult. Police forces in Winnipeg do not necessarily need to know al-Qaida's intentions in the Middle East if there is no clear nexus to Manitoba. Providing a series of alerts without tailoring the advice to those affected can contribute to creating more noise than actionable insight.

Finally, while there is a democratic principle that the public has a right to know about security threats, is this still the case when there is little the public can do about it? This is a problem when there is information that suggests there is a general risk, but no immediate threat.[48] Security agencies appear to be caught in a difficult position: repeated, vague security warnings will have little impact, and may become risible.[49]

However, if warnings are not given and an attack occurs, there can be recriminations of authorities for failing to alert the public to the risk.

Given these challenges, we are left with a series of questions: What does the government want ITAC to be? Is there a future for an integrated threat intelligence centre in Canada? And if so, what should it do? Based upon the post-9/11 experience, national security institutions that seek to provide risk communication on violent extremist threats need to address at least three key questions:

1 Should the centre focus on offering pre-incident/attack analysis (warnings) or post-incident/attack analysis (reassurance and guidance)? The challenge with the former has been discussed above. But while useful information may be provided after an attack to help inform the context of the incident, questions will be asked as to why a warning was not given if information was available.
2 Should ITAC offer strategic (a broad view of large-scale trends) or tactical analysis (more warnings of imminent threats)? The former helps to develop context, but does not offer specific, actionable information. Tactical intelligence warns of specific incidents, but often there will be few cases where all of the warning signs will be known in advance and advice can be given.[50]
3 Should analysis be aimed at government policymakers, the private sector, first responders in provinces/municipalities, or the public? Or some or all of these? Governments have struggled to find a way to answer this question or, if they do, to prioritize who they give information to or how to provide it in a useful and constructive manner.

ITAC seems to have answered these questions by turning away from its original purpose and focusing on senior policymakers. Given the challenges of providing threat warning intelligence, whether to the government or the public, this is understandable. Governments are in the position to actually use and do something with the information they receive. Still, this development is unfortunate as there is a lack of government communications providing useful information to the public on violent extremist threats. Additionally, given that the government already receives advice from CSIS, DND, GAC, and PCO, it is not clear that senior policymakers really need another source of this kind of intelligence. In other words, it seems clear that fifteen years after its founding, ITAC continues to struggle to find its place in the Canadian national security architecture.

NOTES

1 An official speaking in a confidential background interview suggested that this may be the result of concerns that an ITAC social media account would simply compete with the minister of public safety's social media presence and would not add anything of value.

2 ITAC refused multiple requests to provide this information for this chapter, meaning it is the one organization in this book where we have no data on its current resources or number of employees. ITAC had agreed to answer a series of emailed questions but subsequently changed its mind and agreed to one interview in May 2018 over the phone. The spokesperson refused to answer any questions on current resources. At least three individuals with knowledge of ITAC suggested one reason for the Centre's reluctance to discuss its resources is that it has been unsuccessful in recruiting secondees. Given the information in this chapter, the author believes this to be a real possibility, but cannot confirm if this is the case.

3 Government of Canada, "Canada's National Terrorism Threat Levels," last modified 22 January 2018, https://www.canada.ca/en/services/defence /nationalsecurity/terrorism-threat-level.html.

4 See, e.g., Andrew Crosby and Jeffrey Monaghan, "RCMP Files Say 'Violent Aboriginal Extremists' Are Undermining Pipeline Plans," *Vice News*, 4 May 2018, https://news.vice.com/en_ca/article/mbxyw8/rcmp-files -say-violent-aboriginal-extremists-are-undermining-pipeline-plans; Lex Gill and Cara Zwibel, "Why Does Canada Spy on Its Own Indigenous Communities?,", *openDemocracy*, 6 December 2017, https://www .opendemocracy.net/en/surveillance-indigenous-groups-canada/; Carys Mills, "Terrorism Monitor Kept Tabs on Occupy Protests," *Globe and Mail*, 10 April 2012, https://www.theglobeandmail.com/news/national /terrorism-monitor-closely-watched-occupy-protests/article4098990/.

5 Integrated Threat Assessment Centre (ITAC), "Integrated Threat Assessment Centre (ITAC)," backgrounder prepared for the ITAC presentation to the O'Connor Commission of Inquiry, 7 April 2005.

6 Canadian Security Intelligence Service (CSIS), "Backgrounder No. 13: The Integrated Threat Assessment Centre (ITAC)," April 2007. Accessed via the "Wayback Machine" Internet Archive: https://web.archive.org /web/20131120112013/https://www.csis.gc.ca/nwsrm/bckgrndrs /bckgrndr13-eng.asp.

7 Comments by Christian Rousseau, executive director, Integrated Terrorism Assessment Centre, at the Proceedings of the Standing Senate Committee on National Security and Defence, 11 April 2016. Available online: https:// www.sencanada.ca/en/Content/Sen/Committee/421/SECD/03ev-52467-e.

8 Department of the Parliamentary Library (Australia), "The New National
   Threat Assessment Centre," *Research Note* 23 (December 2003), http://
   parlinfo.aph.gov.au/parlInfo/download/library/prspub/0N2B6/upload
   _binary/0n2b66.pdf;fileType=application%2Fpdf#search=%22library
   /prspub/0N2B6%22.
9 New Zealand Government, "Threat Assessment Group Established," 21
   December 2004, https://www.beehive.govt.nz/release/threat-assessment
   -group-established.
10 Security Service MI5 (UK), "Joint Terrorism Analysis Centre," accessed 4
   August 2020, https://www.mi5.gov.uk/joint-terrorism-analysis-centre.
11 Office of the Director of National Intelligence, "History," accessed 4
   August 2020, https://www.dni.gov/index.php/nctc-who-we-are/history.
12 Office of the Auditor General of Canada (OAG), *Report of the Auditor
   General of Canada to the House of Commons, Chapter 3: National Security in
   Canada – the 2001 Anti-Terrorism Initiative* (2004), 16, para. 3.62. Available
   online: http://www.oag-bvg.gc.ca/internet/docs/20040303ce.pdf.
13 Here I define "bureaucratic politics" as the process of compromise and
   competition among civil servants seeking to advance individual and
   organizational preferences.
14 OAG, *Report of the Auditor General*, 16, para. 3.62. Information in this
   paragraph also comes from interviews with two persons formerly at PCO and
   DND, respectively, who were privy to discussions about ITAC at this time.
15 OAG, *Report of the Auditor General*, 15–16, paras. 3.61–3.64.
16 Government of Canada, *Securing an Open Society: Canada's National Security
   Policy* (2004), vii. Available online: http://publications.gc.ca/collections
   /Collection/CP22-77-2004E.pdf.
17 Government of Canada, *Securing*, 11.
18 Government of Canada, *Securing*, 11.
19 ITAC, presentation to the O'Connor Commission of Inquiry.
20 CSIS, "Backgrounder No. 13."
21 OAG, *2009 March Status Report of the Auditor General of Canada: Chapter
   1 – National Security: Intelligence and Information Sharing* (2009), para. 1.25.
   Available online: https://www.oag-bvg.gc.ca/internet/English/parl
   _oag_200903_01_e_32288.html.
22 CSIS, "Integrated Terrorism Assessment Centre," last modified 5 December
   2017, https://www.canada.ca/en/security-intelligence-service/integrated
   -terrorism-assessment-centre.html.
23 Mills, "Terrorism Monitor," A7.
24 ITAC, presentation to the O'Connor Commission of Inquiry.
25 Anonymous interview conducted as a part of an SSHRC-funded project
   on the nexus between intelligence and policymaking in Canada, Ottawa,
   Canada, December 2018.

26 Government of Canada, "Canada's National Terrorism Threat Levels."
27 Government of Canada, "Canada's National Terrorism Threat Levels."
28 Government of Canada, "Canada's National Terrorism Threat Levels."
29 Public Safety Canada, *Public Report on the Terrorist Threat to Canada* (2016), 9–10. Available online: https://www.publicsafety.gc.ca/cnt/ rsrcs/pblctns/2016-pblc-rpr-trrrst-thrt/2016-pblc-rpr-trrrst-thrt-en.pdf. See also Government of Canada, "Canada's National Terrorism Threat Levels."
30 Comments by Christian Rousseau, executive director, Integrated Terrorism Assessment Centre, at the Proceedings of the Standing Senate Committee on National Security and Defence.
31 For example, the National Security and Intelligence Committee of Parliamentarians (NSICOP) cites such an assessment in ITAC's report on Prime Minister Trudeau's visit to India in February 2018 called "Threat Assessment: The Right Honourable Justin Trudeau, Prime Minister of Canada, Will Travel to India, 2018 02 17–24," dated 9 February 2018. NSICOP, *Special Report into the Allegations Associated with Prime Minister Trudeau's Official Visit to India in February 2018* (2018), 9. Available online: https://www.nsicop-cpsnr.ca/reports/rp-2018-12-03/SpecialReport-en .pdf.
32 OAG, *2009 March Status Report*, para. 1.24.
33 Crosby and Monaghan, "RCMP Files."
34 ITAC, presentation to the O'Connor Commission of Inquiry.
35 ITAC, presentation to the O'Connor Commission of Inquiry.
36 OAG, *2009 March Status Report*, para. 1.25.
37 Mike Blanchfield, "Budget 2015: Mounties, CSIS, Border Agency Get Budget Increases," *Global News*, 21 April 2015, https://globalnews.ca /news/1952514/budget-2015-mounties-csis-border-agency-get-budget -increases/.
38 Mills, "Terrorism Monitor."
39 Mills, "Terrorism Monitor."
40 Tia Dafnos, Scott Thompson, and Martin French, "Surveillance and the Colonial Dream: Canada's Surveillance of Indigenous Self-Determination," in Randy K. Lippert, Kevin Walby, Ian Warren, and Darren Palmer, *National Security, Surveillance, and Terror: Canada and Australia in Comparative Perspective* (Cham, Switzerland: Palgrave Macmillan, 2016), 331–2.
41 Postmedia News, "Canada's Spy Agency Kept Close Watch on Rapidly Growing First Nations Protest Movement: Documents," *National Post*, 11 August 2013, https://nationalpost.com/news/canada/canadas -spy-agency-kept-close-watch-on-rapidly-growing-first-nations-protest -movement-documents.

42 Reg Whitaker, Gregory S. Kealey, and Andrew Parnaby, *Secret Service: Political Policing in Canada from the Fenians to Fortress America* (Toronto: University of Toronto Press), 2012.

43 David Pugliese, "Embarrassment to Government among G8, G20 Summit 'Threats'; Canadian Forces Planning Document Based in Part on Ottawa's Integrated Threat Assessment Centre," *Montreal Gazette*, 11 June 2012, A7.

44 The question as to whether or not individuals found ITAC's analysis to be useful was asked to approximately 15 individuals interviewed in 2018–19 who served or were serving in core intelligence and national security agencies and had access to ITAC products in their jobs. This was in relation to a SSHRC project co-investigated with Thomas Juneau on the nature of the intelligence–policy dynamic in Canada. A minority of these spoke somewhat positively as to this aspect of ITAC's mandate. Another noted that ITAC's analysis was often combined with that of other agencies at PCO in order to create products for high-level policymakers, so it was difficult for them to assess ITAC's performance as an individual agency.

45 On the US and UK experience, see Lawrence Freedman, "The Politics of Warning: Terrorism and Risk Communication," *Intelligence and National Security* 20, no. 3 (2005): 379–418; Jacob N. Shapiro and Dara Kay Cohen, "Color Blind: Lessons from the Failed Homeland Security Advisory System," *International Security* 32, no. 2 (2007): 121–54.

46 Shapiro and Cohen, "Color Blind," 130.

47 Shapiro and Cohen, "Color Blind," 128–9.

48 Freedman, "The Politics of Warning," 404.

49 Freedman, "The Politics of Warning," 408.

50 On strategic versus tactical intelligence, see Jack Davis, "Strategic Warning: If Surprise Is Inevitable, What Role for Analysis," *The Sherman Kent Centre for Intelligence Analysis, Occasional Papers* 2, no. 1 (2003).

6 The Financial Transactions and Reports Analysis Centre of Canada (FINTRAC)

JOHN PYRIK

The Financial Transactions and Reports Analysis Centre of Canada (FINTRAC) acts as a clearinghouse, receiving, analysing, and disclosing financial intelligence (FININT) on suspected money laundering (ML), terrorist financing (TF), and threats to the security of Canada. FINTRAC describes FININT as information on financial transactions and accounts linking individuals and businesses that enables police, law enforcement, and national security agencies to refine the scope of their investigations, to shift their sights to different targets, and to identify assets for seizure and forfeiture.[1]

FINTRAC (the "Centre") operates under the *Proceeds of Crime (Money Laundering) and Terrorist Financing Act* (PCMLTFA)[2] and its regulations. It was set up in 2000 so that Canada could meet the international obligations of anti-money-laundering (AML) standards.[3] After the terrorist attacks of 11 September 2001, its mandate was expanded by the *Anti-terrorism Act* (2001) to include combating terrorist financing.[4]

FINTRAC has offices in Ottawa, Montreal, Toronto, and Vancouver. It has a budget of about $55 million and 365 employees. Led by a director nominated by the prime minister and appointed by the governor in council, it is an independent agency that reports to Parliament through the minister of finance.

Approximately 31,000 businesses report to FINTRAC.[5] They include accountants; agents of the Crown; notaries (in British Columbia); casinos; dealers in precious metals and stones; financial entities; life insurance companies, brokers, and agents; money services businesses; realtors; and securities dealers.[6] FINTRAC depends on a sophisticated information technology infrastructure to receive, store, and secure approximately 25 million new financial transaction reports every year.[7]

Mandate

To respond to shortcomings and evolving expectations, the PCMLTFA has been amended 28 times since it was enacted.[8] The significant changes include adding more businesses to the list of those required to comply with the PCMLTFA;[9] expanding the number of organizations to which FINTRAC can make disclosures and the "designated information" that FINTRAC may disclose; allowing FINTRAC to impose administrative monetary penalties (AMPs); requiring money service businesses to register with FINTRAC;[10] allowing attempted (but not completed) transactions to be reported; imposing stronger obligations on reporting entities to know their client and conduct enhanced due diligence on politically exposed foreign persons (PEPs), such as foreign leaders who might be involved in corruption; and authorizing the Office of the Privacy Commissioner to conduct regular reviews.[11]

Despite these amendments, a Senate inquiry concluded in 2013 that Canada was "not really" making progress in combating money laundering and terrorist financing. Furthermore, the "incremental approach" of making changes to fill gaps to meet evolving international recommendations was "not the solution that Canada needs at this time." Instead, the Senate committee suggested it was time to examine "fundamental issues" and called for more cooperation and alignment of priorities among stakeholders.[12]

In 2015, the Financial Action Task Force (FATF), an intergovernmental body founded in 1989 on the initiative of the G7 to develop policies to combat money laundering, assessed Canada. It found that, since its previous 2007 evaluation, Canada had made significant progress and had a comprehensive set of laws and regulations as well as a range of competent authorities to fight ML and TF. However, it also found weaknesses and made 40 recommendations.[13]

Interagency Cooperation

The Royal Canadian Mounted Police (RCMP) is probably FINTRAC's most important partner agency, given that most of its disclosures involve money laundering and the majority go to the RCMP. In 2015, then-RCMP commissioner Bob Paulson said at a parliamentary committee hearing that "the relationship with FINTRAC and the quality of the information that we are receiving is very good."[14]

In addition to the RCMP, FINTRAC may disclose suspected cases of money laundering or terrorism financing to an appropriate police service; the Canada Revenue Agency (CRA); the Communications

Security Establishment (CSE); provincial securities regulators; the Canadian Security Intelligence Service (CSIS); the Canada Border Services Agency (CBSA); the Department of National Defence (DND); or foreign financial intelligence units with which it has a memorandum of understanding for the exchange of information.[15] In 2019, Competition Bureau Canada and Revenu Québec were added to this list.[16]

FINTRAC also produces strategic intelligence about trends and typologies for the Canadian security and intelligence community, federal policy- and decision-makers, reporting entities across the country, international partners, and other stakeholders. Some of these products are posted to its website. In 2008–9, FINTRAC produced three financial assessments on "countries of concern" known for their support for terrorist groups and/or for reportedly having active terrorist groups, and/or for being suspected of proliferating weapons of mass destruction.[17] In 2015, its focus was on the Islamic State of Iraq and the Levant's financing strategies, including the financing available to this terrorist entity through its territorial control.[18] In 2018, it published an operational alert on fentanyl.[19]

Interagency cooperation and interaction are limited, however, by section 40(a) of the PCMLTFA, which specifies that FINTRAC "acts at arm's length and is independent from law enforcement agencies and other entities." The fact that its key partner agencies (police and security services) fall under the portfolio of Public Safety Canada while FINTRAC falls under Finance Canada reinforces this separation.

The arm's-length relationship arose because Canada adopted the administrative model for its financial intelligence unit (FIU). This model involves a centralized, independent administrative authority that receives and processes information from the financial sector and transmits disclosures to judicial or law enforcement authorities for prosecution. In the judicial model and law enforcement model, the financial sector discloses directly to investigative agencies.[20] Essentially, FINTRAC acts as a "buffer" between the financial and law enforcement communities.

The arm's-length relationship helps protect the privacy of Canadians and grants FINTRAC a degree of operational independence, but it also frustrates those who would prefer direct access to FINTRAC's database. Instead, they must file a voluntary information report, then await FINTRAC's response. This delay doesn't exist in the US, where authorized users have direct access to the database maintained by the Financial Crimes Enforcement Network (FinCEN, the US equivalent to FINTRAC).[21] Another consequence of the arm's-length relationship is that it makes it difficult for FINTRAC to get feedback. In 2007, in testimony before the Air India Inquiry, FINTRAC officials admitted that it was unaware of how or even if the intelligence it had provided to CSIS and the RCMP had been used.[22]

To ensure that its disclosures are relevant, FINTRAC has been involved with several committees and groups, including the

- National Coordinating Committee on Organized Crime;[23]
- National Initiative to Combat Money Laundering;
- Canadian Association of Chiefs of Police;
- Canadian Integrated Response to Organized Crime Committee;
- Counter-Terrorism and National Security Committee;[24] and the
- National Inherent Risk Assessment Working Group.[25]

In 2009, FINTRAC announced six strategic priorities, the first being to "align our financial intelligence products more closely with our part-ners' needs."[26] Still, in 2013, a Senate committee commented that FIN-TRAC could suffer "a degree of detachment" and recommended that CRA, CSIS, and the RCMP provide quarterly feedback to FINTRAC.[27] The same problem was noted by a House committee in 2018.[28] How-ever, there remains, at present, no requirement on the part of those that receive disclosures from FINTRAC to report back to FINTRAC on any action taken.

Resources

FINTRAC's funding in 2017–18 was down $4 million from its peak of $59.2 million in 2011–12. Over the same period, it added 24 employees (see Table 6.1). Over the years, additional funding has been periodi-cally provided to cope with the demands of new legislation and, most recently, to update analytic tools.[29]

FINTRAC's 2017–18 departmental plan notes that the agency will "face growing operating pressures due to increasing expenses of imple-menting government-wide technology centric investments and, as a fully reimbursing client of Public Services and Procurement Canada (PSPC), bearing the rising cost of office accommodations, building maintenance and leasehold improvements."[30]

While FINTRAC appears to be adequately resourced, the same can-not be said for the recipients of its financial intelligence. In the wake of the 9/11 attacks, the RCMP largely abandoned its AML work to focus its efforts on terrorism, according to Peter German, former direc-tor general of financial crime for the RCMP.[31] According to the 2016 FATF *Mutual Evaluation Report*, Canadian law enforcement agencies

Table 6.1. FINTRAC budget and number of full-time employees

Budget Year	Actual Spending	Full-time Employees
2011–12	$59,200,000	341
2012–13	$53,993,571	359
2013–14	$51,704,183	343
2014–15	$51,404,430	337
2015–16	$54,952,391	339
2016–17	$55,406,525	353
2017–18	$55,200,000	365

Source: FINTRAC annual reports.

"generally suffer from insufficient resources and expertise to pursue complex ML cases." As a consequence, "law enforcement results are not commensurate with the ML risk and asset recovery is low."[32] In 2018, the attorney general for British Columbia, David Eby, told the House of Commons Standing Committee on Finance that he had no confidence that a report from FINTRAC with the words "HIGHLY SUSPICIOUS" in all caps and triple underlined would result in any enforcement or investigation action from the RCMP or Revenue Canada due to a lack of resources.[33] In 2019, a House committee recommended that "any necessary resources be made available to law enforcement and prosecutors to pursue money-laundering and terrorism financing activities."[34]

Current Challenges

The annual reports published by FINTRAC paint a picture of success, with increasing numbers of disclosures every year. These annual reports include glowing testimonials from recipients and success stories. FINTRAC does, however, face several challenges.

Two risks identified by FINTRAC are increased costs of operation and an aging IT infrastructure.[35] It says that it has been increasingly difficult to efficiently manage the high volume of data it receives.[36] If it was strained before, however, it may now be dealing with a tsunami of information after a change to section 462.31 of the *Criminal Code* in June 2019 that significantly broadened the offence of money laundering.[37] Other challenges include non-compliance with the PCMLTFA, evolving technologies, possible under-utilization of FININT by the Canadian security and intelligence community, impediments to information-sharing, non-reporting by lawyers, and potentially too much oversight by outside bodies.

A Toothless Agency with No AMPerage

FINTRAC's biggest challenge may be that it is not taken seriously by the major Canadian banks. While banks in the US have received major fines for non-compliance with anti-money-laundering regulations, banks in Canada have not. Over the last 18 years, American banks have been fined US$7 billion, while Canadian banks have been fined only $6 million.[38] FINTRAC has also not "named and shamed" all violators. It has issued 95 penalties, but publicly named only 40 reporting entities.[39] In 2016, FINTRAC announced that it had imposed a fine of $1.15 million on a "Canadian federally-regulated financial institution." The decision *not to name* this institution suggested an uneven playing field favouring the major banks.[40] In 2019, the PCMLTFA was amended to *require* FINTRAC to make public the name of the person or entity fined.[41]

Aggressive lobbying may contribute to explain why Canada differs so strongly from the US. In 2017, an investigation by CBC News found that the banking industry had lobbied departmental officials and MPs hundreds of times since the last federal election.[42]

The likely result of a less potent regulatory regime in Canada is under-reporting of suspicious activity and a relatively lax compliance culture. In 2013, the Standing Senate Committee on Banking, Trade and Commerce commented that it was "concerned about non-compliance with the *Act* by reporting entities." In 2017, FINTRAC also reportedly told the minister of finance that there were "significant" problems at six of the nine major banks.[43]

FINTRAC recognizes the need to ensure compliance with the PCMLTFA. To this end, it uses a range of compliance activities to ensure that businesses are fulfilling their obligations. These include observation letters, reporting entity validations, the monitoring of reports, compliance meetings, compliance assessment reports, examinations, follow-up examinations, administrative monetary penalties, and non-compliance disclosures to police.[44] Charges can be laid for non-compliance (see Table 6.2).

In 2017–18, FINTRAC engaged in 94 outreach and engagement activities; issued 374 policy interpretations; conducted 500 compliance examinations; and responded to 6,652 inquiries from businesses.[45] In 2018, FINTRAC provided seven non-compliance disclosures to police.[46] In contrast to other jurisdictions and previous years, however, it did not issue any AMPs.

Table 6.2. Charges laid for non-compliance with the PCMLTFA[47]

	Charges laid for non-compliance with the Act	Charges related to cross-border reporting violations	Guilty Pleas	Convictions
2005–2009	89	68	31	3
2010–2011	34	34	13	0

AMPs are FINTRAC's "big stick" in ensuring compliance with federal anti-money-laundering rules and regulations. Between 2008 and 2016, it issued 95 penalties.[48] However, in 2016 the AMP program was suspended following a decision of the Federal Court of Appeal that found a lack of objective criteria in determining the amount of a penalty.[49] FINTRAC revised and reintroduced the AMP program in early 2019.[50] This might prompt reporting entities in Canada to take steps to improve their compliance regimes, if the penalties are sufficiently large.

Lagging behind Fintech

In 2014, amendments to the PCMLTFA expanded the definition of money service businesses to include persons engaged in the business of "dealing in virtual currencies." It took until 2018 for FINTRAC to publish draft regulations that would capture well-known cryptocurrencies such as Bitcoin.[51]

Virtual currencies are one aspect of a panoply of new and innovative technologies that are dramatically changing financial services and products. Collectively referred to as "fintech," some of this innovation is visible to the public (e.g., virtual currencies and robo-advisors), but much is behind the scenes (e.g., blockchain and artificial intelligence) and relates to infrastructure and business practices. The challenge for regulators has been to keep up.

Government agencies are concerned about public "permissionless" systems such as Bitcoin because they facilitate pseudonymous and fully anonymous cryptocurrency transactions across international borders without third-party oversight or intervention.[52] If banks are removed as financial intermediaries, governments have no one to check whether the parties to the transaction are on a watch-list or prevent the funds from going to embargoed countries. In this context, in 2013, the Senate recommended that the federal government review annually, and update as required, the definition of "monetary instruments" in order to maintain FINTRAC's ability to detect emerging methods of money laundering and terrorist financing.[53]

FINTRAC has been working hard to understand these emerging technologies, track their progress, and assess their vulnerability to criminal exploitation, according to former FINTRAC director Gérald Cossette.[54] In 2018, FINTRAC led the development of a research and typologies report on virtual currencies for the Egmont Group, a global association of 155 international financial intelligence units.[55] The Bank of Canada is also "closely monitoring" fintech developments.[56] The RCMP and CSE are similarly exploring how fintech and blockchain technologies relate to their investigative and intelligence mandates and capabilities.[57]

The New Kid on the Block

Financial intelligence is the newest "collection discipline" of the intelligence community. While human intelligence (HUMINT), signals intelligence (SIGINT), and geo-spatial intelligence (GEOINT) have established their place, FININT is the newcomer. Given its relatively recent appearance on the stage, FININT is likely under-exploited by the Canadian security and intelligence community.

Illustrating this reality, in 2010, the Commission of Inquiry into the Investigation of the Bombing of Air India Flight 182 concluded that FINTRAC and the CRA were not adequately integrated into the intelligence cycle to effectively detect terrorist financing or to provide the best financial intelligence to CSIS and the RCMP.[58]

In 2014–15, to promote FININT, FINTRAC made more than 100 outreach visits and presentations to partner organizations only. As well, FINTRAC exchanged personnel with its regime partners to develop capacity, expertise, and a mutual understanding of legislation and operations.[59] The fact that requests to FINTRAC for information have quadrupled in ten years is a measure of the impact of these efforts.[60]

Legal Impediments to the Sharing of Information

In 2004, the Auditor General stated that the information FINTRAC could disclose to law enforcement and national security agencies and to foreign FIUs was "too limited." Since 2014, amendments to the PCMLTFA have expanded FINTRAC's ability to disclose financial intelligence to regime partners on threats to the security of Canada.[61] FINTRAC can now disclose the grounds on which a person or entity made a report. It can also report the indicators it found of a money laundering offence or a terrorist financing offence.

Oddly, the "designated information" that FINTRAC can disclose still does not include open source information (which could provide vital context), a theory of the crime, or the internal written justification for disclosure. As a result, recipients must redo the analysis and research already done by FINTRAC using the disclosure's "strictly factual information" or use a production order to obtain the full case file.

In 2015, the government tried to encourage and facilitate the sharing of information between federal institutions for purposes of national security with the *Security of Canada Information Sharing Act* (SCISA). That said, FINTRAC took the position that SCISA does not change when, or to whom, it discloses financial intelligence.[62]

Special Treatment for Lawyers

Criminals often seek the involvement of legal professionals in their money laundering schemes. A legal professional can act as a financial intermediary to complete certain transactions or provide specialized legal and notarial skills and services that could assist in laundering the proceeds of crime and in the financing of terrorism.

Despite this, lawyers in Canada are not *legally obligated* to report to FINTRAC, although they may do so voluntarily pursuant to their Model Code of Professional Conduct. Other common law jurisdictions, including the United Kingdom, require financial reporting by lawyers, making Canada an outlier. In the view of the FATF, the situation constitutes a "serious impediment to Canada's efforts to fight ML" and a "significant loophole."[63] The RCMP and the Department of Finance identify the exclusion of lawyers and Quebec notaries from the PCMLTFA as the most significant gap within the AML/CTF (combating terrorism financing) regime.[64]

Surprisingly, this was not an oversight. Lawyers were included in the initial legislation, but the Federation of Law Societies of Canada challenged the provision on constitutional grounds. On 20 March 2003, regulations came into force repealing the provisions that subjected the legal profession to the reporting requirements set out in Part 1 of the PCMLTFA.

The matter of reporting by lawyers remains under active discussion. In February 2018, the Department of Finance published a consultation paper that recommended subjecting lawyers, within constitutional boundaries, to the AML/CTF framework.[65] In 2019, a House report similarly recommended bringing the legal profession into the AML/ ATF regime in a "constitutionally compliant way."[66]

Too Much Review?

The PCMLTFA requires statutory reviews of FINTRAC every five years. It is also subject to review and examination by the Office of the Privacy Commissioner, the Office of the Auditor General, and the parliamentary appropriations process. Externally, its operations have been examined by the FATF, the International Monetary Fund, and the UN Counter-Terrorism Committee. Two more review bodies were recently added to this list: the National Security and Intelligence Review Agency (NSIRA) and the National Security and Intelligence Committee of Parliamentarians (NSICOP). This increased oversight will further tax FINTRAC's resources.

"Effective oversight of public bodies should be encouraged," says Peter German, "provided that it does not foster a culture of timidity and reticence to undertake difficult work, such as the exaggerated attention paid to privacy in the early years at FINTRAC."[67]

Recent Controversies

FINTRAC has seen controversies since its inception. Privacy advocates, in particular, argue that collecting financial intelligence without a warrant from a judge violates *Charter* protections against unreasonable search and seizure.

To assuage these critics, many sections of the PCMLTFA relate to the protection of privacy.[68] If the police or CSIS wish to obtain FINTRAC's "full case analysis," for example, they must obtain a production order from a court. Also, unless it is used in a disclosure, FINTRAC can retain a report in its database for only fifteen years.[69] Between 2003 and 2016, as a result, FINTRAC deleted nearly 35 million reports,[70] while in 2016–17 alone, it deleted nearly 18 million reports.[71]

In 2006, a proposal from the Office of the Privacy Commissioner (OPC) to conduct biannual audits of FINTRAC received Royal Assent as part of Bill C-25. The first review was initiated in 2007–8 and published in 2009. It found that FINTRAC was receiving and retaining personal information beyond its remit because reporting entities were over-reporting – sending in reports under the $10,000 threshold and reports that, in the opinion of the OPC, did not clearly demonstrate reasonable grounds for suspicion.[72] Three years later, during its 2013 audit, the OPC discovered that, despite commitments made by FINTRAC in the wake of the 2009 audit, it continued to accept and retain personal information that the OPC deemed not relevant to FINTRAC's mandate.[73] In 2017, the OPC completed its third review. It found that a new "front-end screening process" had led to improvements, but a "limited number" of reports still did not meet reporting thresholds.[74]

Over-disclosure by FINTRAC may be the issue of greater concern. Since FINTRAC is not a law enforcement agency and has no investigative powers, it must determine on the basis of information provided to it, access to government databases, and open source information whether there are reasonable grounds to suspect money laundering or terrorist financing before it can disclose any transactions. FINTRAC is not authorized to request additional information from any reporting entity.[75] The limits on the scope and depth of the analysis that FINTRAC can conduct may, on occasion, lead to the over-disclosure of information on Canadians because it could not investigate sufficiently to uncover an innocent explanation for an odd transaction.

Conclusion

FINTRAC has come a long way during its relatively short existence. It contributed, for example, to 262 "project-level" investigations in 2018.[76] Information provided by FINTRAC has identified where targets held bank accounts; provided insight into the flow of funds; identified shell companies; confirmed the direction of an investigation; corroborated information previously known; re-evaluated priorities and targets of interest; pieced together financial information located throughout the world; expanded the scope of investigations beyond the initial parties; and identified potential cooperating witnesses and new targets.[77] This information has been "actionable," according to 92 per cent of surveyed recipients.[78]

However, it is unclear *how vital* FINTRAC's contributions have been to investigations. While FINTRAC can provide statistics on disclosures and attestations from clients, the impact of what it does is still not well measured.

In 2010, the Air India Investigation noted that although FINTRAC is the centrepiece of Canada's anti-terrorism-financing program and receives a large portion of the resources available for this purpose, "there has been little evidence of value in FINTRAC's contribution to TF investigations, prosecutions or convictions."[79] In 2013, similarly, a Senate inquiry called the lack of information on results and costs a "significant deficiency."[80] Accordingly, it recommended independent performance reviews every five years and that the government

Figure 6.1. Convictions for terrorist financing; ten jurisdictions with the greatest number of convictions.

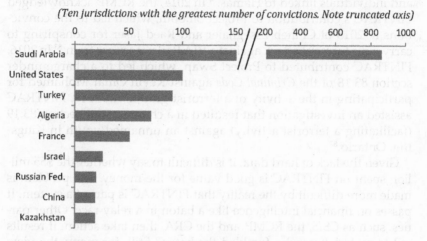

(Ten jurisdictions with the greatest number of convictions. Note truncated axis)

Source: FATF review of review of 194 jurisdictions, 2010–15.

establish a "supervisory body" to report annually to Parliament on the number of investigations, prosecutions, and convictions related to money laundering and terrorist financing in Canada; the amount seized in these cases; the extent to which case disclosures by FIN-TRAC were used in these cases; and the total expenditures by each federal department and agency in combating money laundering and terrorist financing.[81]

One metric that suggests a problem is the high ratio of TF disclosures to charges laid. Between 2003 and 2017, FINTRAC made 1,766 disclosures on terrorist financing and threats to the security of Canada. Over the same period, only seven charges for TF were laid under section 83.03 of the *Criminal Code of Canada*.[82] A ratio of 250:1 suggests that either FINTRAC has set the bar for disclosure too low or that Canada has a chronic inability to mount successful prosecutions for TF.

It should be noted that while seven TF cases over 15 years seems low, it is not unusual in the international context (see Figure 6.1). According to the FATF, relatively few jurisdictions have obtained convictions for terrorist financing.[83]

It should also be noted that FINTRAC has contributed to terrorism investigations that did not involve a charge of terrorism financing. In 2011, for example, FINTRAC helped remove the International Relief

Fund for the Afflicted and Needy Canada (IRFAN) from the CRA list
of registered charities after it funnelled millions of dollars to groups
and individuals linked to Hamas.[84] In 2014, the RCMP acknowledged
FINTRAC's contribution to Project Smooth, which led to the convictions in 2015 of Chiheb Esseghaier and Raed Jaser for conspiring to
carry out a terrorist attack against a VIA Rail passenger train.[85] In 2016,
FINTRAC contributed to Project Swap, which led to a charge under
section 83.18 of the *Criminal Code* against Kevin Omar Mohamed for
participating in the activity of a terrorist group.[86] In 2019, FINTRAC
assisted an investigation that resulted in a charge under section 83.19
(facilitating a terrorist activity) against an unnamed youth in Kingston, Ontario.[87]

Given the lack of hard data, it is difficult to say whether the $55 mil-
lion spent on FINTRAC is good value for the money. The problem is
made more difficult by the reality that FINTRAC is part of a system. It
passes on financial intelligence like a baton in a relay race. Other parties, such as CSIS, the RCMP, and the CRA, then take action. If results
fail to materialize, who fumbled the baton? Still, for many, the view
of Garry Clement, former national director for the Royal Canadian
Mounted Police's Proceeds of Crime Program, prevails: "If FINTRAC
prevents one terrorist attack, it is worth every penny."[88]

NOTES

1 Financial Transactions and Reports Analysis Centre of Canada (FINTRAC),
   Annual Report 2017–18 (2018), 3. Available online: https://www.fintrac
   -canafe.gc.ca/publications/ar/2018/ar2018-eng.pdf.
2 S.C. 2000, c 17.
3 FINTRAC defines money laundering as the process used to disguise the
   source of money or assets derived from criminal activity. It compromises
   the integrity of legitimate financial systems and institutions and gives
   organized crime the funds it needs to conduct further criminal activities.
   FINTRAC, *Annual Report 2017–18*, 2.
4 FINTRAC defines terrorist financing as the act of providing funds for
   terrorist activity. This may involve donations from individuals, businesses,
   and/or charitable organizations, or it may involve funds from criminal
   sources such as the drug trade, the smuggling of weapons and other goods,
   fraud, kidnapping, and extortion. FINTRAC, *Annual Report 2017–18*, 10.
5 FINTRAC, *2016 Annual Report* (2016), 1.
6 FINTRAC, *Annual Report 2017–18*, 7.
7 FINTRAC, *Quarterly Financial Report for the Quarter Ended June 30, 2019*

(2019), s. 3(A). Available online: https://www.fintrac-canafe.gc.ca/publications/finance/fr-rf/20190830-eng.

8   Justice Laws Website, *Proceeds of Crime (Money Laundering) and Terrorist Financing Act*, previous versions, last modified 26 June 2020, https://laws-lois.justice.gc.ca/eng/acts/p-24.501/PITIndex.html.

9   The types of businesses added to the list of reporting entities were public notaries in BC, dealers in precious stones and metals, and real estate developers.

10 A money service business (MSB) transfers funds or exchanges foreign currency. As of March 2016, 833 MSBs were registered with FINTRAC (*2016 Annual Report*).

11 *An Act to Amend the Proceeds of Crime (Money Laundering) and Terrorist Financing Act and the Income Tax Act and to make a consequential amendment to another Act*, SC 2006, c 12.

12 Standing Senate Committee on Banking, Trade and Commerce, *Follow the Money: Is Canada Making Progress in Combatting Money Laundering and Terrorist Financing? Not Really* (2013), 6. Available online: https://sencanada.ca/content/sen/Committee/411/BANC/rep/rep10mar13-e.pdf.

13 Financial Action Task Force (FATF), *Anti-money Laundering and Counter-terrorist Financing Measures – Canada: Mutual Evaluation Report* (2016), 115–200. Available online: https://www.fatf-gafi.org/media/fatf/documents/reports/mer4/MER-Canada-2016.pdf.

14 FINTRAC, *2015 Annual Report* (2015), 1.

15 FINTRAC, *Annual Report 2017–18*, 11, 13.

16 FINTRAC, "@RevenuQuebec and the @CompBureau can now receive financial intelligence disclosures from #FINTRAC following changes to the #PCMLTFA in the Act to implement the federal budget," Twitter, 25 June 2019, 12:20 p.m., https://twitter.com/FINTRAC_Canada/status/1143554470002987009.

17 FINTRAC, *2009 Annual Report* (2009), 15.

18 FINTRAC, *2015 Annual Report*, 1.

19 FINTRAC, *Annual Report 2018–19* (2019), 7. Available online: https://www.fintrac-canafe.gc.ca/publications/ar/2019/ar2019-eng.pdf.

20 Egmont Group, "About," 2018, https://egmontgroup.org/en/content/about.

21 Standing Senate Committee on Banking, Trade and Commerce, *Follow the Money*, A-33.

22 "Agency Unclear How Terror Information Used: Inquiry," *National Post*, 2 October 2007; CPAC, "The Air India Inquiry – October 2, 2007 (Part 1 of 3)," *Inquiries on CPAC*, video, 1:16:50, http://www.cpac.ca/en/programs/inquiries-on-cpac/episodes/90001068.

23 A federal group composed of law enforcement agencies and federal, provincial, and territorial policymakers. The committee determines national policy priorities and assesses emerging concerns in the area of organized crime.

24 FINTRAC, *2015 Annual Report*, 14.

25 FINTRAC, *Annual Report 2018–19*, 10.

26 FINTRAC, *2009 Annual Report*, 24.

27 Standing Senate Committee on Banking, Trade and Commerce, *Follow the Money*, recommendation 6, vii; "The Desired Structure," 8.

28 Standing Committee on Finance, *Confronting Money Laundering and Terrorist Financing: Moving Canada Forward* (2018), 56. Available online: https://www.ourcommons.ca/Content/Committee/421/FINA/Reports/RP10170742/finarp24/finarp24-e.pdf.

29 FINTRAC, *Annual Report 2007* (2007), 30. Available online: https://www.publicsafety.gc.ca/lbrr/archives/cn000029669116-2007-eng.pdf. Government of Canada, *The Road to Balance: Creating Jobs and Opportunities* (2014). Available online: https://www.budget.gc.ca/2014/docs/plan/pdf/budget2014-eng.pdf.

30 FINTRAC, *2017–18 Departmental Plan* (2017). Available online: https://www.fintrac-canafe.gc.ca/publications/dp/2017-2018/2017-2018-dp-eng.pdf.

31 Standing Committee on Finance, *Confronting Money Laundering*, 46.

32 FATF, *Anti-money Laundering and Counter-terrorist Financing Measures – Canada*, 6.

33 Testimony of BC attorney general David Eby, House of Commons Standing Committee on Finance, in relation to the statutory review of the *Proceeds of Crime and Terrorist Financing Act*, 30 March 2018, video, 1:03:51, https://www.facebook.com/dave.eby/videos/1753587104701630/.

34 Standing Committee on Finance, *Confronting Money Laundering*, 6.

35 FINTRAC, *Quarterly Financial Report for the Quarter Ended June 30, 2019*, s. 3(A).

36 FINTRAC, *Quarterly Financial Report for the Quarter Ended December 31, 2018* (2019), s. 3(A). Available online: https://www.fintrac-canafe.gc.ca/publications/finance/fr-rf/20190301-eng.

37 Graydon McGeachy, "AML and Recklessness," *Graydon McGeachy Law LLP* (blog), 9 October 2019, https://gmlegal.ca/blog/aml-and-recklessness/5.

38 Canada data from FINTRAC annual reports (2015 and 2016). From 2008 to 2015, FINTRAC issued seventy-three notices of violation totalling $5,117,710. In 2016, they issued another twenty-two notices of violation and fines totalling $1,150,000. US data from Good Jobs First, "Violation Tracker Summary for Anti-money-laundering Deficiencies," 2020, https://violationtracker.goodjobsfirst.org/offense/anti-money-laundering%20

deficiencies.

39 FINTRAC, *2016 Annual Report*, 8.

40 Dave Seglins, "Manulife Revealed as Bank Fined $1.15M for Violating Anti-money Laundering Reporting Rules," *CBC*, 27 February 2017, https://www.cbc.ca/news/business/fintrac-fine-name-secret-1.3999156.

41 FINTRAC, "Administrative Monetary Penalties Policy," last modified 29 August 2019, https://www.fintrac-canafe.gc.ca/pen/2-eng.

42 Elizabeth Thompson, "Banking Industry Has Lobbied Officials, MPs Hundreds of Times," *CBC*, 12 June 2017, https://www.cbc.ca/news/politics/banks-finance-lobbying-government-1.4155703.

43 Dean Beeby, "Ottawa's Secret Report on Money-Laundering Points Finger at Canada's Banks," *CBC*, 5 April 2018, https://www.cbc.ca/news/politics/money-laundering-banks-terror-1.4603064.

44 FINTRAC, *2016 Annual Report*, 8.

45 FINTRAC, *Annual Report 2017–18*, 11-13

46 FINTRAC, Twitter, 4 October 2019, 10:07 a.m., https://twitter.com/FINTRAC_Canada/status/1180122319110447104

47 Standing Senate Committee on Banking, Trade and Commerce, *Follow the Money*, A-10.

48 FINTRAC, *Annual Report 2017–18*, 9

49 *Canada v. Kabul Farms Inc.*, 2016 FCA 143, [2016] F.C.J. No. 480 (Q.L.).

50 FINTRAC, "News Release: FINTRAC Announces Better Support for Canadian Businesses," last modified 16 August 2019, https://www.fintrac-canafe.gc.ca/new-neuf/nr/2019-02-07-eng.

51 Government of Canada, "Canada Gazette, Part I, Volume 152, Number 23: Regulations Amending Certain Regulations Made Under the Proceeds of Crime (Money Laundering) and Terrorist Financing Act, 2018," 9 June 2018, http://www.gazette.gc.ca/rp-pr/p1/2018/2018-06-09/html/reg1-eng.html.

52 Evangeline Ducas and Alex Wilner, "The Security and Financial Implications of Blockchain Technologies: Regulating Emerging Technologies in Canada," *International Journal* 72, no. 4 (2017): 538–62; Alex Wilner, interview with Canadian intelligence personnel from Communications Security Establishment, 27 June 2016.

53 Standing Senate Committee on Banking, Trade and Commerce, *Follow the Money*, 20.

54 Alexandra Posadzki, "Watchdog Assessing Fintech Startups' Vulnerability to Financial Crime," *Globe and Mail*, 18 August 2016, https://www.theglobeandmail.com/report-on-business/watchdog-assessing-fintech-startups-vulnerability-to-financial-crime/article31459307/.

55 FINTRAC, *Annual Report 2018–19*, 8.

56 Bank of Canada, "Digital Currencies and Fintech: Research," accessed 21

August 2020, https://www.bankofcanada.ca/research/digital-currencies
-and-fintech/fintech-research/.

57 Ducas and Wilner, "The Security and Financial Implications of Blockchain Technologies."

58 Commission of Inquiry into the Investigation of the Bombing of Air India Flight 182, *Air India Flight 182: A Canadian Tragedy*, vol. 5, *Terrorist Financing* (2010), 238. Available online: http://publications.gc.ca/collections/collection_2010/bcp-pco/CP32-89-2-2010-5-eng.pdf.

59 FINTRAC, *Annual Report 2015*, 14.

60 According to FINTRAC's annual reports, voluntary information requests from domestic agencies increased from 547 in 2008 to 2,397 in 2018.

61 FINTRAC, *2017–18 Departmental Plan*, 11.

62 Mr. Gérald Cossette (director, Financial Transactions and Reports Analysis Centre of Canada) at the Access to Information, Privacy and Ethics Committee on 7 February 2017.

63 FATF, *Anti-money Laundering and Counter-terrorist Financing Measures – Canada*, 3.

64 Standing Committee on Finance, *Confronting Money Laundering*, 5.

65 Department of Finance Canada, *Reviewing Canada's Anti-money Laundering and Anti-terrorist Financing Regime* (2018). Available online: https://www.canada.ca/content/dam/fin/migration/activty/consult/amlatfr-rpcfa-eng.pdf.

66 Standing Committee on Finance, *Confronting Money Laundering*, 2.

67 Peter German, email to the author, 3 June 2018.

68 FINTRAC, *2003 Annual Report* (2003), 33.

69 FINTRAC, *Annual Report 2017–18*, 6.

70 FINTRAC, *2016 Annual Report*, 3.

71 FINTRAC, *Annual Report 2017–18*, 6.

72 Office of the Privacy Commissioner of Canada (OPC), *Financial Transactions and Reports Analysis Centre of Canada: Audit Report of the Privacy Commissioner of Canada* (2009), paras. 40–56. Available online: https://www.priv.gc.ca/media/1136/ar-vr_fintrac_200910_e.pdf.

73 OPC, *Financial Transactions and Reports Analysis Centre of Canada: Audit Report of the Privacy Commissioner of Canada* (2013). Available online: https://www.priv.gc.ca/media/1138/ar-vr_fintrac_2013_e.pdf.

74 FINTRAC, *Annual Report 2018–19*, ix, "Highlights."

75 This limitation led the FATF to rate Canada as only "partially compliant" with recommendation 26. FATF, *Third Mutual Evaluation Report on Anti-money Laundering and Combating the Financing of Terrorism – Canada* (2008), 182. Available online: https://www.fatf-gafi.org/media/fatf/documents/reports/mer/MER%20Canada%20full.pdf.

76 FINTRAC, *Annual Report 2018–19*, ii.

77 FINTRAC, *2015 Annual Report*, 17.
78 FINTRAC, *Annual Report 2018–19*, 4.
79 Commission of Inquiry into the Investigation of the Bombing of Air India Flight 182, *Air India Flight 182: A Canadian Tragedy*, vol. 5, *Terrorist Financing*, 244.
80 Standing Senate Committee on Banking, Trade and Commerce, *Follow the Money*, 11.
81 Standing Senate Committee on Banking, Trade and Commerce, *Follow the Money*, 11.
82 From 2005–11, six charges were laid. Standing Senate Committee on Banking, Trade and Commerce, *Follow the Money*, A-32. In 2015, Awso Peshdary was charged.
83 In 2015, only 33 jurisdictions – 17 per cent of those surveyed – reported any convictions for terrorist financing offences. FATF, *Terrorist Financing: FATF Report to G20 Leaders: Actions Being Taken by the FATF* (2015), 2. Available online: http://www.fatf-gafi.org/media/fatf/documents/reports/Terrorist-financing-actions-taken-by-FATF.pdf.
84 Stewart Bell, "Canada Is Seeing a Spike in Behind-the-Scenes Funding for Terrorists, Finance Minister's Office Says," *National Post*, 8 June 2015, https://nationalpost.com/news/canada/terror-financing-cases-doubled-in-a-year-agency-says.
85 FINTRAC, *2015 Annual Report*, 1; Canadian Press, "Suspects Charged in Via Train Terror Plot Have al-Qaida Ties: RCMP," *Maclean's*, 22 April 2013, https://www.macleans.ca/news/canada/arrests-made-in-ontario-quebec-in-alleged-terror-plot-cbc-news/.
86 Royal Canadian Mounted Police (RCMP), "Integrated National Security Enforcement Team Lays Terrorism Charge against Kevin Omar Mohamed," press release, 29 March 2016.
87 RCMP, "Integrated National Security Enforcement Team Lays Terrorism Charge in Ontario," press release, 25 January 2019.
88 Interview with the author, 18 April 2018.

PART THREE

Operations and Enforcement
and Community Engagement

7 The Royal Canadian Mounted Police (RCMP)

KENT ROACH

The Royal Canadian Mounted Police (RCMP) is a key national security actor. It has lead responsibilities in criminal investigations related to national security and is involved in transnational policing. It works with a number of other agencies in the Canadian intelligence community (IC), most notably the Canadian Security Intelligence Service (CSIS).

CSIS took over the RCMP's security intelligence functions when it was created in 1984. This change followed recommendations by commissions of inquiry that had found that the RCMP had engaged in illegal actions in an attempt to disrupt and prevent security threats in the wake of the 1970 October Crisis.

The RCMP's post-9/11 conduct (and in particular its information-sharing practices) was criticized by the O'Connor Commission of Inquiry (otherwise known as the Arar Commission), which recommended major changes to the oversight and review of the RCMP's national security activities. Some, but not all, of the recommendations requiring legislation were implemented in 2013.[1] A revamped national security review system was created in 2019, after enactment of the *National Security Act, 2017*.[2]

The RCMP has to comply with a broad range of ministerial directives, laws, and court decisions, including those requiring broad disclosure of relevant information to the accused, speedy trials, and respect for the rights of individuals, as it discharges its national security mandate. The RCMP continues to face challenges working with other partners in the Canadian IC, including CSIS. It also confronts an urgent need to respond to an evolving threat environment, including concerns about violent extremism, cybersecurity, and foreign influence.

Mandate

Historical

Up until the creation of CSIS in 1984, the RCMP collected intelligence on a range of perceived threats to national security, including Indigenous and labour activists, enemy aliens, and Communists.[3] Indeed, the RCMP was created out of the North-West Mounted Police in 1919 in light of concerns about subversion after the end of the First World War. After the Gouzenko spy affair at the end of the Second World War, the RCMP took on security screening functions and increased its intelligence functions, forming a separate branch.[4]

In the wake of the October Crisis of 1970 and security concerns about the 1976 Montreal Olympics, the RCMP's Security Service engaged in extensive intelligence collection, amassing 1.3 million files on over 800,000 Canadians. It also perpetrated "dirty tricks" as part of its threat disruption activities, including what would become the infamous acts of burning down a barn to prevent a meeting between a suspected terrorist and a member of the Black Panther party and the theft of the separatist Parti Québécois's membership list. In 1981, the McDonald Commission reported on these illegalities, and recommended that the security intelligence function be taken away from the RCMP and transferred to a civilian intelligence agency. It stressed the need to separate the collection of intelligence from the RCMP's law enforcement powers.[5]

Contemporary

The McDonald Commission's recommendations were largely implemented in the 1984 *CSIS Act*.[6] It created CSIS and made it subject to special forms of ministerial and executive watchdog oversight and review that did not apply to the RCMP. The *Security Offences Act*[7] was enacted as parallel legislation. Section 6(1) of the latter act provides that RCMP peace officers (i.e., police officers with prescribed powers, duties, and protections under the *Criminal Code*) "have the primary responsibility to perform the duties assigned to peace officers" with regard to any "alleged offence" that arises out of conduct that also constitutes a threat to the security of Canada as defined under section 2 of the *CSIS Act*, or where the victim of the offence is an internationally protected person, such as a representative of a foreign state or international organization, and their family. These offences include espionage, sabotage, offences under the *Security of Information Act*[8] (formerly the *Official Secrets Act*), and now terrorism offences.

Although it is a little-known act, the *Security Offences Act* gives the RCMP a wide mandate with respect to a broad range of criminal offences that affect national security. The RCMP's duties are not limited to law enforcement, but also include crime prevention and even disruption of national security offences. The RCMP also has a memorandum of understanding with Health Canada to lead investigations into biological, chemical, and nuclear incidents.

Structure

The *RCMP Act* provides that the RCMP is headed by a commissioner who has control and management of the force, but who also holds office "during pleasure" and "under the direction"[9] of the minister of public safety and emergency preparedness. Although the independence of law enforcement decisions from political direction has been recognized as both a common law and constitutional principle,[10] the *RCMP Act* does not attempt to codify police investigative independence from executive direction or to ensure transparency with respect to legitimate political direction to the police on matters of policy.

The national security mandate of the RCMP falls under the deputy commissioner, federal policing, and the assistant commissioner, federal policing, national security and protective policing. The assistant commissioner must approve investigations whenever "academia, politics, religion, media or trade unions" are "the primary focus of the investigation"[11] and in doing so must weigh the objects of the investigation against harm to the sensitive sector of *Charter* rights.

In performing its national security mandate, the RCMP investigates "activities that undermine the security of Canada" by "collecting, analysing, and storing evidence, information, and intelligence related to" national security; "sharing evidence, information, and intelligence with other agencies, both domestic and foreign; investigating offences related to" national security; "pursuing criminal charges and/or disrupting criminal activity; and protecting critical infrastructure."[12] The RCMP also has a national critical infrastructure team that works with other parts of the Government of Canada and the private sector with respect to national-security-related cyber and physical threats.[13]

National security criminal investigations include investigations into crimes involving threats to the security of Canada (i.e., terrorism, espionage or sabotage, foreign-influenced activity, and subversion), an offence against internationally protected persons (such as diplomats), and offences under the *Security of Information Act*.[14] RCMP peace officers are to perform the duties of peace officers "in relation to the preservation of the peace, the prevention of crime and of offences," including "the apprehension of criminals and offenders and others who may be lawfully taken into custody" and the execution of warrants such as wiretap warrants.[15]

National security criminal investigations are conducted by National Security Enforcement Sections (NSESs) within divisions or by Integrated National Security Enforcement Teams (INSETs) located in Ottawa, Montreal, Toronto, Edmonton/Calgary,[16] and Vancouver. INSETs include representatives of the Canada Border Services Agency (CBSA), CSIS, and various provincial and municipal police services.[17] The O'Connor Commission reported in 2006 that the Toronto INSET had 53 RCMP regular members, two RCMP civilians, and 22 others, including those on secondment from the Ontario Provincial Police (OPP) and Toronto, York, Peel, and Durham police services.[18] INSETs are designed to facilitate intelligence-sharing, but also present accountability challenges associated with multijurisdictional fusion centres. Concerns about how CSIS and the RCMP work together, in particular, will be examined below.

All national security investigations are subject to oversight from headquarters, including use of special secure databases. Centralized oversight is meant to ensure that national security investigations follow all relevant laws, directives, and policies, including those with respect to international partnerships and information-sharing and to compliance with the *Canadian Charter of Rights and Freedoms* and the *Privacy Act*.[19] It also enables central prioritization of particular national security investigations and, when necessary, briefing of the minister of public safety and the prime minister.[20]

The RCMP also participates in the no-fly listing process under the *Secure Air Travel Act*.[21] It hosts the National Security Joint Operations Centre (NSJOC), which convenes representatives from the RCMP, the Canada Border Services Agency, CSIS, and Immigration, Refugees and Citizenship Canada to help coordinate agency responses to "high-risk" travellers, especially foreign terrorist fighters.[22]

Resources

At one level, the RCMP is very well resourced. Its overall planned spending for 2017–18 was $3.6 billion.[23] But this number does not tell us much in the national security context; it is the full budget, which includes all of the RCMP's activities, including its contract policing role with the provinces. "Contract policing" exists in eight provinces (where the RCMP is contracted by the province to serve as a provincial police force) and scores of municipalities (where the municipality contracts the RCMP to provide municipal policing). Moreover, as will be seen below, there are scheduled budget cuts in international policing and training that may adversely affect and constrain national security policing.

Criminal Investigations

When urgent cases arise, budgetary constraints do not seem to limit the RCMP's ability to conduct criminal investigations related to national security. For example, in the aftermath of the October 2014 attacks in Saint-Jean-sur-Richelieu and Ottawa, as well as in light of a significant increase in the numbers of foreign fighters, $57 million was spent on RCMP counterterrorism operations in 2014–15, almost six times the originally budgeted figure. About 600 officers were shifted to counter-terrorism from other federal policing responsibilities, most notably serious and organized criminal investigations.[24]

The 2019–20 departmental plan shows main estimates of $881 million for federal policing in 2019–20 and 5,215 full-time equivalents (FTEs). These numbers are expected to drop to $830 million and 5,156 FTEs by 2021–22.[25] Unfortunately, information on how much of the federal policing budget goes to national security policing is not readily available.

Transnational Policing

The 2018–19 RCMP departmental plan provided that 178 FTEs were assigned to international policing with a 2019–20 budget of $51 million, with the projected 2020–21 budget remaining largely static.[26] In 2014, there were 42 RCMP liaison officers in foreign countries at a cost of about $500,000 each per year. About 6 per cent of the requests they handled related to terrorism.[27]

As threats to national security and crime in general become more transnational in nature, one would expect that the resources available for international policing would increase. Unfortunately, this need does not appear to have been anticipated in the RCMP's 2018–19 departmental plan. At the same time, the FTEs and dedicated budgets for RCMP officers stationed outside of Canada do not capture the resources spent on other transnational investigations where RCMP officers in Canada would have worked closely with foreign partners when conducting national security investigations.

Training and Education

Another area of possible underfunding is specialized and continuing national security training. About $459 million was budgeted in 2019–20 for a range of law enforcement services, including not only education and training, but also scientific, technical, intelligence, cybercrime, and investigative services. This figure is expected to dip to $453 million in 2021–22.[28]

National security training is reportedly provided by the RCMP to ensure that members involved in national security investigations "have a full working knowledge of the [governing] policy, and to inform them of the unique operating requirements of the NS [national security] environment."[29] It is not clear, however, where the training is provided. The Canadian Police College does not list national security as one of its seven programs or focus areas.[30]

The RCMP appears to take the position that all members receive adequate national security training so that they can be transferred from other policing duties to national security duties, as indeed occurred with the transfer of 600 people to national security investigations in 2014–15.[31] This transferring raises concerns because of past experiences where inadequately trained officers shifted to national security policing after 9/11. This contributed to inappropriate sharing of information, leading to the detention of Maher Arar by American authorities who eventually sent him to Syria to be tortured, and other inappropriate RCMP dealings with countries, such as Egypt and Syria, with poor human rights records (discussed further below).[32]

Current Challenges

Evolving Threat Levels

Like all national security agencies, the RCMP faces a fluid and evolving threat level. The demands placed on it are even more difficult to predict because of the uncertainty of whether security threats will grow to the point that they come within the RCMP's specific law enforcement mandate. For example, many returnees from conflict zones may not engage in conduct that merits criminal investigation, but an unknown number may. Extremists may quickly move toward violent extremism and the possible commission of terrorism offences. Similarly, it may be difficult to predict when foreign-influenced activity within the purview of CSIS or the Communications Security Establishment (CSE) may cross the line into conduct that should be investigated criminally. The scheduling of international events in Canada further increases demands for protective policing and investigation of possible threats to such events. Other factors identified in the RCMP's Governance Framework for National Security Investigations are growth in transnational investigations and the use of evolving technology in national-security-related crimes.[33]

The national security threat level faced by the RCMP is, in sum, challenging. This raises questions about the adequacy of the training and specialization of the RCMP in relation to many matters, including technology, the context of extraterritorial investigations, and patterns of violent extremism.

A 2015 OPP report found that many previous recommendations to improve security on Parliament Hill had not been implemented before the 22 October 2014 terrorist attack.[34] Unfortunately, both the recommendations made by the OPP in March 2015 and the RCMP's own *After Action Review*[35] in April 2015 are heavily redacted. The effectiveness of the response to this incident might be an appropriate matter for the new committee of parliamentarians with security clearances (the National Security and Intelligence Committee of Parliamentarians) to examine.

The RCMP faces many national security threats, but it also has many legislative tools to respond to evolving threats. These include the mandate to investigate and enforce 15 different terrorism offences (including those relating to terrorist financing, foreign terrorist travel, and advocacy of terrorism), as well as the power to seek peace bonds in response to reasonable fears that a person may commit a terrorist offence, which also includes other offences committed at the direction of or in association with terrorist groups. As peace officers, the RCMP also has a limited power in section 83.3 of the *Criminal Code* of preventive detention, a controversial addition to the *Anti-terrorism Act* (2001)[36] never used to date. There are also a variety of offences relating to foreign influence and communications with foreign powers, especially under the *Security of Information Act*.

The Need for Better Training and Increased Specialization

The RCMP is a traditional police force built on the premise that a constable is a constable. It has typically eschewed specialization, believing that any member of the force should be able to engage in traditional policing activities or be a part of a major national security investigation. However, concerns have been raised over whether or not this is an appropriate model for the RCMP.

A constant theme from both the McDonald Commission and the O'Connor Commission is the need to ensure special national security training so that RCMP officers have particular and detailed understanding of national security threats. Given the inherent complexity of national security investigations, particularly in terms of the employment of advanced techniques such as undercover operations and the handling and use of sensitive information, enhanced and ongoing training for national security operations should be a requirement for RCMP officers working in this area.

Even within national security policing, the skill sets required for terrorism criminal investigations are very different from those required for protective policing, international policing, and community outreach. For example, in terrorism investigations, it is important for officers to be able to separate individuals who are engaged in threat-related activities from those who simply have political or religious views that are outside of the mainstream. The RCMP also requires special skills related to terrorism financing and cybercrime. Yet the RCMP seems to have underinvested in training and has not yet created the advanced specialty courses in national security training that the O'Connor Commission stressed.

Finally, the norm of an all-purpose police constable may not be financially or functionally sustainable, especially in the national security field. At the same time, the RCMP's new unionization environment may make it difficult to contract out part of its activities to civilians with specialized skills.

"Hard" versus "Soft" National Security Policing

Criminal investigations resulting in arrests and prosecutions are the classic work of police – so-called "hard" policing. There are, however, other, "softer" ways for police to stop crime. The RCMP's departmental plan for 2017–18 indicated that it would employ "strategies to counter radicalization to violence, raise awareness and mitigate risks of violent extremism."[37] It is not clear how central this consideration remains for the RCMP – this discussion does not appear in the 2018–19 and 2019–20 departmental plans. (Notably, in 2018, the government created the Canada Centre for Community Engagement and Prevention of Violence, discussed in the chapter by Kubicek and King in this volume.)

At any rate, any focus on crime prevention by targeting "radicalization" presents serious challenges for the RCMP in terms of resources, education, community relations, and respect for human rights. The RCMP has an "intervention team" composed of both officers and civilians with "multidisciplinary experience in the area of radicalization to violence, extremism and violent extremism."[38] Despite this specialization, there are concerns that the RCMP may not be the best-placed agency to deliver such programs because of the type of training its officers receive and because of their law enforcement duties.[39] Focusing on extremism could be criticized as exceeding the RCMP's law enforcement mandate; at the same time, the RCMP does have a crime prevention mandate.

In performing its law enforcement function, the RCMP may face challenges in deciding whether and when it is more appropriate to use alternatives to criminal prosecutions. With respect to illegal forms of foreign influence, including espionage, expulsion may in some cases be quicker and less resource intensive than prosecution. Peace bonds – essentially court restraining orders imposing conditions on a person, short of incarceration – are alternatives to costly and lengthy terrorism prosecutions. They have also been used after terrorism prosecutions. However, they are not perfect: the use of a peace bond in the case of Aaron Driver, notably, failed. While subject to a peace bond, Driver was able to assemble a bomb and almost succeeded in detonating it somewhere in Southern Ontario, before being shot and killed by the police in August 2016.[40] Nevertheless, peace bonds may be more appropriate in other cases, especially in the case of young people who can be dissuaded from various forms of extremist violence.

The success of "softer" forms of policing may be tied to the efficacy of counter-violent-extremism (CVE) programs. More work is required to measure their effectiveness and public acceptability as well as the appropriate role of the police in such programs. The United Nations has stressed the important role that non-state actors should play in CVE, and this suggests that the RCMP should not play a lead role.[41] The public may equate the RCMP and identified national security threats with the need for hard policing that results in criminal prosecutions. RCMP engagement with softer forms of policing may be a proportionate response to some national security threats. Nevertheless, it runs the risk of being criticized both for invading the fundamental freedoms of those targeted and for not incapacitating identified national security risks.

In 2016, the RCMP created a 130-page *Terrorism and Violent Extremism Awareness Guide*. In addition to officially listed terrorist groups, it lists "right-wing" and "left-wing" "extremist groups."[42] Some of the analysis in this guide raises concerns initially expressed by the McDonald Commission that the RCMP as a law enforcement agency may not have the multidisciplinary skills of intelligence professionals and the ability to distinguish extremism from crime. Along similar lines, care should be taken in not conflating the threat from terrorism with extremism, which in many cases will not result in violence.[43] The RCMP may also face dilemmas when attempting to work with community groups. In 2014, it withdrew from a joint project with two Muslim groups to produce a pamphlet, *United against Terrorism*,[44] even though much current thinking suggests that community groups are in a good position to engage in countering violent extremism.

Almost any approach that the RCMP takes to community engagement on national security matters may be controversial. RCMP engagement with communities may be criticized for interfering with civil liberties because of the threat that the RCMP is gathering intelligence and could engage in enforcement, including with respect to speech-based crimes relating to advocacy of terrorism and hate speech. Even if the RCMP manages these tensions and effectively engages in softer strategies, it could also be criticized for not making arrests and contributing to successful prosecutions of known security threats. The challenging national security environment, in sum, can sometimes be seen to be a "no-win" one.

Transnational Investigations

Given the transnational nature of many national security threats, it may be necessary to increase the RCMP's international footprint. Effective and prompt transnational investigations may depend on the RCMP's maintaining a strong international presence, especially through liaison relationships. As discussed above, there are concerns that international policing in the RCMP may be under-resourced. For example, between 1999 and 2003, there was one RCMP liaison officer in Rome who was responsible for both Syria and Egypt at a time when four Canadians were being held and tortured in those countries.[45] International policing can be more resource intensive than other forms of policing. It also may present greater risks to the RCMP's and Canada's reputation than domestic policing. Finally, it also requires more coordination with other agencies, such as Global Affairs Canada (GAC) and CSIS.

Policing Costs

A concern throughout democracies is the sustainability of public policing given rising costs. The main costs in policing are salaries, and police are increasingly highly paid. As a result of successful *Charter* litigation, RCMP officers are also now represented by a union. This will likely drive up labour costs. It might also cause more friction between management and the rank and file over issues such as the use of more specialized civilians.

Governance and Legitimacy

The RCMP remains subject to top-down governance in the form of ministerial guidance and directives and the command of the commissioner. Unlike many other police services, it is not subject to governance through a police board. The limits on ministerial direction to the RCMP depend on case-by-case common law and constitutional adjudication of police independence, which is supposed to prevent political direction of law enforcement decisions. At the same time, the McDonald Commission found that overbroad understandings of police independence from the executive had diminished legitimate ministerial control of and responsibility for the RCMP.[46] As discussed in chapter eleven, the minister of public safety has a very large portfolio, and this, along with the danger of overbroad claims of police independence from government direction, can challenge effective ministerial oversight and direction of the RCMP.

The then-solicitor general (now minister of public safety) introduced an important series of ministerial directives in 2003 in the national security area dealing with investigations of sensitive sectors, including politics, religion, media, unions, and academe; security arrangements with foreign and other agencies; and the conduct of national security investigations.[47] However, unlike some police acts, the *RCMP Act* has not been amended to address such matters or require the public release of such ministerial directives to increase transparency and legitimacy. The publication of directives related to avoiding complicity in torture is now required under the *Avoiding Complicity in Mistreatment by Foreign Entities Act*.[48] This law was enacted in 2019 and will be discussed further below.

The legitimacy of the RCMP is affected by its governance. The RCMP may be involved with some activities of the Cross-Cultural Roundtable on Security (discussed in chapter nine), but such a pan-government approach does not provide a forum for the building of better relations between the RCMP and those groups most affected by national security policing, including Arab, Muslim, and Indigenous communities. Following several recommendations, a 13-person interim management advisory board was created in June 2019. It is concerned with efficient use and management of resources and is not the equivalent of police boards with elected representatives who govern municipal police services. The interim management advisory board does not alter the top-down governance provided by the minister of public safety and the commissioner.[49]

Controversies

The RCMP is a large organization that provides policing for much of Canada. It is fair to say that national security matters are not central to its work. In recent years, there have been a number of other controversies involving sexual harassment, unionization, concerns about whether officers are sufficiently armed, concerns about the future of contract policing, and relations with Indigenous communities. It is difficult to know to what extent these controversies have distracted the RCMP from its national security mandate. At the same time, there is evidence that the RCMP has diverted significant resources to national security investigations in the wake of the October 2014 attacks. The following section examines some of the problems that have plagued the RCMP as it seeks to fulfil its national security mandate.

Information-Sharing and Complicity in Torture

The role of the RCMP, along with CSIS, GAC, and CBSA, in information-sharing about four Canadians who were detained and tortured in Syria after 9/11 was the most significant controversy. The O'Connor Commission found that the RCMP had improperly shared raw investigative data with the United States. Both an immediate post-9/11 sense of threat and fear, as well as a sense that "caveats must be down" to ensure cooperation with the United States, contributed to Maher Arar's detention in the US before he was subject to extraordinary rendition to Syria, where he was tortured before being released in 2003. The RCMP data shared with the United States inaccurately and prejudicially described both Mr. Arar and his wife, Dr. Monia Mazigh, as "Islamic Extremist individuals suspected of being linked to the Al Qaeda terrorist movement."[50]

The subsequent Iacobucci Inquiry considered the RCMP's conduct in relation to three other Canadians held in Middle Eastern prisons. It found that the RCMP had unsuccessfully tried to interview Ahmad Abou-Elmaati in both Syria and Egypt. While the RCMP was concerned with the admissibility of any statement it might obtain in a Canadian court, it was not concerned that he might be tortured in Syria. The RCMP also used information likely obtained from torture to obtain search warrants in this case and then shared the results of the search with American officials. It also sent questions for Syrian officials to ask Abdullah Almalki that contributed to his torture in that country.[51]

In its policy recommendations, the O'Connor Commission urged agencies to ensure they are not complicit with torture and that they engage in better training and oversight of national security investigations. Yet even under new 2011 ministerial directives governing information-sharing, concerns remained about possible RCMP complicity in torture. These concerns were subsequently addressed, at least in part, by new 2017 ministerial directives. Those directives were replaced in 2019 by new orders-in-council, similar in scope to the 2017 instruments, and made public under the terms of the new *Avoiding Complicity in Mistreatment by Foreign Entities Act*,[52] enacted in 2019 as part of the *National Security Act, 2017*. They govern requests for and disclosure of information to foreign entities that would result in a "substantial risk" of torture or other cruel and degrading treatment and the use of information from foreign entities obtained through such mistreatment.[53] One of the purposes of central oversight of RCMP investigations is to prevent complicity in torture. Copies of the information-sharing directives are also given to those responsible for reviewing the RCMP, namely the National Security and Intelligence Review Agency (NSIRA) and the National Security and Intelligence Committee of Parliamentarians (NSICOP, both discussed in chapter fourteen).[54] All of these controls are designed to prevent a repeat of RCMP complicity in torture, but they also present a danger of making the RCMP risk averse in dealing with the many governments in the world that have poor human rights records.

Review and Oversight

Review is the process of auditing agency conduct for compliance with law, and now also standards of reasonableness and necessity. The RCMP has not traditionally been subject to specialized national security review. Rather, it was subject to judicial review in cases involving warrants and criminal proceedings, and to review by an arm's-length complaints body now called the Civilian Review and Complaints Commission (CRCC).

Although the O'Connor Commission concluded in 2006 that the accountability status quo was inadequate, it was not until 2013 that the government enacted the *Enhancing RCMP Accountability Act*.[55] Despite its grand title, the 2013 law fell far short of the O'Connor Commission's recommendations. In principle (but never fully in practice), these changes permitted the CRCC to conduct review audits of the RCMP's national security function.[56] However, the amendments did not provide the CRCC unfettered access to classified information. Rather, they permitted the RCMP commissioner to deny the commission access, triggering a process where a retired judge would offer advice about what should be done.[57] Further, while the commission was given the power to initiate reviews, other provisions prioritized the hearing of complaints.[58] In contrast, the O'Connor Commission had stressed the importance of self-initiated reviews when dealing with secret national security activities, including information-sharing.

Controversies over the complaint- and silo-based RCMP accountability structure arose after the federal government and the RCMP took the lead at the 2010 G20 summit in Toronto, which resulted in over 1,000 arrests, the largest incident of mass arrest in Canadian history. The CRCC concluded that the RCMP had paid proper attention to human rights.[59] This conclusion can be questioned, however, given that the commission received only redacted copies of records of RCMP undercover operations that involved as many as 12 undercover officers in three cities before the summit. Moreover, the commission did not examine how these undercover officers exercised the powers they are given under section 25.1 of the *Criminal Code* to break laws.[60] Finally, the CRCC did not have jurisdiction to examine the role of the many other federal and provincial agencies that the RCMP worked with on the G20 summit.

It remains to be seen how engaged NSICOP will be with respect to matters involving the RCMP. Its mandate is a broad one relating to national security and intelligence, but it is also precluded from accessing "information relating directly to an ongoing investigation carried out by a law enforcement agency that may lead to a prosecution."[61] The McDonald Commission found that inflated claims of police independence had contributed to a lack of ministerial knowledge or supervision of RCMP national security activities. There is some danger that similar concerns might fetter the ability of the new committee to review the efficacy or propriety of the RCMP's national security activities.

Since mid-2019, the RCMP's national security activities have also been subject to review by NSIRA. This change should facilitate reviews of how the RCMP interacts with CSIS and other departments with national security or intelligence responsibilities. The new agency may also hear complaints relating to the RCMP's national security activities, automatically referred to the NSIRA from the CRCC when complaints against the RCMP relate to national security. More generally, NSIRA has a broad mandate to review the RCMP's and other departments' compliance with the law and ministerial directives and the reasonableness and necessity of its use of national security powers.

As with NSICOP, there is some danger that the new review agency may be deterred from investigating how the RCMP discharges its law enforcement national security mandate, perhaps out of caution for matters that may still be the live subject of investigations or court proceedings. Nevertheless, the new review agency, which will effectively replace the CRCC for national security, will have much more national security expertise and more experience in self-initiated reviews than the CRCC. It will also be able to follow the trail and examine RCMP conduct and policy that involve the Canadian intelligence community.[62] (Of note, in early 2020, the minority Trudeau government reintroduced legislation that would create a Public Complaints and Review Commission [PCRC] that would replace the CRCC with a review body that would handle public complaints for both the RCMP and CBSA. This legislation did not pass before the prorogation of Parliament in the fall of 2020. If reintroduced for a third time and passed, the PCRC will not investigate matters related to national security, which will remain the responsibility of NSICOP and NSIRA.)[63]

Hopefully, the new state of affairs in which the RCMP is subject to specialized national security review in Parliament and by an executive watchdog with a mandate to review the entire intelligence community will be effective. It should explore whether those within the RCMP who engage in national security investigations have adequate training, resources, and powers and that they exercise their powers lawfully, proportionately, and in compliance with RCMP policy and directives. Both NSIRA and NSICOP can examine how the RCMP works with other members of the Canadian intelligence community, especially CSIS. As will be discussed below, the courts will also review some, but by no means all, RCMP national security activities.

Challenges to RCMP Conduct in Criminal Trials

RCMP national security activities may be subject to judicial review when they result in warrants being sought or prosecutions commenced. The RCMP acts proactively when conducting criminal investigations into terrorism. This creates legal risks, especially in Canada, where judges, as opposed to juries, decide issues of entrapment. A trial judge stayed a high-profile terrorism prosecution on the basis that the RCMP had entrapped two accused. She found that the RCMP had offered the suspects an opportunity to commit a terrorist crime without a reasonable suspicion that they were involved in terrorist activities and induced them to commit a terrorist crime. This inducement involved pressuring them and exploiting their weaknesses, including their drug and economic dependency, to participate in a planned Canada Day explosion in Victoria.[64] The BC Court of Appeal upheld the stay of proceedings on the basis that the RCMP had manufactured the crime, but held that the RCMP had had reasonable suspicion to offer the accused an opportunity to commit a terrorist crime.[65]

This case is significant from a policy perspective. The trial judge found that CSIS's advisory letter to the RCMP informing them about the two suspects did not even provide reasonable suspicion about the suspects. This raises concerns about the relationship between intelligence and evidence, to be discussed below. The trial judge also ruled that the RCMP had committed several terrorism offences during the elaborate sting. Although (partially) authorized under section 25.1 of the *Criminal Code*, the judge found RCMP illegalities to be an independent basis for staying proceedings on the basis of abuse of process.[66] Finally, the intensive and controversial operation in the case cost over $1 million[67] and was not stopped by the increased centralized oversight of RCMP national security investigations.

Relations with CSIS and the Relationship between
Intelligence and Evidence

The "One Vision 2.0" framework governs investigative relationships between the RCMP and CSIS.[68] It was amended in 2015 to include the need for coordination with CSIS's new threat reduction powers. Nevertheless, it still features a system whereby CSIS retains the discretion to provide any information to the RCMP, and its investigations remain separate and distinct from the RCMP's. Such a bifurcated approach is thought to limit the risk of CSIS's having to disclose its sources and methods, but it was criticized by the commission of inquiry into the 1985 Air India bombing, led by former Supreme Court justice John Major between 2006 and 2010. Major objected to bifurcated investigations on the basis that it gave CSIS too much discretion to withhold intelligence that the RCMP could use in terrorism criminal investigations. He also criticized bifurcation of the prosecutorial and court processes used to determine whether information should be disclosed or sheltered from disclosure to protect national security interests.[69]

CSIS provides the RCMP with minimal investigative tips through disclosure letters, and may also issue more substantive advisory letters. These letters are carefully managed at the headquarters level, which maximizes accountability but not speed. As discussed above, CSIS disclosed so little to the RCMP in one recent investigation that a trial judge held that an advisory letter did not even provide the RCMP with reasonable suspicion to investigate a terrorism offence.[70] This caution reflects Canada's "intelligence-to-evidence" problem – and, specifically, concerns that intelligence products shared with the police may subsequently be subject to disclosure under Canada's broad criminal trial disclosure rules.

Having CSIS and the RCMP pursue separate national security investigations is designed to protect CSIS intelligence from disclosure and minimize the need for uncertain and resource-intensive applications to the Federal Court under section 38 of the *Canada Evidence Act*[71] to obtain non-disclosure orders in order to protect national security interests. Although the constitutionality of this process has been upheld,[72] the Supreme Court has warned that judges should not hesitate to provisionally stay proceedings, in which case the attorney general of Canada would decide whether the prosecution should be abandoned or the classified information disclosed to the accused, something that may require the lifting of caveats or restrictions on disclosure, including those imposed by CSIS or foreign partners.

Both Conservative and Liberal governments did not embrace those Air India commission recommendations critical of the emphasis placed on ensuring that CSIS and RCMP terrorism investigations remain distinct. This siloed investigative approach can have adverse effects not only on terrorism investigations, but also on espionage cases. Unfortunately, there is evidence that CSIS held back from informing the RCMP about Jeffrey Delisle's selling secret information to Russia because of concerns about disclosing intelligence.[73] Another *Security of Information Act* trial was mired in disputes about disclosing CSIS intelligence used to secure the warrant for a wiretap that recorded the accused offering to sell secrets to China.[74] As of 2020, it is also not clear whether intelligence-to-evidence issues will complicate a third *Security of Information Act* prosecution – that involving the alleged illegal information-sharing by an RCMP official, Cameron Ortis.

Problems with moving from secret intelligence to public evidence raise issues about Canada's capacity to conduct national security prosecutions with respect to terrorism and espionage. These concerns could harm Canada's international relations and ability to obtain intelligence from foreign partners. Nearly a decade after Justice Major's scathing report, there seems to be growing recognition in Ottawa that the intelligence-to-evidence problem is not going away.[75] The solution is not better human relations between the RCMP and CSIS, but structural means to reconcile their very different national security mandates.

Terrorism from the Far Right

There are also growing concerns in the wake of the 2017 Quebec City mosque massacre that terrorism laws are applied to Muslim accused, but not others who may engage in politically motivated violence. Greater efforts to prevent right-wing violence may, however, also encounter intelligence-to-evidence challenges. They might also result in debates about whether the RCMP should engage in "soft" forms of policing designed to counter violent extremism or pursue a harder-edged law enforcement strategy. The fact remains that no terrorism charges against extremists on the far right have been laid.[76] Perceptions about discriminatory double standards with respect to terrorism investigations and charges can erode public confidence as well as public support from Muslim and other communities that may be the target of right-wing violence or religious or racial hatred.[77] At the same time, the RCMP has been, and would be, criticized for conducting national security investigations with respect to Indigenous or environmental groups who have also not been charged with any terrorism offence since these offences were created after 9/11. Again, the RCMP's national security mandate is a difficult one, and controversy seems inevitable.

Conclusion

The RCMP has an important national security mandate that includes crime prevention and the investigation of terrorism and other offences involving national security threats, as well as protective policing. Its national security activities are dependent on the evolving threat level, which is affected by the fine line between activities that are threats to the security of Canada within the purview of CSIS and matters that also constitute criminal offences involving national security.

The RCMP has a broad range of legislative tools to discharge its national security mandate, ranging from fifteen terrorism offences and other offences relating to espionage and foreign influence to expanded wiretap powers and peace bonds. The RCMP works with other agencies, but CSIS keeps its terrorism investigations distinct from RCMP investigations in order to protect CSIS sources and methods from disclosure. This presents an intelligence-to-evidence problem that continues to place burdens on both RCMP national security investigations and national security prosecutions.

It is difficult to know whether the RCMP has the resources required to discharge its very important national security mandate. It was able to spend over $1 million in just one terrorism investigation that ended in a finding of entrapment, and it was able to transfer 600 of its officers into terrorism investigations in the wake of two Daesh-inspired terrorist attacks in 2014. Nevertheless, concerns have been raised in this chapter about the adequacy of resourcing for national security training and the static budget for RCMP members who work outside of Canada. There are also concerns about the RCMP's ability to specialize and move away from the one-constable-fits-all model of traditional policing, especially in its newly unionized work environment.

The RCMP faces a number of challenges going forward, including those related to the sustainability of high policing costs, continued governance issues, and the need for national security specialization to match the increasingly specialized oversight and review of its national security activities. There may also be a case for increased national security specialization in the RCMP along the lines of the UK Special Branch, which appears to work more closely with UK intelligence agencies and to better transition from intelligence to evidence. The RCMP also needs to figure out its optimal role in the federal government's nascent CVE strategy and to coordinate with provincial efforts. The RCMP has attempted to develop multidisciplinary intervention teams for CVE, but how these may be reconciled with its law enforcement responsibilities and the need for community involvement remains to be seen.

NOTES

I thank Craig Forcese for valuable suggestions and sharing information with me relating to the RCMP that was obtained by his access to information request.

1 *Enhancing RCMP Accountability Act*, S.C. 2013, c.18.
2 S.C. 2019, c. 13. See chapter by Leah West in this volume.
3 The definitive history is Reg Whitaker, Gregory S. Kealey, and Andrew Parnaby, *Secret Service: Political Policing in Canada from the Fenians to Fortress America* (Toronto: University of Toronto Press, 2012).
4 Commission of Inquiry into the Actions of Canadian Officials in Relation to Maher Arar (henceforth O'Connor Commission), *A New Review Mechanism for the RCMP's National Security Activities* (Ottawa: Public Works and Government Services Canada, 2006), 27. This reference is to the policy report. There is a separate factual report that is cited below. The author served on this inquiry's research advisory committee.
5 Privy Council Office, "Commission of Inquiry Concerning Certain Activities of the RCMP," *Freedom and Security under the Law*, 1981.
6 R.S.C. 1985, c. C-23.

7 R.S.C. 1985, c. S-7.
8 R.S.C. 1985, c. 0-5.
9 R.S.C. 1985, c. R-10, s. 5.
10 *R. v. Campbell*, [1999] 1 S.C.R. 565.
11 Royal Canadian Mounted Police (RCMP), "Governance Framework – National Security Criminal Investigations," document released under ATIP-2018-09837 at 12–13.
12 RCMP, "Governance Framework," 2.
13 RCMP, "Governance Framework," 5–6.
14 RCMP, "Governance Framework," 3.
15 *RCMP Act*, s 18.
16 Edmonton/Calgary is the same office, but in two locations. The main INSET office is in Edmonton, where the officer in charge (superintendent) is located. Calgary has a smaller office with an RCMP inspector in charge, who reports to the Edmonton office.
17 RCMP, "National Security Criminal Investigations Program," last modified 3 June 2020, https://www.rcmp-grc.gc.ca/nsci-ecsn/index-eng.htm.
18 O'Connor Commission, *A New Review Mechanism*, 102.
19 R.S.C. 1985, c. P-21.
20 RCMP, "Governance Framework," 10.
21 S.C. 2015, c. 20, s. 11.
22 RCMP, "Governance Framework," 6.
23 RCMP, *2018–19 Departmental Plan* (2018), 22. Available online: http://www.rcmp-grc.gc.ca/wam/media/2405/original/029c191490ada4f6dd1a71363c52b0c9.pdf.
24 Colin Freeze, "RCMP Shelved Hundreds of Organized-Crime Cases after Terror Attacks," *Globe and Mail*, 17 September 2017, https://www.theglobeandmail.com/news/national/mounties-put-hundreds-of-files-on-hold-in-shift-toward-anti-terrorism/article36285597/; Daniel Leblanc, "A Force in Flux," *Globe and Mail*, 29 June 2017, A8. The latter story reports that fewer than 5,000 officers are in federal policing, including 800 assigned to protective policing. Additional funding for INSETs has come from general RCMP budgets. Alex Boutilier, "Soaring Costs of Terror Fight Hit RCMP," *Toronto Star*, 9 April 2015, A1.
25 RCMP, *2019–20 Departmental Plan* (2019), 10. Available online: http://www.rcmp-grc.gc.ca/wam/media/3217/original/2105314a741c8a1ab58dd4e686660798.pdf.
26 RCMP, *2018–19 Departmental Plan*, 15. The 2019–20 departmental plan does not break-out international policing as a separate item.
27 Office of the Auditor General of Canada, *2014 Fall Report of the Auditor General of Canada*, chap. 2, "Support for Combatting Transnational Crime"

(2014). Available online: http://www.oag-bvg.gc.ca/internet/English
/parl_oag_201411_02_e_39960.html.

28 RCMP, "Governance Framework," 8.

29 RCMP, "Governance Framework," 2.

30 Government of Canada, "Canadian Police College," last modified 24 June
2020, http://www.cpc-ccp.gc.ca/index-eng.htm.

31 Leblanc, "A Force in Flux."

32 See "Information Sharing and Complicity in Torture" below.

33 RCMP, "Governance Framework," 1.

34 RCMP, *RCMP Security Posture, Parliament Hill, October 22, 2014* (2015).
Available online: http://www.rcmp-grc.gc.ca/en/rcmp-security-posture
-parliament-hill-october-22-2014#rec.

35 RCMP, *External Engagement and Coordination: Parliament Hill Incident on
October 22nd, 2014 – After Action Review* (2015). Available online: http://
www.rcmp-grc.gc.ca/en/external-engagement-and-coordination
-parliament-hill-incident-october-22nd-2014-after-action-review.

36 S.C. 2001, c. 41.

37 RCMP, "Governance Framework," 15.

38 RCMP, "Governance Framework," 5.

39 Craig Forcese and Kent Roach, *False Security: The Radicalization of Canadian
Anti-terrorism* (Toronto: Irwin Law, 2015), chap. 13.

40 Elizabeth Thompson, "Foiled Attack Raises Questions about Value of
Peace Bonds," *CBC News*, 11 August 2016, https://www.cbc.ca/news
/politics/terrorism-security-aaron-driver-peace-bonds-1.3717693.

41 Kent Roach, "The Migration and Evolution of Programs to Counter Violent
Extremism," *University of Toronto Law Journal* 68, no. 4 (2018): 588.

42 RCMP, "Terrorism and Violent Extremism Awareness Guide," 2016.

43 Stewart Bell, "What Does It Take to Lay Terrorism Charges? An Internal
Government Document Explains the RCMP View," *Global News*, 27
April 2018, https://globalnews.ca/news/4173552/canada-terrorism
-charges-rcmp-document/. For CSIS's own work in this area, see CSIS,
Mobilization to Violence (Terrorism) Research: Key Findings (2018). Available
online: https://www.canada.ca/content/dam/csis-scrs/documents
/publications/IMV_-_Terrorism-Research-Key-findings-eng.pdf.

44 Forcese and Roach, *False Security*, 483–8.

45 Frank Iacobucci, *Internal Inquiry into the Actions of Canadian Officials in
Relation to Abdullah Almalki, Ahmad Abou-Elmaati and Muayyed Nureddin*
(Ottawa: Public Works and Government Services Canada, 2008), 81.

46 Privy Council Office, "Commission of Inquiry Concerning Certain
Activities of the RCMP," part 3.

47 O'Connor Commission, *A New Review Mechanism*, 89–90.

48 S.C. 2019, c. 13, s. 49.1.

49 Public Safety Canada, "Interim Management Advisory Board for the RCMP," last modified 16 January 2019, https://www.canada.ca/en /public-safety-canada/news/2019/01/interim-management-advisory -board-for-the-royal-canadian-mounted-police.html.

50 O'Connor Commission, *Report of the Events Relating to Maher Arar: Recommendations and Analysis* (2006), 13. Available online: https:// ccrjustice.org/sites/default/files/attach/2015/05/ARAR_AR _English.pdf.

51 Iacobucci, *Internal Inquiry*, 137–51, 374–9, 411; O'Connor Commission, *A New Review Mechanism*, 15.

52 S.C. 2019, c. 13, s. 49.1.

53 *Avoiding Complicity in Mistreatment by Foreign Entities Act*, s. 3.

54 *Avoiding Complicity in Mistreatment by Foreign Entities Act*, s. 6.

55 S.C. 2013, c. 18.

56 The CRCC announced a "strategic investigation" into the RCMP's implementation of the O'Connor Commission's recommendations in 2016. It seems to have abandoned this initiative prior to the National Security and Intelligence Review Agency assuming review jurisdiction over the RCMP's national security activities.

57 *RCMP Act*, s. 45.41.

58 *RCMP Act*, s. 45.34.

59 Civilian Review and Complaints Commission for the RCMP, *Public Interest Complaint into RCMP Member Conduct Related to the 2010 G8 and G20 Summits, Final Report* (2012). Available online: https://www.crcc -ccetp.gc.ca/en/public-interest-investigation-rcmp-member-conduct -related-2010-g8-and-g20-summits-0.

60 Kent Roach, "Post-9/11 Policing of Protests," in *Putting the State on Trial: The Policing of Protest during the G20 Summit*, ed. Margaret Beare, Natalie Des Rosiers, and Abigail C. Deshman (Vancouver: University of British Columbia Press, 2015), 73–4.

61 *National Security and Intelligence Committee of Parliamentarians Act*, S.C. 2017, c. 15, s. 14(d).

62 For my previous arguments for the need for a "super Security Intelligence Review Committee" that would include the RCMP, see Kent Roach, "Review and Oversight of Intelligence in Canada: Expanding Accountability Gaps," in *Global Intelligence Oversight: Governing Security in the Twenty-First Century*, ed. Zachary Goldman and Samuel Rascoff (New York: Oxford University Press, 2016), 194–7; Forcese and Roach, *False Security*, chap. 12.

63 See Bill C-3, *An Act to amend the Royal Canadian Mounted Police Act and the Canada Border Services Agency Act and to make consequential amendments to other Acts*, 2020, https://www.parl.ca/LegisInfo/BillDetails.aspx? Language=E&billId=10613928.

64 *R. v. Nuttall*, 2016 B.C.S.C. 1404.

65 *R. v. Nuttall*, 2018 B.C.C.A. 479.

66 *R. v. Nuttall*, 2016 B.C.S.C. 1404, 620.

67 Farrah Merali, "RCMP Spent Over 1 Million on Victoria Terror Probe," *CBC News*, 17 January 2018, http://www.cbc.ca/news/canada/british -columbia/rcmp-investigation-cost-more-than-one-million-1.4491219.

68 "One Vision 2.0: CSIS-RCMP Agreement for Cooperation," *Secret Law Gazette*, 24 November 2015. Available online: http://secretlaw.omeka.net /items/show/21.

69 Commission of Inquiry into the Bombing of Air India Flight 182, *Air India Flight 182: A Canadian Tragedy*, vol. 3, *The Relation between Intelligence and Evidence and Terrorism Prosecutions* (Ottawa: Commission of Inquiry into the Investigation of the Bombing of Air India Flight 182, 2010). The author was the research director for this commission of inquiry.

70 *R. v. Nuttall*, 2016 B.C.S.C. 1404.

71 R.S.C. 1985, c C-5, s 38.

72 *R. v. Ahmad*, [2011] 1 S.C.R. 110.

73 Jim Bronskill and Murray Brewster, "Jeffrey Delisle Case: CSIS Secretly Watched Spy, Held File Back from RCMP," *Toronto Star*, 26 May 2013, https://www.thestar.com/news/canada/2013/05/26/jeffrey_delisle _case_csis_secretly_watched_spy_held_file_back_from_rcmp.html.

74 *Huang v. Canada (Attorney General)*, 2019 F.C. 1122.

75 In late 2019, the prime minister's mandate letter to the minister of justice and the attorney general of Canada revealed plans to create a director of terrorism prosecutions, which was one of Justice Major's recommendations.

76 Michael Nesbitt, "An Empirical Study of Terrorism Charges and Terrorism Trials in Canada," *Criminal Law Quarterly* 67, no. 1–2 (2019): 123.

77 Forcese and Roach, *False Security*, 278–80.

8 Canada Border Services Agency (CBSA)

CHRISTIAN LEUPRECHT, KELLY SUNDBERG,
TODD HATALEY, AND ALEXANDRA GREEN

State borders are political constructs. However, these political processes are undergoing fundamental changes that are having a major impact on how states manage borders. "Bordering" processes, traditionally determined by territory or historical events, are being disrupted by the effects of technological innovation and globalization, enabling the movement of people and goods on a scale that is unprecedented in both scope and reach. The Canada Border Services Agency (CBSA) is the federal government's expert agency in border management. This chapter is driven by a tension: how to reconcile the mounting "aterritorial" challenges the CBSA confronts in the era of globalization with its mandate of ensuring the integrity of Canada's borders.

The shifting nature of borders is reflected in challenges and controversies in managing and administering borders and related policy. In response, the CBSA has been transformed into Canada's second-largest law enforcement agency in a sprawling web of intergovernmental partnerships: with the Royal Canadian Mounted Police (RCMP), which has been responsible for the border between ports of entry (POEs) since an order-in-council in 1932, and with Immigration, Refugees and Citizenship Canada (IRCC) on inland enforcement. CBSA's National Targeting Centre (NTC) operates as part of the National Border Operations Centre (NBOC), Operations Branch, and works closely with the Canadian Security Intelligence Service (CSIS), the Financial Transactions and Reports Analysis Centre of Canada (FINTRAC), the Communications Security Establishment (CSE), and Global Affairs Canada (GAC).

CBSA falls under the department of Public Safety Canada (discussed in chapter nine), with a minister whose responsibilities include border policy, among their many other responsibilities. It coordinates with provincial and municipal law enforcement and is an integral part of a host of multi-agency fusion centres, such as Integrated National

Security Enforcement Teams (INSETs) in metropolitan cities across the country, as well as the Integrated Terrorist Assessment Centre (ITAC, discussed in chapter five). Over the past twenty-five years, Canada has worked systematically with the United States to advance bilateral coordination, cooperation, and integration, which have given rise to a continental border management paradigm. More generally, it has worked with other like-minded countries on border control, including the remaining three members of the "Border Five" and the Five Eyes intelligence community: the United Kingdom, Australia, and New Zealand. CBSA also has a growing network of liaison officers that spans at least 39 countries.

The 2005 *Canada Border Services Act*[1] codified the most fundamental change in Canadian border security strategy in almost a century. For nearly 90 years, customs, immigration, food inspection, and policing functions had been housed in separate agencies. Unarmed and relatively untrained customs and immigration officers had long assumed responsibility for administering and managing the flow of people and goods through Canada's land, air, and sea ports of entry. But in the aftermath of 9/11, the idea of a "borderless world"[2] was displaced by the fortress state.[3] Protection of the homeland became the priority for border security and immigration officials.[4] By way of an order-in-council on 12 December 2003, the enforcement functions of the Canada Revenue Agency, IRCC, and the Canada Food Inspection Agency were merged into in a single agency under the newly established minister of public safety. Today, CBSA has over 14,000 employees – about 6,500 of whom are uniformed members – working at 1,200 service points across Canada, at POEs, in every major Canadian city, and abroad.[5]

Mandate

CBSA operates at, before, and beyond the border. At POEs, armed and uniformed CBSA officers examine and process persons, goods, and agricultural products to ascertain admissibility in accordance with immigration law, ensure duties and customs are remitted, and identify, intercept, and deny dangerous persons, goods, and agricultural products. Before POEs, CBSA maintains the integrity of Canada's immigration and refugee program, collects intelligence on threats to Canada and its borders, and contributes to Canada's counterterrorism efforts. It reviews and screens visa applications and coordinates with foreign customs, immigration, and agricultural inspection services. Beyond POEs, officers at inland offices throughout Canadian cities investigate inadmissible persons or goods inside the country, arresting, detaining, and removing unlawful non-citizens and seizing contraband goods and agricultural products. CBSA officers also inspect international mail, courier packages, and other shipped goods entering Canada from abroad.

The amalgamation of the legacy customs, immigration, and food inspection functions into the CBSA, discussed above, posed significant challenges. The new organization required policy, infrastructure, crosstraining, equipment, uniforms, et cetera. These changes came at considerable cost and were achieved with few comparative reference points. The initial surge of hiring and training 4,500 new officers, and arming both legacy and new officers, all the while establishing a new institutional culture that reflects yet transcends the traditions of the legacy departments, compounded the challenge. New methods for enforcement ran afoul of the "old ways," resulting in policy being applied inconsistently.[6] The biases arising from these old ways make it more difficult for primary inspection to act on assessments by risk algorithms, for instance, which runs counter to CBSA's purpose as a new, unified, and security-focused organization. Along the way, CBSA has been subject to external and internal constraints beyond its making or control, and confronted with a rapidly changing security environment. It has also matured at a time of mounting uncertainty in Canada's relationship with the United States.[7]

Accomplishments

CBSA excels at inspection and intelligence and in processing refugees. Developed by the United States and Canada in response to the Western Hemisphere Travel Initiative (WHTI), the NEXUS pre-clearance program has proven popular and effective at expediting border crossings for trusted travellers. Similarly, electronic passport readers at Canadian airports are reducing wait times, allowing CBSA to reallocate resources to intelligence and inspection.

In 2016, CBSA linked the Canadian Police Information Centre (CPIC) to its Field Operations Support System (FOSS). Subsequently, under the Beyond the Border accord, Canada and the United States agreed to share entry/exit data on travellers entering by air, sea, and land. CBSA sought to dispel initial concerns over privacy and to convince Canadians of the merits of legitimate information-sharing and the benefits of greater domain awareness, and that these outweigh risks associated with the legal aggregation of data.

When the Canadian government implemented the Syrian Refugee Horizontal Initiative in November 2015, CBSA had to fulfil its regular mandate of normal volumes of immigration and border crossings while coordinating with other government partners to process 25,000 Syrian refugees within four months and ensuring compliance with health and security requirements. It deployed 54 staff overseas to support the selection process and opened two temporary ports of entry to process refugees. Many refugees arrived during the holiday travel season; so, CBSA also allocated ninety-nine border services officers to relieve congestion at airports.[8]

Resources

The volume of travellers crossing the border by land never recovered after 9/11. However, CBSA projects air travel to increase by 50 per cent by 2030 and cross-border shipping continues to increase due to online shopping. Concomitantly, the changing nature of threats as exemplified by irregular migration, foreign terrorist fighters, and transnational drug networks have made the work of CBSA much more complex. Yet, like all federal agencies, CBSA has been subject to fiscal restraint and constraint: more work for CBSA is ever-more complex, while resources remain constant in absolute terms and decline relative to growing traffic and complexity. In consequence, CBSA has to rethink the way it does business: shifting from labour to capital by deploying more technology; optimizing the allocation of scarce resources across the country; and managing risk better.

Figure 8.1 depicts changes in CBSA's spending from 2004 (the first full fiscal year after it was created) through 2017. The graph shows that, corresponding to an evolving threat environment, growing expectations, and a trajectory of greater accountability of government agencies and their spending, CBSA's spending was on the rise over those 13 years. Nonetheless, spending has been bucking that general trend since 2014. Whether this is an aberration (as in 2012/2013) or an emerging trend remains to be seen. If the latter, then CBSA will have no choice but to change the way it does business if it is to meet its mandate.

The 2006 budget allocated $1 billion over a span of 10 years to the "Arming Initiative," which armed CBSA officers.[9] However, that merely accounted for the start-up costs of providing arms; the organization had to absorb secondary costs associated with the reclassification of officers. Arming CBSA members triggered a reclassification at a higher rate of pay. The surge in CBSA spending shown in Figure 1 is, therefore, indicative of more staff at higher rates of pay. That surge also reflects the number of CBSA officers to be armed, from an initial plan of 4,800 to 6,774 by March 2014. Numbers are expected to continue to grow because arming each CBSA officer gives

Figure 8.1. CBSA spending 2004–17. Data compiled from various departmental performance reports.

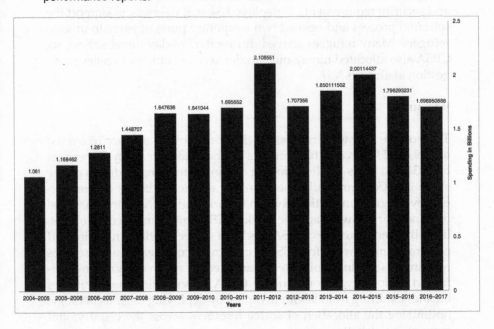

the organization greater flexibility in postings: officers can move to different locations without having to retrain.[10] But as the graph shows, flexibility comes at a cost.

Similarly, CBSA struggles with information technology. Its Strategic Technology Plan proposed a master data management (MDM) system to convert data from different sources into a standardized, readable format for CBSA officials. However, the agency decided to build two separate MDM systems, intending to merge the traveller portfolio MDM system, at $14.3 million, and the commercial portfolio, at $11.7 million, into a single system. This duplication proved costly and inefficient: costs associated with the expertise and time required to merge the two systems were not taken into account.[11] Tepid progress in closing the gap between CBSA's institutional culture, on the one hand, and a globalized world where data is ubiquitous, on the other hand, means the delta between the two continues to widen and makes it ever more difficult for CBSA to keep pace, let alone catch up to a rapidly evolving digital, threat, and trade environment.

Controversies

Auditor General's Report on Corruption

The Auditor General of Canada found in 2017 that CBSA does not sufficiently oversee internal controls to prevent or detect corruption. For example, the investigation found

> examples of improper (though not necessarily corrupt) actions ... that were similar to known violations of code-of-conduct scenarios. For example, agency border services officers at land border crossings did not follow all policies or practices consistently ... we estimated that over a 12-month period, about 300,000 of 19 million vehicles entering Canada [2 per cent] entered without undergoing all elements of a required inspection by border staff.[12]

Although CBSA has measures in place to mitigate corruption, such as randomly assigning border services officers, awareness training, et cetera, it does not mine the data it collects about officers. While CBSA collects information on officers, such as the officer's location and the particular land border crossing to which the officer is assigned, it does not use this information to identify instances of corruption. Instead, corruption is detected by co-workers or the public. Not only are instances of corruption potentially being overlooked, but reporting relies largely on qualitative observations.[13]

Spending Practices

CBSA has been subject to allegations of overspending and poor performance. A former director of CBSA's Toronto office released to the public a 23-page letter that criticized CBSA's spending processes and concluded, "Simply put, more money was spent to produce less."[14] While the percentage of irregular immigrants removed from Canada dropped by 26 per cent, CBSA experienced a "30% increase in the cost of detaining people who are inadmissible to Canada" in the fiscal year ending in March 2014, compared to the previous one.[15] These figures are indicative of a broader trend. From 2012–14 the cost of detaining immigrants increased by 10 per cent – although fewer people were being held.[16]

The two detention centres CBSA runs in Montreal and Toronto aside, in most of the country volumes make it more efficient for CBSA to outsource the detention function. Consequently, "the rise in costs for immigration detention is due to a number of factors, including an increase in operations costs."[17] It is standard practice for CBSA to have provincial jails host detainees. Jail space rented from the provinces varies in price, from $184 per day in Quebec to $448.69 for women in New Brunswick.[18] Although this revelation was intended to assuage the public's concern that CBSA was not deliberately inflating the costs of detention, it ended up stoking controversy surrounding detainees.

Detention

Critics question not only the cost of detaining individuals, but also the number of people who are detained. In May 2017, for example, of the 113 individuals that CBSA held in detention, only 27 were deemed a danger to public safety. The rest were detained until the government obtained sufficient information to ascertain admissibility, settled disputes regarding identity (such as in cases where someone seeking entry into Canada was unable to identify him/herself to the satisfaction of CBSA), or deported them. Costs are a function of the number of detainees and how much time they spend in jail, which can be indefinite in some cases.[19] According to data released by the House of Commons, many detainees are released within 48 hours. Some, however, are held for years: 38 detainees were held between one and two years, and 16 between two and five years.[20] Lengthy detention is ripe with controversy: Why are some individuals being detained for so long? Should CBSA be allocating scarce resources to long-term detention?

Deportations and Removals

Before 2016, CBSA had warrants out for 44,000 inadmissible individuals for failing to comply with removal orders and 15,000 deportation orders for foreign nationals from 180 countries.[21] At the same time, the number of deportations was in decline, from 18,992 in 2012–13 to 7,364 in 2016.[22] During fiscal years 2017–18 and 2018–19, the agency deported 723 failed claimants from a total of 68,000 asylum seekers who had crossed into Canada irregularly since 2017.[23] By 2019, the backlog of Canada's deportation inventory was about 18,000 cases, composed overwhelmingly of failed refugee claimants. Yet fewer than 3,000 people (down from 5,300 in October 2018) had an actionable removal order with no known impediment to deportation.[24] That discrepancy was a function of legal recourse, proceedings, and appeals, temporary stays of removal to countries that were experiencing armed conflict or environmental disasters, court sentences, medical issues, pre-removal risk assessments, and recalcitrance by some countries to issue travel documents.

CBSA also lacks sufficient resources to remove higher-risk "deports."[25] When countries refuse to issue travel documents, then the Government of Canada has to apply diplomatic pressure and persuasion – a notable challenge for smaller states such as Canada with a relatively modest diplomatic corps and limited influence.[26] A shortage of federal judges also exacerbates legal and administrative delays,[27] while inland immigration enforcement has fewer CBSA officers than do ports of entry. In other words, CBSA's problems are not all of its own making. At the same time, many of the operational approaches used by CBSA to identify, arrest, and remove non-citizens living in Canada in contravention of the *Immigration and Refugee Protection Act*[28] are ineffective:[29] tips to the Border Watch Line are notoriously inaccurate and unreliable, inland immigration enforcement officers typically conduct investigations only during regular work hours, and a sizable number of inland immigration enforcement officers are assigned to administrative or clerical functions rather than enforcement, such as booking flights for removals, attempting to secure travel documents, et cetera.

Challenges

Terrorism

Since 9/11, keeping Canada's border with the US open has been an overriding priority for the Government of Canada. To this end, it has to ensure that people and goods from Canada do not pose a threat to the US. CBSA is on the front line of that effort because it is responsible for people and goods entering Canada. CBSA defines terrorist activities as the "risk that individuals/groups with links to terrorism, or materials to support terrorist activities, will enter, exit, or transit Canada."[30] To mitigate the threat posed by terrorist activities, CBSA launched the Interactive Advance Passenger Information (IAPI) initiative in 2016 to implement Immigration, Refugees and Citizenship Canada's electronic travel authorization (eTA) requirements for "visa exempt foreign nationals flying to Canada ... by enabling CBSA to issue 'board and no-board' messages to commercial air carriers, the IAPI expands the existing Advance Passenger Information/Passenger Name Record Program by identifying and minimizing the risk of improperly documented persons from boarding flights to Canada."[31] The eTA effectively expands the scope of the border beyond the border to flag people who are inadmissible or travelling with improper documentation long before they reach the actual borderline. To make the process more manageable, the largest single number of travellers, US citizens, are exempt.

Migration

The eTA, better intelligence-sharing, and a proliferation of other data-reporting requirements have made it much more difficult for aspiring migrants to enter Canada irregularly by plane or boat, leaving only the option of crossing by land to prospective entrants who would otherwise be deemed inadmissible.

After changes in US immigration and refugee policies under the Trump administration, Canada in irregular border crossings surged in areas that are not official POEs, notably Roxham Road in Québec.[32] These crossings exploit a loophole in Canadian law that can help aspiring migrants avoid being turned away at the border. Under Canada's Safe Third Country Agreement with the United States, which, at the time of publication, is subject to ongoing litigation, asylum seekers cannot choose where to lodge their claim; they must do so in the country in which they first set foot. In this way, if they are making a claim, they must do so in the US as it is a "safe" country in which to do so. Therefore, anyone seeking asylum in Canada arriving from the US will likely be turned away at any legal POE.

Under Canadian law, crossing the border between points of entry, without making a legal declaration, is an offence under the Customs Act,[33] and anyone doing so may be arrested. However, in Singh v Canada (1985),[34] Justice Wilson found that foreigners have the right to protection under the Charter once on Canadian soil, allowing irregular migrants access to the immigration and refugee system once they have arrived on Canadian territory, even if they have arrived irregularly or been arrested.[35] In this way, asylum seekers are able to circumvent normal border and immigration procedures. The surge in migrants, as well as a growing number of unexplained inland claims (i.e., from persons who crossed irregularly somewhere and were not detained but then lodged a refugee claim inland),[36] have caused concern about fairness of the immigration and refugee process. Moreover, it has also increased CBSA's workload as the agency is responsible for screening individuals once they make a claim, and tracking and monitoring failed asylum claimants.

Data

The Auditor General concluded in a 2015 report that CBSA lacks sufficient information and controls to fulfil its enforcement duties.[37] Poor information is exacerbated by the sources of information. The agency relies heavily on export declarations, which are often the sole method by which high-risk shipments are identified. Owing to time constraints, CBSA does not review all declarations. Exporters are required to produce their export declarations only two hours before loading for planes and 48 hours for ships. This narrow window poses a challenge for risk assessments, especially when a container that was meant to be shipped by rail is moved to a plane. Although CBSA has seen some success with this model, the agency struggles to recognize high-risk shipments because it does not optimize data analytics (which its IT backend does not currently facilitate). The Auditor General also found that "the Agency did not examine approximately 20 percent of the high-risk shipments that had been identified by its centralized targeting units" during the period spanned by the audit.[38]

Crime

Transaction costs at the border seem low for organized crime, which has shown itself to be quite resilient.[39] Common smuggling routes for contraband include a corridor between British Columbia and Washington state, and the Akwesasne region.[40] Illegal firearms used to commit criminal offences in Canada overwhelmingly originate in the United States.[41] Conversely, transnational organized crime capitalizes on markets of opportunity to move drugs such as ecstasy and cannabis, which have lower penalties in Canada, from Canada to the US, and the amount of illicit trade from Canada to the Eastern US seaboard suggests that risks associated with crossing the border are low.[42]

Privacy and Technology

By legislation, common standards of privacy and reasonable grounds within Canada do not apply at the border, at least not in the same way: legislation allows officials to search (almost) anyone and anything unconditionally (with notable exceptions such as travellers on a diplomatic passport), and to detain individuals until their admissibility and identity can be established to the satisfaction of the Canadian official. For CBSA, this includes the ability to search mobile electronic devices such as smartphones and computers. Some travellers have challenged CBSA's sweeping interpretation of its powers and its application of legislation. Current legislation leaves CBSA in limbo, as the *Privacy Act*[43] and the relevant provisions in the *Customs Act* predate the digital revolution. With respect to smartphones, "the Supreme Court has clearly established that the greater the intrusion on privacy, the greater the constitutional protections and a greater justification is required. And while there may be a diminished expectation of privacy at the border, this expectation is not completely extinguished."[44] The Privacy Commissioner of Canada has investigated CBSA's procedure related to personal devices. Commissioner Therrien pointed out the difficulty in searching personal electronic devices, since the information they contain is extremely personal in nature (implying that they are more than mere goods).[45] By contrast, even the most personal physical searches (pat-downs, strip searches, body cavity searches) convey little about the subject's personal life. Yet CBSA has to balance this difficulty against digitally enabled crime: digital devices can be used for nefarious purposes and thus allow for identification of people with malicious intent.

The issue is somewhat analogous to new screening machines at airports whose first generation effectively revealed a person's body shape to an officer but allowed for ready detection of concealed items a traveller may be carrying, making them controversial when they first appeared in 2010. The software was tweaked to render a person's body shape more generic, and CBSA ran an education campaign so travellers understood how these machines were actually making travel safer. Travellers are given the alternative of a pat-down, but most now opt for the enhanced scanners as they are more efficient and less intrusive. This episode shows that public education and efficiency can go a long way toward travellers' accepting new ways of doing business.

With the adoption of biometric passports, international travel has become increasingly reliant on biometric identification. Digital fingerprint machines at the border submit data to the RCMP. In Canada, NEXUS now uses facial recognition technology to validate members of the pre-approved program. Widely lauded as a "fix-all" solution for identity assurance, biometrics are also implemented at borders because of their convenience and an assumed reduction in wait times. However, bioidentifiers also raise competing perspectives on privacy. On the one hand, biometrics are not so different from current methods of identification: biometrics can actually help protect individuals from identity theft and fraud. On the other hand, biometrics can jeopardize privacy, as their use at the border can blur the distinction between private and public spheres.[46] Storing bioidentifiers also bears new privacy risks: if there is a data breach of documents, government-issued identification can be readily replaced, which is not the case for faces and fingerprints.

The technological disruption of the distinction between public and private spheres also affects perceptions of the border. The use of technology and biometrics to identify and monitor individuals can take place away from the physical border. Biometrics create "a border which is 'everywhere.'"[47] This "delocalization" and change in perception have implications for privacy. CBSA is grappling with the convenience and assurance provided by biometrics while addressing the implications for the separation of public and private spheres, and privacy concerns.

Review

Despite its central importance in Canadian national security and law enforcement, until recently, CBSA has not been subject to independent review or oversight of its activities. This changed with the creation of the National Security and Intelligence Committee of Parliamentarians (NSICOP) in 2017 and the National Security and Intelligence Review Agency (NSIRA) in 2019 (both discussed in chapter fourteen). However, these agencies have a mandate to review only CBSA's national security functions, not the operations of the organization as a whole. In early 2020, the Canadian government reintroduced legislation to create the Public Complaints and Review Commission (PCRC), which will handle public interest reviews and individual complaints for both CBSA and the RCMP for all of their other functions. (This legislation did not pass before the prorogation of Parliament in the fall of 2020, and it is unclear when it may be reintroduced at time of publication.)

The establishment of three new bodies with review powers over CBSA is intended to improve transparency and accountability and enhance public trust and confidence in the agency. At the same time, it will be a major change for an organization not used to independent scrutiny and in many ways operating in the shadows, even as it makes its presence at the border felt. Moreover, so far the government has provided little in the way of resources to assist the organization with making the adjustment or to assist it in complying with the demands of review. Navigating this new series of responsibilities will be a short-term challenge, even if they provide long-term benefits.

Conclusion

Costly post-9/11 security reforms and initiatives notwithstanding, how CBSA would make the border work better or more secure was not immediately apparent when the agency was established. The Standing Senate Committee on National Security and Defence observed in 2005 that "the money [spent on security] is inadequate and a sense of urgency [on behalf of the Government of Canada toward security improvements] is missing."[48] Then-Senator Colin Kenny also voiced concerns about CBSA's organizational culture. In response, CBSA rebranded its image and enhanced the leadership capacity among its front-line force, in the process reinforcing the ethos among its personnel and advancing a culture that respects the history of its legacy agencies.

As noted above, during this period CBSA has had to shift its administrative focus from parochial to global. Gone are the times when a frontline border officer simply had to know the *Immigration Act* or *Customs Act*, for example. That same officer is now responsible for calculating duties and taxes on imported goods or generating paperwork for a foreign visitor. Once-distinct customs, immigration, and food inspection officers became Border Services Officers (BSOs) in 2003. In Canada as elsewhere, many legacy BSOs never intended to join uniformed law *enforcement*: they had joined the legacy customs, immigration, or food inspection agencies to *administer* law as civilian public servants.[49]

In this way, the culture of border officers has shifted significantly: for nearly a century unarmed officers typically administered travellers or goods with the aim of facilitating trade and commerce; now armed BSOs screen travellers and goods for contraband and risk before, at, and beyond the border.[50] Nevertheless, changing how it does business is the only way for CBSA to manage surging and variable movements of travellers and goods crossing borders while confronting a rapidly changing international security environment and stagnating fiscal resources. Shifting challenges, successes, practices, and business models deployed by CBSA provide ample evidence to that effect.

NOTES

The authors acknowledge the SSHRC Borders in Globalization Partnership Grant for support in preparing this chapter.

1 S.C. 2005, c. 38.
2 Kenichi Ohmae, *The Borderless World: Power and Strategy in the Interlinked Economy* (New York: HarperCollins), 1999.
3 Peter Andreas, "A Tale of Two Borders: The US-Mexico and US-Canada Lines after 9/11" (working paper no. 77, University of California-San Diego, La Jolla, California, 2003). Available online: https://cloudfront .escholarship.org/dist/prd/content/qt6d09j0n2/qt6d09j0n2.pdf. Peter Andreas and Thomas J. Biersteker, *The Rebordering of North America: Integration and Exclusion in a New Security Context* (New York: Routledge, 2014).
4 Emmanuel Brunet-Jailly, *Borderlands: Comparing Border Security in North America and Europe* (Ottawa: University of Ottawa Press, 2007).
5 Canada Border Services Agency (CBSA), *2016–17 Departmental Results Report* (2017). Available online: https://www.cbsa-asfc.gc.ca/agency -agence/reports-rapports/dpr-rmr/2016-2017/report-rapport-eng.pdf.

6 Karine Côté-Boucher, "Of 'Old' and 'New' Ways: Generations, Border Control and the Temporality of Security," *Theoretical Criminology* 22, no. 2 (2017): 149–68.

7 Christian Leuprecht, Joel J. Sokolsky, and Thomas Hughes, *North American Strategic Defence in the 21st Century: Security and Sovereignty in an Uncertain World* (New York: Springer, 2018).

8 Government of Canada, "Asylum Claimants Processed by Canada Border Services Agency (CBSA) and Immigration, Refugees and Citizenship Canada (IRCC) Offices, 2011–2016," last modified 16 June 2020, https://www.canada.ca/en/immigration-refugees-citizenship/services/refugees/asylum-claims/processed-claims.html.

9 Government of Canada, *Evaluation of CBSA Arming Initiative* (2017). Available online: https://www.cbsa-asfc.gc.ca/agency-agence/reports-rapports/ae-ve/2017/arm-arme-eng.html.

10 Government of Canada, *Audit of Arming* (2015). Available online: https://www.cbsa-asfc.gc.ca/agency-agence/reports-rapports/ae-ve/2015/arm-eng.html.

11 Office of the Auditor General of Canada (OAG), *Report 5 – Information Technology Investments – Canada Border Services Agency* (2015). Available online: http://www.oag-bvg.gc.ca/internet/English/parl_oag_201504_05_e_40351.html.

12 OAG, *Report 3 – Preventing Corruption in Immigration and Border Services*, 2017. Available online: http://www.oag-bvg.gc.ca/internet/English/parl_oag_201705_03_e_42225.html.

13 OAG, *Preventing Corruption.*

14 Adrian Humphreys, "Canada's Immigration Enforcement System Suffers from 'Orchestrated Mismanagement,' Whistleblower Claims," *National Post*, 10 July 2014, http://nationalpost.com/news/canada/former-border-services-manager-blowing-whistle-on-alleged-orchestrated-mismanagement-of-canadas-immigration-enforcement.

15 Humphreys, "Canada's Immigration Enforcement System."

16 Amy Minsky, "Feds Spend $265 Million Over 5 Years on Controversial Detainee Program: Documents," *Global News*, 24 June 2015, https://globalnews.ca/news/2070097/feds-spend-265m-over-5-years-on-controversial-detainee-program-documents/.

17 Minsky, "Feds Spend $265 Million."

18 Patrick Cain, "Feds Pay Over $22,000 a Day to Jail Non-dangerous Immigration Detainees in Ontario," *Global News*, 31 May 2017, https://globalnews.ca/news/3491853/feds-pay-over-22000-a-day-to-jail-non-dangerous-immigration-detainees-in-ontario/.

19 Cain, "Feds Pay Over $22,000."

20 Minsky, "Feds Spend $265 Million."

21 Standing Senate Committee on National Security and Defence, *Vigilance, Accountability and Security at Canada's Borders* (2015). Available online: https://sencanada.ca/content/sen/committee/412/secd/rep /rep16jun15a-e.pdf .

22 Kathleen Harris, "15,000 on Canada's Deportation List, But Some 'Unco-operative' Countries Won't Take Their Citizens Back," *CBC News*, 20 November 2017, http://www.cbc.ca/news/politics/deportation -uncooperative-countries-1.4405383.

23 Maura Forrest, "CBSA Has Increased Deportations, Though Removals of Irregular Asylum Seekers Remain Low," *National Post*, 7 July 2019, https:// nationalpost.com/news/politics/cbsa-has-increased-deportations-though -removals-of-irregular-asylum-seekers-remain-low.

24 Forrest, "CBSA Has Increased Deportations."

25 Stewart Bell and Andrew Russell, "Canada Is Failing to Deport Criminals. Here's Why It Can Take Years and Sometimes Decades," *Global News*, 20 March 2018, https://globalnews.ca/news/4087292/canada-deporting -dangerous-criminals-ineffective-still-here/.

26 Steven Chase and Shawn McCarthy, "Leaked Internal Report Warns of Canada's Declining World Influence," *Globe and Mail*, 25 March 2017, https:// www.theglobeandmail.com/news/national/leaked-document-says-canadas -world-influence-has-declined/article26556418/; Bruce Mabley, "How to Fix Canada's Broken Foreign Service," *OpenCanada*, 25 April 2016, https://www .opencanada.org/features/how-fix-canadas-broken-foreign-service/.

27 Judy Trinh, "Judge Shortage Forcing Ottawa Courts to Prioritize Criminal Trials Over Civil Cases: Currently 43 Vacancies for Federally Appointed Judges, with 12 More Set to Retire," *CBC News*, 9 January 2017, http:// www.cbc.ca/news/canada/ottawa/federal-judge-shortage-puts-criminal -cases-at-risk-delays-civil-trials-1.3925304.

28 S.C. 2001, c. 27.

29 Kelly W. Sundberg, "Comparing Approaches to Internal Immigration Enforcement: A Study of Canada and Australia" (doctoral thesis, Monash University, 2013).

30 CBSA, *2016–17 Departmental Results Report*.

31 CBSA, *2016–17 Departmental Results Report*.

32 Dan Levin, "A Surge of Migrants Crossing into Quebec Tests Canada's Welcome," *New York Times*, 10 August 2017, https://www.nytimes .com/2017/08/10/world/americas/a-surge-of-migrants-crossing -into-quebec-tests-canadas-welcome.html.

33 R.S.C. 1985, c. 1 (2nd Supp.).

34 *Singh v. Minister of Employment and Immigration*, [1985] 1 S.C.R. 177.

35 At the same time, Justice Wilson explained that any right to a refugee hearing is context specific, i.e., not unconditional.

36 Christian Leuprecht, *The End of the (Roxham) Road: Seeking Coherence on Canada's Border-Migration Compact* (Ottawa: Macdonald-Laurier Institute, 2019). Available online: https://www.macdonaldlaurier.ca/making-sense -of-surging-irregular-border-crossings-new-mli-study/.

37 OAG, *Report 2 – Controlling Exports at the Border* (2015). Available online: http://www.oag-bvg.gc.ca/internet/English/parl_oag_201602_02_e _41059.html.

38 OAG, *Controlling Exports at the Border.*

39 Christian Leuprecht, Andrew Aulthouse, and Olivier Walther, "The Puzzling Resilience of Transnational Organized Crime Networks," *Police Practice & Research* 17, no. 4 (2016): 376–87; Christian Leuprecht, *Smoking Gun: Strategic Containment of Contraband Tobacco and Cigarette Trafficking in Canada* (Ottawa: Macdonald-Laurier Institute, 2016).

40 Royal Canadian Mounted Police, *Canada–United States Integrated Border Enforcement Teams Threat Assessment* (2007); Leuprecht, *Smoking Gun.*

41 Christian Leuprecht and Andrew Aulthouse, "Guns for Hire: Mapping Canada-US Cross-Border Gun Trafficking Networks," *Journal of Criminology, Criminal Justice, Law and Society* 15, no. 3 (2016): 57–74.

42 Todd Hataley and Christian Leuprecht, *Organized Crime beyond the Border* (Ottawa: Macdonald-Laurier Institute, 2013).

43 R.S.C. 1985, c. P-21.

44 Canadian Bar Association (CBA), *Privacy of Canadians at Airports and Borders,* 2017. Available online: https://www.cba.org/CMSPages/GetFile .aspx?guid=04e96564-b5b6-441b-b6de-20b3e0874975

45 CBA, *Privacy of Canadians.*

46 Benjamin J. Muller, "Borders, Bodies and Biometrics: Towards Identity Management," in *Global Surveillance and Policing,* ed. Elia Zureik and Mark Salter (Abingdon: Taylor and Francis, 2013), 95–108.

47 Katja F. Aas, "Getting Ahead of the Game: Border Technologies and the Changing Space of Governance," in *Global Surveillance and Policing,* ed. Elia Zureik and Mark Salter (Abingdon: Taylor and Francis, 2013), 194–214.

48 John Geddes and Charlie Gillis, "How Safe Are We?," *Maclean's,* 15 July 2005, 21.

49 Sundberg, "Comparing Approaches to Internal Immigration Enforcement."

50 Karine Côté-Boucher, "Of 'Old' and 'New' Ways."

9 Public Safety Canada (PSC)

ALEX WILNER

Public Safety Canada (PSC) – formerly Public Safety and Emergency Preparedness Canada (PSEPC) but otherwise legally known as the Department of Public Safety and Emergency Preparedness – was (nominally) created in 2003. Its creation was a direct result of the national security concerns and intelligence considerations that stemmed from al-Qaida's attack on the United States on 9/11. Canada, like the United States with the creation of the Department of Homeland Security in November 2002, sought to establish a federal coordinating body to manage the nexus between intelligence, policy, and action. And yet, in Canada's case, before Public Safety's official establishment under the *Department of Public Safety and Emergency Preparedness Act* of April 2005,[1] many of the organizations embedded within the newly established department had previously existed within the Department of the Solicitor General of Canada, including, most notably, the Correctional Service of Canada (CSC), the Parole Board of Canada (PBC), the Royal Canadian Mounted Police (RCMP), and the Canadian Security Intelligence Service (CSIS). As such, at its inception Public Safety subsumed existing bodies and further expanded the Solicitor General's original base by adding other pre-existing organizations that addressed Canadian border security (the Canada Border Services Agency, CBSA) and infrastructure protection.

Mandate

Under Public Safety's constituting statute, the minister of public safety and emergency preparedness has the powers, duties, and functions in "all matters over which Parliament has jurisdiction – and that have not been assigned by law to another department, board or agency of the Government of Canada – relating to public safety and emergency preparedness."[2]

The *Emergency Management Act* (2007)[3] outlines Public Safety's emergency preparedness responsibilities in greater detail, the core of which are centred on the department's coordinating function to assist provinces and territories in responding to emergencies when requested to do so, and to harmonize the way the federal government responds in kind. To some degree, Public Safety shares this coordinating function with other organizations, namely the National Security and Intelligence Advisor (NSIA) to the Prime Minister, subsumed within the Privy Council Office (PCO, as discussed in chapter one). The logic embedded within Public Safety's very establishment, however, is to "eliminate the potential for confusion" among disparate actors when responding to emergencies in periods of crisis, and to "provide a federal point for coordination" of whole-of-government responses.[4] To these ends, the act calls upon Public Safety to provide leadership in developing and evaluating federal plans, responsibilities, policies, and responses to all types of emergencies (i.e., "all hazards") by promoting a standard and shared approach to emergency preparedness among all relevant partners and by educating and training partners in emergency management and best practices. Public Safety is also tasked with monitoring emergencies, in real time when necessary, and sharing information with relevant parties in order to better coordinate responses at all levels of government, including with provinces, and through them, with municipalities.

Public Safety's statute also instructs the minister to coordinate the activities and priorities of many of the Canadian departments and agencies that fall within the national security (and public safety) rubric.[5] Reporting to the minister, five agencies and three separate review bodies have joined the department within the larger Public Safety portfolio. The former are the CBSA, RCMP, CSIS, the CSC, and the PBC, while the latter are the Civilian Review and Complaints Commission for the RCMP, the Office of the Correctional Investigator, and the RCMP External Review Committee. (Other review bodies, such as the National Security and Intelligence Review Agency, discussed elsewhere in this book, issue reports to the minister. See chapter fourteen.)

More recently, cybersecurity and cybercrime concerns have likewise been added to the mix. Structurally, Public Safety is composed of five branches: Emergency Management and Programs, Community Safety and Countering Crime, Portfolio Affairs and Communications, National and Cyber Security, and Corporate Management.[6] This chapter outlines

Public Safety's many roles, discusses its function and mandate, illustrates the nature of its work, and provides a contextual exploration of the department's core challenges.

Resources

In terms of expenditures, together, the Public Safety portfolio acquires an annual budget of over $6 billion. Public Safety's annual estimated budgets, between 2016–17 and 2018–19, however, were roughly $1.1 billion.[7] Expenditures are captured by the department's four major programs – national security, border strategies, countering crime, and emergency management – and by internal services. The bulk of Public Safety's budget goes first to emergency management programs, which account for over 70 per cent of the department's annual budget, and to countering crime, which absorbs another 20 per cent of the annual budget. By comparison, the national security program consumes less than 3 per cent of the department's spending. The discrepancy between Public Safety's stated priorities and the department's spending is largely attributed to the fact that the department's emergency management program includes the Disaster Financial Assistance Arrangements (DFAA) contribution program, in which Public Safety, on behalf of the federal government, provides financial assistance to provincial and territorial governments in the event of natural and man-made disasters. For instance, in recent years, through DFAA, Public Safety has provided hundreds of millions of dollars annually to various provincial governments to help cover the cost of ice storms (Toronto, Ontario, 2013), train derailments and explosions (Lac-Mégantic, Québec, 2013), flooding (Assiniboine River, Manitoba, 2011), forest fires (Fort McMurray, Alberta, 2016), and other such events.[8] Thus, simply following the money does not provide a clear picture as to Public Safety's core priorities. Nor does the lopsided nature of Public Safety's spending habits tell us how well resourced the department is to fulfil its various duties.

A somewhat better assessment is afforded by tracking Public Safety's actual workforce. While the Public Safety portfolio employs some 60,000 individuals, the department itself in 2017–18 employed about 1,140 full-time employees. The employment breakdown among Public Safety's four major programs is much more evenly spread than the way Public Safety spends its budget: the national security, countering crime, and emergency management programs each have the same number of personnel, or roughly between 220 and 250 employees. That leaves the fourth program, border strategies, with 24 employees, and internal services with 410 employees, as outliers.[9]

Cooperation

Besides its internal coordinating function within the Government of Canada, Public Safety works with a range of other governments and municipalities (including foreign ones), multilateral forums, private sector entities, first responders, communities, and individuals. For purposes of illustration, consider these various examples.

At the international level, falling within its counterterrorism mandate, Public Safety is involved with a number of multilateral organizations, including the G7, the Global Counterterrorism Forum (GCTF), and the Global Coalition against Daesh. The GCTF, established in 2011, is constituted of 29 countries and the European Union, and has a mandate of "reducing the vulnerability of people worldwide to terrorism" by sharing experiences, best practices, and expertise.[10] The organization likewise supports the UN's Global Counter-Terrorism Strategy, working closely with various UN bodies, and focuses heavily on counterterrorism programs in West and East Africa. The Global Coalition, formed in 2014, is a consortium of 75 states and representatives of international organizations (such as NATO and Interpol) dedicated to countering and defeating the Islamic State internationally.[11] In all of these cases, Public Safety both provides Canada's perspective on global counterterrorism initiatives and priorities and coordinates Canada's internal policy and strategic response back home. Likewise, in terms of critical infrastructure protection, Public Safety was instrumental in convening the Critical Five, an international forum first established in 2012 that brought public safety agencies and representatives from the Five Eyes intelligence community – Canada, the United States, the United Kingdom, New Zealand, and Australia – together. The Critical Five helped develop a shared understanding of critical infrastructure across the group, and – building off Canada's long-standing bilateral engagement with the US on critical infrastructure – sought to "strengthen cooperation" and information-sharing between members in addressing common threats.[12] In these various examples, Public Safety represents Canada on the international stage, where global security concerns are addressed and managed.

At the provincial level, Public Safety runs 13 regional offices, organized into five regions across Canada, from the Atlantic Region to British Columbia and the North. Each regional office provides Public Safety with a means to coordinate its work and implement its various programs across Canada with other Canadian jurisdictions and Indigenous communities. Public Safety's work with other Canadian jurisdictions is perhaps best encapsulated in its work on emergency management.

As noted, the 2007 *Emergency Management Act* spells out Public Safety's precise role: "The Minister is responsible for exercising leadership ... by coordinating, among government institutions and in cooperation with the provinces and other entities," including by establishing emergency preparedness "policies, programs, and other measures," establishing "arrangements with each province," and "coordinating the provision of assistance to a province in respect of a provincial emergency."[13] Public Safety's role was further developed in the 2011 emergency management strategy produced in concert between the federal, provincial, and territorial governments: *An Emergency Management Framework for Canada* adopts an "all-hazards approach" to emergency preparedness, covering both natural and man-made disasters. The framework is built around four components: prevention, preparedness, response, and recovery. Public Safety is to provide leadership across all four platforms by establishing national strategies and mechanisms in coordination, communication, and response.[14] It does so, in part, by harmonizing the activities of its regional offices with those led by the emergency management organizations (EMOs) representing each territory and province.

At the community level, Public Safety engages with Canadians in a number of ways. For instance, through its Cross-Cultural Roundtable on Security (CCRS) – a mechanism first proposed in *Securing an Open Society: Canada's National Security Policy* (2004)[15] – the department actively brings together community leaders and representatives of Canada's many cultural and religious communities to discuss issues and concerns that have an "impact on Canada's diverse and pluralistic society."[16] Over the past decade, the CCRS has covered a range of issues in meetings held across Canada, including marine security (Vancouver, 2006); online hate crime (Ottawa, 2017); disinformation (Halifax, 2019); terrorist financing (Ottawa, 2009); border security (Montreal, 2009); cybersecurity (Niagara Falls, 2012); and violent extremism (Halifax, 2014).[17] Summaries of each meeting are then used to inform the minister of public safety and the attorney general of Canada, and provide advice on future programs and policies. To some degree, the CCRS's outreach and collaboration activities have resonated with members of the Public Safety portfolio in building what Public Safety calls "mutual understanding" between the Government of Canada and Canadian communities on national security issues.[18] For illustration, in 2014, Tom Venner, assistant director (policy and strategic partnerships) at CSIS, noted in his public comments to the Standing Senate Committee on National Security and Defence that while CSIS did not have a "legal mandate to engage directly in outreach," it was nonetheless a "strong proponent" of the CCRS. By participating in CCRS events, Venner continued, CSIS had acquired "access to representatives from various communities, creating opportunities to raise awareness and to learn more about some of the communities we serve."[19]

More recently, Public Safety has sought community engagement in addressing the specific concern of radicalization. Through its newly established Canada Centre for Community Engagement and Prevention of Violence – the CCCEPV, but better known as the Canada Centre – Public Safety engages with NGOs and not-for-profit, youth, and community organizations, along with educators and academics (see chapter ten).[20] It does so across Canada (and internationally, too) in order to help society and governments better understand and manage the risks and threat of violent radicalization (or, as it is referred to in the parlance of the times, radicalization leading to violence). The Canada Centre helps guide Canada's application of the *National Strategy on Countering Radicalization to Violence* (published in 2018), helps fund and promote research, including research funded by the CCCEPV's predecessor, the Kanishka Project, and supports programming through the Community Resilience Fund, which offers financial assistance to local groups countering extremism and violence within their communities.[21]

With the private sector, Public Safety's engagement crosses a number of its mandates, including in, most notably, counterproliferation, critical infrastructure protection, and, until 2018, cybersecurity. More specifically, the department works with representatives of all of Canada's 10 critical infrastructure sectors – health, food, finance, water, information/communication technology, safety, energy/utilities, manufacturing, government, and transportation – most of which are largely privately owned.[22] In cybersecurity the department's Canadian Cyber Incident Response Centre (CCIRC) played a central role in coordinating with private sector actors and other organizations (including international counterparts from the Five Eyes community) to collect information on cybersecurity threats, monitor their evolution over time, and coordinate a pan-Canadian response that spanned the public and private sectors. To that effect, the CCIRC provided regular, open-sourced cybersecurity bulletins to Canadians on "potential, imminent, or actual threats, vulnerabilities or incidents affecting Canada's critical infrastructure," along with practical advice on mitigating emerging cybersecurity concerns.[23] In October 2018, following the publication of Canada's *National Cyber Security Strategy*, Canadian cybersecurity leadership was consolidated and transferred to the Communications Security Establishment (CSE).[24] CCIRC – along with the Get Cyber Safe public awareness campaign, Shared Services Canada's Security Operations Centre, and CSE's Information Technology Security Branch – were rolled into the newly established Canadian Centre for Cyber Security.[25] The Cyber Centre has largely assumed Public Safety's role of unifying Canada's cybersecurity strategy and response.

Finally, with the general public, the department engages Canadians regularly with information and social media campaigns and provides free access to relevant and useful information and data. In the latter case, consider Public Safety's Canadian Disaster Database (CDD). It provides detailed information on over 1,000 "natural, technological and conflict events (excluding war)" that have affected Canadians over the past 118 years.[26] The database is useful both to Canadians considering emergency preparedness in their communities and to academics exploring Canada's history of emergency management and response. In the former case – until leadership over cybersecurity awareness was ultimately transferred to CSE – Public Safety provided a number of programs to educate Canadians about cybersecurity through the Get Cyber Safe program. It provided user-friendly information on the types of risks and threats ordinary Canadians face while shopping, gaming, or banking online, downloading and sharing files, or using mobile and Internet of things (IoT) devices. The department also promoted several awareness campaigns, including Data Privacy Day (28 January), Safer Internet Day (6 February), World Backup Day (31 March), Fraud Prevention Month (March), and World Password Day (3 May)."[27] The Get Cyber Safe program was subsumed within CSE's Canada Centre following the 2018 reshuffling of Canada's cybersecurity leadership.

Controversies

Ethics and conduct: Guidance from within

Public Safety's *Departmental Code of Conduct* is at the core of the department's guidelines for establishing a safe and ethical work environment for the department's various employees that meets the high demands of Canada's democratic institutions, principles of law, public accountability, and national service. The document meets Public Safety's requirement to establish an organizational code as stipulated by the *Public Servants Disclosure Protection Act* of 2005.[28] Public Safety's code reads, "As the Department with the mission of building a safe and resilient Canada, we have a special obligation to ensure that everything we do in our work, whether in an administrative, policy, coordination, advisory or other capacity, ultimately contributes to the safety and security of the Canadian public."[29]

By outward appearances, Public Safety affords its code of conduct a great deal of importance. This is perhaps best illustrated by the fact that Public Safety reserves a section of its publicly available "About" page at https://www.publicsafety.gc.ca/cnt/bt/index-en.aspx for a lengthy discussion of its code of conduct. The code is placed front and centre, sandwiched between mentions of the department's core mandate and a description of Canada's Public Safety portfolio and agencies. Any visitor to Public Safety's website would find it difficult to miss. By comparison, neither the RCMP, nor CSIS, nor CBSA highlights a code of conduct on its own "About" or "Home" page. Perhaps they need not to, given that each agency falls within Public Safety's larger portfolio and is thus covered by the department's code of conduct. And yet the discrepancy is nonetheless jarring. For example, while the RCMP does provide relatively straightforward access to a page titled "Results and Respect in the RCMP Workplace" stemming off its "About" webpage at www.rcmp-grc.gc.ca, respect in the workplace is not the same as adherence to a code of conduct. Finding the RCMP's own code was achieved only via a third-party search engine. Without reading too much detail into all of this, perhaps Public Safety's showcasing of its organizational code of conduct is indicative of a public service culture that is missing within these related agencies that largely fulfil front-line policing and intelligence services. Or perhaps, as the concluding section illustrates, the code is a product of the challenging internal dynamics Public Safety has grappled with over the past decade.

Challenges

There are at least four challenges PSC will have to confront in the near future: the department's internal dynamics, its evolving purpose and mandate, the nature and degree of its cooperation and collaboration with others, and its overall size.

First, Public Safety's development and growth has, at times, produced internal challenges. Two episodes stand out. First, in 2009, a report published by the Auditor General of Canada concluded that the department was slow in developing and implementing policies and programs for coordinating all-hazards emergencies, critical infrastructure protection, and cybersecurity. Part of the underlining problem, the report suggests, rested on the department's inability to attract, recruit, and retain qualified employees. Staff shortages, high turnover rates, and retention issues marred the department's work. The problem was especially acute with senior managers: the report found that in 2008–9, nearly 40 per cent of senior manager jobs in emergency management were vacant. Worse, for two straight years, the department had failed to spend one-third of its budget for emergency management, a clear signal, the Auditor General concludes, that "Public Safety Canada has been unable to develop its capacity for emergency management."[30] And second, in April 2014, an employee submitted an anonymous letter to the deputy minister, complaining that Public Safety's National and Cyber Security Branch was suffering from a number of problems, including a toxic work environment. The department responded by appointing Norman Inkster, a former commissioner of the RCMP, to investigate the complaint. In interviews conducted within the department, Inkster uncovered a range of issues: "the vast majority" of interviewees found their work at Public Safety "particularly unpleasant"; fear of reprisals, including public denigration, limited debate and the expression of dissenting views; favouritism, elitism, and a lack of information-sharing marked Public Safety's work culture; and qualified individuals "quit the department to take on less significant ... work just to escape the work atmosphere." The "current situation," Inkster's report concludes, "is, at best, unhealthy."[31]

Second, while Public Safety Canada might have a clear purpose, it also has an ever-expanding mandate. This fact reflects the way emerging concerns, risks, and challenges are approached and tackled by states, with a whole-of-government, and at times a whole-of-society, response. While the whole-of-government mantra may be a tired one, the idea is straightforward and still relevant. Some contemporary public safety and security concerns are so broad, multifaceted, and complex that tackling them effectively requires that different government departments and agencies work closely together toward a common goal and outcome. Coordination across government requires leadership. Public Safety was originally established to provide that very leadership, to guide Canada's response to knotty problems that required the participation and input of various departments and agencies. In the wake of 9/11, then, the department provided guidance in countering international terrorism that necessitated crossing the divide between policing, border security, intelligence, national security, and defence. It was to provide similar guidance in times of emergencies and in critical infrastructure protection, bridging federal, provincial, local, and private sector responses.

The issue is that the types of challenges requiring a coordinated federal government response have evolved over time and expanded in number. Public Safety is busier than ever. For example, its original counterterrorism mandate recently expanded to include countering violent extremism (CVE) – or preventing violent extremism (PVE) – and dealing with foreign fighters and "high-risk" travellers (individuals who have travelled overseas to participate in or facilitate terrorism). Public Safety will also have an important role to play in addressing the issue of prison radicalization, a concern that may grow in the coming years as Canadian foreign fighters and domestic terrorists are incarcerated in greater numbers. As the threat of terrorism evolves, so, too, does Public Safety's mandate.

Public Safety's original focus on critical infrastructure protection likewise expanded to include the cyber domain. Up until the formation of the Cyber Centre, cybersecurity had been an explosive growth industry for the department. In response, its leadership expanded from simply guiding federal departments and agencies to guiding the private sector and ordinary Canadians alike. This expansion in its mandate will continue as new concerns and threats emerge in the coming decade. Who, for instance, is better suited than Public Safety to provide the public–private coordination that the Government of Canada will need in responding to public safety concerns stemming from emerging disruptive technologies like artificial intelligence, quantum computing, the Internet of things, and blockchain, and who else has the appropriate bird's-eye view of how traditional challenges, like weapons proliferation, dual-use technology, and foreign investments, continue to evolve? On several counts, Public Safety has led the way, launching a nationwide counterproliferation dialogue in 2018 for updating Canada's approach to weapons of mass destruction, and a cross-agency policy discussion on blockchain technologies, cryptocurrencies, and national security.[32]

Third, and relatedly, as Public Safety's mandate has evolved and expanded over time, so, too, has the nature of its cooperation and collaboration with others. As noted, its primary function is a coordinating one. The department is meant to help synchronize federal departments, agencies, and partners in their collective management of and responses to national emergencies. By some standards, the department has struggled to do so. For illustration, consider, once again, the Auditor General's 2009 report. It found that Public Safety had not yet "exercised the leadership necessary to coordinate emergency management activities, including critical infrastructure protection." It had failed to "clarify its leadership ... role" for emergency management. And the department's plans for coordinating national responses to emergencies were themselves hazy: they did not properly define the "roles, responsibilities, and capabilities" shared by the community of partners needed for a collective response to emergencies.

The degree to which Public Safety is meant to coordinate federal efforts remains underdefined. The 2009 report captures this tension by describing the way in which Public Safety diverges from the other organizations within, and beyond, the larger Public Safety portfolio. When a federal department or agency, the report notes, has a mandate to respond to a particular emergency and is responsible to act given its legislative powers, that partner "is the subject matter expert." The RCMP, then, takes the primary lead in responding to terrorist attacks, whereas the Public Health Agency of Canada leads in crises involving infectious diseases, and Natural Resources Canada might lead in the event of a major power outage. Public Safety's leadership is called upon in the event emergencies escalate such that the expertise of other departments is needed in responding appropriately. Herein, Public Safety is to coordinate the collective response by ensuring that partners have developed, tested, and shared emergency management plans with all relevant departments and agencies, and, during periods of crisis, by sharing information among relevant partners and various levels of government to ensure a coordinated response. The trouble, the Auditor General clarifies, is that Public Safety "does not assume control over other departments or tell them how to do their jobs." Each partner is distinct in its ability and responsibility. While Public Safety determines the manner in which different responses will be coordinated, each department nevertheless "determines whether it will assist during an emergency, what its role will be, and how it will operate with other federal, provincial, or territorial partners."[33] A certain amount of institutional autonomy exists, then, between the different federal organizations that constitute the Public Safety portfolio, complicating the way in which Public Safety accomplishes its mandate.

And yet, while Public Safety's original function may have largely involved coordinating the practices, policies, and protocols of various federal Canadian agencies and departments, in practice, it increasingly coordinates the activities of a range of other actors as well. Given the very diversity of these actors, coordinating federal-level departments and agencies might be considered the easy part. As illustrated, across its various mandates Public Safety works with other federal departments representing foreign states and international organizations; governments from all levels of Canadian jurisdiction, including Aboriginal governing bodies; NGOs, community activists, and representatives from various cultural or religious associations; first responders; academics and researchers; private sector entities and associations; and ordinary Canadians. To think of Public Safety as solely a coordinator of (federal) government action is shortsighted.

Fourth and finally, given the expansion of its role and function, it is worth exploring Public Safety's overall size. Is the department too big? The answer depends on how you approach the question. From the perspective of scope, the department's function has expanded quite a bit since its creation in 2003, as the two preceding points illustrate. And yet Public Safety's core purpose has remained relatively constrained – that is, to coordinate policy and strategy within and beyond the federal government both inside and outside Canada, and to engage non-government actors, the private sector, communities, and individuals as needed. At issue is that the very notion of public safety captures a lot of territory; Public Safety's role expands accordingly. But in other ways, the department is rather small. Its annual budget of $1.1 billion shrinks considerably if you subtract what it spends on disaster relief through the DFAA ($770 million). By comparison, the RCMP's planned spending for 2017–18 was $2.7 billion. A similar conclusion can be made when it comes to the workforce. Public Safety's 1,140 full-time employees pale in comparison to the RCMP's 29,000.[34] Obviously, these comparisons are between apples and oranges, given the RCMP's role of policing communities across Canada, a resource- and labour-intensive endeavour. Still, Public Safety's actual footprint is small. In sum, while Public Safety's role as Canada's coordinator for public safety has expanded, its core purpose has remained unchanged, and its relative size is small when compared to the agencies it represents with which it works.

Conclusion

As Public Safety closes in on its second decade of existence, it has been forced to adapt to a growing array of national security challenges, from cybersecurity to the threat of foreign fighters. This is on top of its responsibilities for emergency management in an era of increasing numbers of climate-change-fuelled disasters and concerns over the presence of serious organized crime within Canada. Over this period, there have been some successes for Public Safety, such as the establishment of the Canada Centre, but there have also clearly been growing pains that were bound to affect a department created out of an amalgam of agencies and institutions, with a diverse array of responsibilities in the post-9/11 era. Nevertheless, given the fluidity of the international environment, and the growing importance of security issues across a broad range of government priorities, such as foreign investment, trade policy, and digital innovation, the role of Public Safety is not likely to diminish anytime soon.

NOTES

1 S.C. 2005, c. 10.
2 *Department of Public Safety and Emergency Preparedness Act*, s 4.
3 S.C. 2007, c. 15.
4 Office of the Auditor General of Canada (OAG), *2009 Fall Report of the Auditor General of Canada*, chap. 7, "Emergency Management – Public Safety Canada" (2009). Available online: https://www.oag-bvg.gc.ca /internet/English/parl_oag_200911_07_e_33208.html.
5 *Department of Public Safety and Emergency Preparedness Act*, s 5.
6 Public Safety Canada (PSC), *2017–18 Departmental Plan*, 5–6 (2017). Available online: https://www.publicsafety.gc.ca/cnt/rsrcs/pblctns /dprtmntl-pln-2017-18/dprtmntl-pln-2017-18-en.pdf.
7 PSC, *2017–18 Departmental Plan*, 29–31.
8 PSC, *2016–17 Evaluation of the Disaster Financial Assistance Arrangements: Final Report* (2017). Available online: https://www.publicsafety.gc.ca/cnt /rsrcs/pblctns/vltn-dsstr-fnncl-ssstnc-2016-17/vltn-dsstr-fnncl-ssstnc -2016-17-en.pdf. Government of Canada, Office of the Parliamentary Budget Officer, *Estimate of the Average Annual Cost for Disaster Financial Assistance Arrangements Due to Weather Events*, 2016. Available online: http://www.pbo-dpb.gc.ca/web/default/files/Documents/Reports /2016/DFAA/DFAA_EN.pdf
9 PSC, *2017–18 Departmental Plan*, 32–3.
10 Global Counterterrorism Forum: https://www.thegctf.org/.
11 Global Coalition against Daesh: http://theglobalcoalition.org/en/home/.
12 Critical 5, *Forging a Common Understanding for Critical Infrastructure: Shared Narrative* (2014). Available online: https://www.publicsafety.gc.ca/cnt /rsrcs/pblctns/2016-frgng-cmmn-ndrstndng-crtcalnfrstrctr/2016-frgng -cmmn-ndrstndng-crtcalnfrstrctr-en.pdf. See the various resources available at PSC, "Canada-United States Cooperation on Critical Infrastructure," last modified 19 May 2020, https://www.publicsafety.gc.ca/cnt/ntnl-scrt /crtcl-nfrstrctr/cnd-ntd-stts-cprtn-en.aspx.
13 S.C. 2007, c. 15.
14 PSC, *An Emergency Management Framework for Canada: Ministers Responsible for Emergency Management*, 2nd ed. (2011). Available online: https://www .publicsafety.gc.ca/cnt/rsrcs/pblctns/mrgnc-mngmnt-frmwrk/index-en .aspx.
15 Government of Canada, *Securing an Open Society: Canada's National Security Policy* (2004). Available online: https://www.publicsafety.gc.ca/cnt/ntnl -scrt/crss-cltrl-rndtbl/index-en.aspx.
16 PSC, "Connecting with Canadian Communities: Cross-Cultural Roundtable on Security (CCRS)," last modified 13 November 2019,

https://www.publicsafety.gc.ca/cnt/ntnl-scrt/crss-cltrl-rndtbl/index-en
.aspx#a02.

17 PSC, "Cross-Cultural Roundtable on Security: Previous Meeting Summaries,"
last modified 26 February 2018, https://www.publicsafety.gc.ca/cnt/ntnl
-scrt/crss-cltrl-rndtbl/mtng-smmrs-en.aspx.

18 PSC, *2007–08 Departmental Performance Report* (2008), 25. Available online:
https://www.tbs-sct.gc.ca/dpr-rmr/2007-2008/inst/psp/psp-eng.pdf.

19 Senate of Canada, *Proceedings of the Standing Senate Committee on National
Security and Defence Second Session, Forty-first Parliament, 2013–14,* "Issue
11 – Evidence – Meeting of November 17, 2014." Available online: https://
sencanada.ca/en/Content/SEN/Committee/412/secd/11ev-51734-e.

20 PSC, "Canada Centre for Community Engagement and Prevention of
Violence," last modified 6 September 2019, https://www.publicsafety
.gc.ca/cnt/bt/cc/index-en.aspx.

21 PSC, "Canada Centre for Community Engagement and Prevention of
Violence."

22 PSC, "Critical Infrastructure," last modified 19 May 2020, https://www
.publicsafety.gc.ca/cnt/ntnl-scrt/crtcl-nfrstrctr/index-en.aspx.

23 Canadian Centre for Cyber Security (CCCS), "Information & Guidance,"
last modified 3 June 2020, https://cyber.gc.ca/en/information-guidance.

24 PSC, *National Cyber Security Strategy: Canada's Vision for Security and
Prosperity in the Digital Age* (2018). Available online: https://www
.publicsafety.gc.ca/cnt/rsrcs/pblctns/ntnl-cbr-scrt-strtg/ntnl-cbr-scrt
-strtg-en.pdf.

25 CCCS, "About the Cyber Centre," last modified 6 August 2019, https://
www.cyber.gc.ca/en/about-cyber-centre.

26 PSC, "The Canadian Disaster Database," last modified 19 September 2019,
https://www.publicsafety.gc.ca/cnt/rsrcs/cndn-dsstr-dtbs/index-en
.aspx.

27 PSC, "Counting Down the 12 Days of Cyber Safety for 2018," last modified
4 January 2019, https://www.getcybersafe.gc.ca/cnt/blg/pst-20180104
-en.aspx.

28 S.C. 2005, c. 46.

29 PSC, "Public Safety Canada Code of Conduct," last modified 21 January
2019, https://www.publicsafety.gc.ca/cnt/bt/cd-cndct-en.aspx.

30 OAG, *2009 Fall Report,* chap. 7.

31 Vincent Larouche, "Anti-terrorism Branch of Public Safety Ministry
Dysfunctional Prior to Terror Attacks, Top Secret Probe Finds," *Toronto
Star,* 5 September 2015; Vincent Larouche, "Culture de Peur à la Section
Antiterrorisme," *La Press,* 5 September 2015.

32 The author took part in both initiatives. PSC, *Strengthening Canada's
Counter-proliferation Framework* (2018). Available online: https://www

.publicsafety.gc.ca/cnt/rsrcs/pblctns/2018-strngthnng-cntr-prlfrtn
-frmwrk/2018-strngthnng-cntr-prlfrtn-frmwrk-en.pdf. Alex Wilner,
"Why Canada's Counter-proliferation Framework Needs an Update,"
Hill Times, 18 March 2019; PSC, Blockchain and National Security
Conference, Ottawa, Canada, October 2018.

33 OAG, *2009 Fall Report*, chap. 7.

34 Royal Canadian Mounted Police, *2016–17 Report on Plans and Priorities*
(2016), 13. Available online: http://www.rcmp-grc.gc.ca/wam/media
/748/original/35576926127499960eda4474d8fb359c.pdf.

10 The Canada Centre and Countering Violent Extremism

BRETT KUBICEK AND MICHAEL KING

Housed within the Department of Public Safety Canada, the Canada Centre for Community Engagement and Prevention of Violence (the Canada Centre) is the newest federal organization to join Canada's national security community. Created to lead, support, and coordinate efforts to counter violent extremism (CVE), the Canada Centre is the product of prior investments in research, lessons learned from allied countries, and a recognition that prevention measures can help mitigate the threat of terrorism.

Many countries around the world have sought to complement their traditional security and intelligence responses to terrorism with measures to prevent radicalization to violence, as well as interventions for individuals who are radicalized, all under various labels such as CVE, preventing violent extremism (PVE), and terrorism prevention. And over the last 15 years, Canada has been involved in a number of CVE efforts in areas of policy, research, and evaluation, as well as in programming and operational settings. While financial investment over this period has been limited in contrast to a number of allied countries, Canadian officials, CVE practitioners, and subject matter experts have been regularly involved in dialogue with their international counterparts as the field has developed. Drawing on this experience, as well as the growing body of practice and research domestically, the federal government established the Canada Centre, formally launched in June 2017, to significantly expand support and coordination of Canada's various CVE efforts. It brings together policy development and research to better understand how radicalization to violence occurs and how best to counter it, with investments in programming – often at the local level as well as online – along with a strong emphasis on monitoring and evaluation.

This chapter provides a brief survey of some influential developments in the field of CVE, both globally and locally, that laid the foundations for the creation of the Canada Centre and continue to inform the design and implementation of CVE in Canada. This chapter also outlines the policy, research, and programming activities of the Canada Centre, as well as how Canada has operationalized CVE.

Global Precursors: Events, Responses, Learning, and Adaptation

The creation of the Canada Centre, as well as the various CVE activities that preceded and followed it, should be seen in the context of events, responses, and lessons learned in countries abroad, especially countries closely aligned with Canada that have similar societal contexts.

As a member of the Five Eyes, the G7, the Global Counterterrorism Forum (GCTF), and other international partnerships aimed at collaborating on shared security and public safety interests, Canada has been privy to the CVE efforts of other countries, including their successes and failures, as well as their efforts to improve and adapt.[1] Failures have tended to receive the most attention, and these lessons have informed the design and work of the Canada Centre. This chapter will review some of these challenges, yet the emphasis will be on the progress achieved throughout the field of CVE in Canada.

The International Context

In the field of national security, a major shift toward terrorism prevention occurred in the mid-2000s, following incidents such as the 2004 train bombings in Madrid, the 2004 murder of film director Theo van Gogh in Amsterdam, and the 2005 "7/7" attacks in London, as well as foiled plots like the "Toronto 18" case in 2006. In this context, Western countries began to expand their counterterrorism tactics to include "softer" approaches.[2] At its core, the shift was driven by a need to better understand and address "homegrown" violent extremism, as an increasing proportion of violent extremists were born and raised in the very country they sought to attack, in contrast to prior high-profile terrorist incidents that involved foreign actors. And so began the search for warning signs within domestic social networks and for ways of intervening prior to attack.

In Europe, the very first CVE programs were "exit" programs designed to help people leave violent far-right extremist movements. As CVE programs multiplied, some programs were built on broad concepts of resilience, borrowing from other areas of social policy. The UK is often recognized as the first Western country to establish a *comprehensive* CVE program with the launch of Prevent, which first appeared as part of their 2006 counterterrorism strategy, known as CONTEST.[3] However, UK's Prevent is also sometimes described as an example of how CVE efforts can go wrong, yield unintended negative consequences, and draw public criticism.

Meanwhile, the United States focused its initial CVE efforts abroad through international programming led by the State Department and the US Agency for International Development (USAID). A part of these efforts was the Global Futures Forum (GFF), a US-led multinational, multidisciplinary initiative to support an (unclassified) international dialogue for the intelligence community, involving a wide range of non-government experts and practitioners, to identify and assess emerging transnational threats. The GFF featured work streams on CVE-related issues.[4]

Unlike Europe and the UK, the US invested relatively little domestically in CVE programming until 2011, when it issued its White House strategy, *Empowering Local Partners to Prevent Violent Extremism in the United States*. This strategy led to (1) the creation of a CVE task force with representatives from the four lead domestic national security federal agencies (the Department of Homeland Security [DHS], Department of Justice, FBI, and National Counterterrorism Centre); (2) CVE pilot programs in three cities; and (3) launching the GCTF, a new international partnership to bridge policy and program efforts.[5] In 2016, DHS launched a first national granting program to invest in local terrorism prevention initiatives.

These international CVE efforts provided Canada with many lessons to draw upon for developing its own CVE strategy. The first of such lessons was the danger of haste-making. Indeed, many CVE programs were built quickly, driven by a sense of urgency, to the detriment of program design. As a result, these programs rarely produced any clear impact on the specific factors, needs, and vulnerabilities purported to increase the risk of violent extremism.

Second, where initiatives were found to be effective, there were few ways to share best practices or lessons learned. A regular finding from researchers studying the experiences of CVE practitioners is that it can be a niche endeavour, where professionals are working largely in isolation, with few colleagues to compare lessons with or reach out to for help. This situation would prove to be especially germane to Canada. Indeed, because terrorism is a smaller issue in Canada than in its allied countries, its counterterrorism community – and CVE community – is correspondingly small.

Third, the American experience demonstrated the value of involving researchers to gather evidence in support of policy and practice. The

National Institute of Justice (NIJ) within the Department of Justice, for example, is a world leader in supporting evaluations of crime prevention programs. Similarly, the social and behavioural science teams at DHS Science and Technology have extensive experience in aggregating evidence to build intervention models and guidelines. These exemplify the culture of evidence in American national security, which has translated into robust evaluation efforts of the White House CVE strategy pilot programs.[6]

Fourth is the importance of program design and transparency, which became clear following the perceived failures of the UK's Prevent program. Initial Prevent efforts targeted specific communities with the hope of fostering better relationships with police, which in turn were expected to yield increased cooperation from communities to identify and report early signs of radicalization to violence. However, researchers and critics noted negative unintended consequences of Prevent's first iteration, such as exacerbating distrust and creating new grievances in the course of labelling whole communities as "at risk." A government review acknowledged these issues, stating that Prevent had actually funded the very extremist organizations Prevent should have been countering in a failed attempt to leverage its perceived credibility.[7] Part of the problem, it seemed, was that some Prevent activities were based on intuitive borrowing of practices from other fields of prevention and community safety and well-being, rather than on clearly defining goals specific to countering radicalization to violence, along with the actors, activities, and relationships needed to achieve them.

Since the first iteration of Prevent, academics and researchers have become increasingly involved in independently assessing whether its front-line programs – including the intervention program Channel – are achieving their stated goals. The UK government has published more information about Prevent, and, at a minimum, the public discourse around these programs now includes much more evidence to inform debate and analysis, including the voices of front-line intervention practitioners. In tandem, the purpose and design of programs like Channel and the more community-focused efforts at education and capacity-building have increasingly become more amenable to evaluation.

Canadian Precursors to the Canada Centre

Policy and Operational Responses

Concurrent with these international developments were efforts in Canada to revise the approach to national security. A prominent example was *Securing an Open Society*, a federal action plan published in 2004 aimed at taking a more holistic approach to safety and security that included an increased involvement of community partners.[8] This was followed by the creation, in 2005, of the Cross-Cultural Roundtable on Security (CCRS), designed to increase dialogue about national security between the federal government and prominent figures from ethno-cultural communities across Canada. Over time, the CCRS regularly discussed CVE, in part to address how best to engage communities on issues of security.

In parallel, a number of police services were working to adapt community-policing principles to engage communities on national security issues, including prevention. The RCMP's National Security Community Outreach Program was a leader in this area, and was directed in 2008 by the Canadian Association of Chiefs of Police to study the UK's Prevent model in order to inform a counter-radicalization framework for Canada.[9] Collaboration with American partners on this issue increased, with a new work stream under the Beyond the Border initiative[10] entitled the Canada–US Bilateral Working Group on CVE.[11] Moreover, Canada was invited to join the European Policy Planners Network on Countering Radicalisation and Polarisation as an observer, and later as a full member (forcing the network to change its name). The Policy Planners Network (PPN) provided a regular opportunity for CVE practitioners and policymakers to learn from each other and develop relationships with non-government experts and activists.[12]

In early 2012, the Government of Canada published its first counterterrorism (CT) strategy, entitled *Building Resilience against Terrorism: Canada's Counter-terrorism Strategy*. The strategy outlined the four elements that underpinned the government's CT activities: Prevent, Detect, Deny, and Respond. The Prevent element was the government's first publicly communicated intent to "prevent individuals from turning to terrorism." In line with CVE efforts in other countries, the strategy promised to address "the factors that may motivate individuals to engage in terrorist activities, and building resilience to withstand violent extremist ideologies and challenge those who espouse them."[13]

Canada also started investing in research on CVE. For example, Defence Research and Development Canada focused on psychosocial and behavioural aspects of public safety and security, including radicalization to violence and building community resilience. To address early interest from domestic policy and operational circles on developing CVE in Canada, much of the work came through participation in international initiatives such as the GFF and PPN. This led to incorporating Canada as the fifth country into a major study led by the UK think tank Demos on violent versus non-violent radicalization.[14]

Separately, CVE components were brought in to the Metropolis Project Canada, an initiative led by Citizenship and Immigration Canada (now Immigration, Refugees and Citizenship Canada) in partnership with the Social Sciences and Humanities Research Council.[15] While the core of Metropolis was policy-relevant research on migration, diversity, and integration, in the 2007–12 phase, a research stream was added on justice, policing, and security, with Public Safety Canada acting as government lead. Metropolis served as a venue for Public Safety to convene ongoing, sometimes difficult dialogue among non-traditional partners, often on CVE-related topics. Events brought together representatives from sectors like policing and security with community-serving organizations, health and social service practitioners, and researchers from domains well outside those normally involved with departments like Public Safety, but relevant to CVE, including its impact on communities. A notable result is the 2014 edited volume *Religious Radicalization and Securitization in Canada and Beyond*, which was conceived through exploratory workshops organized during the annual Metropolis conference.[16]

Building Research Capacity: The Kanishka Project Research Initiative

Canada's first program dedicated to terrorism and CVE research was a direct result of the 2006–10 Commission of Inquiry into the Investigation of the Bombing of Air India Flight 182. The commission identified a significant need for evidence in order to better understand terrorism and to support counterterrorism efforts in Canada, which in turn underscored the need to build a community of researchers outside government who could inform and challenge policy and practice. In this context, the Air India Victims' Families Association called for creation of a memorial initiative to address this research gap, and the government of the time agreed.

Started in 2011, the Kanishka Project research initiative[17] was a five-year, $10-million investment in terrorism-focused research funded by the Government of Canada. Through Kanishka, the federal government funded policy-relevant projects that aimed to better understand terrorism in the Canadian context, how it had changed over time, and how policies and programs could best counter terrorism and violent extremism in Canada. The Kanishka Project funded close to 70 projects and contributed to hosting a range of events bringing together officials, researchers, practitioners, and community members to share knowledge on counterterrorism and building a sustainable community of practice.[18]

For example, the Kanishka Project funded the first academic survey of far-right violent extremism in Canada,[19] which continues to shape policy and research as well as public discourse. It also funded a study of Western foreign terrorist fighters travelling to Syria and Iraq that has been regularly consulted by international policymakers and established new methodologies for using social media to better understand individuals and networks involved in violent extremism.[20] Support was also given to several projects testing online counter-narrative campaigns and assessing the effectiveness of counter-speech and social media tools.[21] Lastly, the Kanishka Project funded the development of the Canadian Network for Research on Terrorism, Security and Society (TSAS),[22] which built on relationships and lessons learned from the Metropolis Project and whose experts are regularly called upon to brief government agencies.

Much of the current CVE research and programming is led by experts who participated in Kanishka-funded projects, such as the Research and Action on Social Polarization (RASP) team from Montreal, with RASP members now leading the Canadian Practitioners Network for the Prevention of Radicalization and Extremist Violence, a network of front-line health and social service professionals who work on CVE. Lastly, the Kanishka Project, with its funding model and its network of academics and practitioners, formed the basis for building the Canada Centre.

First Programs to Conduct CVE

While reports of CVE initiatives arose as early as 2009,[23] it was not until 2015 that fully fledged programs emerged in Canada. Some of the first programs to offer CVE interventions were Calgary's ReDirect (2015), the Centre for the Prevention of Radicalization Leading to Violence in Montreal (2015), the RASP team in Montreal (2015), and FOCUS Toronto (2017).

Creating the Canada Centre

It is in the context of the following three concurrent factors that the Government of Canada sought to take an active role to counter radicalization to violence:

- Globally: many Western countries had instituted government-led CVE programs, with progressively better approaches and designs.
- Historically: the Kanishka Project had helped build a community of scholars and practitioners.
- Locally: several Canadian CVE programs had emerged.

Finally, another important factor in the development of CVE in Canada was the emergence of political will. More specifically, during the 2015 election, all three national parties committed to either extend the Kanishka Project (Conservative Party of Canada) or expand it to prioritize community outreach and counter-radicalization (New Democratic Party and Liberal Party of Canada).[24] After winning the election, Prime Minister Justin Trudeau mandated the minister of public safety to establish the Office of the Community Outreach and Counter-radicalization Coordinator.[25]

Resources

Work to set up the office started in 2016. That year, the federal budget assigned $35 million over five years to create the office and administer the Community Resilience Fund (CRF), a funding vehicle for research and programming aimed at better understanding and countering radicalization to violence.[26] While setting up, the office changed its name to the Canada Centre for Community Engagement and Prevention of Violence, now commonly referred to as the Canada Centre.

The establishment of the Canada Centre has progressed in stages and is based on an integrated approach to policy, research, and program funding. Through the CRF, the centre allocated $1.2 million for research projects and programming in its first fiscal year of activity, and $2.4 million in the second fiscal year. It planned $4.4 and $7 million for 2018–19 and 2019–20, respectively. The federal budget allotted an ongoing $10 million per year to the Canada Centre after the first five years, of which $7 million is to be allocated through the CRF for existing and new research and programming projects.[27]

The CRF is a cornerstone of the Canada Centre because funding is the main mechanism that enables the Government of Canada to support organizations that conduct CVE programming and research. The Canada Centre itself does not conduct CVE programming, nor is it involved in specific cases or case management, but it plays an active role in providing help to front-line practitioners and researchers, such as through connections to relevant resources and potential partners, as well as through providing expert guidance.

Early Days

The Canada Centre was officially launched in June 2017 with early emphasis on investing in front-line CVE initiatives. While there was limited media attention to the launch, there was some focus on the lack of a "coordinator,"[28] eventually clarified to be a "special adviser" to the minister of public safety, a politically appointed position to nominally head the Canada Centre, as alluded to in the original name (i.e., the Office of the Community Outreach and Counter-radicalization *Coordinator*). Nonetheless, from the outset, core operations had been led by Public Safety staff assigned to the Canada Centre, and they carried on the initial work, including national consultations to support the creation of a national strategy. The results of these consultations were published in early 2018, and the *National Strategy on Countering Radicalization to Violence* was released in December 2018. In February 2019, the government announced the launch of a National Expert Committee on Countering Radicalization to Violence, made up of 10 individuals with diverse expertise and experience – relevant to various aspects of CVE, from policing and health, to issues of preventing hate and violence, to impact on children and communities – who are to fulfil the role of providing independent advice to the minister and help ensure that the Canada Centre meets the objectives of the national strategy.

At the time of writing, the Canada Centre counts approximately 15 full-time employees, a number that can vary with hosting staff seconded from other agencies. Much of the staff is dedicated to policy work, and some dedicated to research, while staff in the Programs Branch at Public Safety Canada support Community Resilience Fund recipients, including regional staff in different parts of the country.

Mission

The Canada Centre was designed to develop and provide expertise in understanding radicalization to violence and the most effective ways to counter it, across all forms of ideologically motivated violent extremism in Canada. Its approach, informed by public health and crime prevention, includes early prevention, intervention, and reintegration.

Early prevention efforts are aimed at the general population and have the objective of preventing violent radicalization from occurring in the first place. This includes raising awareness about violent extremism to enable front-line workers, such as police officers and social workers, to better distinguish it from simply holding radical or objectionable views. Similarly, awareness raising can help peers and family members, as well as the public and media, better recognize meaningful signs of behaviour change of individuals potentially at risk, and avoid needlessly raising fear. Early prevention can also include increasing critical thinking skills and digital literacy so that people are less vulnerable to the manipulation and influence of terrorist and violent extremist messaging online.

Interventions are for individuals who are in the process of radicalizing to violence, and aim to redirect them away from a path that, if continued, might lead to terrorist activity. While each intervention program is slightly different, their interventions are often very similar. These interventions are led by health or social service professionals who address the needs and vulnerabilities of the individual. Because programs have access to professionals from various disciplines, and depending on the needs and vulnerabilities of the individual, interventions can involve professionals from the health sector, employment, housing, law, mental health, education, or child welfare services. For complex cases, multiple professionals from various disciplines may come together to coordinate an intervention. This multidisciplinary approach generally works to help individuals disengage from violent ideologies without directly challenging the ideology. That said, violent ideologies can be directly addressed when requested by the individual, or when deemed necessary by the practitioner leading the intervention. In these cases, credible mentors, religious experts, or former extremists can be called upon to assist with the ideological component of the intervention. This multidisciplinary approach to CVE interventions resembles that of the Channel program, for which the UK government has reported high success rates.[29]

Reintegration efforts are aimed at individuals who have become directly involved in ideologically, religiously, or politically motivated violence. These can include individuals on terrorism peace bonds or parole conditions, or returning from conflict zones. Reintegration work generally involves the same professionals and approach involved in CVE intervention, but often carries the additional complexity of navigating the criminal justice system. Reintegration, which also includes initiatives to help individuals exit from violent extremist groups, is another way of mitigating the potential threat posed by these individuals.

In sum, the Canada Centre's mission is to support and coordinate efforts across all three types of CVE activities: early prevention, intervention, and reintegration. This mission is pursued through four types of activities: policy guidance, promoting collaboration, research support, and programming.

Policy Guidance

Given its recent creation, much of the Canada Centre's policy work is still early in progress. It did carry out its first major policy achievement by publishing Canada's *National Strategy on Countering Radicalization to Violence*.[30] The strategy defines the government's approach to prevent and counter radicalization to violence and sets out the first order of priorities to counter violent extremism in Canada: building, sharing, and using knowledge; addressing radicalization to violence in the online space; and supporting interventions. A notable area of focus for the Canada Centre's policy work is providing support for international dialogue on addressing violent extremist and terrorist use of the internet, including through international fora such as the Five Country Ministerial and the G7, as well as support for the Christchurch Call to Eliminate Terrorist and Violent Extremist Content Online.

Promoting Coordination and Collaboration

A large part of the work done by staff at the Canada Centre is to help various initiatives across Canada build capacity. Mirroring successful practices in Europe, the Canada Centre helps front-line CVE practitioners connect with each other and with researchers, academics, and potential sources of funding. A notable example is one of the first initiatives funded through the CRF: the Canadian Practitioners Network for Prevention of Radicalization and Extremist Violence (CPN-PREV), a network to foster collaboration and support among CVE practitioners and develop excellence in countering violent radicalization.[31] The Canada Centre also organizes events to share best practices about assessment, case management, prevention, intervention, and addressing violent extremism online, as well as measurement and evaluation.

Funding, Planning, and Coordinating Research

The Canada Centre works closely with a number of domestic and international partners on developing the evidence base to better understand radicalization to violence and how best to counter it.[32] Also, through the Community Resilience Fund, the Canada Centre supports research addressing the needs of practitioners, such as building better tools to evaluate CVE programs, understanding the role of extremist content online in violent radicalization,[33] and identifying the scope of violent extremist movements in parts of Canada.[34] To do so, the Canada Centre maintains strong working relationships with initiatives like TSAS, for whom the Canada Centre acts as the lead representative of the federal government.

Supporting Programs

A significant role of the Community Resilience Fund is to invest in programs aimed at countering radicalization to violence in Canada. Some programs focus on early intervention, implementing activities in the hope of inoculating individuals against violent extremism. Other programs deliver interventions: tailored health and social services to individuals to stop, and reverse if possible, their radicalization toward violence.

Funding is a crucial type of support offered to these programs. However, it is not the only type. The Canada Centre helps facilitate training and connects practitioners to useful research and CVE tools. In addition, through organizing events and workshops, the Canada Centre facilitates exchanges between practitioners, fostering learning and the development of best practices.

Cooperation

Given its mission, the Canada Centre collaborates with federal departments and agencies whose mandates include, or are relevant to, tackling violent extremism. These include the Canadian Security Intelligence Service (CSIS), the Royal Canadian Mounted Police (RCMP), Global Affairs Canada (GAC), Justice Canada, Correctional Service Canada (CSC), Women and Gender Equality Canada, Canadian Heritage, Statistics Canada, Defence Research and Development Canada, the Privy Council Office (PCO), and Innovation, Science and Economic Development Canada (ISED), as well as Immigration, Refugees and Citizenship Canada (IRCC). For example, there exists an increasing collaboration between the Canada Centre and the Department of Canadian Heritage in areas that overlap with CVE, such as new initiatives to prevent and counter hate and disinformation. At the time of writing, Canadian Heritage had prioritized efforts to address online disinformation and hate speech though *Canada's Anti-racism Strategy 2019–2022*.[35] Part of this strategy confers $0.9 million to the Canada Centre to support the development of a national framework and evidence-based guidelines to respond to hate crimes, hate incidents, and hate speech.

The Canada Centre also relies on other government departments to help select which proposals submitted to the CRF should be considered for funding, as well as provide expert feedback to funding recipients, coordinate participation in their projects, and connect stakeholders to new networks and resources. For this kind of collaboration, the Canada Centre has established both working and senior-level committees to bring together a cross-section of stakeholders, to better inform and coordinate work on safety, security, social cohesion, and community resilience and well-being, that cuts across federal departments and agencies.

For specific policy priorities such as addressing radicalization to violence in the online space, the Canada Centre similarly benefits from a partnership approach. In some cases, the Canada Centre is the lead for the Government of Canada, but draws on partners from organizations like ISED, the RCMP, and GAC for support, as well as partners from policy centres at Public Safety that cover areas like community safety and national security. These include the Christchurch Call, Global Internet Forum to Counter Terrorism, and Five Country Ministerial working groups devoted to engaging with digital industry for online CVE. In other cases, the Canada Centre provides an important supporting role for lead departments like ISED and GAC in the context of broader initiatives that include elements related to online CVE, such as the Internet & Jurisdiction Policy Network and the Organisation for Economic Co-operation and Development (ISED lead), and the Freedom Online Coalition (GAC lead).

The Challenge Ahead

A number of challenges have already been suggested throughout this chapter, not least the ways in which sensitive issues involving terrorism and counterterrorism can lead to fear and social polarization. Other challenges for the Canada Centre include keeping up with the evolving nature of violent extremism, its different forms, and how it can affect different segments of Canadian populations differently. That said, one of the immediate challenges facing the Canada Centre and CVE in Canada, as well as close counterparts internationally, is measuring the effectiveness of CVE initiatives.

Efficacy and Evaluation

Assessing the impact of CVE programs is widely acknowledged as a conundrum. While methodological recommendations for such assessments are plentiful, there have been few successful applications. Moreover, there is currently limited consensus on which metrics should be used to measure the desired outcomes for CVE, such as reducing risk and increasing protective factors for those potentially or already involved in violent extremism.[36] These measurement challenges increase the urgency to verify the efficacy of the burgeoning number of CVE programs in Canada.

It is important to note, however, that while progress is being made toward measuring outcomes,[37] other types of evaluation are taking place. These focus on process, measuring the implementation and operation of CVE programs and assessing whether activities align with objectives. These process evaluations are now central to a growing number of CVE programs in Canada.

For example, researchers have touted Canada for using "situation tables," a multidisciplinary approach to clients with complex health and social needs, for CVE.[38] While there is some evidence that situation tables can reduce crime in complex cases, their effectiveness is largely assumed, and not yet proven, for countering violent extremism.[39] Consequently, this assumption is the focus of one of the first CRF-funded research projects. Led by Ryerson University, the study examines the performance of situation tables in Toronto, alongside other program models, to counter radicalization to violence in Canada.

CVE as a whole, however, will probably never be deemed effective or not. That is because CVE, as is the case with other more established fields of prevention, encompasses different activities that have different objectives.[40] Rather, evidence is emerging for the effectiveness of specific CVE techniques for specific populations in specific contexts.[41] For example, in the online context, peer-to-peer messaging techniques have shown promise.[42] For in-person interventions, tailored multidisciplinary case management has demonstrated effectiveness.[43]

Now that CVE research and programs have been established, the Canada Centre is poised to accelerate the use of measurement and evaluation, and support the development of the field as it progresses from early emphasis on process evaluation toward assessing the impact on risk and protective factors. Assessing effectiveness not only aligns CVE with the evidence-based policy development approach advocated by the Government of Canada, but more importantly, also helps inform front-line practitioners about promising practices relevant to their local context and anticipate the potential harms that may be incurred by well-intentioned CVE programs.

Conclusion

At the time of writing this chapter, the Canada Centre was in the middle of its first year at full funding capacity, as well as in the midst of putting in place new funding agreements from its second open call for proposals. Considering both the global and domestic precursors to CVE in Canada, the Canada Centre began its work from a position of strength, incorporating best practices, building relationships with actors already well established in the field, and focusing its resources on priority gaps and building new partnerships to help address them. This chapter provides only a limited review of the field of CVE and the Canada Centre's place in it. It is intended to provide an overview of some of the core principles shaping the work of the Canada Centre: the importance of bridging policy and practice, design and transparency, and evidence and evaluation.

NOTES

The views expressed in this chapter are those of the authors and do not necessarily reflect those of Public Safety Canada or the Government of Canada.

1 Peter Romaniuk, *Does CVE Work? Lessons Learned from the Global Effort to Counter Violent Extremism* (Goshen, IN: Global Center on Cooperative Security, 2015). Available online: https://www.globalcenter.org /publications/does-cve-work-lessons-learned-from-the-global-effort -to-counter-violent-extremism/.
2 Shandon Harris-Hogan, Kate Barrelle, and Andrew Zammit, "What Is Countering Violent Extremism? Exploring CVE Policy and Practice in Australia," *Behavioral Sciences of Terrorism and Political Aggression* 8, no. 1 (2016): 6–24.
3 Secretary of State for the Home Department, *Countering International Terrorism: The United Kingdom's Strategy* (2005). Available online: https:// assets.publishing.service.gov.uk/government/uploads/system/uploads /attachment_data/file/272320/6888.pdf.
4 See, e.g., S. Rajaratnam School of International Studies, *Global Futures Forum General Meeting 2010* (2010). Available online: https://www.rsis .edu.sg/wp-content/uploads/2014/07/ER100912_Global_Futures _Forum_General_Meeting_2010.pdf.
5 For more, see Countering Violent Extremism Task Force, "What Is CVE?," accessed 3 August 2020, https://www.dhs.gov/cve/what-is-cve, and https://www.thegctf.org/.
6 See, e.g., National Academies of Sciences, Engineering, and Medicine, *Countering Violent Extremism through Public Health Practice: Proceedings of a Workshop* (2017). Available online: http://nationalacademies.org/hmd /reports/2017/countering-violent-extremism-through-public-health -practice.aspx.
7 Secretary of State for the Home Department, *Prevent Strategy*, 2011, 1. Available online: https://assets.publishing.service.gov.uk/government/uploads /system/uploads/attachment_data/file/97976/prevent-strategy-review.pdf.
8 See Government of Canada, *Securing an Open Society: Canada's National Security Policy* (2004). Available online: http://publications.gc.ca/collections /Collection/CP22-77-2004E.pdf.

9 CACP Prevention of Radicalization Study Group, *Building Community Resilience to Violent Ideologies: A Discussion Paper* (Ottawa: CACP, 2009).

10 The Beyond the Border initiative was a series of agreements between 2011 and 2016 that sought to improve security cooperation and coordination at the border between the two countries, while expediting trade and travel. For more on Beyond the Border, see Public Safety Canada, "Beyond the Border: A Shared Vision for Perimeter Security and Economic Competitiveness," last modified 15 February 2018, https://www .publicsafety.gc.ca/cnt/brdr-strtgs/bynd-th-brdr/index-en.aspx.

11 See, e.g., Public Safety Canada (PSC), *2014–15 Report on the Beyond the Border Action Plan Horizontal Initiative*, "Initiative 4 (Countering Violent Extremism)" (2015), 5. Available online: https://www.publicsafety.gc.ca /cnt/rsrcs/pblctns/dprtmntl-prfrmnc-rprt-2014-15/btb/index-en.aspx.

12 See Institute for Strategic Dialogue, "Policy Planners Network," accessed 3 August 2020, https://www.isdglobal.org/programmes/policy -government-advisory/policy-planners-network/.

13 Government of Canada, *Building Resilience against Terrorism: Canada's Counterterrorism Strategy* (2012). Available online: https://www.publicsafety.gc.ca /cnt/rsrcs/pblctns/rslnc-gnst-trrrsm/rslnc-gnst-trrrsm-eng.pdf.

14 Jamie Bartlett, Jonathan Birdwell, and Michael King, *The Edge of Violence: A Radical Approach to Extremism* (London, UK: Demos, 2010).

15 For more on Metropolis Canada, see https://web.archive.org/web /20181219002508/https://canada.metropolis.net/policypriority/justice _e.html.

16 Paul Bramadat and Lorne Dawson, eds., *Religious Radicalization and Securitization in Canada and Beyond* (Toronto: University of Toronto Press, 2014).

17 The Kanishka Project is named after the Air India Flight 182 plane, which was bombed on 23 June 1985, killing 329 people, most of them Canadians, in the worst act of terrorism in Canadian history. Kanishka was the name given to the aircraft.

18 For more, see PSC, *2015–16 Evaluation of the Kanishka Project Research Initiatives* (2016). Available online: https://www.publicsafety.gc.ca/cnt /rsrcs/pblctns/vltn-knshk-2015-16/index-en.aspx.

19 Barbara Perry and Ryan Scrivens, "Uneasy Alliances: A Look at the Right-Wing Extremist Movement in Canada," *Studies in Conflict & Terrorism* 39, no. 9 (2016): 819–41.

20 Joseph A. Carter, Shiraz Maher, and Peter R. Neumann, *#Greenbirds: Measuring Importance and Influence in Syrian Foreign Fighter Networks* (London, UK: International Centre for the Study of Radicalisation and Political Violence, 2014). Available online: https://preventviolentextremism .info/sites/default/files/%23Greenbirds-%20Measuring%20Importance%20

and%20Influence%20in%20Syrian%20Foreign%20Fighter%20Networks
.pdf.

21 See, e.g., PSC, "Considerations for Successful Counterspeech," last
modified 8 September 2016, https://www.publicsafety.gc.ca/cnt/ntnl
-scrt/cntr-trrrsm/r-nd-flght-182/knshk/ctlg/dtls-en.aspx?i=119.

22 See www.tsas.ca.

23 For example: Stewart Bell, "Toronto Mosque Offers 'Detox' for Extremists,"
National Post, 11 February 2009.

24 See Liberal Party of Canada, "Bill C-51," 2015, accessible at https://web
.archive.org/web/20151110225858/http://www.liberal.ca/realchange
/bill-c-51/.

25 Justin Trudeau, "Minister of Public Safety and Emergency Preparedness
Mandate Letter," 12 November 2015, https://pm.gc.ca/en/mandate
-letters/2015/11/12/archived-minister-public-safety-and-emergency
-preparedness-mandate.

26 Information about the CRF is available online: PSC, "Community
Resilience Fund," last modified 17 April 2019, http://www.publicsafety
.gc.ca/cnt/bt/cc/fnd-en.aspx.

27 See page 188 of the federal budget: Government of Canada, *Growing the
Middle Class*, 2016, http://budget.gc.ca/2016/docs/plan/budget2016-en
.pdf.

28 Canadian Press, "Liberals Launch Anti-radicalization Centre without
Special Adviser," *Huffington Post*, 26 June 2017, http://www.huffingtonpost
.ca/2017/06/26/liberals-launch-anti-radicalization-centre-without-special
-advis_a_23002566/.

29 Home Office, *Individuals Referred to and Supported through the Prevent
Programme, April 2015 to March 2016: Statistical Bulletin 23/17* (2017).
Available online: https://assets.publishing.service.gov.uk/government
/uploads/system/uploads/attachment_data/file/677646/individuals
-referred-supported-prevent-programme-apr2015-mar2016.pdf. Home
Office, *Individuals Referred to and Supported through the Prevent Programme,
April 2017 to March 2018: Statistical Bulletin 31/18* (2018). Available online:
https://assets.publishing.service.gov.uk/government/uploads/system
/uploads/attachment_data/file/763254/individuals-referred-supported
-prevent-programme-apr2017-mar2018-hosb3118.pdf.

30 See PSC, *National Strategy on Countering Radicalization to Violence* (2018).
Available online: https://www.publicsafety.gc.ca/cnt/rsrcs/pblctns/ntnl
-strtg-cntrng-rdclztn-vlnc/index-en.aspx

31 See https://cpnprev.ca/.

32 For example, the Canada Centre collaborates with its counterparts in the
US, UK, Australia, and Sweden to fund a series of systematic reviews of
evidence carried out by Campbell Collaboration.

33 For example, see Ghayda Hassan et al., "Exposure to Extremist Online Content Could Lead to Violent Radicalization: A Systematic Review of Empirical Evidence," *International Journal of Developmental Sciences* 12, no. 7 (2018): 1–18.

34 Organization for the Prevention of Violence, *Building Awareness, Seeking Solutions: Extremism & Hate Motivated Violence in Alberta,* 2019. Available online: https://preventviolence.ca/publication/building-awareness -seeking-solutions-2019-report/.

35 Canadian Heritage, *Building a Foundation for Change: Canada's Anti-racism Strategy 2019–2022* (2019). Available online: https://www.canada.ca /content/dam/pch/documents/campaigns/anti-racism-engagement /ARS-Report-EN-2019-2022.pdf.

36 Sarah Marsden, James Lewis, and Kim Knott, *Countering Violent Extremism II: A Guide to Good Practice* (Lancaster: Centre for Research and Evidence on Security Threats, 2019). Available online: https://crestresearch.ac.uk /resources/countering-violent-extremism-two/.

37 For example: Adrian Cherney, "Evaluating Interventions to Disengage Extremist Offenders: A Study of the Proactive Integrated Support Model (PRISM)," *Behavioral Science of Terrorism and Political Aggression* 12, no. 1 (2018): 17–36.

38 Eric Rosand, "Congress Should Learn from Canada on Preventing Extremist Violence," Brookings Institution blog, 4 January 2019, https:// www.brookings.edu/blog/order-from-chaos/2019/01/04/congress -should-learn-from-canada-on-preventing-extremist-violence/.

39 Brian A. Jackson et al., *Practical Terrorism Prevention: Appendixes* (Santa Monica: RAND Corporation, 2019), 12.

40 For example, see Romaniuk, *Does CVE Work?*, 8.

41 For example, see Amy-Jane Gielen, "Countering Violent Extremism: A Realist View for Assessing What Works, for Whom, in What Circumstances, and How?," *Terrorism and Political Violence* 31, no. 6 (2019): 1149–67.

42 See, e.g., Ross Frenett, Institute for Strategic Dialogue, and Curtin University, *One to One Online Interventions: A Pilot CVE Methodology* (2015). Available online: http://www.isdglobal.org/wp-content/uploads /2016/04/One2One_Web_v9.pdf

43 Home Office, *Individuals Referred to and Supported through the Prevent Programme, April 2017 to March 2018.*

PART FOUR

Government Departments with National Security Functions

11 The Department of National Defence and the Canadian Armed Forces (DND/CAF)

THOMAS JUNEAU

The defence intelligence function receives relatively limited attention in Canada from either the media or the scholarly community. It deserves more, however, given its size (approximately 3,000 civilian and military employees) and its scope (it is the entity in the Canadian security and intelligence community responsible for conducting the widest range of intelligence activities). Indeed, just like the Canadian Security Intelligence Service (CSIS), it gathers human intelligence and has counter-intelligence as part of its mandate and, like the Communications Security Establishment (CSE), it collects signals intelligence. It also collects multiple other types of intelligence, such as imagery and geo-spatial, and it houses a large analytical function. Defence intelligence, moreover, has been affected by recent structural reforms in the Canadian intelligence community at least as much, if not more, than most of its counterparts. The creation of the National Security and Intelligence Committee of Parliamentarians (NSICOP) and of the National Security and Intelligence Review Agency (NSIRA), in particular, implies that for the first time in its history, defence intelligence is subject to comprehensive external review and oversight.

To shed light on these issues, this chapter begins with a brief outline of the overall defence function by focusing on matters of structure, policy, and budget, before shifting specifically to the defence intelligence enterprise. It follows with an overview of some of the main challenges facing defence intelligence today and for the foreseeable future: managing growth; responding to the evolving threat environment; the consequences of Trumpism; review and oversight; cybersecurity; and gender.

The Defence Function in Canada: Structure, Policy, Resources

The commander-in-chief of the Canadian Armed Forces (CAF) is the governor general, who – acting through the governor in council – is responsible for appointing the chief of the defence staff (CDS) on the recommendation of the prime minister. The minister of national defence, a federal Cabinet minister, presides over all matters relating to the Department of National Defence (DND) and the Canadian Armed Forces, as established by the *National Defence Act*[1] (see Figure 11.1). The deputy minister (DM) – usually supported by one or two associate deputy ministers – is the department's senior civil servant and is responsible for policy, resources, interdepartmental coordination, and international defence relations. Reporting to the deputy minister are a number of assistant deputy ministers, responsible for policy, materiel, finance, infrastructure and environment, and civilian human resources. The CDS is Canada's senior serving officer and is responsible for command, control, and administration of the CAF and for military strategy, plans, and requirements.[2] Reporting to the CDS are the commanders of the three services (Royal Canadian Navy, Royal Canadian Air Force, and Canadian Army), of Military Personnel Command, of the two operational commands (Canadian Special Forces Command, or CANSOF-COM, and Canadian Joint Operations Command, or CJOC), and of the North American Aerospace Defence Command (NORAD), as well as the director of the Strategic Joint Staff (the chief's headquarters staff). Other positions report to both the DM and the CDS: the vice chief of the defence staff, the DND/CAF legal advisor, the commander of Canadian Forces Intelligence Command, and the assistant deputy ministers for public affairs, science and technology, information management, and review services.[3]

The Liberal government of Prime Minister Justin Trudeau released in 2017 its defence policy, *Strong, Secure, Engaged* (SSE).[4] As with other official defence policy documents, it is important to remember that its value is limited. This is not to say that it is of no use: official defence policy documents serve important planning functions internally, and they signal Canada's intentions to its allies and to the Canadian public. A comparison of the outcomes of recent defence policies (the last ones were released in 2008, 2005, and 1994), however, reveals that these documents, after a few years, carry only a partial connection to reality.

There is much continuity in SSE with earlier policies. Like its predecessors, the 2017 policy calls for the CAF to be able to engage in a wide range of activities, from humanitarian assistance and aid to the civil power, to stabilization and peace operations and full-scale combat. In addition, SSE maintains the CAF's three core missions – defend Canada, contribute to the security of North America, and contribute to international peace and security. SSE does distinguish itself at some levels, notably by its stronger emphasis on human resources; the first chapter, strikingly, focuses exclusively on this aspect. SSE also differs from

Figure 11.1. DND/CAF structure.[5]

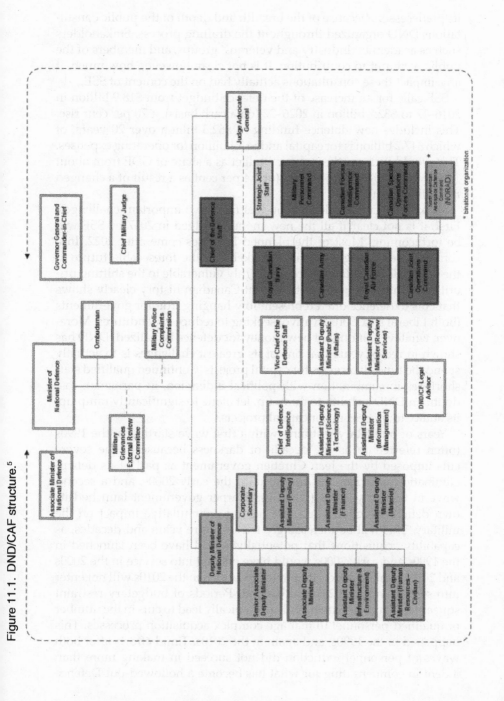

* binational organization

its predecessors because of the breadth and depth of the public consultations DND organized throughout the drafting process. Stakeholders such as academics, industry and veterans' groups, and members of the public were put to contribution. It is not clear, however, how much, if any, impact these consultations actually had on the content of SSE.

SSE calls for an increase of the defence budget from $18.9 billion in 2016–17 to $32.7 billion in 2026–27 (on a cash basis), a 70 per cent rise. This includes new defence funding of $62.3 billion over 20 years, of which $47.2 billion is for capital and $15.1 billion for operating expenses. This would increase the defence budget as a share of GDP from about 1 per cent in 2017 to 1.2 in 2024 (or 1.4 per cent as a result of a changed reporting formula).[6]

Looking ahead, the defence budget faces two important challenges. First, it is not clear if all the new money pledged in 2017 by SSE will be forthcoming. Most of the planned increases come after 2022. In a context where budget deficits are likely for the foreseeable future at the federal level, defence becomes highly vulnerable to the shifting priorities of future governments. Recent Canadian history clearly shows that cuts to defence often represent low-hanging fruit for governments (both Liberal and Conservative) seeking to reduce expenditures. Moreover, whatever amount of new money for defence is realized, DND has shown in recent years that one of its greatest challenges is to actually spend the funds it receives for capital projects. Continued qualified staff shortages in combination with political indecision, in particular, cast doubt on DND's ability to ramp up, let alone to significantly ramp up, its ability to process major capital projects.[7]

Years of budgetary restraint, with a first wave starting in the 1990s (often referred to as the decade of darkness because of the severe cuts imposed by the Jean Chrétien government as part of its deficit-elimination exercise) and lasting until the early 2000s, and a second wave in the early 2010s (when the Harper government launched its own deficit-reduction plan), are having a cumulative impact on the military. This will be increasingly felt in future years and decades, as capability acquisitions that potentially would have been launched in the 1990s and early 2000s would have entered into service in the 2000s and 2010s, while projects that failed to launch in the 2010s will not enter into service in the 2020s and beyond. Periods of budgetary restraint squeeze the capital budget, and also typically lead to cuts in the number of qualified personnel to manage complex acquisition processes. This happened in the 1990s, and again in the 2010s. Timid efforts after both waves of personnel reduction did not succeed in making more than a dent in compensating for what has become a hollowed-out Defence

Team on the materiel side. As a result of these trends – a limited capital budget and cuts to qualified personnel over decades, as well as a dysfunctional procurement system – the CAF are experiencing growing capability gaps, and these are likely to intensify in coming years.

The Intelligence Function in DND/CAF

At the time of the attacks of 11 September 2001, the defence intelligence function was led by the Director General Intelligence.[8] DGInt, as it was known, was widely viewed as a dysfunctional organization with multiple internal human resources problems. It was also a marginal player in the Canadian intelligence community and had limited influence with the senior levels of the department and the Forces. It was mostly operations focused, viewing operational commanders as its main clients.

The recognition that there had been a major erosion of capability from the end of the Cold War to 9/11 reached the Deputy Minister and the Chief of the Defence Staff. With the support of the Defence Management Committee, then the highest-level internal body, they launched a comprehensive, top-to-bottom review. The goal was to overhaul not only the DGInt organization itself, but also the defence intelligence function as a whole (i.e., intelligence activities conducted by other DND/CAF units outside DGInt). The result, the *Defence Intelligence Review* (DIR), was published internally in 2003. It was very forthcoming in raising major problems and vulnerabilities with the defence intelligence function.

The overarching goal of the DIR was to rebuild the intelligence branch and move it into the twenty-first century. Its most visible recommendations were to change the name of the organization to the Chief of Defence Intelligence (CDI) and make its head a two-star officer instead of a one-star. CDI would now be the functional authority over the entire defence intelligence function, which DGInt was not. CDI would also now report to the CDS, as opposed to the deputy chief of the defence staff (DCDS, a position abolished in subsequent reforms), and also to the DM, giving the branch greater visibility and access. The DIR further called for the creation of a new position, the director general for intelligence production (DGIP), a civilian under CDI responsible for analysis (emulating the model of allies, notably the United States and the United Kingdom, where the Defence Intelligence Agency and the Defence Intelligence Staff, respectively, have a similar structure). An important part of the rationale behind the creation of the DGIP position was to steer the organization to look more to the civilian side of the department, which had previously not been much on its radar, and to develop better relations with the rest of the intelligence community in

Ottawa. More broadly, the DIR recommended an increase in the organization's civilian representation, from DGIP down to mid-level managers and analysts. The DIR, moreover, recommended the creation of new defence intelligence capabilities, notably in human, imagery, and geo-spatial intelligence.

The DIR created a new organizational framework with greater accountability and civilian representation. It steered the organization to be better connected with both DND/CAF clients and the broader intelligence community, and to better promote its products. The first DGIP, for example, cancelled DGInt's flagship analytical product, the long and unwieldy *Weekly Intelligence Digest*, in favour of the shorter and more frequent *Daily Intelligence Digest*. Work has since been ongoing to continually improve defence intelligence governance. In particular, DND/CAF later prepared a ministerial directive on roles and responsibilities in the defence intelligence function, as well as new internal policies for the management of the defence intelligence function. CDI, in addition, started producing an annual report to the minister of national defence in which it explains its priorities and how it spends its money. More recently, the organization was restructured and renamed the Canadian Forces Intelligence Command (CFINT-COM). As part of these reforms, the commander of CFINTCOM, notably, gained greater authorities and autonomy. DGIP was also renamed the assistant chief of defence intelligence (ACDI), responsible for a steadily broader remit.

The Ministerial Directive (MD) on Defence Intelligence, along with subsequent other documents, clarified organizational accountability around defence intelligence.[9] In Canada, the authority to deploy military force domestically or internationally rests with the government, which can authorize the use of the CAF through a decision by the prime minister, Cabinet, or one or more ministers (this is referred to as an exercise of the Crown prerogative). The *National Defence Act*, or any other statute, does not contain any provision specifically governing defence intelligence activities. Instead, DND/CAF's position, as expressed in communications with NSICOP, is that the "authority to conduct defence intelligence activities is implicit when the CAF is legally mandated, pursuant to legislation or an exercise of the Crown prerogative, to conduct military operations and other defence activities."[10] The MD further states that there must be "a clear nexus between the nature and scope of the defence intelligence activity and DND/CF's mandated defence operations or activities."[11] This implies, in practice, that DND/CAF considers that defence intelligence activities can be authorized in the conduct of CAF deployments in Canada or abroad.

Today, CFINTCOM is, by some indicators, the organization within the Canadian intelligence community with the broadest mandate: it collects more types of intelligence, in particular, than any other agency (human, signals, open-source, imagery, geo-spatial, medical, and meteorological, among others, while also having counter-intelligence responsibilities). The defence intelligence function, as a whole, employs approximately 3,000 individuals, both civilian and military, with about 1,000 of them working within CFINTCOM. There is no publicly available figure for the defence intelligence budget; in the 2018 annual report of the National Security and Intelligence Committee of Parliamentarians, for example, the number is redacted.[12]

The commander of CFINTCOM, who is still also the chief of defence intelligence, oversees the provision of "credible, timely, and integrated defence intelligence capabilities, products, and services" to support Canada's national security objectives.[13] CFINTCOM has two specific tasks. It collects intelligence, including with deployable capabilities to support CAF operations, through the Joint Imagery Centre, the National Counter-Intelligence Unit, the Mapping and Charting Establishment, the Joint Meteorological Centre, and Joint Task Force X (which collects human intelligence). Its second task is to provide analysis, strategic warning, and threat assessment functions in support of decision-making in DND/CAF and the broader Government of Canada as well as in support of CAF operations.[14]

The commander of CFINTCOM, a two-star officer, is supported in their duties by the ACDI, a civilian with the rank of EX-3 (director-general). The ACDI is responsible for the analytical function of the command, with two directors in support, one for transnational and regional intelligence (DTRI) and the other for scientific and technical intelligence (DSTI). Both positions are civilian, with a majority of their analysts also civilian. The ACDI is also responsible for review and compliance, leading a team in charge of coordinating defence intelligence remits to NSICOP and NSIRA (see chapter fifteen). In addition, the ACDI is responsible for the Directorate of Intelligence Production Management (DIPM), which covers, among other issues, client relations, editing and dissemination of analytical products, and training and professional development.

Other units within DND/CAF also perform defence-intelligence-related functions, notably the J2 (intelligence) units within CJOC and CANSOFCOM; in their cases, the work is more directly geared toward providing analysis in support of, respectively, conventional domestic and international CAF operations and special operations. The three services (Army, Navy, and Air Force) also have their own intelligence units (respectively, G2, N2, and A2). CANSOFCOM includes various units responsible for specific intelligence-related activities, notably Joint Task Force 2 (JTF 2 a high-readiness unit), the Canadian Joint Incident Response Unit (CJIRU, to respond to chemical, biological, radiological, and nuclear threats), the Canadian Special Operations Regiment (CSOR), and 427 Special Operations Aviation Squadron (to provide precision lift to special forces missions).[15] CANSOFCOM units are trained and equipped to accomplish a range of tasks, including hostage rescue, direct action (small-scale raids or other small-scale offensive actions), chemical, biological, radiological, or nuclear crisis response, sensitive-site exploitation, combating weapons of mass destruction, maritime special operations, support to non-combatant evacuation operations, and special protection operations (to ensure the security of VIPs).[16]

Challenges

Managing CFINTCOM's Evolution

CFINTCOM has grown significantly since 2001, when it was known as DGInt. It has also become increasingly civilianized and professionalized: from being a predominantly military organization, it now features a far higher proportion of civilian personnel than in the past. It has also significantly enhanced its efforts to recruit, train, and retain qualified intelligence analysts by offering them a more attractive career path and by investing more in their professional development. The command, in particular, set up a Defence Intelligence Officer Recruitment Program (DIORP), modelled on the successful Policy Officer Recruitment Program (PORP) managed by the Department's Policy Group, to standardize and professionalize its recruitment of civilian analysts.

Recognizing its growing role, SSE pledged to create 300 new positions for defence intelligence, including 120 on the military side and 180 for civilians.[17] This is a significant vote of confidence in the defence intelligence function, but managing this growth raises questions. At the level of human resources, first, it raises issues of hiring, training, and retention. The latter will be a challenge: the pyramidal structure of CFINTCOM narrows rapidly for civilians moving up the hierarchy. It appears that most new positions will not be for analysts, but instead to enhance the collection and corporate sides of CFINTCOM. Nevertheless, if new analysts are hired in the coming years, bandwidth challenges will also arise: it is not clear whether, simply put, there are sufficient topics that are both relevant to CFINTCOM readers and not already covered by analysts in CFINTCOM or in partner intelligence agencies and for which there is appetite at senior levels. SSE rightly highlights the need for more analysis of trends such as hybrid and cyber warfare and influence operations. But CFINTCOM readers – both those on the operational side and the DND/CAF leadership on the strategic side – already have limited free bandwidth for additional inputs into their decision-making.

CFINTCOM has become far more relevant as an actor within the Canadian intelligence community than it was in the past.[18] Partly as a result of the very strong incentives of the combat mission in Afghanistan, it has also emerged as a more influential voice within DND/CAF. CFINTCOM analysts and managers now regularly provide direct oral and written briefings to the minister, deputy minister, and chief of the defence staff, who have come to value its input into the decision-making process. This is, in part, the result of a sustained effort to bring in civilian managers with strong policy experience elsewhere in DND and the security and intelligence world, who, over the years, have been able to steadily steer the command's analytical work toward greater relevance. In this context, one of its main challenges looking ahead is to keep this positive momentum toward greater relevance. To achieve this, the command will need to continue modernizing its human resources practices, make the right strategic choices as it manages its growth, focus on the right priorities as it assesses which threats matter most to Canadian defence, and maintain and further develop the close relations it has steadily developed with senior DND/CAF leadership.

The Evolving Threat Environment

According to SSE, three broad trends shape Canada's security environment:[19]

- the evolving balance of power with, in particular, the shift in relative power from West to East and the renewal of major power competition;
- the changing nature of conflict, especially the growing use of hybrid methods by state and non-state actors (defined as the "the coordinated application of diplomatic, informational, cyber, military and economic instruments to achieve strategic or operational objectives"), the evolution of global terrorism, and the shifting nature of peace operations; and
- the rapid evolution of technology, notably in the space and cyber domains, and their growing use by state and non-state adversaries, and the need for Canada to adapt its own capabilities and doctrines.

SSE's assessment of the international security environment, and of the threats it poses to Canadian defence, is likely to remain relevant, in its broad outline, for the foreseeable future. It is an excessively broad threat assessment, however; it is very challenging for CFINTCOM, given its limited collection and analytical capabilities, to focus on such a wide range of threats. Of course, CFINTCOM, like its other partners in the Canadian intelligence community, heavily relies on its partners, especially the US and other Five Eyes members, to compensate for its finite capabilities.

Nevertheless, looking forward, an important challenge for CFINT-COM will be to continually reassess which specific threats should be priorities for its collection and analytical efforts. This is not an either/or question, of course, but rather one of calibration: In the short, mid, and long term, how should CFINTCOM distribute its scarce resources in terms of supporting counterterrorism operations? How should it rank the relative threats posed by great power competition, hybrid warfare, or failed states? How should it distribute its analytical and collection resources across different regions – in particular, how many resources should be shifted toward the Arctic and East Asia? What are the implications if it chooses to focus less on the Middle East as a result? These questions, and others, are especially relevant and challenging given mounting uncertainty around the long-term role of the United States.

The Consequences of Trumpism

The United States is Canada's closest defence partner, by far. Canada is heavily reliant on the United States for the defence of North America, and many of the CAF's international deployments, especially in combat missions, are reliant on American support (for intelligence, in particular, but also for other enablers such as logistics, specialized capabilities, etc.). As a general rule, when the Government of Canada – whether Liberal or Conservative – weighs the pros and cons of various options to deal with important defence policy decisions, the American variable weighs heavier than most and usually all other variables.

In this context, the disruptive impact not only of the Donald Trump presidency but also, further down the road, of "Trumpism" raises significant questions for Canadian defence intelligence. It remains too early to rigorously assess the long-term effects of Trumpism, the eclectic and unpredictable mixture of protectionism, aggressiveness, unilateralism, and disdain for the liberal international order promoted by the 45th president. From the Canadian perspective, nevertheless, it would be a mistake to simply assume or hope that Trumpism will disappear with President Trump, whether in 2020 or at the latest in 2024. Trump has mobilized and emboldened important constituencies who support parts or all of his agenda, and these are unlikely to completely disappear once he leaves the Oval Office. This potentially has important long-term consequences.

It is important to emphasize that as of 2020, Canada–US bilateral cooperation on defence intelligence matters remains extremely close and has been sheltered from the political storms in Washington.[20] It is not a given, however, that the status quo will continue indefinitely. The US could eventually choose to reduce its cooperation with its northern neighbour on continental defence matters, perhaps as its long-standing simmering frustration with perceived Canadian free-riding would boil over. Alternatively, it could become more difficult politically for Canadian governments to overtly cooperate with the United States on domestic and continental security matters. The Canadian intelligence community, in general and even more so specifically in defence matters, is heavily integrated with its American counterpart. Complications in the bilateral relationship, especially more American protectionism, could thus carry important costs in the longer term, as Canada is a massive net recipient of intelligence from the United States. As such, a deterioration of relations or a more closed and isolationist America could cost Canada some of the extraordinary benefits it derives from its very close intelligence partnership with the United States. This would, in particular, have negative implications for how defence intelligence supports CAF operations.

Oversight and Review

DND/CAF conducts a wide range of intelligence activities, including multiple forms of collection and analysis, involving about 3,000 staff, yet it was never subject to independent, comprehensive oversight and review until recently. It is true that DND/CAF intelligence activities were subjected to DND's internal review services and to other external bodies, such as parliamentary committees, the Office of the Auditor General, and others such as the privacy and information commissioners. But these all have limited mandates, either because they are narrow or specific, or have limited authorities or investigative powers. The establishment of NSICOP and NSIRA, on the other hand, has created a completely new reality. For the first time, defence intelligence activities are subject to comprehensive, external, and independent review and oversight by two bodies with significant authorities. In response, DND/CAF has established internal teams to coordinate relations with NSICOP and NSIRA. Beyond organizational changes, adjusting to the era of review and oversight has also imposed on DND/CAF, and specifically on CFINTCOM, a major cultural shift: never before had the organization had to respond to the multiple demands of such bodies, and then had to deal with the consequences of their findings, notably at the public and political levels.

Indeed, NSICOP's first annual report, published in 2019, contains a full chapter reviewing DND/CAF's intelligence activities.[21] The report aimed to accomplish three tasks: define the nature, scale, and scope of defence intelligence; determine the authority framework under which defence intelligence activities are conducted; and detail the governance structure to ensure oversight and accountability for defence intelligence. The result is a heavily redacted document that nevertheless contains significant amounts of information that had previously been unavailable to the public.

The committee found that there are, in its view, a number of weaknesses in DND/CAF's administrative system of governance for defence intelligence activities. It assessed, in particular, that DND/CAF lacks a standardized process to determine a nexus between an intelligence activity and an authorized mission; that the main governance body, the Defence Intelligence Management Committee, has failed to achieve part of its mandate (it more effectively deals with administrative issues such as policy development and human resources, but because of its overly broad membership and its infrequent meetings, sensitive matters tend to be brought directly to the DM, the CDS, or the minister, and not to the committee); that DND/CAF has made only partial efforts to measure and document compliance with the obligations of the ministerial directive on defence intelligence; and that DND/CAF does not have a standardized process for interdepartmental consultations. Perhaps most controversially, the report also argues that DND/CAF is an anomaly in Canada's security and intelligence community in that it is the only department or agency conducting intelligence activities, similar in kind, risk, and sensitivity to those conducted by CSIS, CSE, and others, under the Crown prerogative and not under clear statutory authorities. On this basis, the committee recommended that the government seriously consider providing explicit legislative authority for the conduct of defence intelligence activities.[22]

Cybersecurity

Canada does not currently face major conventional military threats, and neither is it likely to for the foreseeable future. It does, however, face other significant threats. This is especially the case in the cyber realm, where multiple departments and agencies play a role; importantly, DND and the CAF are only one player among many. Canada lags behind the United States and many of its allies in thinking about the cyber threat and in generating new capabilities and doctrines. Though there has been much movement in recent years, there is, as is often the case in the Canadian context on such matters, only limited information available to the public. After years without clear direction, a new cyber strategy was released in 2018, under the direction of Public Safety Canada.[23] Along with the *National Security Act, 2017*,[24] passed into law in 2019, it brings more clarity to defence's role in the management of the cyber function.[25] Canada's 2017 defence policy also marked an important shift in how Canadian defence views the cyber realm. According to SSE, the key DND/CAF functions in this realm are to provide cyber intelligence, defend the government's networks from cyber-attacks, and generate the capacity to respond should the government task it with mounting a military response to a cyber-attack. SSE also formally calls, for the first time, for the CAF to develop the capacity to conduct offensive cyber operations.[26]

Cybersecurity and defence are clearly, and justifiably, a priority for Canada, yet these recent developments raise important challenges. Developing policies and doctrines, as well as generating the desired assets, first, is complex. The case of offensive cyber operations, in particular, raises multiple novel operational, legal, ethical, and administrative questions. Overall, developing Canada's cyber capabilities also involves difficult coordination within the federal government across multiple levels of government, and with the private sector and civil society. At the level of human resources, moreover, DND/CAF needs to generate the necessary skill sets and fill additional civilian and military positions, notably in the new cyber operator occupation within the CAF. The organization will have to train these individuals, ensure that it offers them an attractive career path, and provide them with competitive salaries – all difficult challenges as the private sector continues to compete for many of the same individuals. Finally, as witnessed by the debate around the *National Security Act, 2017*, the very idea of offensive cyber operations conducted by the Canadian military raises the complex task of managing public perceptions.

Gender

During the First World War, women served in the Canadian military as nurses, and also in mechanical and logistical positions. Even though their roles slowly expanded over the following decades, they maintained a second-class status and were barred from combat positions and paid less than their male counterparts for similar work.[27] All positions, including combat, became formally open to women in 1989. As of February 2019, women represented 15.4 per cent of the regular force and 16.3 per cent of the primary reserve. They are primarily concentrated in intelligence, administrative, and logistical roles, and remain heavily underrepresented in combat roles. The CAF's goal is to increase the number of women by one per cent annually, in order to reach one-quarter by 2026.[28]

Yet sexual harassment and abuse represent a major barrier to women's integration in the Canadian military. The problem has been compounded by decades of institutional denial; the leadership's priority, every time a scandal erupted, was to manage the public fallout and move on. This became especially clear to the public upon the release of the Deschamps Report in 2015, drafted by a former Supreme Court justice (and now member of NSIRA). It found, in particular, that there is an "underlying sexualized culture" within the CAF that is hostile to women and LGTBQ members.[29]

The CAF responded to the Deschamps Report by launching Operation HONOUR, with the mission "to eliminate harmful and inappropriate sexual behavior in the military."[30] A number of programs and initiatives have since been launched, some formalized in SSE. Some indicators suggest that there has already been positive change, including an increase in the number of CAF members released or fired because of inappropriate sexual behaviour. Yet even under the most optimistic scenarios, the depth and breadth of cultural and institutional barriers to full gender equality in the military will continue to suppress female participation for the foreseeable future.

This will come at a great cost for DND/CAF, including for its intelligence function. Studies have shown, for example, that having a greater proportion of female CAF members in intelligence and civil-military roles enhances information-gathering and the ability to gain the trust of local populations in the context of complex peace operations.[31] An organization that largely excludes half the country's population indeed loses out on multiple opportunities for recruiting skilled individuals. And as many specialists have noted, gendered socialization tends to produce in women different distributions of skills than in men. Some of those skills, such as empathy and interpersonal communication, are especially useful for defence intelligence, such as human intelligence collection, civil–military relations, and counterterrorism.[32]

Conclusion

The defence intelligence function in Canada has come a long way: CFINTCOM in 2020 bears only a limited resemblance to DGInt on the eve of the 9/11 attacks. DGInt was insular, operationally focused, dominated by the military, and beset by internal problems. It was not an influential player in the broader Canadian intelligence community, and neither was it perceived as a relevant provider of inputs into senior decision-making in DND/CAF. Today, CFINTCOM includes a stronger civilian component, is better connected across Ottawa, and has developed greater access to the DM, the CDS, and the minister. Its governance has been overhauled and is now better institutionalized, with clearer accountability lines. There remains, of course, much scope for improvement, but the organization can plausibly claim to have evolved in a positive direction in the past 19 years.

As it looks to the future, the defence intelligence function still faces many challenges. The coming years, in particular, will raise difficult and complex questions on the threat environment in which the CAF operates, and on the implications this has for defence intelligence. It is not difficult to come up with an abstract list of threats – terrorism, a revanchist Russia, a rising China, nuclear proliferation, climate change, failed and failing states, et cetera. What is far more difficult, however, is to clearly prioritize these threats and to identify clear, optimal strategies for the collection of intelligence and for analysis. As it continues its evolution, CFINTCOM will also face ongoing challenges in terms of human resources (e.g., hiring and retaining appropriately skilled staff), governance (notably, responding to NSICOP's recommendations), and international relations (especially regarding the future of Canada's relations with the US).

NOTES

1 R.S.C. 1985, c. N-5.
2 Department of National Defence and the Canadian Armed Forces (DND/CAF), *2017–18 Departmental Plan*, "Mandate and Role" (2018), 9. Available online: http://forces.gc.ca/assets/FORCES_Internet/docs/en/dp-2017 -18-_-final_eng.pdf.
3 For more on the roles and responsibilities of each of these functions, see Government of Canada, "Organizational Structure of the Department of National Defence and the Canadian Armed Forces," last modified

21 September 2019, https://www.canada.ca/en/department-national
-defence/corporate/organizational-structure.html. The Defence portfolio
also includes three statutory agencies operating at arm's length and
funded independently (the Communications Security Establishment,
the Military Grievances External Review Committee, and the Military
Police Complaints Commission of Canada) and four intradepartmental
organizations, internal entities operating outside the National Defence
chain of command (the Office of the Chief Military Judge, Defence
Research and Development Canada, the Independent Review Panel for
Defence Acquisitions, and the Office of the Ombudsman); see Government
of Canada, "Defence Portfolio," last modified 10 September 2019, https://
www.canada.ca/en/department-national-defence/corporate/defence
-portfolio.html. On CSE, see the chapter by Bill Robinson in this volume.
4 Department of National Defence (DND), *Strong, Secure, Engaged: Canada's
   Defence Policy* (2017). Available online: http://dgpaapp.forces.gc.ca/en
   /canada-defence-policy/docs/canada-defence-policy-report.pdf.
5 Government of Canada, "Organizational Structure."
6 This is still well short of NATO's oft-quoted target of 2 per cent of GDP. This,
   however, is not a binding target for alliance members; it is merely aspirational.
   Moreover, as Canadian officials often rightly point out, the share-of-GDP target
   is misleading, in that it does not measure actual defence outputs. Canada, by
   this measure, performs relatively better, since it has repeatedly made important
   contributions to NATO-led and like-minded coalitions over the years.
7 David Perry, *2015 Status Report on Major Defence Equipment Procurements*
   (Calgary: Canadian Global Affairs Institute, 2015). Available online:
   https://www.policyschool.ca/wp-content/uploads/2016/03/defence
   -procurement-perry.pdf.
8 Some of the information that follows is taken from interviews that the
   author conducted with Stephanie Carvin as part of their research for
   a forthcoming book on the role of intelligence analysis in informing
   policymaking in Canada.
9 Other mechanisms in the governance and oversight of defence intelligence
   include another MD, on defence intelligence priorities, as well as a
   ministerial direction on avoiding complicity in mistreatment by foreign
   entities. In addition, ministerial authorization must be sought to conduct
   sensitive intelligence activities, notably signals intelligence (SIGINT) and
   human intelligence (HUMINT). See chapter 4 in NSICOP's *Annual Report
   2018* for more detail.
10 National Security and Intelligence Committee of Parliamentarians
   (NSICOP), *Annual Report 2018* (2019), 68. Available online: http://www
   .nsicop-cpsnr.ca/reports/rp-2019-04-09/2019-04-09_annual_report_2018
   _public_en.pdf.

11 NSICOP, *Annual Report 2018*, 77.

12 NSICOP, *Annual Report 2018*, 61.

13 Government of Canada, "Canadian Forces Intelligence Command," last modified 18 December 2016, https://www.canada.ca/en/department -national-defence/corporate/organizational-structure/canadian-forces -intelligence-command.html.

14 In performing these functions, CFINTCOM also has access to vast pools of raw and finished intelligence obtained through information-sharing with partners, especially but not exclusively from the Five Eyes network (Australia, Canada, New Zealand, the United Kingdom, and the United States). Very little has been published in academia on Canadian defence intelligence; for one exception, see Martin Rudner, "The Future of Canada's Defence Intelligence," *International Journal of Intelligence and Counterintelligence* 15, no. 4 (2002): 540–64.

15 Government of Canada, "Special Operations Forces Organizational Structure," last modified 19 November 2019, https://www.canada.ca/en /special-operations-forces-command/corporate/organizational-structure .html

16 Government of Canada, "Mandate of the Special Operations Forces," last modified 17 July 2020, https://www.canada.ca/en/special-operations -forces-command/corporate/mandate.html

17 DND, *Strong, Secure, Engaged*, 65–6.

18 Based on extensive interviews the author conducted with Stephanie Carvin in 2018–19.

19 DND, *Strong, Secure, Engaged*, chap. 4.

20 This is supported by multiple interviews conducted by the author and Stephanie Carvin in Ottawa and Washington, DC, in 2018–19.

21 See chapter 4 in NSICOP, *Annual Report 2018*.

22 During its appearances before NSICOP and in written feedback, DND/ CAF raised several concerns with this option. In its view, in particular, comparisons with entities such as CSIS and CSE were inappropriate, since these are primarily intelligence organizations, whereas defence intelligence is only one, integrated, aspect of the wide spectrum of DND/CAF activities. Of note, the Liberal Party included in its campaign platform for the 2019 federal elections a commitment to move forward with this recommendation. As of this writing in 2020, it is not clear whether the government of Justin Trudeau will move ahead with this pledge.

23 Public Safety Canada, *National Cyber Security Strategy: Canada's Vision for Security and Prosperity in the Digital Age* (2018). Available online: https:// www.publicsafety.gc.ca/cnt/rsrcs/pblctns/ntnl-cbr-scrt-strtg/index-en .aspx. See Alex Wilner's chapter in this volume.

24 S.C. 2019, c. 13.

25 See chapters by Kent Roach and Leah West in this volume.
26 DND, *Strong, Secure, Engaged*, 71–2. See this volume's chapter by Bill Robinson on CSE's role.
27 See Barbara Dundas, *A History of Women in the Canadian Military* (Montreal: Art Global, 2000).
28 DND/CAF, "Backgrounder: Women in the Canadian Armed Forces," 7 March 2019, http://www.forces.gc.ca/en/news/article.page?doc =women-in-the-canadian-armed-forces/izkjqzeu.
29 DND/CAF, *External Review into Sexual Misconduct and Sexual Harassment in the Canadian Armed Forces* (2015). Available online: http://www.forces .gc.ca/en/caf-community-support-services/external-review-sexual -mh-2015/summary.page
30 Government of Canada, "Operation HONOUR," last modified 25 May 2020, http://www.forces.gc.ca/en/caf-community-support-services /sexual-misconduct.page
31 Col. Ellen Haring, "What Women Bring to the Fight," *Parameters* 43, no. 2 (2013): 27-32.
32 Andrea Lane, "Women in the Canadian Armed Forces," in *Canadian Defence Policy in Theory and Practice*, ed. Thomas Juneau, Philippe Lagassé, and Srdjan Vucetic (Cham, Switzerland: Palgrave Macmillan, 2019), 351–64.

12 Global Affairs Canada (GAC)

MICHAEL NESBITT

Today it might be forgotten that for many years, Global Affairs Canada (GAC) held a central national security role in the Government of Canada.[1] Between the end of the Second World War and the fall of the Berlin Wall, what was then the Department of External Affairs was the leading agency when it came to Canada's national security. During this time (until 1995), External Affairs was primarily responsible for bringing together and coordinating the then-smaller number of national security agencies to ensure information-sharing and a collaborative approach to national security matters.

At the time, External Affairs' central role in national security made eminent sense: threats were more state-based during the Cold War, and External Affairs was *the* repository for knowledge about Canada's greatest national security threat at the time, the Soviet Union. National security was seen much more through the lens of fighting communism and subversion than fighting terrorism. Diplomats abroad were – as they are now – the major conduit for the international sharing and receiving of information, which was gathered and sent home to Canada for analysis. Of course, the Canadian Security Intelligence Service (CSIS) did not exist until 1984.[2]

Today, the threat environment and departmental roles and responsibilities have changed. Terrorism, in particular, now plays an outsized role in Canada's national security landscape. Nevertheless, GAC continues to have a major role on the front lines of the national security landscape, though for better and/or worse, that role is necessarily not what it once was.

To place GAC within its current governmental and national security context, this chapter proceeds in three parts. It begins with an overview of GAC as it exists today, including its mandate, legal authorities, structure, resources, funding, and information-sharing authorities and restrictions. The chapter then offers an overview of GAC's primary national security roles and responsibilities. It then proposes six interrelated challenges that GAC faces as it adjusts to a new departmental, security, regulatory, and governmental landscape.

Mandate

External Affairs was renamed and reorganized in 1995 to become the Department of Foreign Affairs and International Trade. Since 1995 the department has gone through numerous other name changes, and with them internal reorganizations and reprioritizations.[3] The changes first separated traditional diplomacy and foreign affairs from international trade and development, as though they were not three of a kind, and then brought them back together again under one roof. It is only since 2015 that the department has been called GAC, and it is now governed by the 2013 *Department of Foreign Affairs, Trade and Development Act* (*Foreign Affairs Act*).[4]

The *Foreign Affairs Act* ensures the incorporation of international trade and development with foreign affairs and brought the Canadian International Development Agency (CIDA) under the formal head of the larger department. Despite this integration of departments under the GAC umbrella, separate ministerial responsibilities for development, trade, and foreign affairs remain, and the actual physical integration of the departments, such as ensuring all those who work on the Middle East are housed together, has been slow.

The ministerial mandate for GAC is found in section 10 of the *Foreign Affairs Act*, which stipulates that it has all of "the powers, duties and functions of the Minister [unless formally granted to another minister] ... relating to the conduct of the external affairs of Canada, including international trade and commerce and international development."[5] In particular, section 10(b) states that, in exercising their powers, the minister is responsible for, among other things, foreign affairs, the maintenance of good international relations, including with regional and international institutions like the United Nations, and international negotiations and trade, as well as consular relations and humanitarian assistance. The minister is also to "foster the development of international law and its application in Canada's external relations" and carry out other duties as assigned.[6]

Formally, there is nothing relating to national security in the legislative mandate or in any of the online descriptions of GAC's activities. However, GAC's 2017–18 departmental plan – like other departmental plans before it – does set out what might, in broad terms, be considered that national security mandate. Specifically, the departmental plan states that GAC "supports global peace and stability and addresses international security threats such as terrorism, transnational organized crime, arms control and the proliferation of weapons and materials of mass destruction."[7] Put another way, GAC continues to engage internationally in order to promote peace and stave off conflict, including addressing threats from aggressive nation states.

But today GAC also has an increasing national security role in collecting and sharing information and coordinating bodies to fight international aspects of terrorism[8] and organized crime,[9] as well as promoting peace through initiatives such as the Landmines Convention[10] (the "Ottawa Convention"), its capacity-building programs to promote peace and prosperity, or its support for the International Atomic Energy Agency (IAEA) and chemical weapons destruction through the Organisation for the Prohibition of Chemical Weapons (OPCW).[11]

Resources

To manage its Ottawa headquarters and diplomatic missions and consulates abroad, GAC has an annual budget of $7.2 billion as forecasted for 2019–20.[12] That budget has been under increasing stress for many years, as illustrated by a chart of the last 20 years of the department's funding[13] and the planned spending for the years to come. As one can see in Figure 1, GAC's resources have been largely stagnant in recent years – with one large increase that coincided with Canada's hosting of the 2010 Winter Olympic Games in Vancouver.

Put into context, as the international threat environment becomes more complex, the Canadian population has grown and become more international, increasing the needs of foreign services and consular assistance, and as the department takes on new initiatives related to terrorism, the budget has remained largely stagnant over a 20-year period, with threats of a major drop-off in the near future. GAC is being asked to do more, in a more complex environment, with a more fractured workforce, all without increasing (and largely without modernizing) its resources.

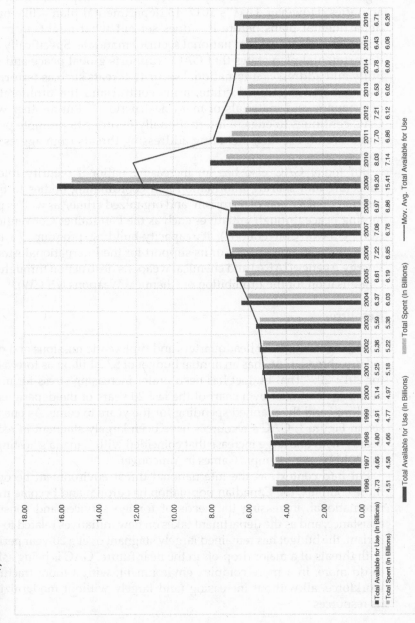

Figure 12.1. GAC spending and budget fiscal years 1996–2016 as per Public Accounts of Canada (adjusted for inflation in 2016 $).

	1996	1997	1998	1999	2000	2001	2002	2003	2004	2005	2006	2007	2008	2009	2010	2011	2012	2013	2014	2015	2016
Total Available for Use (In Billions)	4.73	4.66	4.80	4.91	5.14	5.25	5.36	5.59	6.37	6.61	7.22	7.08	6.97	16.20	8.03	7.70	7.21	6.53	6.78	6.43	6.71
Total Spent (In Billions)	4.51	4.58	4.66	4.77	4.97	5.18	5.22	5.38	6.03	6.19	6.85	6.78	6.86	15.41	7.14	6.86	6.12	6.02	6.09	6.08	6.26

■ Total Available for Use (In Billions) ▨ Total Spent (In Billions) —— Mov. Avg. Total Available for Use

Cooperation

Central to the role of GAC has always been its near-constant collaboration on information-sharing with international partners, as well as interdepartmental collaboration within the Government of Canada. Yet GAC is more dependent on these information-sharing channels than ever before.

Within Canada, GAC has information-sharing agreements with institutions like CSIS, which recognizes GAC as a priority partner.[14] Such agreements delineate the kind of information that can be disclosed and for what purposes, and establish standardized templates for disclosures. Certain GAC employees are cleared to see Top Secret material, meaning that they will be permitted to see materials produced by Canada's security agencies, where these are relevant to the job in which the employee is placed, necessary, and individually authorized.[15]

GAC does not tend to have information-sharing agreements with foreign governments because it would be too complicated – after all, sharing information is what GAC is expected to do, with any partner that will engage. However, GAC does benefit from Canada's participation in the Five Eyes agreement, which allows the United Kingdom, the United States, Australia, Canada, and New Zealand to share intelligence.

There are also limits on the international aspects of GAC's information-sharing. For example, Bill C-59, the *National Security Act, 2017*,[16] introduced the *Avoiding Complicity in Mistreatment by Foreign Entities Act*. It mandates that ministerial directives be issued by the minister of foreign affairs (and other ministers) to regulate the sharing of information between departments like GAC and foreign counterparts, including when such information can be shared. In light of GAC's activities related to – and arguably complicity in – the torture of Maher Arar,[17] Adullah Almalki, Ahmad Abou-Elmaati, and Muayyed Nureddin,[18] oversight by future ministerial directives and GAC's compliance therewith will be crucial.

Finally, the growth of information-sharing agreements between other Canadian departments, like CSIS, and their foreign counterparts, like MI5 and MI6 in Britain or the Federal Bureau of Investigation (FBI) and Central Intelligence Agency (CIA) in the United States, has affected GAC's operations. (Though of course a number of information-sharing agreements, particularly between Canada's closest allies, have been in place for many decades, including between Canada and the signals intelligence agencies in Britain and the United States.) Whereas international information once flowed through GAC as a matter of course, and often in the first instance, today GAC is but one player in the broad flow of international intelligence between government agencies. This means that GAC is left in the dark on a variety of national and international security matters, intelligence which might once have flowed through the department. As a corollary, GAC is increasingly dependent on information-sharing agreements with other Canadian government departments and the goodwill of those agencies.

National Security Responsibilities and Activities

Broadly speaking, GAC's national security responsibilities can be broken down into three main categories: supporting global peace and security; addressing international threats such as terrorism, organized crime, and the proliferation of weapons of mass destruction; and protecting individual Canadians abroad, including diplomatic staff and embassies.

Supporting Global Peace and Security

Supporting global peace and security – and promoting prosperity at home and, arguably, abroad – has historically been GAC's core mission. Most of the activities that one would impute to a diplomat fall under this category: trade negotiations to improve prosperity and thus decrease conflict; fostering healthy diplomatic and, hopefully, pacific relations; working through the United Nations and other multilateral bodies for a more interlinked global governance, to improve security worldwide and to prevent or respond to conflict; addressing humanitarian disasters; and so on. In fact, just about all of GAC's officially mandated activities can be seen, through one lens or another, as promoting national security, even if that is not the primary objective in each case.

Addressing International Threats

GAC is on the front lines of Canada's efforts to address a host of international threats, from transnational crime to the proliferation of chemical or biological weapons, disease outbreaks, or even international peace talks. GAC works through allied countries, partner agencies, and international organizations like the United Nations, the World Health Organization, the International Red Cross, and others to deliver humanitarian assistance and respond to myriad types of threats.

Protecting Individual Canadians and Canadian Interests Abroad

GAC is responsible for the safety and security of its staff and embassies and other property abroad; not surprisingly, it conducts threat assessments to ensure their safety and have emergency and evacuation plans in place. But GAC is also primarily responsible for evacuating Canadian citizens if necessary, as it did in Lebanon during the 2006 Israel–Hezbollah War. Moreover, GAC helps to coordinate Canada's response to hostage-takings when they involve Canadian citizens, such as when Robert Fowler and Louis Guay were held hostage by al-Qaida operatives in Mali in 2009.

Primary Actors and Sections within GAC Dealing
with National Security

GAC's efforts on these three national security fronts are supported by a number of internal "bureaus" or sections created to address discrete problems or threats. GAC is far too big an institution to allow for a comprehensive overview of its activities here. Furthermore, as an institution it has been too amorphous and lacking in transparency in recent years to properly elaborate on all that it is doing. The bureaus within GAC are constantly changing their names (and associated acronyms) and with them their mandates, making it difficult from inside government to know who works where doing what at any one time, and almost impossible to know from the outside. Still, some relatively stable bureaus exist that are worth canvassing, even if their precise names have changed over time – and will undoubtedly change in years to come.

First, GAC has an assistant deputy minister for "International Security", which houses the three broad shops, including the "Counter-Terrorism, Crime and Intelligence Bureau." This bureau is again subdivided into "international crime and terrorism," "threat assessment and intelligence services," "counter-terrorism and anti-crime capacity building programs," and "technical security and communications" sections. These various sections perform a number of central national security functions, including foreign mission security, which includes preparing intelligence assessments with regard to foreign countries, embassies, and other facilities; managing the expulsion of diplomats; managing responses to foreign terrorist activities; acting as a central hub for the sharing of information – particularly receiving inbound information – from Canada's security agencies like CSIS and CSE; liaising with domestic intelligence agencies to coordinate information-sharing, express informational or assistance needs, and request information; and helping to coordinate Canada's response to hostage situations.[19]

Housed within the Counter-Terrorism, Crime and Intelligence Bureau[20] is the Global Security Reporting Program (GSRP). According to the Security Intelligence Review Committee (SIRC, CSIS's former review agency, discussed in chapter fourteen), which offered one of the few minor publicly available insights into the GSRP, the program "was created post-9/11 to generate increased reporting on terrorism, non-proliferation and other security issues. GSRP officers, who are not intelligence officers, collect information on security and stability issues, assess the evolving threat and risk environment at missions and work with whole-of-government reaction teams during crisis situations."[21] GSRP produces reports for GAC on issues related to national security and conflict, international security, and international trade and investment issues. Designating staff with this particular agenda on information gathering and sharing, and keeping out of their portfolios many of the other tasks that keep diplomats abroad busy, like preparing for state visits or more mundane state-to-state meetings, was seen as a way to maintain a necessary diplomatic capacity within the Foreign Service. In this way, the GSRP program insulates a small number of employees from many modern bureaucratic responsibilities.[22] It ensures that some people, in some places (usually countries seen as security threats or hotbeds of terrorist activity, like Pakistan, Afghanistan, or Venezuela), are able to focus on information collection and reporting. Over 1,000 such reports were produced by GSRP between 2015 and 2016.[23]

GAC has also taken on new responsibilities with coordinating Canada's cyber foreign policy. The 2019 *National Cyber Security Action Plan* announced an "International Strategic Framework for Cyberspace," which called for the creation of a "cyber unit" within GAC, the "International Cyber Policy" team.[24] Although the unit is new and small, it has considerable responsibilities, including the development of an international cyber strategy, developing an attribution policy, and promoting Canadian interests and values on cyber issues, including cybersecurity, in international fora.

GAC also coordinates Canada's platform functions, meaning any department that wants to send someone abroad will go through GAC to arrange the posting. A good example is the "Liaison Officer" program. Liaison officers are individuals from other Canadian departments, including CSIS, who work out of Canada's embassies abroad to liaise with their counterpart institutions and ensure the smooth flow of information nation to nation and department to department. For example (as discussed in chapter three), Canada has CSIS officers in its embassy in Washington to liaise with the intelligence community and particularly the CIA, report back to Canada, and try to ensure the smooth coordination of activities and information.

GAC also houses a Weapons of Mass Destruction Threat Reduction Program, which directs funds to organizations like the OPCW.[25] Other GAC bureaus have piecemeal obligations that relate directly or indirectly to national security. For example, GAC is responsible for Canada's sanctions regime under the *Special Economic Measures Act* (SEMA)[26] and for import and export trade restrictions under the *Export and Import Permits Act* (EIPA).[27] Under the SEMA, geographic departments have traditionally been responsible for the listing process, whereby entities or individuals are listed, or sanctioned. Given that the purpose of sanctions under the SEMA is to counter "a grave breach of international peace and security"[28] or "gross and systematic human rights abuses,"[29] the listing process is, in theory, crucial to supporting Canada's diplomatic stick (sanctions) used in response to international threats. Similarly, under the EIPA, GAC (by way of the Trade Control Bureau) controls the flow of goods named in the Import, Export, and Area Control Lists.[30] These lists restrict the goods that can be imported or exported, including to certain countries or geographic regions. While the exports controls, for example, might include limitations on textiles or agricultural products (not necessarily national security related), the controls also limit the sale of weapons or munitions.

There are also plenty of bureaus that would seem to have little direct link to national security, yet may nevertheless be tied to security issues. For example, for several years GAC housed a "Direct Diplomacy" shop, now called the "Digital Inclusion Lab." Initially, the idea was that the conduct of diplomacy was increasingly happening not just in person, but online, and GAC had to engage in that virtual space. Further, there were areas of the world where GAC was not active, such as in post-2012 Iran, or where GAC needed to be more active, such as with respect to non-state actors. GAC needs eyes and ears even where it cannot operate, and, in some ways, it needs them most where it cannot operate. With that said, the scope of Canada's digital diplomacy initiative, its connection to the International Cyber Policy team, and the extent to which digital diplomacy is being effectively implemented and monitored is unclear. Despite a promise in 2008 to articulate its digital foreign policy and a 2017 evaluation by Public Safety Canada calling for digital foreign policy to be fully developed, GAC has thus far failed to do so.[31]

Challenges

Human Resourcing, Expertise, Staffing, and Training

Like so many government departments, GAC's budget presents challenges. As it stands, GAC's employees are slotted into a variety of work streams: Foreign Affairs, composed primarily of employees or political officers in the Foreign Service (FS) stream; International Trade, traditionally composed mainly of FS-stream employees in the economic officers' sub-stream; and International Development, composed of former CIDA employees. There are also a whole host of non-foreign-service employees who occupy positions across all sections of work (employees in the Economic and Social Sciences [EC] stream and Commerce Officer [CO] stream), as well as a growing number of contract employees and a stable contingent of Department of Justice lawyers. These employees are neither hired through the foreign service recruitment process nor given the standard training required of all FS-stream employees.

This brings us to training, where GAC has fallen behind on almost all counts. Most training is done through the Canadian Foreign Service Institute (CFSI) and, as with all federal government employees, the Canada School of Public Service. As it stands, COs entering GAC are required to take very little training, while FS-stream employees go through the diplomatic training. But all groups are often tasked with doing substantively the same work depending on the employment "box" that they fill. It is an open secret that competition for advancement is more extreme within GAC than some other departments, so if one wishes to become a senior manager one should go elsewhere and transfer into GAC at the managerial (EX, or executive) level. For better or worse, the upper ranks of GAC are thus increasingly populated with individuals who have spent at least a portion of their careers elsewhere.

As a result, one of two scenarios must be true, neither of which paints a particularly compelling picture. Either GAC is employing people to do diplomatic work for which they are not properly trained, even at senior levels, or GAC does not have training programs in place that substantially benefit its diplomatic employees, such that other people cannot simply step in and do the same jobs. In this second scenario, GAC is also then requiring its diplomatic corps to undergo training that it may later tacitly admit is of little benefit to adequate performance.

Diplomacy versus Security versus Humanitarianism versus Trade

GAC is still finding its footing as a department that has amalgamated what was alternatively the Department of Foreign Affairs and International Trade with CIDA under one roof. An existential battle bubbles within GAC over its modern raison d'être. In practical terms, trade is institutionally separated from political affairs, which are in turn separated from humanitarianism, a neat compartmentalization of responsibilities that fits cleanly within the major work streams that together form GAC. The result is an employment structure that prioritizes different – sometimes competing – conceptions of what a diplomatic corps should strive to achieve.

Should humanitarian aid be "politicized," that is, follow political priorities, or should it be distributed purely to the neediest? Similarly, to what extent should trade-stream employees working on import and export regulations consider national security imperatives, and how should those concerns be balanced with the more traditional trade imperatives of opening free markets and increasing transparency?[32]

Surely these are difficult questions and not prone to simplified, generalized answers. Yet the structure of GAC has shifted so much through the past 25 years, introducing competing priorities and conceptions of the department, and even competing employment streams, that answering them internally is no easy matter. At some point GAC will have to grapple with these competing priorities and conceptions of the department. How GAC defines itself, and how its diverse employees define it, will be a challenge in the years to come.

Transparency

Despite its best efforts, transparency has long eluded GAC. Over the years, GAC has tended to provide little but generalities on the activities that it undertakes.[33] It promotes peace through democracy-building programs, but whether that is through dialogue or the funding of foreign dissident groups is often unclear. GAC runs a controversial GSRP program, but it has no mandate that can be found, its budget and dealings remain elusive, and it has historically had little external oversight or review.

Consider as another example GAC's management of the sanctions files. Unlike the *Criminal Code*'s listing process,[34] Canadians currently know next to nothing about how GAC lists entities in its various sanctions regimes, what (due) process it follows, or the legal basis for its listings. It is evident that GAC periodically updates its sanctions listings, but GAC does not offer public reasons or an explainer, as the United States' Office of Foreign Assets Control does as a matter of course.[35] More concerning is the fact that, unlike the United States, Canada provides little to no guidance to Canadian businesses and often refuses to conduct outreach or even talk with businesses to help explain its sanctions or its listings.[36] It is hard to imagine this situation standing were an external body to conduct an efficacy or propriety review of GAC's processes. But given the historic lack of external review or oversight, GAC is left with an inefficient, ineffective,.and opaque sanctions process that is unlikely to change without the new review bodies taking a close look.

Review (Times Two) for the First Time and Other Recent Legislative Amendments

Until now, GAC has been subject only to occasional reviews by, for example, the Privacy Commissioner, but never a specific, designated body such as the Security Intelligence Review Committee (SIRC).[37] Yet since 2017, GAC has been subject to (potential) review by the NSICOP, as will be other federal government departments carrying out activities that might relate to national security and intelligence.[38] With the June 2019 passage of the *National Security Act, 2017*, the NSIRA also has the power to review GAC. These formal – and mandatory – review and reporting requirements are completely novel to GAC and its employees. It will require not just a cultural adjustment to become accustomed to these new review bodies, but also a structural readjustment within a department already in need of modernization.

The *National Security Act, 2017* also enacted the *Communications Security Establishment Act*, which provides another major new obligation for the minister of global affairs: they must be "consulted" whenever CSE undertakes any of its new "defensive cyber operations," and they must request or consent to any exercise of the CSE's "active," or offensive (hacking), cyber operations.[39] This new authority contemplates a good deal of new collaboration and information-sharing between not just CSE and GAC, but any other departments that might have relevant information upon which a foreign minister would want to draw. Moreover, the CSE minister may issue offensive or defensive cyber authorizations only if they have "reasonable grounds to believe ... that the objective of the cyber operation could not reasonably be achieved by other means."[40] They will then have certain reporting obligations with respect to the types of activities authorized, length thereof, etc.[41] As a result, GAC may well be involved in the justification of some of CSE's cyber decisions – a process that will be overseen by a new Intelligence Commissioner and NSIRA, and possibly by NSICOP.

In many ways, GAC will be forced to become more transparent even if (or as) it resists. That process will neither be an easy one, nor will it come naturally, as GAC has neither the culture nor the infrastructure or procedures in place to comply seamlessly with increased transparency requirements. As with so many other departments, GAC is already struggling to keep pace with access to information requirements. Adding review compliance obligations will take time, and a structural – and cultural – readjustment. Moreover, that adjustment may not come easily given the budget crunch that seems to follow GAC and the staffing and training issues that already exist. Simply put, there will be structural and cultural reasons why review will create internal problems of compliance for GAC, which will be borne by employees who have little power individually to meaningfully change that which requires change.

In the meantime, there is little doubt that these new review, reporting, and information-sharing requirements will reveal a host of unforeseeable problems, whether they be structural and already in existence, or the result of future programs or initiatives that attract scrutiny. The fact that GAC has not had meaningful reviews in the past surely means that there is some catching up to do, both because of the need to make up for lost time (by solving inefficiencies and resolving any ongoing improprieties) and simply because GAC will have to put the infrastructure in place to cope with a new level of oversight. GAC should probably expect a review of its listing and sanctions programs at some point, as well as the GSRP and digital diplomacy initiatives. External review of GAC is a net positive and long overdue – if for no other reason than the need to challenge long-standing practices to improve efficacy. But such review may cause a cascading series of problems, big and small, that will not necessarily have easy or simple solutions.

An Increasingly Complex and Multipolar International
Security and Diplomatic Environment

We no longer live in a bipolar world, with the United States and Russia as two opposing powers keeping stability worldwide,[42] or even a unipolar world dominated by the United States. Instead, we live in a multipolar world with countries like China and Germany exercising increased influence. India, Brazil, and other rising economic powerhouses are likewise flexing their might. This multipolar world is increasingly complex – and dangerous. The so-called fourth industrial revolution has brought about rapid technological change; slow-footed bureaucratic departments struggle to keep pace with international adversaries that are at times able to act more nimbly.[43]

With relatively fewer resources and continuing problems with staffing, training, and identity, GAC is tasked with leading Canada's response in this increasingly complex world. How GAC manages these internal pressures and external challenges will have a great impact on Canada's place in the world – and perhaps the country's security.

Short-Termism versus the Long Game

The problem here is both systemic and existential: in a system that prioritizes quick responses and short catchphrases, where answers are demanded of politicians immediately and there is little appetite for a misspoken word or misunderstood conflict, how does GAC avoid getting dragged into the mundane political activities and short-termism of modern politics in the information age? This problem is particularly acute for GAC because it is a department that deals with complex international issues often misunderstood at home and subject to competing narratives abroad. What politician wishes to wade into a complex question about Gaza, or the US moving its Israeli embassy to Jerusalem, without safe talking points from GAC? A department can lose days of person power responding to one such request, not to mention the need for mission briefs, Question Period notes, take-note debates, which are written in the first instance by the bureaucrats, and myriad other "communications" products.

An ever-growing GAC headquarters, which is based in Ottawa, means a similarly growing focus on domestic, Ottawa-centric matters; a good deal of time is increasingly spent on responsive measures to little questions that require specific answers, all to avoid big problems. Long-term planning is put on the back-burner, in favour of the short-termism of politics and the vagaries of the information age. At the same time, Canada's international adversaries are able to take a long-term view in a way that can be near impossible for democracies: authoritarian regimes in China or Russia can afford to look well into the future, or to plan for resource depletion or migration decades in advance, because they do not have to worry about bad press or losing that next election. So while the multipolar world includes a number of increasingly powerful authoritarian adversaries able to take a long-term view, Canada is stuck in the short-termism of democratic politics and, more poignantly, the information age in which we live, where answers are demanded immediately and mistakes are unforgiveable.

Conclusion

GAC is a department with a key role to play in Canada's national security landscape, even if its mandate and, occasionally, its priorities fail to adequately recognize this. It tackles issues like international terrorism and organized crime directly, while its daily activities promote peace and prosperity worldwide. But GAC rarely works alone. It is increasingly interrelated with, and interdependent on, key international allies and national government departments, particularly in the field of national security.

GAC collects information from others, but it does not do national security investigations in the way that CSIS, the RCMP, or even CSE do; as such, it is imperative that GAC work cooperatively with all its partners to meet increasingly complex challenges. Six of these interrelated challenges have been identified in this chapter. Surely many more challenges could be identified. How GAC tackles them will dictate not only the fate of the department as a "central" agency in the years to come, but its place in the business of keeping Canada safe and prosperous.

NOTES

1 For a detailed history of the iterations of GAC, see John Hilliker, *Canada's Department of External Affairs*, vol. 1, *The Early Years, 1909–1946* (Toronto: Institute of Public Administration of Canada, 1990); John Hilliker and Donald Barry, *Canada's Department of External Affairs*, vol. 2, *Coming of Age, 1946–1968* (Montreal: McGill-Queen's University Press, 1995); John Hilliker, Mary Halloran, and Greg Donaghy, *Canada's Department of External Affairs*, vol. 3, *Innovation and Adaptation, 1968–1984* (Toronto: University of Toronto Press, 2017).

2 Instead, on the home front, the Royal Canadian Mounted Police (RCMP) was then responsible for policing and for intelligence gathering primarily related to sedition and espionage. The *CSIS Act* of 1984 established the service as separate entity from the RCMP; see the *Canadian Security Intelligence Service Act*, R.S.C. 1985, c. C-23, s. 1.

3 The names are as follows: Department of External Affairs from 1909 to 1995; Department of Foreign Affairs and International Trade (DFAIT) from 1995 to 2003; Foreign Affairs Canada from 2003 to 2006; Foreign Affairs and International Trade Canada from 2006 to 2013; Department of Foreign Affairs, Trade and Development (DFATD) (this is also when CIDA was added) from 2013 to 2015; Global Affairs Canada (GAC) from 2015 to present.

4 S.C. 2013, c. 33, s. 174.
5 *Department of Foreign Affairs, Trade and Development Act*, S.C. 2013, c. 33, s. 10(1).
6 *Department of Foreign Affairs, Trade and Development Act*, s. 10(2)(J).
7 GAC, *Departmental Plan 2017–18* (2017). Available online: http://international.gc.ca/gac-amc/publications/plans/dp-pm/dp-pm_1718.aspx?lang=eng#a3.
8 For example, GAC is responsible for administering the *United Nations Al-Qaida and Taliban Regulations*, SOR/99-444, and the *Regulations Implementing the United Nations Resolutions on the Suppression of Terrorism*, SOR/200-360.
9 For example, as a part of GAC's Anti-crime Capacity Building Program (available online: https://www.international.gc.ca/gac-amc/publications/evaluation/2016/eval_accbp_ctcbp-eval_arclcc_arca.aspx?lang=eng), GAC has contributed to security system reform in El Salvador, Honduras, and Guatemala in an effort to fight organized crime. See GAC, *Departmental Performance Report 2015–16* (2016). Available online: https://www.international.gc.ca/gac-amc/assets/pdfs/publications/plans/dpr-rmr/dpr-rmr_2015-2016-eng.pdf.
10 United Nations Office at Geneva, "Convention on the Prohibition of the Use, Stockpiling, Production and Transfer of Anti-Personnel Mines and on their Destruction," *Treaty Series*, vol. 2056 (3 December 1997, entry into force 1 March 1999), 211. Available online: https://www.unog.ch/80256EDD006B8954/(httpAssets)/8DF9CC31A4CA8B32C12571C7002E3F3E/$file/APLC+English.pdf.
11 Canada contributes roughly $16 million annually to the International Atomic Energy Agency (IAEA) with the expectation that the agency's actions and decisions will pay dividends to the Canadian nuclear industry and remain in step with Canadian foreign policy. See GAC, *2018–19 Departmental Plan* (2018), "Supplementary Information Tables," 44. Available online: https://www.international.gc.ca/gac-amc/assets/pdfs/publications/plans/dp-pm/dp-pm_1920_en.pdf?_ga=2.161222269.1925144423.1595283098-772590767.1595037877.
12 GAC, *2020–21 Departmental Plan* (2020), "Spending and Human Resources," 32. Available online: https://www.international.gc.ca/gac-amc/assets/pdfs/publications/plans/dp-pm/dp-pm_2021_en.pdf?_ga=2.239553862.452843355.1598761634-772590767.1595037877.
13 The figures for each year include the following institutions: GAC/DFATD/DFAIT, and CIDA.
14 See Office of the Privacy Commissioner of Canada, *Review of the Operationalization of the Security of Canada Information Sharing Act, Final Report 2017* (2017). Available online: https://www.priv.gc.ca/en/opc-actions-and-decisions/audits/ar-vr_scisa_2017/.

15 For more on what Top Secret security clearance means and how one
gets it, see Government of Canada, *Policy on Government Security* (2019)
(available online: https://www.tbs-sct.gc.ca/pol/doc-eng.aspx?id=16578);
Government of Canada, *Standard on Security Screening* (2014) (available
online: https://www.tbs-sct.gc.ca/pol/doc-eng.aspx?id=28115).

16 S.C. 2019, c. 13.

17 See Commission of Inquiry into the Actions of Canadian Officials in
Relation to Maher Arar (O'Connor Inquiry), *Report of the Events Relating to
Maher Arar*, vols. 1–3 (2006). Available online: http://publications.gc.ca
/site/eng/9.688875/publication.html.

18 For more on the torture of Almalki, Elmaati, and Nureddin in Syria, see
generally Frank Iacobucci, *Internal Inquiry into the Actions of Canadian
Officials in Relation to Abdullah Almalki, Ahmad Abou-Elmaati and Muayyed
Nureddin* (Ottawa: Public Works and Government Services Canada,
2008). Available online: http://publications.gc.ca/site/eng/9.699757
/publication.html.

19 For more information on these duties, see Craig Forcese, *National Security
Law: Canadian Practice in International Perspective* (Toronto: Irwin Law,
2007), 100.

20 This bureau was previously known as the Security and Intelligence
Bureau, which was responsible for providing "intelligence to support
policy and operational decisions." It also was said that it "advises the
Minister on intelligence activities" and that "the Bureau is also responsible
for the security of the department's personnel, physical assets and
information systems in Canada and around the world." See Government
of Canada, *The Canadian Security and Intelligence Community: Helping
Keep Canada and Canadians Safe and Secure* (Ottawa: Privy Council Office,
2001), 11. These tasks have obviously been subsumed by the International
Security Branch and its bureaus, though the tasks performed by the
branch's successor and other bureaus in the International Security Branch
have expanded since the 2001 PCO report.

21 See Security Intelligence Review Committee (SIRC), *Lifting the Shroud of
Secrecy: Thirty Years of Security Intelligence Accountability: Annual Report
2013–2014*, "Review of a CSIS Foreign Station" (2014), 24–6. Available
online: http://www.sirc-csars.gc.ca/anrran/2013-2014/index-eng
.html#sc2-7.

22 The program has not been without its controversies. First and foremost,
the distinction between GSRP and CSIS officers might at times be blurry.
The solution has been to mandate that GSRP use traditional diplomatic
information-gathering techniques. In practice, this means GSRP officers
use their real names, identify their positions, and do not throw bags of
money at sources or resort to other forms of covert tradecraft. There is

little publicly available data on the GSRP program or how it is working, so the extent to which the program is viewed as a success or remains controversial with CSIS or other agencies is difficult to say.

23 GAC, *Departmental Performance Report 2015–16*; GAC, *Departmental Results Report 2016–17* (2017). Available online: https://www.international.gc.ca /gac-amc/assets/pdfs/publications/plans/dpr-rmr/drr-rrm_1617-eng .pdf.

24 Public Safety Canada (PSC), *National Cyber Security Action Plan 2019–2024* (2019), 17. Available online: https://www.publicsafety.gc.ca/cnt/rsrcs /pblctns/ntnl-cbr-scrt-strtg-2019/ntnl-cbr-scrt-strtg-2019-en.pdf.

25 For a detailed account of Canada's contributions to the OPCW, see Government of Canada: Embassy of Canada in the Netherlands, "Statement of Canada Circulated to the Twenty-Second Conference of the State Parties to the Chemical Weapons Convention," The Hague, 28 November 2017. Available online: https://www.opcw.org/fileadmin /OPCW/CSP/C-22/national_statements/Canada_11-28.pdf.

26 S.C. 1992, c. 17, s. 6(1).

27 R.S.C. 1985, c. E-19.

28 *Special Economic Measures Act*, s. 4(1.1)(b).

29 *Special Economic Measures Act*, s. 4(1.1)(c).

30 GAC, Import and Export Controls, "About Us," last modified 2 October 2013, http://www.international.gc.ca/controls-controles/about-a_propos /index.aspx?lang=eng.

31 PSC, *Horizontal Evaluation of Canada's Cyber Security Strategy: Final Report* (2017), 18. Available online: https://www.publicsafety.gc.ca/cnt/rsrcs /pblctns/vltn-cnd-scrt-strtg/vltn-cnd-scrt-strtg-en.pdf.

32 These are no small questions. In 2018, section 25 of the *Investment Canada Act* was invoked to prevent the sale of Aecon to a Chinese state-owned enterprise, China Communications Construction Company (CCCC), on the basis of national security. See Lally et al, "Proposed Acquisition of Aecon by CCCI Blocked on National Security Grounds," *Osler, Hoskin & Harkourt LLP – Cross Border Markets*, 24 May 2018, https://www.osler .com/en/resources/cross-border/2018/proposed-acquisition-of-aecon -by-ccci-blocked-on-national-security-grounds. Section 25.4(1)(a) of the *Investment Canada Act* specifically allows the governor in council to disallow an investment by a non-Canadian that it believes to be injurious to the national security of Canada. See *Investment Canada Act*, R.S.C. 2013, c. 33, s. 25.4(1)(a). So does national security trump big business, or should we look the other way for business opportunities? Similar concerns have recently sprung up regarding Chinese telecom giant Huawei. See comments from John Adams, Ward Elcock, and Richard Fadden – former heads of CSIS and CSE – in Robert Fife and Steven Chase, "Former Top

Canadian Security Officials Warn Ottawa to Sever Links with China's Huawei," *Globe and Mail*, 19 March 2018, https://www.theglobeandmail.com/politics/article-former-top-canadian-security-officials-join-call-for-ottawa-to-nix/.

33 The Integrated Foreign Affairs and Development Policy spent $76,329,133.00 in the 2015–16 year, but there is not a more specific breakdown of that spending. While more specific breakdowns of GAC's budget allocations are available via Public Accounts of Canada and the government's InfoBase resource, these still do not provide a completely accurate picture of which specific programs GAC is funding. See GAC, *Departmental Performance Report 2015–16*; GAC, *Departmental Results Report 2016–17*. Information on year-over-year funding to the dozens (at the very least) of GAC's important and potentially controversial subprograms, such as the GSRP, is thus impossible to find. It is similarly impossible to determine how many full-time equivalents (FTEs) are employed by any such subprograms.

34 See *Criminal Code*, R.S.C. 1985, c. C-46, s. 83.05. See also the Department of Justice's list of terrorist entities: PSC, "Currently Listed Entities," last modified 21 June 2019, https://www.publicsafety.gc.ca/cnt/ntnl-scrt/cntr-trrrsm/lstd-ntts/crrnt-lstd-ntts-en.aspx.

35 For a more robust discussion of this problem, see Michael Nesbitt, "Canada's '"Unilateral"' Sanctions Regime under Review: Extraterritoriality, Human Rights, Due Process, and Enforcement in Canada's Special Economic Measures Act,", *Ottawa Law Review* 48, no. 2 (2017): 554–5, 561.

36 At least the reason is fairly clear, even if it is not expressly articulated by GAC: its Legal Bureau has traditionally taken the lead on the sanctions file, though it does not have the capacity to determine who should be listed. So the Legal Bureau works with the geographic departments – and as of the summer of 2019, the sanctions coordination unit housed within GAC – to come up with a list of entities that might be sanctioned. But traditionally, by the Legal Bureau's maintaining ultimate responsibility for all interpretative functions on the file, all questions about SEMA sanctions must go through it. And being made up of lawyers, the Legal Bureau does not think it proper to provide "legal advice" to private industry. Thus, the structure of GAC has traditionally limited outreach with Canadian businesses in a way not seen with allied governments. For a more robust discussion of this problem, see Michael Nesbitt, "Canada's 'Unilateral' Sanctions Regime under Review: Extraterritoriality, Human Rights, Due Process, and Enforcement in Canada's Special Economic Measures Act," *Ottawa Law Review* 48, no. 2 (2017): 554–5, 561.

37 In its former iterations, GAC was the subject of ad hoc reviews. The O'Connor Inquiry, for example, detailed DFAIT's knowledge of the

detainment and eventual torture of Mr. Arar. See generally all four
volumes of the O'Connor Inquiry, *Reporting on the Events Relating to
Maher Arar* (2006). Available online: http://publications.gc.ca/site
/eng/9.688875/publication.html. In its 2014 report, SIRC reviewed
GAC's relationship with CSIS and found the relationship between the
two to be positive on the whole. The report also notes that after the
O'Connor Inquiry, "CSIS and DFATD signed a protocol concerning
cooperation in respect of consular cases involving Canadians detained
abroad with national security or terrorism-related implications." SIRC
however noted that there were still issues with respect to disclosure
protocols and deconfliction process between the two institutions.
See SIRC, *Annual Report 2014–2015: Broader Horizons: Preparing the
Groundwork for Change in Security Intelligence*, "CSIS's Relationship
and Exchanges with the Department of Foreign Affairs, Trade and
Development" (2015), s. 2. Available online: http://www.sirc-csars
.gc.ca/anrran/2014-2015/index-eng.html.

38 *National Security and Intelligence Committee of Parliamentarians Act*, S.C.
2017, c. 15. The mandate of the Committee is found at section 8(1)(a)–(c)
of the act. Section 8(b) states that the committee is to review "any activity
carried out by a department that relates to national security or intelligence,
unless the activity is an ongoing operation and the appropriate Minister
determines that the review would be injurious to national security."

39 See Bill C-59, cl. 76, *An Act to establish the Communications Security
Establishment*, at cls. 30(2) and 31(2), respectively, online: http://www
.parl.ca/DocumentViewer/en/42-1/bill/C-59/second-reading.

40 Bill C-59, cl. 76 at cl. 35(4).

41 Bill C-59 cl. 76 at cls. 35(1)–(4) and 36.

42 See Joseph S. Nye Jr., "The Future of American Power: Dominance and
Decline in Perspective," *Foreign Affairs* 89, no. 6 (2010): 2–12; Andrew F.
Cooper and Daniel Flemes, "Foreign Policy Strategies of Emerging Powers
in a Multipolar World: An Introductory Review," *Third World Quarterly* 34,
no. 6 (2013): 943–62.

43 Klaus Schwab, *The Fourth Industrial Revolution* (New York: Crown Business,
2016). See also Chen Liu, "International Competitiveness and the Fourth
Industrial Revolution," *Entrepreneurial Bus & Economics Review* 5, no. 4
(2017): 111–33.

13 The Department of Justice Canada (Justice Canada)

CRAIG FORCESE AND JENNIFER POIRIER

Introduction

This chapter addresses the role of Canada's Department of Justice (Justice Canada) in national security. While Justice Canada is not a national security agency *per se*, it is intimately involved in Canada's approach to national security. In Canada's liberal democracy, all state activities, including those implicating national security, are expected to comply with the rule of law. This means that no agency may act without a legal basis, anchored typically in statute and sometimes in royal prerogative or other forms of common law. It also means that no agency is above the law and that all are expected to act in accordance with it.

This chapter describes the role of Justice Canada generally, and then those groups within Justice Canada most closely implicated in national security matters. It then addresses key Justice Canada functions: Justice Canada's legal advisory role; its legislative drafting and policy work; and its role as counsel in litigation. We intersperse these discussions with observations on professionalism challenges associated with Justice Canada's role in national security.

Because one of the authors (Poirier) of this chapter is a Justice Canada lawyer, there are occasions in this chapter where the opinions expressed are attributed specifically to the other author (Forcese).

Mandate of Justice Canada

Justice Canada is a statutory department headed by the minister of justice.[1] By law, the minister of justice is also the attorney general of Canada. In the first role, the minister manages and directs Justice Canada. The minister is also the "official legal advisor to the Governor General and the legal member of the Queen's Privy Council for Canada," which makes the minister the chief law officer to Cabinet. Among other things, the minister must "see that the administration of public affairs is in accordance with law."[2]

In her or his role as attorney general, the minister inherits the traditional powers and duties belonging to the office of the attorney general of England "by law and usage, to the extent applicable to Canada." Most importantly, the attorney general conducts litigation for or against the Crown or any department within federal jurisdiction.[3] This litigation may arise in provincial courts or in the Federal Courts (i.e., the Federal Court and Federal Court of Appeal). Because most national-security-related litigation occurs in Federal Courts, this chapter confines its focus to litigation before that body.

Inter-agency Issues in Criminal Law

The federal attorney general also oversees prosecutions in Canada's criminal justice system. By long-standing constitutional tradition, the attorney general is expected to be above partisan concerns in supervising prosecutions, creating an independence within executive government not shared by other members of Cabinet.[4] Prosecutorial independence is a carefully protected expectation in Canadian law.[5] At the federal level, it is reinforced within the Justice portfolio by a statute that separates Justice Canada and the Public Prosecution Service of Canada (PPSC). Under the supervision of its own director, the PPSC conducts most federal prosecutions, and its law imposes transparency requirements where the attorneys general themselves assume the conduct of a prosecution or direct its initiation or conduct.[6] Federal prosecutions generally do not include *Criminal Code* matters arising in the provinces, as provincial Crowns prosecute these crimes. However, the federal attorney general has concurrent jurisdiction over many national security offences, including terrorism,[7] and may assert primacy in prosecuting them.[8]

In practice, PPSC conducts most – if not all – terrorism and espionage prosecutions. In 2017, PPSC was pursuing 8 ongoing terrorism prosecutions (down from 17 the year before) and one espionage prosecution. It reported in 2017 that "understandings with the provincial Attorneys General ensure seamless cooperation and the availability of the full range of investigative and prosecution options to address the dangers posed by terrorism."[9]

Prosecutorial independence also means that the PPSC is institutionally independent of the police and investigative agencies. Police or other investigators cannot compel the initiation or abandonment of a prosecution.[10] However, national security cases especially may involve close coordination between prosecutors and police. Not least, terrorism and espionage criminal proceedings require the attorney general's consent,[11] in practice given by the director or deputy director of PPSC.[12] Coordination challenges also arise between the Canadian Security Intelligence Service (CSIS, in collecting intelligence) and the Royal Canadian Mounted Police (RCMP, in collecting evidence). This cooperation between CSIS and the RCMP also engages Justice Canada (in advising government agencies and performing the litigation roles discussed below) and PPSC (in prosecuting criminal trials).

Justice Canada and National Security

In the balance of this chapter, we focus on the role of the Department of Justice (as opposed to the PPSC) in national security. Justice Canada supports the dual mandates of the minister of justice and attorney general of Canada. To this end, Justice Canada generally organizes itself into four broad areas of work: advisory and legal services; litigation (both in terms of providing litigation support and conducting actual litigation on behalf of the attorney general); legislative drafting; and policy development. Justice Canada's work in these four areas contributes to Canada's national security.

Justice Canada lawyers work in the department's central offices, where they support Justice Canada's policy development and legislative drafting roles; in regional offices from which they support the conduct of litigation; in specialized advisory units focused on particular areas of practice (e.g., labour and employment law, public law, commercial law, etc.); and from offices co-located with other government departments and agencies where Justice Canada lawyers provide most advisory and legal services.

Resources

For 2020–21, Justice Canada anticipated approximately 4,400 full-time equivalent employees, with almost three-quarters providing legal services. Most employees were in the national capital region, while the others worked from regional offices across the country. The department's anticipated budget in 2020–21 was $718 million.[13] No specific figures are available publicly on the resources allocated specifically to national security matters.

Justice Canada's Advisory Role

Providing Legal Advice

Justice Canada is effectively the government's law firm: it is responsible for providing advisory services to all government departments and agencies.[14] This centralized model for government legal advice aims to promote consistent and high-quality legal services in support of the policy objectives of the government as a whole.

Most advisory and legal services are delivered through department legal service units (DLSUs), co-located with each department or agency. While the Justice counsel who staff these DLSUs may be physically situated in another department or agency, they remain Justice Canada employees. This has the advantage of allowing Justice Canada to "speak with one voice" on legal issues. There may, however, be legal matters requiring referral to other sections within Justice Canada with specialized subject-matter expertise (e.g., constitutional law issues). Inevitably, giving legal advice requires balancing between DLSUs (who may have thorough knowledge of the institutions with which they are co-located and the factual concerns underlying their legal advice) and subject-matter specialists (with focused expertise, but less familiarity with the client departments and the factual issues).

Each of the departments or agencies with a national security mandate has its own, on-site DLSU to provide daily advice and, in some cases, other specialized legal services. Most of these DLSUs form part of the Public Safety, Defence and Immigration (PSDI) Portfolio at Justice Canada (Global Affairs Canada and the Financial Transactions and Reports Analysis Centre of Canada fall within different portfolios because their core mandates are not as national security focused). This portfolio acts as a coordinating body for the range of advisory, litigation, and legislative services that its legal counsel offer in support of client departments and agencies.

Certain specialized national security law issues also arise within Justice Canada's National Litigation Sector, a high-level branch within the department headed by an assistant deputy attorney general who coordinates federal litigation. Within this unit, the National Security Group (NSG) provides specialized advice and conducts litigation in relation to all matters that fall under section 38 of the *Canada Evidence Act*.[15] Section 38 governs the handling of sensitive and potentially injurious information related to international relations, national defence, or national security, during judicial and other proceedings. The NSG's advisory role is both inward and outward facing: it not only provides advice in relation to section 38 matters to all government departments and agencies, but it also provides advice to the attorney general with regard to their role under section 38.[16]

Policy Development and National Security

The principal responsibility for national security policy development rests with other departments in the Government of Canada, such as the Department of Public Safety and Emergency Preparedness (Public Safety Canada). However, Justice Canada does support the development of national security policy in two important ways.

First, Justice Canada supports the development and implementation of national security policy through its counsel who are co-located with the departments who have national security mandates. As noted above, these DLSU counsel are generally responsible for providing advisory services to the department or agency where they are co-located, and this includes advice on the development or implementation of national security policy.

Second, one of Justice Canada's own core policy responsibilities is criminal justice. This is done through the department's Criminal Law Policy Section (CLPS), which is the department's centre of expertise in this area. Counsel in CLPS provide legal and policy advice to the minister of justice and other government departments, including on the development and implementation of criminal justice policy in relation to national security. Much of CLPS's work also involves the development of amendments to major federal criminal statutes, including the original 2001 Anti-terrorism Act.[17]

Legislative Drafting and National Security

Justice Canada is responsible for drafting all government bills and most regulations, whatever the sponsoring department or agency. Its Legislative Service Branch has bilingual and bijural (i.e., expert in both the common and civil law traditions) counsel who do drafting in tandem, and who also provide legal and legislative policy advice to departments or agencies during the development of legislative proposals.

Because Justice Canada counsel who work in DLSUs develop an intimate knowledge of the mandates of the departments and agencies they serve, counsel from DLSUs are also be present when legislation is being drafted by the Legislative Service Branch to provide subject-matter-specific advice. In the context of major national security legislation, like Bill C-59 (the National Security Act, 2017),[18] counsel from each of the DLSUs whose departments or agencies are affected by the proposed legislation work with the policy experts and legislative drafters to ensure that the government policy objectives are attained. In some cases, where the legislative proposals touch on several departments or agencies, counsel from various DLSUs also work in teams.

Professionalism Considerations and Controversies

All lawyers advising clients "must be honest and candid and must inform the client of all information known to the lawyer than may affect the interests of the client in the matter."[19] The lawyer is obliged to give a "competent opinion" based on the facts, applicable law, and the lawyer's own experience and expertise. That advice "must be open and undisguised and must clearly disclose what the lawyer honestly thinks about the merits and probable results."[20]

Government lawyers are not formally subject to different rules of professionalism.[21] However, they are differently situated from their private sector counterparts, as they advise on the exercise of state power. This may create special public duties on government lawyers. For one thing, Justice lawyers are public servants and are bound by the same values and ethics that apply to the public service. In his report on this topic, former deputy minister of justice John Tait noted that Canada's public institutions are established under law and must administer and uphold law. To achieve this objective,

> the public service and individual public servants should be animated by an unshakable conviction about the importance and primacy of law, and about the need to uphold it with integrity, impartiality and judgement. Because so many public servants are engaged, one way or another, in acts of what might be called discretionary justice, they must possess a due sense of the solemnity and exigencies of this role.[22]

More than this, Justice lawyers exercise powers delegated by the minister of justice.[23] As noted, the latter is obliged to "see that the administration of public affairs is in accordance with law." More generally, the 1968 McRuer Report into Civil Liberties in Ontario concluded that attorneys general have duties to "exercise constant vigilance to sustain and defend the rule of law against departmental attempts to grasp unhampered arbitrary powers."[24] The Federal Court of Appeal has described attorneys general as "guardians of the public interest in the administration of justice," "constitutionally obliged to exercise their discretionary authority in good faith, objectively, independently, and in the public interest."[25]

John Tait concluded that, as a result of these types of ministerial responsibilities, "Justice lawyers have a special mandate within government to uphold the rule of law, a crucial principle of democracy which is, among other things, a protection for citizens against the 'despotism' of officials – our clients and public service lawyers themselves."[26] This imposes an obligation of objectivity in the interpretation of the law: "There must be a fair inquiry into what the law actually is. The rule of law is not protected by unduly stretching the interpretation to fit the client's wishes."[27] The Justice lawyer's advisory role, Tait argued, has three aspects:

> His or her role is to advise, first on the Constitution and the law, which is one representation of the public interest; second, on the ethical matters deriving from the duties of the Minister and public servants, which are often of a fiduciary nature; and third, on the policy wisdom or public interest from a government lawyer's perspective (not just his personal views) and not in a way that fails to respect the client department's mandate and expertise.[28]

The divide between policy and law may not, therefore, be as stark as in a private sector context. In Tait's words:

> Public law is replete with issues of values and morals for the solicitor to consider on behalf of the client, often relating to the big picture of how government must use their power in a Parliamentary democracy. A public service lawyer does not try to play the role of the client, but knows what the duties of the client are and what factors must be considered, and brings them to the attention of the client.[29]

These considerations may be particularly acute in the national security area. As Forcese has regularly noted, Canada's national security laws are rarely amended and updated.[30] In consequence, they may not keep pace with changes in the threat or technological environment. While this is not something that Justice Canada can address directly given its mandate, there is nevertheless a concern that Justice lawyers may be left to advise on how operational square pegs fit into legal round holes. Forcese has urged that a more regular updating of legal authorities – of the sort represented by Bill C-59 and that is commonplace in close allied countries – would be a welcome addition to Canada's practice of national security law.

Regular updating, coupled with careful law-making, would address another challenge stemming from uncertain or outdated law: transparency.

246 Craig Forcese and Jennifer Poirier

Forcese worries that Justice Canada legal opinions construing the scope of vague, open-textured statutory powers have the *de facto* effect of legislating the practical reach of those powers. These opinions are clothed in solicitor–client privilege – leading Forcese to worry that rules designed to permit frank advice between lawyer and client have the consequence of diminishing public access to a true understanding of how the government interprets its legal powers.[31] It must be acknowledged that the government regularly asserts solicitor–client privilege in all areas, but in the context of national security, Forcese is concerned that Justice Canada legal advice often is the last say: the covert nature of national security activities means that no one may be aware of how these powers are being used, and able to adjudicate the true scope of the law in front of an impartial magistrate. In the hothouse of internal government deliberations, established legal positions may become difficult to dislodge. Forcese has worried that subsequent legal interpretations of agency powers may build on earlier, undisclosed legal positions, producing outcomes that those outside of government may find difficult to understand.[32]

To its credit, however, the government has recently embraced greater proactive transparency in the Justice Canada area. In June 2017, the government announced a "national security transparency commitment." This commitment includes a pledge: "Departments and agencies will explain how their national security activities are authorized in law and how they interpret and implement their authorities in line with Canadian values, including those expressed by the Charter."[33] Since then, the government has published online its "Charterpedia" summary of *Canadian Charter of Rights and Freedoms* jurisprudence. And it now discloses *Charter* analyses of bills before Parliament, making its reasoning transparent to the legal and broader community.

Justice Canada's Role in Litigating National Security Cases

Overview

The federal government is almost always represented in litigation by lawyers from Justice Canada's National Litigation Sector. Thus, litigation implicating national security is usually led by counsel from the Justice Canada regional office most closely situated to where the litigation will commence. For example, the lead counsel in many of the immigration security certificate litigations (representing the ministers of immigration and public safety) came from Justice Canada's regional offices. Regional counsel who take the lead in civil litigation cases are assisted by Justice Canada counsel who work in the relevant DLSU. These latter lawyers provide litigation support, acting as a link between their relevant department or agency and the regional litigators and assisting in the collection of documents for discovery purposes.

However, there are certain specialized areas of practice involving national security where counsel from elsewhere in Justice Canada take the lead in litigating. For example, as noted above, counsel in NSG are responsible for litigating all proceedings under section 38 of the *Canada Evidence Act*.[34] Similarly, counsel in Justice Canada's National Security Litigation and Advisory Group are responsible for bringing all CSIS warrant applications pursuant to sections 21 and 21.1 of the *Canadian Security Intelligence Service Act*.[35]

Proceedings under these acts differ from typical civil or criminal litigation in several ways. This novelty obliges counsel with a more specialized litigation practice. As discussed next, national-security-related litigation may also pose specific professionalism challenges different from regular areas of practice.

Professionalism in National-Security-Related Litigation

Lawyers representing a client in litigation are obliged to act "resolutely and honourably" within the limits of the law.[36] This "duty of commitment to the client's cause (sometimes referred to as 'zealous representation')"[37] requires a lawyer, in an adversarial proceeding, "to raise fearlessly every issue, advance every argument and ask every question, however distasteful, that the lawyer thinks will help the client's case and to endeavour to obtain for the client the benefit of every remedy and defence authorized by law."[38] The lawyer is expected to be "openly and necessarily partisan" and generally need not "assist an adversary or advance matters harmful to the client's case."[39]

On the other hand, counsel "must discharge this duty by fair and honourable means, without illegality and in a manner that is consistent with the lawyer's duty to treat the tribunal with candour, fairness, courtesy and respect and in a way that promotes the parties' right to a fair hearing in which justice can be done."[40]

These responsibilities raise special problems in national security litigation, mostly because of the classified nature of the information often at issue. National security litigation may be protracted and especially burdened with delay, sometimes controversially, as issues surrounding the disclosure of this information in open court are resolved.[41]

Even more dramatically, many national security proceedings are held in the absence of a party other than the government (*ex parte*), behind closed doors (*in camera*). Here, where the adversarial system no longer exists, rules of professional conduct impose a robust duty of candour on lawyers, and by extension their clients: "The lawyer must take particular care to be accurate, candid and comprehensive in presenting the client's case so as to ensure that the tribunal is not misled."[42] In *ex parte* proceedings, there is a duty of utmost good faith,[43] and the "evidence presented must be complete and thorough and no relevant information adverse to the interest of that party may be withheld."[44] The party relying on evidence in an *ex parte* proceeding must "conduct a thorough review of the information in its possession and make representations based on all of the information including that which is unfavourable to their case."[45] The duty also obliges "an ongoing effort to update, throughout the proceedings, the information and evidence regarding" the excluded party subject to the proceedings (for instance, the "named person" in immigration security certificate proceedings).[46] (There is, however, no obligation on government lawyers to argue against their own case.)[47]

Ex parte proceedings – usually done also *in camera* – are rare in regular legal proceedings, not least because Canada embraces the principle of "open courts," in which parties know the case to be met and the merits of the case are tested in a fully adversarial process. In the criminal context, an exception to these principles is made with warrant and other search authorizations, where the police seek to invade a person's reasonable expectation of privacy to further a criminal investigation. *Ex parte/in camera* proceedings (which we shall simply call closed proceedings) in warrant applications reflect investigative need. For instance, a covert wiretap is unlikely to produce evidence of guilt if the target is apprised of it. Subsequently, however, the substance of that warrant and the materials supporting it are disclosable in any criminal prosecution. And even in the absence of a criminal trial, the existence of a wiretap authorization must, following the conclusion of an investigation, be revealed to the target according to legislated timetables.

Closed proceedings are much more commonplace in the national security area. They may (and in some cases, must) arise as part of threat-reduction or invasive surveillance warrants under the *CSIS Act*; proceedings under section 38 of the *Canada Evidence Act* to protect from disclosure information over which the government claims national security confidentiality in criminal, civil, or administrative matters; adjudication of the reasonableness of security certificates under the *Immigration and Refugee Protection Act*;[48] appeals from passport revocations under the *Prevention of Terrorist Travel Act*;[49] judicial review of listings on Canada's terrorist entity list under the *Criminal Code*;[50] and appeals from listings on Passenger Protect, Canada's no-fly list, under the *Secure Air Travel Act*.[51]

The justification for closed proceedings varies slightly among these matters. A common theme in all national security closed proceedings is the need to protect classified information from disclosure in what would otherwise be open court proceedings. The fact that information is "classified" is not, itself, a legal justification for denying disclosure. The government must justify non-disclosure based on various tests that vary between statutory frameworks, with that under section 38 of the *Canada Evidence Act* being the most complex. Here, the Federal Court must balance the national security interest in confidentiality against other interests, not least fair trial rights. In so doing, the court is concerned with the prejudice that would stem from disclosure, and especially potential harm to intelligence sources, means, and methods.

These preoccupations are supplemented by investigative need in CSIS warrant applications. That need may be even more important here than in the criminal context. While classic criminal investigations are time limited, involving the collection of information in service of a prosecution, intelligence investigations may be indefinite, involving the collection of information to guide government action. Disclosing government knowledge of this information might prompt targets to change their behaviour, defeating the point of acquiring intelligence. For these reasons, CSIS warrants and the information supporting them (contained in affidavits sworn by CSIS officers) are almost never disclosed. Unlike *Criminal Code* wiretap authorizations, *CSIS Act* warrants are only occasionally at issue in criminal proceedings – usually when information collected under such a warrant is then shared with police and supports a police search warrant or authorization.[52] They do not, therefore, generally become public as part of criminal proceedings. Moreover, the *CSIS Act* contains no obligation that a target be notified of the existence of a wiretap, even on completion of an investigation.

Some closed proceedings – most notably, immigration security certificate adjudications and passport revocation, no-fly, and terrorist listing appeals – enable the government to use non-disclosed classified information as evidence on the merits of the case. These raise even more complex issues about procedural fairness and open courts. In the security certificate context, a trilogy of Supreme Court cases has obliged on constitutional grounds the participation of security-cleared "special advocates," tasked with representing the interests of the "named person" in the closed proceedings.[53] Special advocates restore an element of adversarialism, although they do not compensate fully for the absence of the party and their own lawyers. In other proceedings, including some *Canada Evidence Act* and CSIS warrant application matters, the Federal Court has exercised its own discretion in appointing *amicus curiae* – or friends of the court – to test the government's case or perform other functions to assist the court in the closed proceedings.[54]

The presence of special advocates or *amicus curiae* does not, however, negate government counsel's duty of candour. Indeed, statutory and constitutional expectations in immigration security certificate contexts impose a substantial obligation on government to disclose relevant information to the court and special advocate,[55] a process that closely implicates Justice counsel.

Controversies

In several recent decisions, the Federal Court raised concern about the degree of candour exhibited by CSIS in closed proceedings before it.[56] In its 2016 decision in the so-called ODAC (Operational Data Analysis Centre) matter, the Federal Court wrote:

> CSIS, through its elevated duty of candour must inform the Court fully, substantially, clearly and transparently of the use it makes or plans to make of the information it collects through the operation of Court issued warrants. ... The CSIS must have the confidence of the Court when it presents warrant applications. In the present file, it has certainly not enhanced the Court's trust. ...
>
> I find that the CSIS has breached its duty of candour by not informing the Court of its associated data retention program [ODAC].[57]

In the wake of this decision, Justice Canada retained Murray Segal to study the issue of candour in CSIS warrant proceedings.[58] His detailed report, containing 21 reform recommendations, was then reviewed by John Sims, a former deputy attorney general.[59] Mr. Sims's study explored how the Segal recommendations might be implemented. Justice Canada then issued an action plan to address CSIS warrant practices.[60] The action plan included a new policy on the duty of candour in *ex parte* proceedings.[61] This policy establishes several governing principles: "information must be presented completely, accurately, fairly and fully"; "counsel and affiants must be transparent" (a requirement of "frankness"); "errors in the authorization or its execution must be brought to the court's attention promptly";[62] "the [CSIS officer] affiant must be experienced, authoritative and independent"; and "counsel must understand and carry out the role of the Attorney General" (independence from CSIS and objectivity). The policy also provides guidelines on the practical application of these principles, both for drafting

affidavits supporting warrants and providing adequate legal and factual context to the court.

Conclusion

It is easy to overlook Justice Canada's role in national security and to
focus on those of operational agencies. However, Canada's national
security practices are infused with law, a pattern that has acceler-
ated with time. In these circumstances, lawyers increasingly sit at the
metaphorical elbow of security agencies, and their advice shapes the
conduct of national security in Canada. To advance national security
in a society governed by the rule of law, Justice Canada must be
able to adapt to and evolve in a dynamic environment while simultaneously ensuring that "the administration of public affairs is in
accordance with law." It is a challenging task, but one that representatives of the attorney general of Canada acknowledge and organize
to achieve. The principles discussed in the Murray and Sims reports,
and that form the basis of the new policy on the duty of candour,
are part of the foundation ensuring Justice Canada can meet these
challenges.

NOTES

Jennifer Poirier is an employee of Justice Canada. The views represented in
this article should not be taken to represent the views of Justice Canada.

1 *Department of Justice Act*, R.S.C. 1985, c. J-2, s. 2.
2 *Department of Justice Act*, s. 4.
3 *Department of Justice Act*, s. 5.
4 *Krieger v. Law Society of Alberta*, 2002 SCC 65 at para. 30.
5 See *Hinse v. Canada (Attorney General)*, 2015 SCC 35 at para. 40.
6 *Director of Public Prosecutions Act*, S.C. 2006, c. 9, s. 121 at ss. 10 and 15.
7 *Criminal Code*, R.S.C. 1985, c. C-46, ss. 2(b.1)–(g).
8 *Security Offences Act*, R.S.C. 1985, c. S-7, ss. 2–5.
9 Public Prosecution Service of Canada (PPSC), *2017–18 Departmental Plan*
   (2017), 21. Available online: https://www.ppsc-sppc.gc.ca/eng/pub/dp
   -pm/2017_2018/index.html. PPSC, *Report on Plans and Priorities 2016–17*
   (2016), 21. Available online: https://www.ppsc-sppc.gc.ca/eng/pub/
   rpp/2016_2017/index.html. No numbers on terrorism prosecutions are
   reported in the two most recent departmental plan reports.
10 PPSC, *Deskbook* (2014–20), 7. Available online: https://www.ppsc-sppc
   .gc.ca/eng/pub/fpsd-sfpg/fps-sfp/tpd/d-g-eng.pdf.

11 *Criminal Code*, s. 83.24; *Security of Information Act*, R.S.C. 1985, c. O-5, s. 24.
12 PPSC, *Deskbook*, 4.
13 Department of Justice Canada, *2019–20 Departmental Plan* (2019), 30. Available online: https://www.justice.gc.ca/eng/rp-pr/cp-pm/rpp/2019_2020/rep -rap/dp-pm.pdf.
14 A caveat to this: the Office of the Judge Advocate General serves as the lead legal advisor on military law. *National Defence Act*, R.S.C. 1985, c. N-5, s. 9.1. The legal advisory office in Global Affairs Canada also constitutes a separate centre of legal advice (at least on international law).
15 R.S.C. 1985, c. C-5.
16 Where an appropriate claim exists, the government will assert this privilege, which leads to bifurcation between the court that has jurisdiction over the prosecution (typically a Superior Court of a province) and the Federal Court of Canada. In matters stemming from criminal prosecutions, it may also bifurcate legal teams between Justice Canada's NSG and PPSC prosecutors.
17 S.C. 2001, c. 41.
18 S.C. 2019, c. 13.
19 Federation of Law Societies of Canada (FLSC), *Model Code of Professional Conduct*, rule 3.2-2 (2019), 21. Available online: https://flsc.ca/wp-content /uploads/2019/11/Model-Code-October-2019.pdf.
20 FLSC, *Model Code*, rule 3.2-2, commentary 2, 21.
21 There is, however, controversy on this point. See Adam Dodek, "Lawyering at the Intersection of Public Law and Legal Ethics: Government Lawyers as Custodians of the Rule of Law," *Dalhousie Law Journal* 1, no. 33 (2010): 1–53.
22 Task Force on Public Service Values and Ethics, *A Strong Foundation: Report of the Task Force on Public Service Values and Ethics* (Ottawa: Canadian Centre for Management Development, 1997), 42.
23 For a discussion on this point, see Dodek, "Lawyering at the Intersection of Public Law and Legal Ethics," 18.
24 Ontario, *Royal Commission into Civil Rights*, vol. 2 (Toronto: Queen's Printer, 1968), 945. See discussion in Dodek, "Lawyering at the Intersection of Public Law and Legal Ethics," 20.
25 *Cosgrove v. Canadian Judicial Council*, 2007 F.C.A. 103 at para. 51.
26 John Tait, "The Public Service Lawyer, Service to the Client and the Rule of Law," *Commonwealth Law Bulletin* 23, no. 1–2 (1997): 543.
27 Tait, "The Public Service Lawyer," 543.
28 Tait, "The Public Service Lawyer," 544.
29 Tait, "The Public Service Lawyer," 544.
30 See, e.g., Craig Forcese, "Oh, What Tangled Webs the CSIS Act Weaves: The Federal Court's Latest Decision on CSIS's Foreign Intelligence Mandate," *Craig Forcese* (blog), 19 July 2018, https://www.craigforcese

.com/blog/2018/7/19/oh-what-tangled-webs-the-csis-act-weaves-the
-federal-courts.html.

31 For a critique of Justice Canada's views on the scope of solicitor–client
privilege in this sort of context, see Dodek, "Lawyering at the Intersection
of Public Law and Legal Ethics," 44.

32 See discussion in Craig Forcese, "Armchair Metalawyering Metadata:
CSEC's Mandate and the Latest Snowden Release," *National Security Law
Blog*, 4 February 2014, http://craigforcese.squarespace.com/national
-security-law-blog/2014/2/4/armchair-metalawyering-metadata-csecs
-mandate-and-the-latest.html. Both of these uncertainties are addressed
in Bill C-59.

33 Government of Canada, "Executive Transparency," last modified 2 July
2019, https://www.canada.ca/en/services/defence/nationalsecurity
/national-security-transparency-commitment/executivetransparency.html.

34 R.S.C. 1985, c. C-5.

35 R.S.C. 1985, c. C-23 (*CSIS Act*).

36 FLSC, *Model Code*, rule 5.1-1, 79–80.

37 *R. v. Neil*, 2002 SCC 70 at para. 19.

38 FLSC, *Model Code*, rule 5.1-1, commentary 1, 79.

39 FLSC, *Model Code*, rule 5.1-1, commentary 3, 79.

40 FLSC, *Model Code*, rule 5.1-1, commentary 1, 79.

41 See, e.g., the issues of delay discussed in *Almalki v. Canada (Attorney General)*,
2012 O.N.S.C. 3924.

42 FLSC, *Model Code*, rule 5.1-1, commentary 6, 79.

43 *Ruby v. Canada (Solicitor General)*, [2002] 4 S.C.R. 3, 2002 SCC 75 at para. 27.

44 *Canada (Citizenship and Immigration) v. Harkat*, 2014 SCC 37 at para. 101.

45 *Harkat* at para. 101, citing *Almrei (Re)*, 2009 FC 1263 at para. 500.

46 *Harkat* at para. 102.

47 *Canada (Attorney General) v. Almalki*, 2011 FCA 54 at para. 22

48 S.C. 2001, c. 27, division 9.

49 SC 2015, c. 36, s. 42.

50 R.S.C. 1985, c. C-48, s. 83.05 *et seq.*

51 SC 2015, c. 20, s.11, s. 16 *et seq.*

52 See, e.g., *R. v. Jaser*, 2014 ONSC 6052.

53 *Charkaoui v. Canada (Citizenship and Immigration)*, 2007 SCC 9; *Charkaoui v.
Canada (Citizenship and Immigration)*, 2008 SCC 38; *Harkat.*

54 For a discussion of the role of *amici*, see Murray D. Segal, "Review of CSIS
Warrant Practice" (December 2016), *Secret Law Gazette*. Available online:
http://secretlaw.omeka.net/items/show/76.

55 *Immigration and Refugee Protection Act*, SC 2001, c. 27, s. 85.4.

56 The "ODAC" judgment, 2016 FC 1105; *Re X*, 2013 FC 1275, aff'd 2014 FCA
249; *Almrei (Re)*, 2009 FC 1263.

57 2016 FC 1105 at paras. 107–8.

58 Segal, "Review of CSIS Warrant Practice."

59 John H. Sims, "Advice on Implementing the Recommendations of Murray Segal's Review of CSIS Warrant Practice" (March 2017), *Secret Law Gazette*. Available online: http://secretlaw.omeka.net/items/show/77.

60 Justice Canada, "Action Plan of the Department of Justice and the Canadian Security Intelligence Service to Address Practices in Warrant Matters before the Federal Court of Canada," last modified 12 April 2017, http://www.justice.gc.ca/eng/rp-pr/cj-jp/antiter/doc-odf/p2.html.

61 "Policy of the Department of Justice Canada and the Canadian Security Intelligence Service on the Duty of Candour in *Ex Parte* Proceedings" (23 February 2017), *Secret Law Gazette*. Available online: http://secretlaw .omeka.net/items/show/78.

62 This principle can be compared with that governing *Criminal Code* warrants, which are oftentimes subject to subsequent review during a trial, as noted above.

PART FIVE

The Evolving National Security Review Landscape

14 Review and Oversight of National Security in Canada

LEAH WEST

Introduction

The earlier chapters of this volume tell the story of Canada's security and intelligence agencies. Through them we have learned that beginning in 1984, and especially from 2001 onward, those agencies grew in size, mandate, and budget. We also learned that as technology evolved and extended the reach of asymmetrical threat actors, those tasked with protecting Canada's national security acquired increasingly powerful and intrusive means of investigation.

For almost two decades, the reach of Canada's intelligence and security community continued to expand in this vein without any significant enhancement to the review bodies that served as a check on its power. Until 2019, only the Royal Canadian Mounted Police (RCMP), the Canadian Security Intelligence Service (CSIS), and the Communications Security Establishment (CSE) were subject to regular national security review, while other organizations like the Canada Border Services Agency (CBSA), the Department of National Defence (DND), and Global Affairs Canada (GAC) underwent sporadic review by commissions of inquiry established to investigate catastrophic failures in the system, commissions that consistently identified Canada's siloed approach to national security review as a priority for reform.[1]

This chapter begins by setting out the definition of review and oversight, followed by a brief history of Canada's review bodies. It then details the dramatic remodelling of review and oversight in Canada and describes the structure, mandates, and resources of the National Security and Intelligence Committee of Parliamentarians (NSICOP), the National Security Intelligence Review Agency (NSIRA), and the Office of the Intelligence Commissioner. Because it is too early to identify the impact these reforms will have on Canada's intelligence and security community, this chapter concludes with a brief discussion of the factors that could affect their success.

Review versus Oversight

Before delving too far into a discussion of Canada's national security review and oversight bodies, we must first define what these terms mean.

Often misused, the term "oversight" describes real-time operational command and control over the conduct of an organization. In the most basic sense, oversight can be explained as the need to get the proverbial "green light" from an arm's-length body or office before proceeding with a course of action. Until very recently, oversight in Canada was almost entirely a function of the executive branch, with an exception for the use of certain intrusive investigative techniques (e.g., search warrants) or the deployment of certain threat disruption measures by CSIS, which both require prior judicial authorization.[2]

Review, on the other hand, is a retrospective performance audit; past security service activity is scrutinized and then measured against specific criteria, most often compliance with law, policy, and regulations.[3] In Canada, review bodies are a means of bringing agency practices to light and holding decision-makers and agencies accountable to both Parliament and the public. Hallmarks of an effective review body include

(1) independence from the agency they evaluate;
(2) access to that agency's personnel, records, and systems;
(3) trust from both the security agency and the public;
(4) transparency and accountability to Parliament and the citizenry; and
(5) teeth, meaning that the recommendations and findings of the review body commonly result in a change in practice or some form of response by the security agency.[4]

Still, even the most robust review bodies are a fraction of the size of the security agencies for which they are responsible, and as such, are capable of validating only a sample of that organization's conduct. However, when done right, a strong system of accountability can enhance the public's trust in their security organizations and their faith in the security of the nation.

History of Security and Intelligence Review in Canada

The Security Intelligence Review Committee (SIRC) was the first permanent review body of a security agency in Canada. Established at the same time as CSIS in 1984, both organizations were a response to findings by the Commission of Inquiry Concerning Certain Activities of the Royal Canadian Mounted Police (McDonald Commission), which called for the establishment of a security intelligence agency separate from the RCMP and the creation of an independent advisory council.[5] SIRC's mandate was threefold: (1) monitoring and reporting on the activities of CSIS to Parliament; (2) investigating complaints made regarding any act or thing done by the Service; and (3) serving as the appeals tribunal regarding the provision of federal security clearances.

Under its review mandate, SIRC conducted thematic and sometimes geographic assessments of CSIS activities within Canada and abroad.[6] Findings were reported to the minister of public safety annually, with an unclassified version subsequently made available to Parliament and the public. SIRC had no capacity, nor the authority, to evaluate and guide CSIS's actions in real time.

Before 2012, review of CSIS was also conducted by the inspector general (IG), a statutory position established under the *CSIS Act*[7] to ensure there was sufficient ministerial accountability over CSIS's operations.[8] The office of the IG was an independent body whose judgments and certificates were not subject to direction or control by the CSIS director, SIRC, or even the minister or deputy minister of public safety.[9] The IG was commonly understood as the minister's "eyes and ears" inside CSIS. For 30 years, the office of the IG maintained a small expert staff to monitor the Service's compliance with its operational policies. In 2012, as a cost-cutting measure, the Harper government abolished the office and transferred the IG's reporting and certification functions to SIRC.[10]

Even before acquiring that additional role from the IG, SIRC had raised concerns that its capacity and authorities were "falling increasingly out of step with the *modus operandi* of contemporary intelligence."[11] It its 2012 annual report, SIRC noted that it "must be ready with the legislative tools and matching government resource commitments to ensure that the checks and balances enshrined in the Committee remain relevant and effective."[12] Specifically, the report warned that preventing and investigating threats to national security in the globalized digital age demanded swift information-sharing between Canadian agencies and their foreign partners. Yet Canada's review bodies, explained SIRC's former executive director Michael Doucet, were "constrained from following the information of the agency they examine into other Government of Canada institutions and from performing joint reviews."[13] Such legislative constraints, noted Doucet, "made it increasingly difficult for [SIRC] to provide robust assurances on CSIS's activities to Parliament and Canadians."[14]

Unfortunately, after raising these concerns, the problem got worse, not better, with the passage in 2015 of the *Security of Canada Information Sharing Act* (SCISA). SCISA authorized more than 100 government agencies to share information regarding activities that "undermine the security of Canada" with 17 federal departments and agencies so long as the disclosure of that information contributed to the fulfilment of their national security mandate.[15] All the while, SIRC's jurisdiction remained confined to the siloed review of CSIS information and conduct.

SIRC was not the only one to identify this issue; the Commission of Inquiry into the Actions of Canadian Officials in Relation to Maher Arar noted the challenges of coordinated review between review bodies.[16] Of particular and growing concern was SIRC's inability to *follow the thread* of CSIS information and investigations when partnering with CSE.

The Office of the Communications Security Establishment Commissioner (OCSEC) was founded in 1996 to review the activities of CSE and determine whether they conformed to the law, as well as to receive and investigate complaints about CSE actions. For six years, the commissioner executed these functions under the authority of orders-in-council, but in 2001 amendments were made to both the *National Defence Act* (NDA) and the *Security of Information Act*[17] to entrench the mandate of OCSEC in legislation.[18]

The NDA amendments codified the mandate of OCSEC, which included (1) reviewing the legality of CSE's activities;[19] (2) validating that the actions taken by CSE under ministerial authorization were compliant with the authority granted by the minister of national defence;[20] and (3) investigating complaints brought against CSE.[21] The legislation also stipulated that the commissioner had to be either a supernumerary or retired judge.[22]

To fulfil its tripartite mandate, OCSEC had complete access to CSE facilities, files, systems, and personnel, and the power of subpoena to compel individuals to answer questions.[23] Despite the broad scope of OCSEC's powers, the commissioner had no authority to investigate whether the signals intelligence or operational assistance provided by CSE to CSIS was being leveraged by CSIS appropriately and in compliance with the law.

This limitation became the source of considerable controversy in 2013 after Justice Richard Mosley of the Federal Court read OCSEC's 2012–13 annual public report. Through this report, Justice Mosley learned that CSIS was not merely relying on technical assistance from CSE to collect information under the top-secret warrants he and others had issued to CSIS since 2009.[24] Rather, other Five Eyes partners had also been collecting the private communications of Canadians abroad on behalf of CSIS, a detail never revealed to the court during the original application or subsequent renewals.[25] For its part, OCSEC found CSE had complied with the law. Nevertheless, concerned by the outsourcing of signals collection beyond CSE, the commissioner recommended that CSIS inform the Federal Court.[26]

Given that the court had issued the warrants to CSIS and not CSE and that OCSEC had no authority to investigate CSIS's conduct, the commissioner had a single option: he noted his recommendation in the annual report and sent it to SIRC.[27] Apparently, neither SIRC nor CSIS acted on the commissioner's recommendation, leading Justice Mosley and the Federal Court to learn about the outsourcing of Canada's security intelligence collection with the rest of the Canadian public. Subsequently, Justice Mosley, having found that CSIS had breached its duty of candour to the court, set conditions on the issuance of further warrants.[28] The attorney general appealed Justice Mosley's finding, which was ultimately upheld by the Federal Court of Appeal.[29] This incident of "accidental accountability" exemplified the need for a review body with not just the capacity to investigate a single agency, but the authority to review how Canada's security agencies work together.

Calls for stronger review also came after the bombing of Air India Flight 182 in 1985 and the terrorist attacks in Saint-Jean-sur-Richelieu and on Parliament Hill in October 2014. All three plots raised questions about intelligence-sharing between CSIS and the RCMP as well as serious concerns regarding the agencies' interoperability and efficiency when conducting counterterrorism investigations. Instead of heeding these concerns, the Canadian government responded to the 2014 attacks by introducing SCISA and giving CSIS additional powers to act on their own to disrupt threats to national security.[30] Disappointingly, review of Canada's newly empowered agencies remained siloed and limited to CSE, CSIS, and the RCMP.

Review of the RCMP's national security mandate had been, in practice, almost non-existent. Before the passage of Bill C-59, the *National Security Act, 2017*, the Mounties were subject only to independent review by the Civilian Review and Complaints Commission (CRCC). The primary mandate of the CRCC was and remains the reception of complaints from the public about the conduct of RCMP members, and review of the RCMP's investigation into those complaints.[31] The commission also has the mandate to conduct strategic investigations in the public interest and review specified activities. However, it may undertake such investigations only after assuring the minister of public safety that the CRCC has sufficient resources to handle both the proposed review and its complaint function.[32] Given the body's meagre budget, it is perhaps unsurprising that only one investigation related to national security was ever approved. Moreover, that lone review, which began in 2016 and sought to identify whether the RCMP had implemented the recommendations of the Arar Commission,[33] was still underway (and apparently stalled) when the CRCC lost jurisdiction to review activities related to national security matters following the coming into force in 2019 of the *National Security and Intelligence Review Agency Act (NSIRA Act)*.[34] In January 2020 the Trudeau government introduced Bill C-3, *An Act to amend the Royal Canadian Mounted Police Act and the Canada Border Services Agency Act and to make consequential amendments to other Acts*. If passed, the legislation will modify the CRCC to also cover the CBSA, effectively creating an independent review and complaints function for both the RCMP and CBSA. This revised entity will be branded the Public Complaints and Review Commission (PCRC). Importantly, the PRCC will review non-national security functions of these agencies. Its functions are, therefore, outside the scope of this chapter. Ultimately, C-3 was not passed before the proroguing of Parliament in the fall of 2020. It is believed a similar bill will be re-introduced sometime in the government's mandate, although at time of publication, this is not guaranteed.

Review and Oversight Today

NSIRA

Canada's siloed approach to national security review finally came to an end in 2019 with the passage of the *National Security Act, 2017* and the establishment of NSIRA. Unlike Canada's previous review bodies, NSIRA's mandate includes the review of any activity carried out by CSIS and CSE, and any activity carried out by a department of the government that relates to national security and intelligence, including the Canadian Armed Forces.[35] NSIRA is also mandated to review any matter related to national security and intelligence referred to it by a minister of the Crown and investigate complaints made against CSIS and CSE, as well as the RCMP where the complaint relates to national security.[36]

Additionally, NSIRA is responsible for investigating complaints related to the denial of security clearances required for either employment or the provision of goods and services to the Government of Canada.[37] Lastly, the agency investigates reports made to it by a minister under the *Citizenship Act*[38] that a person should be denied citizenship on the ground that they pose a risk to national security or are involved in organized crime.[39]

With the creation of this new "super-SIRC," the resources and staff of OCSEC and SIRC were wholly collapsed and reconstituted into NSIRA, while the RCMP commission retained its jurisdiction to receive and review all complaints against the RCMP except those related to national security.[40] Along with the staff and budget of the former review bodies, NSIRA inherited all of SIRC'S and OCSEC's ongoing complaints, investigations, and pending litigation.[41]

The *NSIRA Act* stipulates that the agency shall include a chair and no fewer than three and no more than six additional members.[42] Under the act, the governor in council appoints all members upon the recommendation of the prime minister (PM).[43] Before making the recommendation, the prime minister must consult with every leader of every caucus and every recognized group in the Senate, the leader of the Opposition and any other party having at least 12 seats in the House, and the leader and Opposition leader of the Senate.[44] Upon appointment, members can serve for a term of no more than five years and may be reappointed for one additional term.[45] Members may also be designated to hold their office on a full- or part-time basis.[46] Like its predecessor agencies, NSIRA is assisted by a secretariat led by an executive director who has all of the powers of a deputy head of a department and is appointed by the governor in council for a maximum term of five years, with the possibility of a single reappointment.[47]

To fulfil its whole-of-government review mandate, NSIRA is entitled to access any information in the possession or under the control of any department, including information otherwise subject to solicitor–client privilege.[48]

Annually, NSIRA is required to undertake specific reviews and file a number of reports. First, it must review at least one part of CSIS's conduct under its threat disruption mandate and may make any finding or recommendation it considers appropriate. Second, it must submit a report to the minister of public safety outlining CSIS's compliance with the law and ministerial direction and the reasonableness and necessity of CSIS's exercise of its powers. NSIRA must also deliver a third report to the minister of national defence detailing the same information in relation to CSE.[49] Fourth, the agency may submit a report to the minister responsible at any other department that was subject to review and must do so if it is of the opinion that the department's activities may not be compliant with the law.[50] When such a "compliance report" is submitted, the appropriate minister must provide a copy to the attorney general, along with their comments, as soon as feasible.[51] Fifth, the agency must submit a report to the minister of public safety regarding the disclosure of information under the *Security of Canada Information Disclosure Act*,[52] replacing the earlier *Security of Canada Information Sharing Act*. Finally, NSIRA must provide a report to the PM regarding its activities, as well as the findings and recommendations offered by the agency throughout the year.[53] Once submitted, the PM must file NSIRA's report in Parliament within the first 15 days of the House sitting calendar.[54] In addition to filing these reports, the chair of NSIRA must meet with the ministers of national defence and public safety at least once every 12 months to brief them on the performance of their respective agencies.[55]

When preparing any report, NSIRA must consult with the heads of the security agencies or the deputy head of a relevant department to ensure that they do not contain information that, if disclosed publicly, would be injurious to national security, or any information that might jeopardize the independence of a peace officer investigating an allegation of non-compliance.[56]

The most novel function of NSIRA is perhaps its role in ensuring CSIS complies with new provisions of the *CSIS Act* when collecting, retaining, and using datasets. Under the dataset framework, CSIS is required by law to establish record-keeping requirements outlining the rationale for its collection and retention, and the details and results of all queries and exploitations.[57] CSIS must also conduct random checks to ensure that its use of datasets accords with the law and must submit any report prepared following a verification of this kind to NSIRA.[58] What's more, CSIS must inform NSIRA when it removes information from a foreign dataset that relates to a Canadian or person in Canada, and also provide the agency with a copy of the director's decision to conduct a query of an unauthorized dataset under exigent circumstances.[59]

If upon review of this reporting, NSIRA believes that CSIS's use of a dataset was not compliant with the law, the agency shall complete a compliance report and submit it to the director of CSIS, who must in turn file that report with the Federal Court of Canada.[60] We might call this "the Justice Mosley Rule." In effect, this legal requirement creates a direct line of reporting from NSIRA to the Federal Court and will work to ensure that, in the future, judges will not have to wait to learn about a review body's concerns through a public report (at least in this one area).

Intelligence Commissioner

Along with NSIRA, the *National Security Act, 2017* also established the Office of the Intelligence Commissioner (IC), a quasi-judicial office that engages in limited oversight of both CSE and CSIS. Based on the recommendation of the prime minister, the first IC, Jean-Pierre Plouffe, was appointed in July 2019 by the governor in council.[61] Plouffe had served as the commissioner of CSE from 2013 until the dissolution of the body with the establishment of NSIRA. Like members of NSIRA, the IC is appointed for a term of not more than five years and may be reappointed for one additional term.[62] Under the *Intelligence Commissioner Act*, the IC has the power to determine CSE's and CSIS's human resource requirements and hire employees.[63]

The *Intelligence Commissioner Act* also stipulates that the IC must be a retired judge of a superior court.[64] The reason for this is that the IC's responsabilities include approving authorizations issued by a minister before CSE or CSIS can engage in certain conduct. This duty carries important constitutional consequences and is much more analogous to a judge issuing a warrant than an independent review body conducting *ex post facto* analysis.

Concerning CSIS, the IC has oversight responsibilities related to the organization's dataset and justification regimes. A dataset is "a collection of information stored as an electronic record and characterized by a common subject matter."[65] An online telephone book is a basic example of a dataset. Only datasets that contain personal information are governed by the *CSIS Act*, and their collection is authorized on a statutory basis. The IC performs an oversight role in relation to the retention of datasets not composed of publicly available information that predominantly relate to non-Canadians or persons outside of Canada.

In particular, the IC is responsible for reviewing the reasonableness of the minister of public safety's decision to allow CSIS to collect certain classes of datasets and is also mandated to review the minister's authorization to retain foreign datasets.[66] To complete their review, the IC must be supplied with the written decision of the minister and any material they relied upon when making that determination. If the IC concludes that the minister's decision was reasonable and approves the authorization, it is at that moment that the authorization takes effect and CSIS may proceed with the requested activity.[67] Similarly, the IC must review and approve the minister of national defence's authorization for CSE to conduct foreign intelligence collection or access a federal institution's infrastructure or specially designated non-federal infrastructure in furtherance of its cybersecurity mandate.[68]

The IC's approval of an elected official's decision is crucial to ensuring the constitutionality of CSE's and CSIS's data collection regimes, which may either deliberately or incidentally result in the acquisition of personal information about Canadians and persons in Canada that attracts a reasonable expectation of privacy. Section 8 of the *Canadian Charter of Rights and Freedoms* protects everyone from unreasonable search and seizure.[69] When conducting surveillance or leveraging intrusive investigative techniques, security and law enforcement officials typically ensure the reasonableness of their searches as required by section 8 by obtaining prior judicial authorization. While a search warrant issued by a judge is the ideal means of ensuring a search's reasonableness, it is not constitutionally required so long as prior authorization has been given by a neutral and impartial actor capable of acting judicially.[70]

As arguably a Cabinet minister is neither neutral nor impartial,[71] the IC's review is intended to ensure CSIS and CSE activities are constitutionally compliant in a more expedient and deferential manner than bringing applications before the courts. Nevertheless, this form of "double-lock" authorization system has yet to be challenged in court, meaning the constitutionality of CSE's and CSIS's bulk collection regimes remains an open question.

NSICOP

Another significant and recent development was the passage of Bill C-22, the *National Security and Intelligence Committee of Parliamentarians Act* (*NSICOP Act*), in June 2017.[72] With this legislation, Canada established its first parliamentary review body with a mandate to conduct national security review and oversight, joining the ranks of the United States, the United Kingdom, Australia, and New Zealand, who have long held their intelligence community accountable to elected officials.[73]

NSICOP is a non-partisan committee comprised of nine security-cleared representatives: seven members of Parliament (four from the government and three from opposition parties) and two senators.[74] The prime minister appoints all members following consultation with party leaders, and the governor in council designates the chair of the committee based on the prime minister's recommendation.[75]

Section 8 of the *NSICOP Act* sets out the broad mandate of the committee, which includes review of

(a) "the legislative, regulatory, policy, administrative and financial framework for national security and intelligence";

(b) "any activity carried out by a department that relates to national security or intelligence," unless that activity relates to an ongoing operation; and

(c) any matter relating to national security or intelligence referred to the committee by a minister of the Crown.

Importantly, NSICOP is not limited to review of specific departments or agencies, and the committee has the mandate to examine the administrative and financial aspects of the security and intelligence community's work, which has always been beyond the remit of Canada's independent review bodies. Though there is some overlap with the responsibilities assigned to NSIRA, under the *NSIRA Act* the two bodies are required to take "all reasonable steps to cooperate with each other to avoid unnecessary duplication of work."[76]

To carry out their review function, committee members have the right to all information under the control of a department related to its mandate, and this right is not limited by any other act of Parliament, such as the *Privacy Act*.[77] The latter would normally act as a barrier to sharing the personal information of Canadians.[78] Unlike most committees, however, NSICOP does not have the right to subpoena witnesses or documents, and witnesses do not testify under oath. This means that those called before the members are not at risk of being charged with either perjury should they lie or contempt if they fail to comply. This is because NSICOP is a "Committee of Parliamentarians," not a parliamentary committee, which would have the power to send for persons, papers, and records.[79] Testifying before the Standing Senate Committee on National Security and Defence, then public safety minister, Ralph Goodale, explained the reasoning behind the committee's structure:

> There is a need to ensure that the operational independence of government agencies in the security and intelligence field is not infringed. This legislation provides that the deputy head of the agency will decide who in that department or agency is best placed to speak to an issue identified by the committee, and it's very important that this authority remain with the deputy head for operational reasons.[80]

The practical impact of the limits placed on the committee's authority is unknown at this time but likely minimal. Instead of the power to compel information, the *NSICOP Act* creates a legal obligation for the responsible minister to disclose requested information in a timely fashion so long as the information relates to the committee's mandate.[81] That said, unlike NSIRA, NSICOP is entitled to request and receive only information that is under an agency's "control,"[82] a term of art in the security world. Conventionally, or through the use of caveats, law enforcement and intelligence agencies understand that the "originator control" rule prohibits the further use or dissemination of intelligence beyond the intended recipient agency (this rule generally applies to all intelligence-sharing partners regardless of whether they are formal allies or not). Thus, information may be in the *possession* of an intelligence or security agency, but it remains under the *control* of the originator unless permission for further use or disclosure is sought and granted.

Section 8(b) of the *NSICOP Act* also bars the committee from reviewing ongoing operations. To take advantage of this exception, the responsible minister must establish not only that the information relates to an ongoing operation, but that review of the information would be injurious to national security.[83] The minister must inform NSICOP of their decision to prohibit review and give reasons.[84] Once those criteria are satisfied, the minister's determination is final.[85] The minister does not, however, hold an absolute veto. The *NSICOP Act* requires that as soon as the operation ceases and review of the information no longer poses a risk to national security, the committee be informed. Therefore, in effect, the exception in section 8(2) serves as a delay rather than an outright prohibition on the committee's review of operational information.

Other limits on information that the committee may review, even where it falls within NSIRA's mandate, include Cabinet confidences, information on persons under federal protection and confidential sources, and material related to an ongoing criminal investigation that may lead to prosecution.[86] The reason for this final limitation is to safeguard law enforcement's independence from political interference; whether this prohibition extends to information held by other agencies, like CSIS or CSE, who may be supporting RCMP investigations is unclear.[87]

Not surprisingly, the *NSICOP Act* prohibits committee members and secretariat staff from disclosing any information to which they have access that the government is taking measures to protect, and adds the committee and the secretariat to the list of entities whose members are permanently bound to secrecy under the *Security of Information Act*.[88] What some do find shocking is that committee members cannot claim immunity based on parliamentary privilege in any proceeding against them relating to the disclosure of information reviewed in the course of carrying out their committee duties, even if they make that disclosure before Parliament or another parliamentary committee.[89]

The committee may communicate its findings only through reports to Parliament. Under the act, NSICOP is required to complete an annual report for the prime minister and may draft "special" reports for the prime minister and other Cabinet ministers.[90] Upon review, the prime minister has the authority to direct the committee to provide a revised version of the report before tabling it in the House and Senate.[91] If the prime minister issues such a direction, the revised version must clearly indicate that it is not the original report, as well as the extent of and reasons for the revisions.[92] Once the prime minister receives the report (or the revised report), he must submit the committee's findings to Parliament within the first 30 days during which the House is sitting.[93]

To date, NSICOP has submitted one special report to the prime minister related to security concerns arising from his official visit to India in 2018.[94] When made public in December 2018, the report was heavily redacted to protect the intelligence sources used. Unfortunately, this meant that the majority of the recommendations were also redacted, so it is difficult to assess the impact of the committee's report. Nevertheless, the report did identify several failings with the RCMP's decisions regarding handling threat-related information.[95]

Conclusion

The establishment of NSICOP in 2017, and of NSIRA and the IC in 2019, has remodelled Canada's national security review and oversight structure entirely. Not only have the silos been broken down, the *NSIRA* and *NSICOP Acts* also provide the executive and the Federal Court with more tools to hold the intelligence community accountable.

Each of these bodies is vitally important to the protection of civil liberties, and for strengthening the trust between citizens and the agencies responsible for protecting us and the rights and values we cherish as Canadians. Reliable and robust scrutiny is necessary to finding and maintaining the elusive balance between security and liberty as agencies like CSIS and CSE increasingly leverage the new powers given to them by Parliament under Bills C-51 (the *Anti-terrorism Act, 2015*) and the *National Security Act, 2017*.

What remains to be seen is how effective these bodies will be at holding Canada's security agencies and officials accountable. Review without real accountability to Parliament, the Federal Court, and the public is a worthless endeavour. In the future, the government must ensure that NSIRA and the IC are competently staffed and adequately resourced, and Parliament must guard against NSICOP becoming a forum for political partisanship and finger-pointing. Failure in either regard would not only be a disservice to the agencies under their supervision, but also put all Canadians at risk.

NOTES

1 For example: the 1977 Royal Commission into Certain Activities of the Royal Canadian Mounted Police, the 1995 Commission of Inquiry into the Deployment of Canadian Forces to Somalia, the 2004–06 Commission of Inquiry into the Actions of Canadian Officials in Relation to Maher

Arar (Arar Inquiry), the 2006–08 Internal Inquiry into the Actions of
Canadian Officials in Relation to Abdullah Almalki, Ahmad Abou-Elmaati
and Muayyed Nureddin, and (perhaps most notoriously) the 2006–10
Commission of Inquiry into the Investigation of the Bombing of Air India
Flight 182 (Air India Inquiry).

2 See, e.g., *Canadian Security Intelligence Service Act (CSIS Act)*, R.S.C. 1985,
c. C-23, s. 21.

3 For more on the distinction between review and oversight, see Arar
Inquiry, *Report of the Events Relating to Maher Arar* (2006), 456–7. Available
online: http://publications.gc.ca/site/eng/9.688875/publication.html.

4 Craig Forcese, Kent Roach, and Leah West, "Bill C-51 Backgrounder #5:
Oversight and Review: Turning Accountability Gaps into Canyons?"
(2015), 25. Available online: https://papers.ssrn.com/sol3/papers
.cfm?abstract_id=2571245.

5 The reports of the Commission of Inquiry Concerning Certain Activities
of the Royal Canadian Mounted Police (McDonald Commission) are
available online: https://epe.lac-bac.gc.ca/100/200/301/pco-bcp
/commissions-ef/mcdonald1979-81-eng/mcdonald1979-81-eng.htm.

6 For the history of SIRC's first 20 years, see SIRC, *Reflections: Twenty Years
of Independent External Review of Security Intelligence in Canada* (2005).
Available online: https://www.publicsafety.gc.ca/lbrr/archives
/cn000031056742-eng.pdf.

7 R.S.C. 1985, c. C-23.

8 Centre for International Policy Studies (CIPS), "CSIS Inspector General
Certificate – 2008," 8 May 2012, http://cips.uottawa.ca/publications/csis
-certificate-report-2008/.

9 CIPS, "CSIS Inspector General Certificate."

10 Canadian Press, "Axing CSIS Watchdog 'Huge Loss,' Says Former
Inspector General," *CBC News*, 10 August 2012, http://www.cbc.ca
/news/politics/axing-csis-watchdog-huge-loss-says-former-inspector
-general-1.1143212.

11 SIRC, *Annual Report 2012–2013: Bridging the Gap* (Ottawa: Public Works
and Government Services Canada, 2012), 9.

12 SIRC, *Annual Report 2012–2013*, 10.

13 Standing Senate Committee on National Security and Defence, Evidence of
Michael Doucet, 41st Parliament, 2nd Session, 23 April 2015.

14 Standing Senate Committee, Evidence of Michael Doucet.

15 S.C. 2015, c. C-20, s. 5 (originally introduced as the *Security of Information
Sharing Act* as part of Bill-51, the act and its title were significantly amended by
Bill C-59. As a result, SCISA is now the Security of Information Disclosure Act).

16 Commission of Inquiry into the Actions of Canadian Officials in Relation
to Maher Arar, *A New Review Mechanism for the RCMP's National Security*

Activities (2006), recommendation 11. Available online: https://epe.lac-bac
.gc.ca/100/206/301/pco-bcp/commissions/maher_arar/07-09-13/www
.ararcommission.ca/eng/EnglishReportDec122006.pdf.

17 R.S.C. 1985, c. O-5.
18 *Anti-terrorism Act*, SC 2001, c. 4.
19 *National Defence Act*, R.S.C. 1985, c. N-5, s. 273.65(2)(a).
20 *National Defence Act*, s. 273. 65 (8).
21 *National Defence Act*, s. 276.63 (2)(b).
22 *National Defence Act*, s. 273.63(1).
23 *National Defence Act*, s. 276.73.
24 *X(Re)*, 2013 FC 1275.
25 *X(Re)*, 2013 FC 1275.
26 Office of the Communications Security Establishment Commissioner, *Annual Report 2012–2013* (Ottawa: Public Works and Government Services Canada, 2013), 24.
27 *X (Re)*, 2009 FC 1058.
28 *X(Re)*, 2013 FC 1275
29 *X (Re)*, 2014 FCA 249.
30 Section 12.1 of the *CSIS Act*, authorizing the use of threat disruption measures, was added with the passage of the *Anti-terrorism Act, 2015*, S.C. 2015, c. 20 (Bill C-51).
31 *Royal Canadian Mounted Police Act*, R.S.C. 1985, c. R-10, s. 28.
32 *Royal Canadian Mounted Police Act*, s. 43.34.
33 See Civilian Review and Complaints Commission for the RCMP, "Review of the RCMP's Implementation of Justice O'Connor Recommendations Concerning National Security Activities," 8 December 2016.
34 S.C. 2019, c. 13, s. 2.
35 *NSIRA Act*, s. 8(1)(a)–(b).
36 *NSIRA Act*, s. 8(1)(c)–(d).
37 *NSIRA Act*, s. 8(d)(i).
38 R.S.C. 1985, c. C-29.
39 *NSIRA Act*, s. 8(1)(d)(iii)
40 Bill C-59, cl. 5, cls. 7–10.
41 Bill C-59, cls. 11–13, cl. 15–17.
42 *NSIRA Act*, s. 4.
43 Bill C-59, cl. 11–13.
44 *NSIRA Act*, s. 4(1)–(2).
45 *NSIRA Act*, s. 4(3)–(4).
46 *NSIRA Act*, s. 4(5).
47 *NSIRA Act*, ss. 41–42.
48 *NSIRA Act*, s. 9(2).
49 *NSIRA Act*, s. 32–33.

50 *NSIRA Act*, s. 34.
51 *NSIRA Act*, s. 35.
52 *NSIRA Act*, s. 39.
53 *NSIRA Act*, s. 38(1), 40(1).
54 *NSIRA Act*, s. 38(2), 40(2).
55 *NSIRA Act*, s. 37.
56 *NSIRA Act*, s. 53–54.
57 *CSIS Act*, s. 11.24(1)(b), (3)(d).
58 *CSIS Act*, s. 11.24(d).
59 *CSIS Act*, s. 11.25.
60 *CSIS Act*, s. 27.1.
61 *Intelligence Commissioner Act (IC Act)*, S.C. 2019, c. 13, s. 50 at s. 4(1).
62 *IC Act*, s. 4(1).
63 *IC Act*, s. 6.
64 *IC Act*, s. 4(1).
65 *CSIS Act*, s. 2.
66 *CSIS Act*, s. 16–17.
67 *CSIS Act*, s. 11.23.
68 *IC Act*, s. 13–14.
69 *Canadian Charter of Rights and Freedoms*, Part I of the *Constitution Act, 1982*, being Schedule B to the *Canada Act 1982* (UK), c. 11, s. 8.
70 *R. v. A.M.*, [2008] 1 S.C.R. 569, 2008 SCC 19 at para. 13; *Hunter et al. v. Southam Inc.*, [1984] 2 S.C.R. 145, 1984 CanLII 33 (SCC) at p. 1621.
71 For further discussion on this point, see Tamir Israel, "Foreign Intelligence in an Inter-Networked World: Time for a Reevaluation," in *Law, Privacy and Surveillance in the Post-Snowden Era*, ed. Michael Geist (Ottawa: University of Ottawa Press, 2015), 77.
72 S.C. 2017, c. 15.
73 Forcese, Roach, and West, "Bill C-51 Backgrounder #5," 15.
74 *NSICOP Act*, s. 4.
75 *NSICOP* Act, s. 5(1).
76 *NSIRA Act*, s. 13.
77 R.S.C. 1985, c. P-21.
78 *NSICOP Act*, s. 13(1).
79 *NSICOP* Act, s. 4(3).
80 Standing Senate Committee on National Security and Defence, Evidence of Ralph Goodale, 42nd Parliament, 1st Session, 5 June 2017, 5–6.
81 *NSICOP Act*, s. 15(3).
82 *NSICOP Act*, s. 13(1), 15(1), 16(1).
83 *NSICOP Act*, s. 8(b).
84 *NSICOP Act*, s. 16(1).
85 *NSICOP Act*, s. 31(2).

86 *NSICOP Act*, s. 14.
87 Standing Senate Committee on National Security and Defence, Evidence of Ralph Goodale, 5.
88 *NSICOP Act*, s. 41.
89 *NSICOP Act*, s. 12 (2). (The constitutionality of this provision was challenged in the Ontario Superior Court in *Alford v. Canada (Attorney General)*, 2018 ONSC 3984. However, the court ruled that the applicant, a law professor at Lakehead University, did not have standing to bring the challenge, and the application was dismissed.
90 *NSICOP Act*, s. 21(2).
91 *NSICOP* Act, s. 21(5). (Revisions may result only from the PM's finding that the report contains information the "disclosure of which would be injurious to national security, national defence or international relations or is information that is protected by litigation privilege or by solicitor-client privilege or the professional secrecy of advocates and notaries.")
92 *NSICOP Act*, s. 21(5)(1).
93 *NSICOP Act*, s. 21(6).
94 NSICOP, "Media Advisory – National Security and Intelligence Committee Report on PM'S Visit to India Delivered to PM," 31 May 2018, http://www.nsicop-cpsnr.ca/press-releases/pr-cp-2018-05-31/pr-cp-2018-05-31-en.html.
95 NSICOP, *Special Report into the Allegations Associated with Prime Minister Trudeau's Official Visit to India in February 2018* (2018). Available online: http://www.nsicop-cpsnr.ca/reports/rp-2018-12-03/intro-en.html.

15 The Media and National Security Reporting in Canada

ALEX BOUTILIER

Nobody gets into national security reporting in Canada because it's easy.

Intelligence and security agencies are incredibly secretive – often understandably, sometimes reflexively – and the sources of information on them are few. The issues are immensely complex and take time, a precious commodity in the news industry, to get a handle on.

Taking the time to get a proper grasp on the issues is critical, given the stakes are extremely high. National security reporting is reporting on threats to Canadian lives, on the balance between state power and fundamental civil liberties, on the relationship between governments and internet giants, on war and cyber war.

Despite its challenges, the beat feeds addictions many journalists share: the need to figure things out, to reveal information the public doesn't know but should, and to hold to account people who wield immense power.

"What draws me to reporting on national security/policing/privacy-related topics is the same thing that draws me to most of my reporting," said Matthew Braga, a reporter with the CBC in Toronto. "A desire to take things that few people know about or understand and try and put it into context. ... Partly a right-to-know thing, partly an education thing, and partly because I'm personally drawn to wanting to understand how things work."[1]

Unlike the other chapters in this book, this will not be an overview or critique of a particular facet of Canada's national security framework. Instead, I was asked to share my experience in covering national security issues in Canada. I spoke with three other reporters who report on national security and law enforcement to broaden that perspective.

This won't be a fiery polemic about the need for more transparency – although I would argue more transparency is desperately needed.

Canada's national security will not be threatened by granting an interview or a background chat every now and then. Instead, it may actually strengthen it by encouraging factual, comprehensive reporting with context and accountability.

The Basics

For the vast majority of Canadians who have not spent time in a news-room, even the very basics of how the sausage gets made every day can be a bit of a mystery. So that might be a helpful place to begin.

First, yes, it's true: reporters don't write the headlines.

Second, outside of a major attack or hot-button political issue, it's been my experience that national security reporting in Canada is largely self-directed work. Successive editors at the *Toronto Star* have trusted me to pursue what I think needs pursuing, and I'm required to make the case for why something like the debate around encryption is something our readers need to know. It should be noted that this freedom is a privilege.

That freedom also means a lot of what gets reported depends on the individual reporter. They have to decide where to focus, figure out how to forage for the information they need, and make the case to editors why this or that issue needs highlighting or pursuing. And when a national security story pops up in another news outlet, a press release, or court ruling, they have to explain why they should or should not "match" or "advance" the story.

Third, while yes, this is a scoop-driven industry where everybody wants to be first, accuracy and fairness are still taken immensely seriously in any newsroom I've been a part of. While media organizations routinely fall short of that ideal, especially in the wake of a major incident, it nevertheless remains the goal every day.

Finally, reporters rarely have the whole picture of any issue they're covering, despite their best efforts. This is especially true in national security reporting.

"Covering most beats is like doing a jigsaw puzzle," said veteran Canadian Press reporter Jim Bronskill. "Covering the security and intelligence beat is like doing a jigsaw puzzle in the dark."[2]

That means, to those inside the intelligence community, coverage might be puzzling or seem incomplete or even unfair.

But when faced with the question of publishing something you know to be accurate (if incomplete) or withholding that information from the public, my guess is most reporters are going to choose the former.

That seems to me a compelling argument why it's in intelligence agencies' self-interest to share more of the puzzle publicly. Academics and researchers are much, much more accessible for in-depth interviews than the agencies themselves. Journalists will work with the pieces of the puzzle we have.

Learning Curve

Many of the academics and former practitioners in this book have spent their careers analysing particular aspects of the Canadian intelligence apparatus. The vast majority of journalists asked to report on national security issues – especially in the wake of an attack or tragedy – do not have that depth of experience and understanding.

Instead, in the case of the immediate aftermath of a terrorist attack or major security incident, most of the reporters working the story will have little to no national security background or sources.

For example, Michelle Shephard's first national security assignment at the *Toronto Star* was covering the aftermath of 9/11. I had virtually no background in cybersecurity or intelligence reporting until the Snowden disclosures in 2013.

This is not to say that national security reporting should be limited to reporters who specialize in it. Journalists are obliged to report accurately and fairly on any number of issues we don't have particular expertise in.

But the learning curve with national security reporting can be particularly steep, and few younger reporters receive guidance from within their own ranks.

"My introduction to the terrorism file came essentially on September 11, 2001," said Shephard, who won multiple awards for her national security reporting published in the *Star* between 2001 and 2018. "I remember my first task was just having to learn the acronyms of the various agencies. I would have a cheat sheet in my notebook that I could refer to during interviews."[3]

Shephard said that breaking into the national security beat "as a rookie" reporter was near impossible, so she instead focused on the abuse of power or civil liberties issues. After 9/11, there was plenty to focus on.

"Civil rights lawyers became my best sources," Shephard said. "I covered every day of the Arar inquiry and was a pretty vocal critic of our security agencies, most especially the RCMP and CSIS. It seems counter-intuitive, but this coverage opened doors at both agencies – perhaps for no other reason than their own damage control, but it had benefits for me."

The learning curve will only become steeper as more espionage – and military action – is conducted in cyberspace. The debate around the growing importance of cyber operations to Canadian security and defence agencies is badly needed, and the public needs reliable information to facilitate that debate.

We're not there yet – everyday denial-of-service attacks are still called "hacks" in headlines and television hits – but we're getting there.

Secret Agents, Man.

So, yes, one of the barriers to getting to an informed debate on intelligence issues is how news organizations treat issues. Using imprecise terms like "hack" for a broad range of online activity doesn't help the public's understanding of cyber threats, and it's difficult to present a scholarly overview of intelligence mandates in a two-minute news clip. It also doesn't make for a very compelling story.

But the unwillingness of the intelligence community to publicly discuss these issues is another barrier.

"The secrecy of these agencies is ludicrous," Shephard said. "There is no doubt there are legitimate security concerns and information that would be dangerous if disclosed publicly. But Canada is notorious for its censorship and secrecy. If in doubt, an interview is declined or a document redacted."

Because of this, Canada is one of Shephard's "least favourite" countries to report on. For reference, here's a partial list of countries where Shephard has worked as a reporter: Afghanistan, Pakistan, Syria, Somalia, Yemen, and – of course – the United States' outpost at Guantanamo Bay.

Bronskill is slightly more diplomatic.

"The security community, by necessity, works largely in secret. And secrecy can breed mistrust among the public, including among journalists. So I'm afraid it's an occupational hazard for those in the community," he said. "Having said that, I think part of my job is to point out not only when things go wrong, but also when things go right – being fair and telling all sides of the story."

I think there's a broad agreement among journalists who cover national security issues that some methods, information, and ongoing operations should and must remain secret. Details that would put Canadian public servants' lives at risk or compromise the safety of the Canadian public obviously must be treated with extreme care.

But that is the extreme end of the spectrum. There's a lot of information kept secret for no good reason, and a lot of discussions the security and intelligence community seems only too happy to avoid.

Take the issue of IMSI catchers, or "Stingrays." We've known for years that Canadian law enforcement was using Stingrays, but it took Herculean efforts on the part of Braga and our colleagues to prove it.[4]

For a more recent example, take the discussion around so-called "active cyber operations," which the Communications Security Establishment (CSE) is authorized to use under Bill C-59,[5] the Liberal government's 2017 national security overhaul. CSE is more than happy to talk about how they're defending Canadian networks from attacks. When it comes to how they'll launch attacks of their own they're much less chatty.

There has been very little debate in Canada about cyber-attacks and their implications, for example, of the potential for escalation, of cyber war's tendency to blur the lines between military strikes and intelligence operations, or of the moral and legal questions around targeting civilian infrastructure.

Part of that is on our tribe, frankly. Too few reporters spread too thin over too many issues. But when we ask about these issues, we're often met with canned media lines, a refusal to answer direct questions, and a sudden breakout of "vacations" among anyone who might be able to speak to the issues on background.

Just because a discussion is uncomfortable doesn't mean it is top secret. To paraphrase Bronskill's earlier point, secrecy for its own sake breeds mistrust among the public. And we only need to look south of the border to get a taste of what extreme mistrust of government and intelligence agencies can lead to.

The News Business

The challenges facing the news industry in Canada are well known, and there's no reason to go in-depth into them here. I do, however, want to highlight a few aspects of our industry I believe are pertinent to this discussion.

First, the bad news: Canada's legacy print media outlets continue to decline. A 2017 report from the Public Policy Forum estimated that since 2010, 225 weekly and 27 daily newspapers had been either closed or absorbed into other newspapers. Fewer newsrooms meant the number of journalism jobs in this country had been slashed by a third since 2010, the report estimated.[6] Advertising revenues have been permanently lost to the internet behemoths, and subscription revenues alone will not keep legacy media afloat.

National security reporting, like any specialized beat, requires time and resources. In the newspaper context, that requires other reporters covering breaking news, politics at all three levels, entertainment, sports, human interest – you name it – so someone like me can toil away filing access to information requests.

As newsrooms continue to shrink, specialized beats are becoming harder and harder to maintain. That's an issue not just for national security journalists, but for anyone who wants informed debate on national security issues in Canada.

Now, the slightly less bad news: as legacy media declines, specialty news and information outlets have sprung up all over the internet.

This is especially true in the United States. Websites like War on the Rocks and Lawfare provide in-depth, specialized reporting on national security and defence, and podcasts like *Deep State Radio* bring in former practitioners as well as journalists and academics to reflect on whatever foreign policy crises befall Washington, DC, in a given week.

Although there are fewer examples in Canada, there are some notable ones. Stephanie Carvin and Craig Forcese, in addition to being two of the driving forces behind this book, maintain *A Podcast Called INTREPID*. The podcast provides a sorely needed deep dive on Canadian national security issues, as well as secures sit-downs with senior members of the intelligence community for in-depth interviews – interviews that elude most workaday journalists.

Bill Robinson, another contributor to this book, provides an indispensable resource for those of us who cover CSE. His blog, *Lux Ex Umbra*, includes not only fascinating elements of CSE's history, but analysis of news and developments related to the increasingly crucial and central agency.

Other groups and researchers, like the CitizenLab at the University of Toronto and the Canadian Civil Liberties Association, have been generous in assisting reporters understand the ins-and-outs of complicated technical or legal issues. Their own research often has strong news value, as well.

These organizations can never replace the reach of legacy mass media, and some on the activist side of the spectrum don't strive for the same kind of balance as traditional journalism. But it certainly beats a void.

Adversarial Relationship, Shared Goal

Now for the good news – and there is good news.

Both Canada's intelligence community and the mainstream press enjoy high levels of credibility among the Canadian public. A 2018 Ipsos survey found that 65 per cent of Canadians had trust in the media, while 79 per cent of respondents said they would side with the media over the government should the government take issue with the accuracy of news reports.[7]

An Ekos poll released earlier this year showed that 57 per cent of respondents believed the federal government could be trusted to both keep them safe and protect their civil liberties. The same poll found that 95 per cent of respondents believed the Canadian Security Intelligence Service's work is important, even if 40 per cent were concerned about the information intelligence agencies gather on them.[8] That's a fairly strong endorsement.

Why are those findings important to a discussion on national security reporting in Canada? Because to be effective in their work, both sides of the fence – journalists and intelligence agencies – depend on public trust. Again, we only need to look to the United States, and the crisis of public confidence in that country, for proof.

Journalists need to continue to earn the public's confidence, or be treated as just one more piece of information alongside YouTube conspiracy theorists, partisan blogs, and state propaganda campaigns. If we don't have that confidence, we can't serve as the public's watchdog and advocate.

The security and intelligence community needs the public's confidence for their findings and threat assessments to be taken seriously – not dismissed as politically motivated hit jobs or nefarious "deep state" puppet mastery. Canada will be less safe if the community does not command that confidence.

The relationship between the Canadian security and intelligence apparatus and the journalists who cover it must remain adversarial – we're here to hold power to account, not to reinforce it.

But both sides have a stake in maintaining the public's confidence. And it may be that, in the extraordinary context we find ourselves in, we need to re-evaluate our relationship and methods to ensure that we do.

NOTES

1 Personal communication with author.
2 Personal communication with author.
3 Personal communication with author.
4 Kate Allen, Jayme Poisson, and Wendy Gillis, "Two Years after They Said They Didn't, Toronto Police Admit They Use Stringray Cellphone Snooping Device," *Toronto Star*, 5 March 2018, https://www.thestar.com/news/gta/2018/03/05/two-years-after-they-said-they-didnt-toronto-police

-admit-they-use-stingray-cellphone-snooping-device.html; Matthew Braga, "Spies More Free to Use Cellphone Surveillance Tech without Warrant, under Court Ruling," *CBC*, 28 November 2017, https://www.cbc.ca/news /technology/csis-court-stingray-imsi-catchers-1.4423871.
5 *National Security Act, 2017*, S.C. 2019, c. 13.
6 Bruce Campion-Smith and Alex Ballingall, "Media Cuts Are a Threat to Canadian Democracy, New Report Warns," *Toronto Star*, 26 January 2017, https://www.thestar.com/news/canada/2017/01/26/media-cuts-are-a -threat-to-democracy-new-report-warns.html.
7 Rebecca Joseph, "Trust in the Media Fell 4% in Past Year: Ipsos Poll," *Global News*, 25 May 2018, https://globalnews.ca/news/4230242/trust-in-media -poll/.
8 Monique Scotti, "Trust in Intelligence Agencies Is Up, but a Third of Canadians Have Never Heard of CSIS: Poll," *Global News*, 18 July 2018, https://globalnews.ca/news/4336428/csis-trust-intelligence-agencies -canada-poll/.

Conclusion

STEPHANIE CARVIN, THOMAS JUNEAU, AND CRAIG FORCESE

In drafting this book, the authors and editors have tried to paint a picture of the activities and challenges faced by Canada's national security and intelligence agencies, some of the consumers of their products, and those tasked with their review and oversight. As noted in the introduction, Canada is going through the greatest changes to its national security architecture in almost four decades. And yet, as is clear from the chapters in this volume, it still seems that there is ample room for further reform and evolution.

Therefore, in concluding this volume, the editors wish to highlight three overarching themes that connect the chapters, as well as point to future issues the Canadian national security and intelligence community will face: challenges posed by current trends, the need for greater transparency, and the need to balance security with democratic principles.

Current Trends

While each national security institution faces its own particular challenges, there are a number of trends that cut across the chapters in this volume worth highlighting here.

Fluid environment: Every national security and intelligence agency in Canada is affected by an extremely dynamic international environment and new security challenges. In some cases, the challenges arise from the (re-)emergence of China and Russia, strategic competitors who engage in a range of adversarial activities. Domestically, the rise of far-right extremist groups has created the need for organizations that have been largely focused on al-Qaida- and Islamic State–inspired movements to reassess the threat of violent extremism. In other cases, challenges are emerging from technological change: while organizations like the Royal Canadian Mounted Police (RCMP) grapple with encrypted applications and the "going dark" problem, John Pyrik notes that the Financial Transactions and Reports Analysis Centre of Canada (FINTRAC) is challenged in trying to keep up with the latest "fintech" innovations. And while these national security agencies are forced to keep up with these changes, older challenges, like the threat of foreign fighters, are not going away. Prioritizing investigations and resources in such an environment is difficult.

Mandates: Within this fluid environment, national security and intelligence agencies are required to operate within the limits of their mandates while fulfilling their responsibilities in playing their part to keep Canada safe. If some organizations, such as the Department of National Defence and the Canadian Armed Forces (DND/CAF), have a relatively clear mandate, others are confronted with mandates that are expanding quickly, such as Public Safety Canada (PSC), or that need to be balanced against a growing list of responsibilities. As Michael Nesbitt discusses in his chapter, Global Affairs Canada (GAC) is responsible for a large and growing array of national-security-linked activities, including cyber-diplomacy. Bill Robinson discusses in his chapter the growing responsibilities of the Communications Security Establishment (CSE) since 2001, including support for law enforcement and now "active" and "defensive" cyber operations.

At the same time, some chapters highlight how mandates are increasingly insufficient for the world we are now living in. As Jez Littlewood notes in his chapter, the Canadian Security Intelligence Service (CSIS) has been called out by the courts on several occasions for engaging in activities deemed to go beyond the mandate created for it in 1984. Indeed, if intelligence and national security agencies need to change with the times, the courts have made it clear that it needs to be done through legislative change – if politicians, occupied by other concerns, can be bothered with such change at all.

New kids on the block: However, some chapters have made it clear that change and reform do not always produce results. In particular, chapters on newer intelligence and national security institutions explain that there are problems in terms of fitting in, especially in terms of working out their relations with other departments and agencies. As John Pyrik observes in his chapter on FINTRAC, financial intelligence reports produced by the agency tend to be under-utilized at best and ignored at worst by law enforcement agencies such as the RCMP. The chapter by Stephanie Carvin notes that the Integrated

Terrorism Assessment Centre (ITAC) has seemingly failed to find its footing within the Canadian intelligence and national security community. Although designed to be a fusion centre comprising secondees from across the Canadian government to provide information to first responders, ITAC has increasingly hired its own staff and now also provides high-level briefings to senior policymakers. Today, it is still not clear it has fully found its place.

These are only two cases. But they suggest that within Canada, when governments make major changes such as reforming or creating institutions, they may need to do a better job of ensuring that other departments and agencies are prepared to make adjustments as well. Using one of the examples above, it is good that there was a new institution created to provide financial intelligence analysis to others in the community, including the RCMP. But without providing the RCMP with resources and expertise to act on this information, little has changed in Canada's ability to prosecute the financial support of violent extremism overall.

Human resources and training: While all government departments face human resources (HR) and training challenges, several intelligence and national security agencies are confronted with either outdated or broken recruitment models (such as GAC) or serious workplace environment and employee retention problems (PSC). Recently, CSIS has been embroiled in its own human resources controversies, stemming from a seemingly toxic workplace in the Toronto office.[1] Even where organizations may be getting hiring right, security clearances often take months, sometimes years, to be obtained, meaning talented individuals may decide to go elsewhere in their careers rather than wait for an unclear and uncertain process to complete. In the case of ITAC, an individual may wait longer for a clearance than the duration of their secondment to that organization. In addition, both the chapter on GAC and Kent Roach's chapter on the RCMP note the problems those organizations have in training their staff: training budgets are usually one of the first line items to be eliminated when cuts are looming.

While it is, perhaps, easy to be cynical about government HR issues, if we want a safe and secure Canada, it is vital that our national security agencies have strong, transparent, and fair hiring and talent management practices, as well as robust training to ensure that employees are well prepared to encounter the fluid threat environment discussed above. Unfortunately, the Canadian national security and intelligence community appears to have a lot of work to do to make this a priority and a reality.

Cooperation: Despite these challenges, at the end of the day it also seems that the work of national security in Canada is getting done – although Canada does far less in this space than many of its Western allies. There is grumbling and frayed nerves, but there are few documented instances of serious conflict between the different organizations.

Of course, there are instances where a failure to cooperate has produced tragedy. The Air India disaster was an early, tragic example of a failure to cooperate between the RCMP and the then newly created CSIS. This failure, however, did bring about some reforms. As noted in the CSIS chapter, today the Service and the RCMP deconflict their national security activities through a process known as the "One Vision" framework. This is important, particularly as the Service is now engaging in "threat reduction measures" that could disrupt national security investigations and/or attempts to prosecute individuals for terrorism offences.

Nevertheless, today, reporting on tension in the relationship between different organizations remains relatively rare. In 2019, for example, there were reports of conflicts in the foreign investment review process under the *Investment Canada Act*.[2] However, for the most part, these stories are the exception rather than the rule. While American national security agencies tend to be fierce bureaucratic fighters, utilizing the media when necessary, Canadian disagreements tend to be kept mostly behind closed doors.

In that sense, though it may not be possible to get a full idea of the scope and efficacy of cooperation between the different national security and intelligence agencies, it appears that at a minimum there is a consensus that such fights should not be played out in front of the media. And while there are clashes of personality and interests, especially in the relatively small world of Canadian national security, where initiatives are frequently personally driven, this is not different from the bureaucratic politics found in other government departments and agencies in Canada and throughout the world. Perhaps one day the enhanced review of the National Security and Intelligence Review Agency (NSIRA) and the National Security and Intelligence Committee of Parliamentarians (NSICOP) will add insight into the efficacy of inter-agency cooperation.

One interesting emerging trend is that national security and intelligence agencies are cooperating not only with each other, but also increasingly with non-traditional partners as the threat environment changes. CSE is now working with Elections Canada to secure our democratic institutions from online foreign influence. Heritage

Canada's broadcasting responsibilities mean that it is increasingly a partner of Public Safety and the Canada Centre in terms of a broad Government of Canada strategy to counter extremism. And CSIS has been heavily engaged with Innovation, Science and Economic Development (although not always happily, as noted above) in thinking through Canada's foreign investment strategy. As the threat environment changes further, it will be important for review agencies, journalists, and scholars to follow the extent to which the traditional national security and intelligence agencies in Canada lean on the expertise of non-traditional partners and share information with them. A possible, if idealistic, by-product of such collaboration could be improved intelligence-to-policy and policy-to-intelligence literacy within a bureaucracy that has hitherto been largely removed from national security matters.

Transparency and the Canadian Intelligence and National Security Community

Many chapters in this volume directly or indirectly touch on the issue of transparency. Leah West's chapter, in particular, explains how the establishment of NSICOP and NSIRA will vastly enhance review and oversight of Canada's national security and intelligence community. Relations with these two new bodies have been, and will continue to be, especially challenging for organizations that have not historically been the object of intrusive review and oversight, such as the Canadian Forces Intelligence Command (CFINTCOM) and the Canada Border Services Agency (CBSA). Other chapters, such as Michael Nesbitt's analysis of GAC, have also highlighted how other individual departments do not perform well in terms of transparency.

Indeed, the Canadian national security and intelligence community as a whole has traditionally not been very transparent. Senior Canadian intelligence officials, for example – until recently at least – very rarely gave public speeches. And when they did speak in public, they famously said little. Other indicators, such as the limited amount of detail in official public documents (such as annual reports, threat reports, or departmental reports on plans and priorities), the severe extent of redactions in documents released through access to information requests, and the absence of a formal declassification strategy for archived documents, all illustrate the lack of transparency in security and intelligence matters in Canada.

This matters for multiple reasons. In a democracy, first, transparency is – or should be – an end in itself. Much information in the hands of government institutions, in general and even more so in the national security and intelligence realm, should remain classified and away from the public's eyes, for justifiable reasons. That said, there is a strong ethical and moral case to be made that the default position should, as a rough rule of thumb, be that information should be released and made public *unless* there is a compelling reason to protect it. Unfortunately, in Canada, it is the opposite approach that has historically tended to dominate – that information should not be released, unless it is deemed safe to do so.

There is also a strong pragmatic and utilitarian case in favour of greater transparency in the national security and intelligence community. Law enforcement and intelligence agencies need the buy-in of the society they seek to protect: when they have the trust of the population, it is far easier to gather information, to build and maintain collaborative ties with key communities, and, ultimately, to do their jobs. Yet when security agencies are closed and perform poorly in terms of transparency, it is more difficult for citizens to trust them, and it opens space for erroneous information, misperceptions, and conspiracy theories to circulate. This reinforces a dynamic of mistrust and suspicion.

Greater transparency in the form of enhanced scrutiny and accountability should, in time, contribute to enhancing the performance of security and intelligence agencies. When required to respond to the requests of review and oversight bodies, government institutions are pressured to, for example, work harder to become more effective (since more openness brings greater attention to their successes and failures) and improve record-keeping (to be able to provide access to internal documents to review and oversight bodies with intrusive investigative powers). This is certainly time consuming and labour intensive, and can come at a cost – especially if agencies do not receive sufficient additional resources to deal with review and oversight. If well done, however, greater transparency as a result of enhanced review and oversight can and should provide strong net benefits.

As this volume has shown, despite Canada's lacklustre performance in terms of the transparency of its national security and intelligence community, the situation is steadily changing in a positive direction. NSICOP and NSIRA, in particular, will, as noted, greatly enhance transparency in the national security and intelligence community. Their public reports, perhaps most strikingly, will contribute to public debate on national security and intelligence matters in a unique and transformative way. The first annual report by NSICOP, notably, probably contained more information on CFINTCOM than any other publicly available official document ever has, even if it was heavily redacted. The ability of these two bodies' leading officials, including parliamentarians, to bring serious attention to security and intelligence issues will also enhance public debate in Canada.

Alongside the major legislative changes that led to the establishment of NSICOP and NSIRA, the government published its "Six Principles of National Security Transparency," which outline how it aims to fulfil its commitment to increased transparency in national security and intelligence.[3] The principles are divided into three categories: information transparency (how to provide more information to Canadians on the activities of departments and agencies), executive transparency (how to better explain to Canadians the legal framework underpinning the national security architecture, and how this framework shapes the decision-making processes and activities of departments and agencies), and policy transparency (how to better inform Canadians about the strategic issues affecting the country's national security and the government's responses, and how to better consult stakeholders and citizens in policy development). The leading initiative coming out of this National Security Transparency Commitment (NSTC) has been the National Security Transparency Advisory Group (NS-TAG). This new body, created in 2019, is tasked with advising the deputy minister of public safety and other government officials on the implementation of the NSTC.[4]

These initiatives – NSICOP, NSIRA, the NSTC, and NS-TAG – are positive developments. Nevertheless, even if there is a clear trend toward greater transparency in Canada's national security and intelligence community, these multiple reforms raise important challenges. Staff with different skill sets need to be hired, both in the new review and oversight bodies as well as in departments and agencies to deal with the new entities. Existing staff also need to be trained for their new responsibilities and, more broadly, to change some of their ways of doing business given this new reality. More abstractly, the prevailing culture of secrecy and of limited transparency in the community needs to shift. This will take time, and requires more than new professional development courses; it requires leadership by example from senior management, in particular. Cultural change will also, inevitably, be the result of friction: the inherently conflictual relation between overseer and overseen will often be difficult, especially early on, and will lead to controversies, many of which will not reach the public eye. But it is through this constant tension that, in theory at least, the national security and intelligence community will learn, change some of its procedures, and steadily become more transparent.

Balancing Security and Democracy

A final question is the extent to which Canada's security and intelligence community has succeeded in securing an open, rights-observing liberal democracy. As Canada's one-and-only national security policy statement noted in 2004, there is "no greater role, no more important obligation for a government, than the protection and safety of its citizens."[5] Canada is unusually blessed by geography, removed from the traditional perils of land invasion that have driven the security policies of other states. It is not, however, immunized for distance-spanning modern threats – globalized terrorism, cyber threats, foreign interference, weapons of mass destruction, and the knock-on effects of instability in distant places. For the first time in a generation, it risks collateral damage (or more) in an era of renewed great power competition.

In the final analysis, and as noted above, Canada's generally peaceable status suggests that, through good fortune, constant vigilance, or a mix of both, Canada's security and intelligence services have so for generally been successful in their core security objectives. That success requires a security and intelligence sector equipped with adequate means, resources, and legal authorities. For some critics, those means, resources, and legal authorities are excessive and have come at the cost of rights and liberties, with security and rights in opposition as a trade-off. Of course, security primacy achieved at the expense of rights and liberties would inevitably produce a state not truly worth securing. No careful assessment could, however, conclude that Canada has abandoned rights in its quest for security. Instead, like other liberal democracies, it partakes in a dynamic balancing act of maintaining rights and security simultaneously, not unlike trying to keep an umbrella balanced on the tip of one's finger.

It does so imperfectly, of course. At various points, this book has mentioned the McDonald, Arar, Iacobucci, and Air India inquiries, provoked by security service errors and misdeeds, and mentioned the criticisms of the review bodies charged with assessing (historically a subset of) the agencies discussed in this book. Still, it is notable that the inquiries and reviews over the last two decades have rarely identified outright unlawfulness by the security and intelligence services. The agencies have suffered from their share of incompetence, bureaucratic bungling, and examples of poor foresight, sometimes most easily assessed with the benefit of hindsight. Not every employee has met the ethical expectations of the organization for whom they work. A microcosm of society, the agencies have struggled with organizational culture – including with gender and racial bias, homophobia, and Islamophobia in the workplace.[6] But as much as there has been limited reporting about inter-agency infighting, there also have been few recorded examples of outright malice in the agencies' conduct of their national security functions. The Arar commission's conclusions that people in the government were seeking to tar Mr. Arar's reputation during that judicial inquiry is one of the few examples of a review entity finding the government intended to do harm through a deliberate, wrongful act.[7] In 2020, it is hard to imagine a repeat of the RCMP Security Service's "dirty tricks" campaign of the 1970s – that is, an orchestrated campaign of unlawfulness.

Some readers may be sceptical of these conclusions, pointing to periodic security and intelligence "scandals" – often the by-product of criticisms levelled by review bodies or the courts. However, a careful probing of the record in these cases – difficult to do for those not able to see classified history – is more likely to reveal an agency confronting a genuinely hard dilemma and choosing a path that hindsight reveals to be controversial, ineffectual, unwarranted, or unwise. More difficult to sustain on close examination of the facts is the narrative of a rogue agency, unmoored from legal or ethical concerns and predisposed to violate the rights of persons.

This discussion is not an apologia for the security and intelligence agencies. Nor do we intend to diminish the consequences of ill-conceived, bungled, or inept security agency conduct. It remains the case that the security and intelligence services wield enormous powers. Any limitations on a right or liberty they cause are just that, limitations, even if not the product of malevolence. The security and intelligence community must, therefore, observe the "Spider-Man rule": with great power comes great responsibility. The challenge for the Canadian security and intelligence community remains, therefore, organizing its affairs to meet the prerequisites for national security activities in a liberal democracy: that those activities be lawful, effective, efficient, proportionate to the threat, and necessary in the context.

In the 2020s, it seems Canada will continue to confront adversaries unencumbered with these sorts of limits, or more generally by the "rule of law." Canada's generally rule-compliant security and intelligence sector is, in some respects, analogous to an accountant in competition with buccaneers. Still, those less rule-observant, autocratic competitor states confront threats from which Canada is mostly immunized – not least threats from a domestic population kept in uneasy check through authoritarian tools. The social licence Canada's security and intelligence agencies enjoy is a considerable advantage. Preserving it is a constant task. In this way, a challenge for government remains to deepen the public's understanding of the workings of the national security sector. Canadians (and indeed, their political leaders) must have context to avoid swinging wildly from indifference to panic when security events occur. Likewise, transparency and national security literacy help citizens tease apart real scandals from the noise. More generally, Canadians shall need to develop a renewed understanding of the hard dilemmas that frequently arise in securing a free and democratic state. It is our hope this book provides a partial step toward this objective.

NOTES

1 Michelle Shephard, "CSIS Settles Multimillion-Dollar Lawsuit with Employees Who Claimed Workplace Islamophobia, Racism and Homophobia," *Toronto Star*, 14 December 2017, https://www.thestar.com /news/canada/2017/12/14/csis-settles-multimillion-dollar-lawsuit-with -employees-who-claimed-workplace-islamophobia-racism-and-homophobia .html.
2 Robert Fife and Steven Chase, "Canadian Intelligence Agencies at Odds over Whether to Ban Huawei: Official," *Globe and Mail*, 12 November 2019, https://www.theglobeandmail.com/politics/article-canadian-intelligence -agencies-disagree-on-whether-to-ban-huawei-from/.
3 Background information on the six principles is available here: Government of Canada, "National Security Transparency Commitment," last modified 18 June 2020, https://www.canada.ca/en/services /defence/nationalsecurity/national-security-transparency-commitment .html.
4 For background on the NS-TAG, and information on its membership as of February 2020, see Government of Canada, "The National Security Transparency Advisory Group (NS-TAG)," last modified 13 July 2020, https://www.canada.ca/en/services/defence/nationalsecurity/national -security-transparency-commitment/national-security-transparency -advisory-group.html. One of the editors of this volume (Juneau) is the NS-TAG's non-government co-chair.
5 Government of Canada, *Securing an Open Society: Canada's National Security Policy* (2004), vii. Available online: http://publications.gc.ca/collections

/Collection/CP22-77-2004E.pdf. See also *Charkaoui v. Canada*, 2007 SCC 9
at para. 1.
6 See, e.g., Shephard, "CSIS Settles Multimillion-Dollar Lawsuit."
7 Commission of Inquiry into the Actions of Canadian Officials in Relation to
Maher Arar, *Report of the Events Relating to Maher Arar* (2006), 263. Available
online: http://publications.gc.ca/site/eng/9.688875/publication.html.

Contributors

Alex Boutilier – Media
Alex Boutilier is a national security and politics reporter with the *Toronto Star* in Ottawa. Boutilier writes about privacy and security issues, how political parties and government agencies are harnessing new digital tools, and where politics and the internet intersect. He has covered "lawful access" debates and telecom transparency, Conservative and Liberal anti-terrorism bills, foreign affairs, and the evolving debate around cyberwarfare in Canada and abroad. Boutilier has a combined honours (BAH), University of King's College (Contemporary Studies) and Dalhousie University (Political Science).

Stephanie Carvin – Integrated Terrorism Assessment Centre
Stephanie Carvin is an associate professor of international relations at the Norman Paterson School of International Affairs. Her research interests are in the areas of national security, foreign policy, critical infrastructure protection, terrorism, and technology. Stephanie holds a master's and PhD from the London School of Economics, and her most recent book is *Science, Law, Liberalism and the American Way of Warfare: The Quest for Humanity in Conflict* (Cambridge University Press, 2015), co-authored with Michael J. Williams. In 2009, Carvin was a visiting scholar at George Washington University Law School and worked as a consultant to the US Department of Defense Law of War Working Group at the Pentagon. From 2012 to 2015, she was an analyst with the Government of Canada working on national security issues. She is the author of the forthcoming book *Stand on Guard: Reassessing Threats to Canada's National Security* (University of Toronto Press, 2020).

Craig Forcese – Department of Justice
Craig Forcese is a full professor at the Faculty of Law (Common Law Section), University of Ottawa. He is also an adjunct research professor and

Senior Fellow, Norman Paterson School of International Affairs, Carleton University, and a National Security Crisis Law Fellow, Center on National Security and the Law, Georgetown Law (Washington, DC). At the University of Ottawa, Forcese teaches public international law, national security law, administrative law, and constitutional law. Forcese has a BA from McGill University, an MA from the Norman Paterson School of International Affairs, Carleton University, an LLB (JD) from the University of Ottawa, and an LLM from Yale University. Forcese is the author of several books on Canadian national security law, including (with Kent Roach) *False Security* (Irwin Law, 2015) and *National Security Law* (Irwin Law, 2007).

Greg Fyffe – Privy Council Office

Greg Fyffe is currently a facilitator at the Telfer Centre for Executive Leadership, and teaches courses in policy leadership, security and intelligence leadership, and strategic thinking. He co-teaches the Summer Course on Intelligence at the University of Ottawa Centre for Public Management and Policy. He is currently serving as the president of the Canadian Association for Security and Intelligence Studies (CASIS), and from 2000 to 2008 he was executive director of the Intelligence Assessment Secretariat in the Privy Council Office. He is a consultant and editor on security and intelligence issues. Fyffe's range of high-level positions within the public service and national security community, as well as his position as president of CASIS, makes him uniquely placed to speak to the core themes of this book.

Alexandra Green – Canada Border Services Agency

Alexandra Green is a graduate of Carleton University's Master of Infrastructure Protection and International Security (IPIS) program, where she was awarded a Social Sciences and Humanities Research Council (SSHRC) grant to fund her research into target selection and extremism. During her undergraduate studies at Queen's University, she was awarded an undergraduate fellowship, the John Rae award, the Women in Defence and Security Scholarship, and the Chancellor's Scholarship, and was placed on the Dean's List with Distinction. She has been engaged in research projects on border security, terrorist resourcing, countering violent extremism, policing, signals intelligence, and critical infrastructure. She has been published in the *Journal of Money Laundering Control* and in the SERENE-RISC digest.

Todd Hataley – Canada Border Services Agency

Todd Hataley is a professor in the School of Justice and Community Development at Fleming College. He is a retired member of the Royal

Canadian Mounted Police. During his tenure as a federal police officer he conducted investigations into money laundering, organized crime, national security, extraterritorial torture investigations, and the cross-border smuggling of drugs, weapons, and humans. Dr. Hataley is also an adjunct associate professor at the Royal Military College of Canada. His research currently focuses on the management of international boundaries, public safety, Indigenous policing, and transnational crime.

Thomas Juneau – Department of National Defence
Thomas Juneau is an associate professor at the University of Ottawa's Graduate School of Public and International Affairs. His research focuses on the Middle East, in particular Iran and Yemen, and on Canadian foreign and defence policy and international relations theory. He is also currently conducting a number of research projects on the relationship between intelligence analysis and policymaking in Canada. He is the author of *Squandered Opportunity: Neoclassical Realism and Iranian Foreign Policy* (Stanford University Press, 2015), editor of *Strategic Analysis in Support of International Policy Making: Case Studies in Achieving Analytical Relevance* (Rowman & Littlefield, 2017), and co-editor of *Canadian Defence Policy in Theory and Practice* (Palgrave Macmillan, 2019) and of *Iranian Foreign Policy Since 2001: Alone in the World* (Routledge, 2013). He has published book chapters and articles in, among other publications, *International Affairs*, *Political Science Quarterly*, *Nonproliferation Review*, *Orbis*, *International Journal*, *Canadian Public Administration*, *Canadian Foreign Policy*, *Middle East Policy*, and *International Studies Perspectives*. From 2003 until 2014, he worked with Canada's Department of National Defence, mostly as a policy analyst covering the Middle East. He also acts as a consultant for various departments with the Canadian government and is a frequent commentator in Canadian and international media. He tweets @thomasjuneau.

Michael King – Organization for the Prevention of Violence
Michael King is the director of research at the Organization for the Prevention of Violence. He is also an adjunct professor in the Department of Political Science at the University of Toronto. Michael held several positions in the field of counterterrorism within the Government of Canada; most recently as senior research advisor at the Canada Centre for Community Engagement and the Prevention of Violence, housed within Public Safety Canada, from 2017 to 2020. Previously, Michael has done contract work for community-based NGOs, think tanks, and Canada's Department of Defence and Ministry of Public Safety. He

completed a PhD in social psychology from McGill University, where he researched how individuals legitimize the use of terrorism.

Brett Kubicek – Canada Centre for Community Engagement and the Prevention of Violence
Brett Kubicek is the manager of research at the Canada Centre for Community Engagement and Prevention of Violence, Public Safety Canada. Formerly, he was the manager responsible for Public Safety's Kanishka Project, a five-year, $10-million Government of Canada initiative investing in research on terrorism and counterterrorism. He has served as the Government of Canada's representative for the Canadian Network for Research on Terrorism, Security and Society since its inception in 2012 and from 2007 to 2016 served as Public Safety's liaison for the National Justice Statistics Initiative. He joined the Canadian public service in 2005 after completing his PhD in political science at the Massachusetts Institute of Technology and a postdoctoral fellowship at Ohio State University, as well as a BA from the University of British Columbia.

Christian Leuprecht – Canada Border Services Agency
A leading authority on the comparative study of national security, Christian Leuprecht is an expert on borders and crime. He is Class of 1965 Professor in Leadership, Department of Political Science and Economics, Royal Military College of Canada; director of the Institute of Intergovernmental Relations, School of Policy Studies, Queen's University; adjunct research professor at the Australian Graduate School of Policing and Security, Charles Sturt University, and the Centre for Crime Policy and Research, Flinders University; and Munk Senior Fellow in Security and Defence at the Macdonald-Laurier Institute. He is a former Fulbright Research Chair in Canada-US Relations at the School for Advanced International Studies at Johns Hopkins University and Eisenhower Fellow at the NATO Defence College. A recipient of the Royal Military College of Canada's Cowan Prize for Excellence in Research and an elected member of the College of New Scholars of the Royal Society of Canada, he has held visiting positions in North America, Europe, and Australia and is regularly called as an expert witness to testify before committees of Parliament. He holds appointments to the boards of the German Institute for Defence and Strategic Studies, the Police Services Board of the City of Kingston, and the Polar Research and Policy Initiative.

Meredith Lilly – Prime Minister's Office
Meredith Lilly is an associate professor at Carleton University, where she holds the Simon Reisman Chair in International Affairs, focusing on

trade policy. She previously served as foreign affairs and international trade advisor to Canadian prime minister Stephen Harper. She is a Fellow with the Canadian Global Affairs Institute, academic advisor to the Canadian Centre for Trade Policy and Law, and a frequent media commentator on North American trade relations. She earned a postdoctoral certificate in economics from McMaster University, a PhD in health services research from the University of Toronto, and an honours BA in international development from the University of Toronto.

Jez Littlewood – Canadian Security Intelligence Service
Jez Littlewood is a policy analyst based in Alberta. He was formerly an assistant professor in the Norman Paterson School of International Affairs at Carleton University, where he led the Intelligence and National Security (INS) concentration of the MA program. His research encompasses terrorism and counterterrorism, proliferation of weapons of mass destruction, and national security intelligence, and his most recent research grant studied chemical, biological, radiological, and nuclear terrorism under the Kanishka Project Contribution Program. His peer-reviewed work on biological weapons controls is complemented by publications related to intelligence and national security issues. He served previously with the UK Foreign & Commonwealth Office, the United Nations, and Her Majesty's Forces in the UK. He is a regular guest speaker on issues related to terrorism and intelligence in Ottawa.

Michael Nesbitt – Global Affairs Canada
Michael Nesbitt teaches and researches in the areas of criminal law, national security law, and international organizations at the University of Calgary, Faculty of Law. He is a Senior Fellow with the Centre for Military, Security and Strategic Studies, a Fellow with the Canadian Global Affairs Institute, and a senior research affiliate with the Canadian Network for Research on Terrorism, Security and Society (TSAS). Before joining the University of Calgary's Faculty of Law in July 2015, he practised law and worked on Middle East policy, human rights, international sanctions, and terrorism for Global Affairs Canada. Previously, he completed his articles and worked for Canada's Department of Justice, where his focus was criminal law. Nesbitt has also worked internationally for the United Nations' International Criminal Tribunal for the former Yugoslavia in the Appeals Chamber. He would like to thank Bassam Saifeddine and Ian Wylie for truly exception research assistance in the preparation of this chapter.

Jennifer Poirier – Department of Justice
Jennifer Poirier has been counsel with the Department of Justice since 2007. In April 2012, Jennifer joined the department's National Security Litigation and Advisory Group (NSLAG). Her primary client is the Canadian Security Intelligence Service (CSIS), for whom she provides litigation support in national security civil litigation cases and advice on CSIS operations, and represents CSIS in national security warrant applications before the Federal Court. Jennifer obtained a BA in communication studies from Concordia University in Montreal, following which she spent two years as a cartoon sound editor. Jennifer then returned to school and obtained an MA in international peace and conflict resolution from Arcadia University in Philadelphia before attending law school at McGill University in Montreal, where she obtained both civil law and common law degrees.

John Pyrik – Financial Transactions and Reports Analysis Centre of Canada
John Pyrik spent 27 years in government. As an analyst at FINTRAC, he uncovered money laundering and terrorism financing. He has also worked in counterterrorism and counter-proliferation. As a securities investigator, he investigated market fraud, broker misconduct, and insider trading. In mid-career, he created and managed a program at the Privy Council Office to improve the tradecraft of intelligence analysis. He then spent five years in charge of analytic training at the Canadian Security Intelligence Service (CSIS). Since retiring, he has become more involved in academia. He is the treasurer for the Intelligence Studies Section of the International Studies Association and teaches part time in the graduate studies program of the Justice Institute of British Columbia (JIBC).

Kent Roach – Royal Canadian Mounted Police
Kent Roach is a professor of law and Prichard-Wilson Chair of Law and Public Policy at the University of Toronto Faculty of Law. In 2015, he was appointed a Member of the Order of Canada. He is the author of 13 books, including *The 9/11 Effect: Comparative Counter-terrorism* (Cambridge University Press, 2011; winner of the Mundell Medal) and (with Craig Forcese) *False Security* (Irwin Law, 2015; winner of the Canadian Law and Society Association best book prize). Professor Roach has served as research director for the Commission of Inquiry into the Investigation of the Bombing of Air India Flight 182, and he served on the research advisory committee for the inquiry into the rendition of Maher Arar.

Bill Robinson – Communications Security Establishment
Bill Robinson is a Research Fellow at the Citizen Lab, an interdisciplinary laboratory at the Munk School of Global Affairs and Public Policy at the University of Toronto, and writes the blog *Lux Ex Umbra*, which focuses on Canadian signals intelligence (SIGINT) activities past and present. He is frequently consulted by journalists about Canadian SIGINT activities, helped the CBC analyse the Snowden revelations, and has provided research assistance to the British Columbia Civil Liberties Association for its legal challenge to Communications Security Establishment (CSE) monitoring of Canadians. From 1986 to 2001 he was on the staff of the Canadian peace organization Project Ploughshares.

Kelly W. Sundberg – Canada Border Services Agency
Kelly Sundberg is an associate professor in the Department of Economics, Justice, and Policy Studies at Mount Royal University and an adjunct professor at both the University of Calgary and University of Adelaide, and serves as a Fellow with the Canadian Global Affairs Institute. Prior to his academic career, Kelly served over 15 years in various enforcement, investigation, policy development, and advisory roles with what is today the Canada Border Services Agency (CBSA). He has been qualified as an expert witness by the Provincial Court of Alberta (Criminal Division) on matters relating to immigration enforcement and border security, has written numerous academic and government articles and reports on migration management and border security, and regularly is quoted by the national and international media on border and national security issues. Kelly's BA in political science is from the University of Victoria, his MA in justice and public safety leadership and training from Royal Roads University, and his doctor of philosophy in political and social inquiry (specialization in criminology) from Monash University.

Leah West – Oversight and Review
Leah West is a lecturer at the Norman Paterson School of International Affair at Carleton University. She is also an SJD candidate at the University of Toronto Faculty of Law, where she studies the application of national security, international humanitarian, and constitutional law in cyberspace. She is also currently co-authoring the second edition of *National Security Law*, with Craig Forcese. Leah was formerly counsel with the National Security Advisory and Litigation Group (NSLAG) of the Department of Justice, and served as the judicial law clerk to the Honourable Justice Richard Mosley of the Federal Court of Canada. Before attending

law school, Leah served as an armoured officer in the Canadian Armed Forces. She is a graduate of the Royal Military College and also holds advanced degrees in law and intelligence.

Alex Wilner – Public Safety Canada
Dr. Alex S. Wilner is an associate professor at the Norman Paterson School of International Affairs, Carleton University. Professor Wilner's research primarily focuses on the application of deterrence theory to contemporary security issues, like terrorism, cybersecurity, and radicalization. His latest project – AI Deterrence – received two IDEaS grants from the Department of National Defence (2018–21). His books include *Deterring Rational Fanatics* (University of Pennsylvania Press, 2015) and *Deterring Terrorism: Theory and Practice* (Stanford University Press, 2012). Dr. Wilner has held a variety of positions at Policy Horizons Canada, the Munk School of Global Affairs at the University of Toronto, the National Consortium for the Study of Terrorism and Responses to Terrorism (START) at the University of Maryland, and the ETH Zurich in Switzerland.

Index

mandate, 4, 18, 205–8, 283; PCO
and, 26; review and oversight,
211–12, 216n9, 217n22, 257;
structure, 202, *203*, 205–6; threat
environment, 209–10; Trumpism
and, 210–11. *See also* Canadian
Armed Forces; Canadian Forces
Intelligence Command; Defence
Research and Development Canada
Department of Natural Resources
(Natural Resources Canada), 75, 176
Department of Public Safety and
Emergency Preparedness. *See*
Public Safety Canada
*Department of Public Safety and
Emergency Preparedness Act* (2005),
166
Department of the Environment
(Environment Canada), 75, 77
Department of the Solicitor General
of Canada, 7, 92, 166
Department of Transport (Transport
Canada), 10, 18, 75, 77, 92
deportations and removals, 156–7
Deputy Ministers Intelligence
Assessment committee (DMIA),
25–6
Deputy Ministers National Security
Committee (DMNS), 25
Deputy Ministers Operations
Committee (DMOC), 25
Deschamps Report (2015), 214
digital foreign policy, 227
Digital Inclusion Lab, 227
Directorate of Intelligence Production
Management (DIPM), 207
Director General Intelligence (DGInt),
205, 215. *See also* Canadian Forces
Intelligence Command
Disaster Financial Assistance
Arrangements (DFAA)
contribution program, 168, 177

Doucet, Michael, 259
Driver, Aaron, 135

Eby, David, 110
Egmont Group, 113
Elcock, Ward, 26
Elections Canada, 10, 285
electronic travel authorization
(eTA), 157
Emergency Management Act (2007),
167, 170
emergency preparedness, 167, 169–70
*Empowering Local Partners to Prevent
Violent Extremism in the United
States* (2011 strategy), 183
end product reports (EPRs), 72–3, 75,
85n13, 86n17
Enhancing RCMP Accountability Act
(2013), 139–40
Environment Canada (Department
of the Environment), 75, 77
Esseghaier, Chiheb, 118
European Policy Planners Network
on Countering Radicalisation and
Polarisation, 185
ex parte (closed) legal proceedings,
247–50
Export and Import Permits Act (EIPA,
1985), 227
export declarations, 158–9
extremism. *See* Canada Centre for
Community Engagement and
Prevention of Violence; countering
violent extremism

Fadden, Richard, 20, 21, 26
Finance Canada (Department of
Finance), 75, 108, 114
Financial Action Task Force (FATF),
107, 114, 115, 117, 122n75
financial intelligence (FININT),
106, 113

Office of Critical Infrastructure
Protection and Emergency
Preparedness, 7, 92
Office of the Communications
Security Establishment
Commissioner (OCSEC), 82,
260–1, 262
Office of the Community Outreach
and Counter-radicalization
Coordinator, 188. *See also* Canada
Centre for Community Engagement
and Prevention of Violence
Office of the Correctional
Investigator, 167
Office of the Intelligence
Commissioner (IC), 83, 89n48,
257–8, 264–6, 269
Office of the Judge Advocate
General, 252n14
Office of the Privacy Commissioner
(OPC), 107, 115–16, 160, 230. *See
also* privacy issues
Official Secrets Act. See *Security of
Information Act*
"One Vision" and "One Vision 2.0"
frameworks, 55, 142, 285
Operational Data Analysis Centre
(ODAC), 60, 250
Organisation for Economic Co-
operation and Development, 193
Organisation for the Prohibition of
Chemical Weapons (OPCW),
221, 227
organized crime, 17, 159, 221, 234n9
Ortis, Cameron, 143
oversight. *See* review and oversight

Parliament Hill terror attacks (2014),
37, 39, 133, 261
Parole Board of Canada (PBC),
166, 167
Paulson, Bob, 107

peace, global, 224
peace bonds, 135, 190
Plouffe, Jean-Pierre, 264
A Podcast Called INTREPID, 279
policy development, 243
Policy Planners Network (PPN), 185
political staff, 29–30. *See also* Prime
Minister's Office
politicization, of security and
intelligence, 36–7
Prevent (UK countering violent
extremism program), 182–3, 184, 185
preventing violent extremism (PVE).
See countering violent extremism
Prevention of Terrorist Travel Act
(2015), 248
preventive detention, 8, 133
prime ministers, 20, 30, 37
Prime Minister's Office (PMO):
introduction and conclusion, 10–11,
29–30, 40–1; Cabinet process
and, 33–4; crisis management
and, 37–8, 40; CSE relations, 75;
mental health considerations,
38–9, 40; "need to know" vs.
"interesting" intelligence, 31–4,
40; political staffers as intelligence
assets, 35–7, 40; Security and
Intelligence Secretariat and, 23
priority-setting, intelligence, 25, 74,
85n8
Privacy Act (1985), 130, 159, 267
privacy issues: introduction,
6; CBSA, 159–61; CSE, 82–4;
datasets, 9, 47, 61, 264, 265;
FINTRAC, 115–16. *See also* Office
of the Privacy Commissioner
private communications, 73–4, 76,
82, 260–1
Privy Council Office (PCO):
introduction and conclusion,
10, 15, 27; Canada Centre

26–7; coordination role, 18–20,
28n1; CSE relations, 75; Foreign
and Defence Policy (FDP)
Secretariat, 21, 22, 23–4, 25;
Integrated National Security
Assessment Centre (INSAC)
and, 92; Intelligence Assessment
Secretariat (IAS), 20, 22, 23,
26; intelligence priority-setting
and, 74; national security and
intelligence advisor (NSIA), 15,
20–2; NSIA committee structure,
24–6, 28n3; Public Safety Canada
and, 5; Security and Intelligence
Secretariat (PCO-S&I), 22–3, 25,
26; staffing, 26–7
*Proceeds of Crime (Money Laundering)
and Terrorist Financing Act*
(PCMLTFA, 2000), 106, 107, 108,
111, 112, 113, 114, 115
professionalism, in Justice Canada,
244–6, 247–50
Project Smooth, 118
Project Swap, 118
prosecutions, 240–1
Public Complaints and Review
Commission (PCRC), 141, 161, 262
Public Policy Forum, 278
Public Prosecution Service of
Canada (PPSC), 240
Public Safety, Defence and
Immigration (PSDI) Portfolio, 242
Public Safety Canada (PSC):
introduction and conclusion, 11,
166, 177; budget, 168; challenges,
173–7; community-level
cooperation, 170–1; controversies,
172–3; cooperation and
coordination role, 18–19, 169–72,
175–6, 286; critical infrastructure
protection, 169; CSE relations,

75; cybersecurity, 171–2, 175,
213; emergency preparedness,
167, 169–70; establishment, 7,
166; ethics and conduct code,
172–3; internal challenges,
173–4; international cooperation,
169; mandate, 5, 166–7, 174–5,
283; Metropolis Project Canada
and, 186; policy development,
243; private sector engagement,
171; provincial cooperation,
169–70; public engagement,
172; resources, 168; size issues,
177; staffing, 168, 173–4, 284;
structure, 167; terrorism and, 169,
174–5. *See also* Canada Centre for
Community Engagement and
Prevention of Violence
*Public Servants Disclosure Protection
Act* (2005), 172
*Public Service Rearrangement and
Transfer of Duties Act* (1985), 7

Quebec City mosque shooting
(2017), 144

radicalization. *See* Canada Centre
for Community Engagement and
Prevention of Violence; countering
violent extremism
RCMP Act (1985), 129, 137
ReDirect, 187
*Religious Radicalization and
Securitization in Canada and Beyond*
(Bramadat and Dawson), 186
Research and Action on Social
Polarization (RASP), 187
Revenu Québec, 108
review and oversight: introduction
and conclusion, 12, 257–8, 269;
history of, 258–62; NSICOP, 266–9;
NSIRA, 262–4; Office of the

The Institute of Public Administration of Canada Series in Public Management and Governance

Making Medicare: New Perspectives on the History of Medicare in Canada, edited
   by Gregory P. Marchildon
*Overpromising and Underperforming? Understanding and Evaluating New
   Intergovernmental Accountability Regimes*, edited by Peter Graefe, Julie M.
   Simmons, and Linda A. White
Governance in Northern Ontario: Economic Development and Policy Making, edited
   by Charles Conteh and Bob Segsworth
Off and Running: The Prospects and Pitfalls of Government Transitions in Canada,
   David Zussman
Deputy Ministers in Canada: Comparative and Jurisdictional Perspectives, edited by
   Jacques Bourgault and Christopher Dunn
The Politics of Public Money, Second Edition, David A. Good
Commissions of Inquiry and Policy Change: A Comparative Analysis, edited by
   Gregory J. Inwood and Carolyn M. Johns
*Leaders in the Shadows: The Leadership Qualities of Municipal Chief Administrative
   Officers*, David Siegel
*Funding Policies and the Nonprofit Sector in Western Canada: Evolving Relationships
   in a Changing Environment*, edited by Peter R. Elson
Backrooms and Beyond: Partisan Advisers and the Politics of Policy Work in Canada,
   Jonathan Craft
Fields of Authority: Special Purpose Governance in Ontario, 1815–2015, Jack Lucas
*A Quiet Evolution: The Emergence of Indigenous–Local Intergovernmental
   Partnerships in Canada*, Christopher Alcantara and Jen Nelles
*Canada's Department of External Affairs, Volume 3, Innovation and Adaptation,
   1968–1984*, John Hilliker, Mary Halloran, and Greg Donaghy
*Federalism in Action: The Devolution of Canada's Public Employment Service,
   1995–2015*, Donna E. Wood
Distributed Democracy: Health Care Governance in Ontario, Carey Doberstein
*Top Secret Canada: Understanding the Canadian Intelligence and National Security
   Community*, edited by Stephanie Carvin, Thomas Juneau, and Craig Forcese